Praise for Jumpstart! A Workbook for Writers . . .

"When the new edition is available, I will be first in line to adopt the text for my courses."

Paul D. Martin, Pasadena City College

"The second edition of Barbara Clouse's workbook for writers, *Jumpstart!*, continues its excellent tradition of providing multiple tools to basic writers. As an instructor for ESL students, I find the textbook to be my first choice after numerous semesters of trying one textbook after another."

Jeanne P. McAllister, Richard J. Daley College

"**Photo Gallery** is positively the best thing I've seen anyone do for a writing textbook ever. **Getting in Gear** is absolutely fantastic. I like the progressive approach and find the prompts to be current, engaging, and relevant to students. It's nice to see some thoughtful, creative, and original ideas for writing."

Theresa Zeleznick, Cuyahoga Community College—West

"This text's special features, such as the **If English is Your Second Language** feature and the study skills tips, place it uniquely above others I've seen."

Carlotta W. Hill, Oklahoma City Community College

"**Tips** are great. Cross references for the curious or serious student and those who are finding the other concepts difficult are especially good."

Leslie Mohr, Casper College

"One of my favorite [features] is the **Connect** feature. The tips are practical and speak to the need to integrate learning in this course to other areas."

Lucia Partin, Faulkner State Community College

"I would use *Jumpstart!, 2E* in a heartbeat."

Maria C. Villar-Smith, Miami-Dade Community College

. . . *and for* Jumpstart! with Readings

"I find the readings particularly impressive. Not only do they come from culturally diverse authors, but also the topics are quite diverse. The issues are real and practical. Overall, the [reading] features have brought back my enthusiasm for including readings in a [writing] text."

Carlotta W. Hill, Oklahoma City Community College

"With the inclusion of reading passages from such renowned writers as Maya Angelou, Maria Muñiz, and Andrew Lam, Clouse brings reading skills into the writing classroom. **Connecting the Readings,** which asks students to relate these professional passages to one another and to their own lives, is an exciting addition that puts Barbara Clouse's textbook into the superb category. I enthusiastically recommend both *Jumpstart!* and *Jumptstart! with Readings.*"

Jeanne P. McAllister, Richard J. Daley College

"I like the way **Strategies for Thoughtful Reading** provides students with a structure for focusing on author, purpose, topic, and main points; for responding critically; and for marking problems."

Vicki Covington, Isothermal Community College

JUMPSTART!
WITH READINGS

A WORKBOOK FOR WRITERS

JUMPSTART!
WITH READINGS

A WORKBOOK FOR WRITERS

ANNOTATED INSTRUCTOR'S EDITION

Barbara Fine Clouse

Boston   Burr Ridge, IL   Dubuque, IA   Madison, WI   New York   San Francisco   St. Louis
Bangkok   Bogotá   Caracas   Kuala Lumpur   Lisbon   London   Madrid   Mexico City
Milan   Montreal   New Delhi   Santiago   Seoul   Singapore   Sydney   Taipei   Toronto

McGraw-Hill Higher Education

A Division of The **McGraw-Hill** *Companies*

JUMPSTART WITH READINGS: A WORKBOOK FOR WRITERS
Published by McGraw-Hill, an imprint of The McGraw-Hill Companies, Inc. 1221 Avenue of the Americas, New York, NY, 10020. Copyright © 2002, by The McGraw-Hill Companies, Inc. All rights reserved. No part of this publication may be reproduced or distributed in any form or by any means, or stored in a database or retrieval system, without the prior written consent of The McGraw-Hill Companies, Inc., including, but not limited to, in any network or other electronic storage or transmission, or broadcast for distance learning.

Some ancillaries, including electronic and print components, may not be available to customers outside the United States.

This book is printed on acid-free paper.

1 2 3 4 5 6 7 8 9 0 QPD/QPD 0 9 8 7 6 5 4 3 2 1

ISBN: 0-07-241470-7 (Annotated Instructor's Edition ISBN: 0-07-249964-8)

Editorial director: *Phillip A. Butcher*
Executive editor: *Sarah Touborg*
Developmental editor: *Alexis Walker*
Marketing manager: *David S. Patterson*
Senior project manager: *Christine A. Vaughan*
Production supervisor: *Rose Hepburn*
Coordinator freelance design: *Artemio Ortiz, Jr.*
Cover design: *Artemio Ortiz, Jr.*
Interior design: *Cindy Crampton*
Photo research coordinator: *Judy Kausal*
Supplement producer: *Susan Lombardi*
Media technology producer: *Todd Vaccaro*
Compositor: *Carlisle Communications, Ltd.*
Typeface: *10/12 Sabon*
Printer: *Quebecor World Dubuque Inc.*

www.mhhe.com

About the Author

Barbara Clouse is a seasoned writing instructor who has taught all levels of college composition, first at Youngstown State University in northeastern Ohio and then at Slippery Rock University in western Pennsylvania. She has written a number of composition texts for McGraw-Hill, including *The Student Writer: Editor and Critic, Patterns for a Purpose: A Rhetorical Reader, Transitions: From Reading to Writing,* and *Working It Out: A Troubleshooting Guide for Writers.* In addition, she has developed *Cornerstones II: Readings for Writers,* which is a short prose developmental reader that is part of Primis Online, McGraw-Hill's electronic database that allows instructors to build their own textbooks. Barbara's publications also include *Progressions* for Allyn & Bacon and *Conventions and Expectations: A Brief Handbook and Guide to Writing* for Longman. Barbara is a frequent presenter at national and regional conferences, and she often conducts workshops for writing teachers.

McGraw-Hill Titles by Barbara Clouse

JUMPSTART! A Workbook for Writers, Second Edition
ISBN: 0-07-230074-4 (2002)

JUMPSTART! WITH READINGS: A Workbook for Writers, First Edition
ISBN: 0-07-241470-7 (2002)

TRANSITIONS: From Reading to Writing, Third Edition
ISBN: 0-07-240521-X (2002)

WORKING IT OUT: A Troubleshooting Guide for Writers, Third Edition
ISBN: 0-07-236748-2 (2001)

THE STUDENT WRITER: Editor and Critic, Fifth Edition
ISBN: 0-07-043486-7 (2000)

PATTERNS FOR A PURPOSE: A Rhetorical Reader, Second Edition
ISBN: 0-07-011980-5 (1999)

CORNERSTONES II: Readings for Writers
Build your own *text with McGraw-Hill Primis Online!*
(www.mhhe.com/primis)

In memory of Justine Greenman—
a gentle teacher, an elegant woman,
and a good friend

ix

Brief Contents

Contents

If English Is Your Second Language

A GUIDE TO CONTENTS

Preface

Aimed at helping basic writers achieve the proficiency necessary for success in their college courses, *Jumpstart! with Readings: A Workbook for Writers* focuses on both sentence-level concerns and whole discourse. Its primary focus, however, is on the sentence-level problems common to basic writers. Unlike other worktexts that focus on sentence proficiency, *Jumpstart! with Readings* connects learning to writing in other classes, so students understand its importance across the disciplines. Also unlike similar worktexts, *Jumpstart! with Readings* offers abundant support for multilingual students.

FEATURES OF *JUMPSTART! WITH READINGS*

Because *Jumpstart! A Workbook for Writers* was extensively used and widely reviewed in its first edition, the McGraw-Hill team was able to craft a new edition with readings based on what has been shown to work. In this new edition, we have incorporated changes that both instructors and students agreed would enhance an already successful text. The result is a thoughtful new edition that incorporates the best of the previous edition of *Jumpstart!* with engaging new features.

Reading and Writing Support for Students

Every feature of *Jumpstart! with Readings* is designed to support and encourage students.

- Chapter goals listed at the beginning of every chapter allow students to preview material.
- Explanations are clear and concise.
- Important grammar terminology is defined in easy-to-understand, jargon-free language.
- Abundant, varied exercises provide ongoing reinforcement and practice. Review exercises are strategically placed for additional reinforcement.
- *Grammar Alerts, Spelling Alerts,* and *Punctuation Alerts* highlight pitfalls for students to avoid.
- Marginalia labeled *Connect* help students see the application of what they are learning to writing across the curriculum and in the workplace.
- Marginalia labeled *Tip* suggest helpful strategies.
- At the end of each chapter, *Recharge* sections highlight the main points for easy review.
- A generous number of varied writing activities ensure that every student can find a topic of interest.
- Help for nonnative users appears under the heading *If English Is Your Second Language.*

The Exercises

The high-interest exercises are varied and abundant.

- A generous number of whole discourse exercises (in paragraphs) and continuous discourse exercises (in sequenced sentences developing a single topic) are given on a range of topics, including space junk, the origin of common expressions such as "spitting image," the history of credit cards, how lie detectors work, and the evolution of the ball.
- A number of exercises involve sentence combining to help students build syntactic fluency.
- Chapter review exercises appear at the end of every chapter.
- Unit review exercises focusing on multiple skills appear at the end of every unit.
- Group activities are offered for collaborative learning experiences.
- Supplemental activities labeled *Power Up* appear in the margins.

Whole Discourse and the Writing Process

Because grammar must be learned in the context of writing, *Jumpstart! with Readings* emphasizes both process and product.

- Chapter 1, "Your Writing Process," focuses on the writing process with
  - tips for managing writing tasks
  - specific strategies for idea generation, considering audience and purpose, drafting, revising, editing, and proofreading
  - specific strategies for giving and receiving reader response
  - tips for composing at the computer and writing e-mail
  - an emphasis on journal writing
- Chapter 2, "Writing a Paragraph," focuses on both process and product with
  - an explanation and illustration of the characteristics of an effective paragraph
  - ways to develop effective supporting details
  - an explanation of how to use transitions
  - an explanation of concise, specific word choice
  - strategies for coming up with a topic sentence idea
  - strategies for discovering supporting details
  - strategies for revising
- Chapter 3, "Writing an Essay," focuses on both process and product with
  - an explanation and illustration of the characteristics of an effective essay
  - a comparison of essay and paragraph structure
  - specific strategies for writing an essay, from idea generation through editing
- Each chapter closes with three sequenced writing activities that move students from idea generation to whole discourse.

Writing Opportunities

Each chapter closes with a three-part set of thematically related writing activities, labeled *Getting in Gear.*

- A *Thinking in Writing* prompt for a discovery writing.
- A *Writing from Experience* prompt for whole discourse based on an experiential writing topic.

- A *Writing in Context* prompt for whole discourse based on an analytic topic given in full rhetorical context.

Photo Gallery

This unique section of the text offers a collection of arresting photographs with accompanying writing assignments.

The Marginalia

The marginalia in *Jumpstart! with Readings* offers students a little "something extra."

- The *Power Up* marginalia offer individual and group activities related to the skill under discussion.
- The *Connect* marginalia explain how the skills under consideration apply beyond the writing classroom—across the curriculum, in the workplace, and in the real world. They also offer study skills applications.
- *Tips* offer additional information, helpful reminders, and cross-references.

The Readings

The readings offer the students an opportunity to read and respond in writing, much as they will be asked to do in other classes.

- The thirteen selections are on a range of themes by diverse authors.
- "Strategies for Thoughtful Reading" explains the active reading process.
- A sample marked essay illustrates the active reading process.
- Each essay is accompanied by helpful apparatus that includes
  - a headnote with information about the author and selection
  - marginalia that glosses potentially difficult vocabulary
  - *On Writing* marginalia that points out a previously studied grammar, usage, or rhetorical feature of the selection
  - two sets of questions, one set to check reading comprehension and one to provide critical thinking opportunities
  - a set of three sequenced writing assignments that move progressively from discovery to experiential writing to analytic writing in rhetorical context
  - "Connecting the Readings" assignments calling upon the students to write about two readings

COMPREHENSIVE SUPPLEMENTS PACKAGE

For Instructors

- An *Annotated Instructor's Edition* (ISBN 0-07-249964-8) consists of the student text complete with answers to all exercises.
- The *Instructor's Manual and Testbank* (ISBN 0-07-250061-1) includes abundant testing material, tips on using the text in class, and additional writing assignments and exercises (including ESL exercises).
- An *Online Learning Center* (www.mhhe.com/jumpstart) offers a host of instructional aids and additional resources for instructors, including a computerized test bank, an electronic version of the Instructor's Manual, online resources for writing instructors, and more.
- An *Instructor's CD-ROM* (0-07-249953-2) offers all of the resources of the Instructor's Online Learning Center in a convenient offline format.

- *PageOut!* helps instructors create graphically pleasing and professional web pages for their courses, in addition to providing classroom management, collaborative learning, and content management tools. *PageOut!* is **FREE** to adopters of McGraw-Hill textbooks and learning materials. Learn more at http://www.mhhe.com/pageout/.

For Students

- Our *Online Learning Center* (www.mhhe.com/jumpstart) offers a host of instructional aids and additional resources for students, including self-correcting exercises with feedback for right and wrong answers, writing activities for additional practice, a PowerPoint grammar tutorial, guides to doing research on the Internet and avoiding plagiarism, useful web links, and more.
- *AllWrite!* 2.0, User's Guide with Password for Online Access (0-07-244992-6), also available on CD-ROM (0-07-236207-3), is an interactive, browser-based grammar and editing tutorial program that provides an online handbook, comprehensive diagnostic pre-tests and post-tests, and extensive practice exercises in every area.
- *WebWrite!* is an interactive peer-editing program that allows students to post papers, read comments from their peers and instructor, discuss, and edit online. To learn more, visit the online demo at http://www.metatext.com/webwrite.

Please consult your local McGraw-Hill representative or consult McGraw-Hill's website at **www.mhhe.com/english** for more information on the supplements that accompany *Jumpstart!, 2E* and *Jumpstart! with Readings, 1E.*

ACKNOWLEDGMENTS

I am deeply appreciative of the help I received throughout the development of this text. At McGraw-Hill, Sarah Touborg and Alexis Walker guided the editorial process gently and wisely, while Christine Vaughan shepherded a tricky manuscript through production with considerable good humor. Deborah Barberousse and Jennifer Bradner developed the Instructor's Manual, testbank, and website material. I take the liberty of calling them friends and valued colleagues, and I thank them for their good work.

Many instructors generously lent their precious time and considerable expertise to the development of this text. I owe them a great deal and thank them profoundly. The following reviewers read the manuscript in its various stages and offered the best possible advice—the kind that comes from experience and respect for students.

Karlene Alexander, Miami-Dade C.C.–Wolfson; Margery L. Brown, SUNY Farmingdale; Beverly K. Burch, Vincennes University; Lawrence Carlson, Orange Coast College; Vicki Covington, Isothermal C.C.; Jeanine Edwards, University of Memphis; Lulie E. Felder, Central Carolina T.C.; Carlotta W. Hill, Oklahoma City C.C.; Peggy Hopper, Walters State C.C.; Glenn Klopfenstein, Passaic County C.C.; Laura Knight, Mercer County C.C.; Patsy Krech, University of Memphis; Paul D. Martin, Pasadena City College; Joan Mauldin, San Jacinto College–South; Jeanne P. McAllister, Richard J. Daley College; Leslie Mohr, Casper College; Mindy Morse, University of Akron; Karen O'Donnell, Finger Lakes C.C.; Sharon Owen, U. of Texas at El Paso; Clair Juenell Owens, Vincennes University; Jeanette B. Palmer, Motlow State College; Lucia Partin, Faulkner State C.C.; Mark Polnoroff, Penn State/Capital–Schuylkill; Harvey Rubinstein, Hudson County C.C.; Jennifer Scheidt, Palo Alto College; Johanna Seth, Edison C.C.; Lynette Shaw-Smith, Springfield College in Illinois; Karen Sidwell, St. Petersburg J.C.; Maria C. Villar-Smith, Miami-Dade C.C.; Dorothy Ward, University of Texas–El Paso; and Theresa Zeleznick, Cuyahoga C.C.–West.

The following survey respondents also helped guide the course of this project, and I thank them as well:

David Adelman, C.C. of Allegheny County; Karlene Alexander, Miami-Dade C.C.; Kathleen Anderson, Southern Ohio College; Kathleen Andrew, Springfield Technical C.C.; Linda Bagshaw, Briar Cliff College; Lori Baker, Southwest State University; Robert Begiebing, New Hampshire College; Laureen Belmont, North Idaho College; Denise Bostic, Nicholls State University; Lynda Brooks, Kilgore College; Margery Brown, SUNY–Farmingdale; Harry Card, Cabrillo College; Debra Cherson, C.C. of Vermont; Kenneth Cooney, Shasta College; Sue Cross, Mission College; Norma Cruz-Gonzales, San Antonio College; Stephen DeGiulio, New Mexico State University; Margaret Desjardins, Edison C.C.; Jeannine Edwards, University of Memphis; Margaret Fox, Oregon State University; James Fuller, Midland College; Eddye Gallagher, Tarrant County Junior College; Reginald Gerlica, Henry Ford C.C.; Deborah Gilbert, Cleveland State University; Peggy-Joyce Grable, Walla Walla C.C.; Richard Grande, Penn State University; Patrick Haas, Glendale C.C.; Judy Haberman, Phoenix College; Muriel Harris, Purdue University; William Helmls, Vermilion C.C.; Suzanne Henne Mayer, West Illinois University; Beth Hewett, C.C.BC Essex; Marion Heyn, Los Angeles Valley College; Mark Hillringhouse, Passaic County College; Maureen Hoffman, Central C.C.; Pamela Howell, Midland College; Michael Hricik, Westmoreland County C.C.; Kendra Humphrey, John A Logan College; Barbara Huval, Lamar-Port Arthur; Tom Hyder, Piedmont Virginia C.C.; Faye Jones, Nashville State Tech; Reevelyn Jones, University of Arkansas; Dawn Keane, Salem C.C.; Dennis Keen, Spokane C.C.; Patsy Krech, University of Memphis; Dennis Kriewald, Laredo C.C.; Keith Kroll, Kalamazoo Valley C.C.; A. L. Star, C.C. of Baltimore County; Laura Lamalie, Tiffin University; Bill Lamb, Johnson County C.C.; Linda Lane, Foothill College; Bert Lorenzo, Miami-Dade C.C.; Gordon Madson, Crafton Hills C.C.; Becky Mann, Wilkes C.C.; Susan Marsala, Cuesta College; Randy Maxson, Grace College; Jean Miller, DeAnza College; Suzanne Moore, St. Clair C.C.; Harold Morrell, Fulton-Montgomery C.C.; Carol Orban, Vermillion C.C.; Juenell Owens, Vincennes University; Sandra Pass, University of St. Francis; Patricia Patterson, C.C. Allegheny County; Betty Payne, Montgomery College; Myra Peavyhouse, Roane State C.C.; Fritz Pointer, Contra Costa College; Mark Polnoroff, Penn State; Clara Radcliffe, Southwestern Oregon C.C.; Jim Read, Allan Heacock College; Joan Reeves, Northeast AL C.C.; Kathy Routon, Lassen C.C.; Harvey Rubinstein, Hudson County C.C.; Anne Ruder, Maysville C.C.; Julia Ruengert, Ozarks Technical C.C.; Andrea Sanders, Waltes State C.C.; Lew Sayers, Mountain View College; Jim Scholten, Morningside College; Lynette Shaw-Smith, Springfield College; Sharon Small, Golden Gate University; Barbara Smith, College of Mt. St Vincent; John Snyder, Queens Borough C.C.; Carol Solon, Norwalk C.C.; Pat Sterling, New Mexico State U.-Alamogordo; Marjorie Sussman, Miami-Dade C.C.; Carol Swain Lewis, Three Rivers C.C.; Ernie Talavera, Miami Dade C.C.; Nancy Trautmann, Northampton C.C.; Sue Tretter, Lindenwood University; Richard Turner, Ozarks Technical C.C.; Sandia Tuttle, Grossmont College; Lani Uyeno, Leeward C.C.; John Valone, Sacramento City College; Martha Vertreace, Kennedy King College; Maria Villar-Smith, Miami-Dade C.C.; Dorothy Voyles, Parkland College; Beverly Walker, North Central Technical College; Glenda Whalon, Cochise College; Steve Whiting, Sinclair C.C.; Jill Widner, Yakima Valley C.C.; Fred Wolven, Miami-Dade C.C.; and Karen Wong, Skyline College.

As always, I thank my amazing husband, Denny, who doesn't find anything peculiar about my peculiar work habits.

Barb Clouse

Developing Your Writing Process and Writing Paragraphs and Essays

PART ONE

CHAPTER **1**

Your Writing Process

CHAPTER GOALS

By the end of this chapter, you will:

Know tips to help you manage your writing tasks.

Know procedures for dealing with the stages of writing.

Like anything else, writing goes better if you approach it in an organized fashion. This chapter will help you do that by describing specific procedures you can follow and by offering helpful tips.

TIPS FOR MANAGING YOUR WRITING TASKS

1. BEGIN RIGHT AWAY AND WRITE EVERY DAY. The instant you learn about your writing project, begin thinking about it. Consider ideas, approaches, and possibilities as you go about your normal routine. Then the first chance you have to sit down and write—SIT DOWN AND WRITE. Sit down and write two or three times every day, even if you do not feel like it, until your task is complete. Remember, procrastination is a writer's worst enemy.

2. SET INTERMEDIATE GOALS FOR YOURSELF. Rather than worrying about the whole task looming in front of you, break your writing project down into smaller steps. Tell yourself that the first time you sit down, you will think of two ideas. The next time you will think of two more. Make one day's goal to write a good opening idea with support. Make another day's goal to check spellings, and so forth. As you achieve each goal, you will feel encouraged and successful.

3. WORK WITHOUT INSPIRATION. Many people think writers must be zapped by the lightning bolt of inspiration before they can write. These people wait and wait and wait, and the next thing they know they are staring their deadline in the face, with nothing on paper. If you are not inspired, forget about inspiration and write anyway. You will be surprised at how productive you can be.

4. TALK YOUR IDEAS OVER WITH CLASSMATES, ROOMMATES, COWORKERS, AND ANYONE ELSE WHO WILL LISTEN. Also, the phone, e-mail, and message boards can work as well as direct contact.

5. MEET WITH YOUR INSTRUCTOR. If you share your work with your instructor once or twice over the course of the project, your teacher can monitor your progress, make suggestions, help you solve problems, and keep you pointed in the right direction.

6. VISIT YOUR CAMPUS WRITING CENTER. There you will be in the company of other writers who can keep you motivated. You will also find sensitive readers to help you think about your writing and weigh possibilities.

7. EXPECT PROBLEMS. All writers get stuck, so if you hit a snag, do not become discouraged. Walk away from your writing for a while and try again later; experiment with a different approach to the problem; consult the relevant sections

TIP

Writing centers often sponsor workshops on writer's block, readings by authors, and other events that can improve your writing.

of this book; or talk to your instructor. In other words, when a writing problem surfaces, take a break and then take action.

8. EMBRACE YOUR MISTAKES.   Welcome your mistakes and learn from them, because they can help you improve. Each time your instructor comments on your work, study the responses and make note of what to do next time. If you do not know how to overcome a weakness or solve a problem that has been pointed out to you, talk to your instructor.

9. READ EVERY DAY.   The more you read, the more you will learn about how writers operate, and the better writer you will become as a result. In addition to your textbooks, read other things you enjoy—newspapers, magazines, and books (detective novels, romance novels, science fiction—whatever). Of course, as a busy student you have much to do, but reading even 15 minutes every day can make a difference over time.

THE STAGES OF WRITING

Successful writers do not complete a writing task in one sitting. They work through a number of stages over a period of time, leaving and returning to their work often. To be a successful writer, you too should work through the stages of writing described in the rest of this chapter.

STAGE 1: FINDING A WRITING TOPIC

Your instructor may give you a specific writing topic, perhaps something like this:

> Argue for or against abolishing mandatory student activities fees.

More often, however, your instructor will establish a general subject area and you must find a writing topic within that subject area. For example, your instructor might give this assignment:

> Write about stress and the college student.

In this case, you have a broad subject area, but you must discover a specific topic within that subject area. Possibilities include:

- The causes of stress in the college student
- The effects of stress on the college student
- Ways to cope with stress in college
- How to avoid exam anxiety

When you need a writing topic, the following strategies can help. In addition, if you keep a journal, you can consult it for possible topics. Journal writing is discussed on page 9.

Freewriting

To freewrite, you write nonstop for five to ten minutes without worrying about spelling, grammar, neatness, and such. You write whatever occurs to you (even silly ideas) without censoring yourself. If you run out of ideas to write, then write the alphabet or write about how you feel. Soon new ideas will occur to you, and you can write those. Here is an example of a freewriting written to discover a topic.

Man I can't wake up here. What in the world should I write about? I don't have a clue. What what what does she want me to do? All this stress. I can't take it anymore and the semester just began I just don't know how I can do 3 classes and work too but I can't give anything up. What am I going to do? I can't let everyone down. Now what? What to do, what to write. This is hard. Oh well. Does every one else

POWER UP

Join a book group—or organize one yourself. Many websites host book discussions. This site can lead you to many of them: www.bookbrowser.com/Resources/ReadingGroups.html.

feel as stressed out as I do? I'm so tired all the time I'd like to quit work but what will I do for money? Tuition will be due again soon. Maybe I should drop a course. I don't know what to do but I better do something or I'll be a basket case.

This freewriting suggests two possible writing topics: why the writer feels stress and the difficulty of working while attending school.

1.1 ACTIVITY

On a separate sheet, freewrite for about 10 minutes. Do not worry about correctness or how good your ideas are. If you run out of ideas, write the alphabet, names of family members, or "I don't know what to write" until new ideas strike you. When you are finished, read your freewriting and underline ideas that could be shaped into writing topics. Then respond to the following:

1. List the ideas you underlined.

   _____

   _____

   _____

   _____

2. Which idea do you like the best?

   _____

3. Did freewriting help you find a topic? Explain why or why not.

   _____

   _____

   _____

CONNECT

Journalists answer these "journalist's questions" in each news story: who? what? when? where? why? how? Look for the answers to these questions in the next news story you read.

Asking questions

One way to find a writing topic is to ask questions about the subject area your instructor assigns. Here is a list of questions you can ask and the topics they can yield for the subject "stress and the college student."

1. Can I describe something?
   Possible topic: a description of cramming the night before an exam

2. Can I give examples of something?
   Possible topic: examples of ways the college bureaucracy contributes to students' stress

3. Can I explain causes?
   Possible topic: the top 10 reasons students procrastinate

4. Can I explain effects?
   Possible topic: the effects of school pressures on personal relationships

5. Can I compare or contrast something?
   Possible topic: comparing and contrasting stress in school and stress at work

6. Can I place items in groups?
   Possible topic: grouping the kinds of stress in college (exam-related, paper-related, time-related, etc.)

7. Can I tell how something is made or done?
   Possible topic: an explanation of how to cope with school-related stress

8. Can I define something?
   Possible topic: a definition of school-related stress

9. Can I argue something?
   Possible topic: why college officials should be responsible for helping students cope with stress

1.2 ACTIVITY

Ask the above nine questions about one of the following: "television violence" or "working mothers." Write out the answers on a separate sheet. (Do not be concerned if you cannot answer every question.) When you are finished, respond to the following:

1. List the writing topics you discovered.

   _____

   _____

   _____

   _____

   _____

   _____

2. Which topic do you like best?

   _____

   _____

3. Did answering questions help you find a topic? Why or why not?

   _____

   _____

STAGE 2: CONSIDERING YOUR PURPOSE AND YOUR AUDIENCE

Your **purpose** is your reason for writing. You must think about your purpose carefully because it will affect what goes into your writing. For example, say you decide to write about stress and the college student. If your purpose is to make students aware of stress-reduction techniques, you probably will not need to explain to them what stress is. If, on the other hand, you aim to explain to a general audience the effects of stress on the typical college student, you should explain what stress is in that context.

Most writing serves one or more of the following purposes:

- To entertain the reader.
- To express the writer's thoughts and feelings.
- To relate the writer's experience.
- To inform the reader of something.
- To persuade the reader to think or act in a particular way.

Many topics, such as "the causes of stress among college students," lend themselves to a variety of purposes, so you must clarify your reason for writing and choose your details accordingly. Here is a list that shows how different purposes can lead to different details on the topic "the causes of stress in college students."

- If you want to *entertain the reader*, you might include a humorous example of how small dorm rooms create stress.
- If you want to *express your feelings*, you might include an explanation and description of the way you felt the night before your biology final.
- If you want to *relate your experience*, you can tell a story about the time you finished a history paper just minutes before the deadline.
- If you want to *inform the reader of something*, you can explain the most common causes of stress.
- If you want to *persuade the reader to think or act in a particular way*, you can give reasons why changing the general education requirements would reduce stress in college students.

In addition to considering your purpose, you must consider your **audience**, which is your reader. The characteristics of your reader will also influence what goes into your writing. For example, say you plan to argue for a change in the general education requirements. If your audience is the dean of your college, you do not need to define "general education requirements," but you would have to do that if you wrote a letter to the editor of your local newspaper.

1.3 ACTIVITY

Pick one of the topics you discovered in Activity 1.2 and decide on a writing purpose and audience.

Purpose _____

Audience _____

STAGE 3: DISCOVERING IDEAS FOR DEVELOPING A TOPIC

Many students believe that once they have a writing topic they should be able to sit down and spill a draft onto the page. If they can't, they conclude that they do not know how to write. However, this idea is wrong. Before drafting, writers usually must take steps to discover ideas to develop their topics, and they often use the procedures described below. In addition, if you keep a journal, you can consult it for ideas. Journal writing is discussed on page 9.

Listing

To list, write every idea that occurs to you in a column down the page. Do not stop to decide how good your ideas are; just write what you think of. When you run out of ideas to list, you can study what you have and cross out any ideas you do not want to include.

Here is an example of a list developed for a paper about what colleges can do to help students cope with stress. The ideas that are crossed out are ones the writer decided not to include.

make counseling available to students
have stress management workshops
~~test students to learn who is stressed out~~
have "catch-up" days when classes are canceled so students can catch up on their work
train teachers to recognize signs of stress
give out more scholarships so students do not have to work
~~colleges will have fewer dropouts and make more money~~
~~tell profs to lighten up on the work and tough grading~~
show students how to study and take tests

Pick one of the topics you developed for Activity 1.1 or 1.2. If you prefer a different topic, use "why movies are more violent today than ever before." On a separate sheet, write a list to discover ideas for developing the topic. When you are finished, study your list. If there are ideas you do not want to use, cross them out.

The next time you need to discover ideas to develop a topic, will you try listing? Why or why not?

_____

_____

Mapping

CONNECT

If you have trouble remembering how the ideas in a textbook or lecture notes relate to each other, try mapping them for an easier-to-remember visualization.

Many people like mapping because it helps them see how the ideas they discover relate to each other. To map, place your writing topic in a circle in the center of a page, like this:

effects of stress on college students

Then, as each idea occurs to you, connect it to the circle it most closely relates to. A map of ideas for developing a paper about the effects of stress on the college student might look like this:

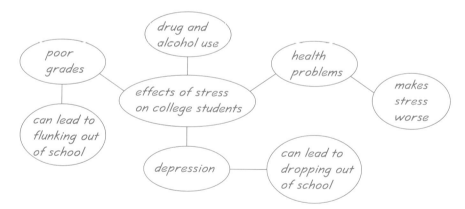

To discover ideas for developing a topic, make a map on a separate sheet, placing in the center one of the topics you developed when you completed Activity 1.2. If you prefer a different topic, use "what I hope to gain from college."

Did mapping help you develop a topic? Why or why not?

_____

_____

Focused freewriting

On page 4, you learned that freewriting can help you find a writing topic. It can also help you discover ideas to develop the topic you settle on. Once again you write non-

CONNECT

Freewriting is an excellent problem-solving technique. What problems are you facing? Are you trying to find time to exercise, decide on a major, or get extra money? Freewrite for 10 minutes, focusing on possible solutions to your problem, and a good one may surface.

stop for five to ten minutes. However, this time, you write everything that occurs to you about your writing topic. You do not worry about how good your ideas are, nor do you think about correctness. Again, if you run out of ideas, write how you feel or write the alphabet until new ideas occur to you. When the time is up, read what you have and underline ideas you can include in your writing.

Here is an example of a focused freewriting on why the writer feels stress, a topic discovered in the first freewriting, which appears on page 4. Notice that usable ideas are underlined.

Why do I feel stress? My parents are on me all the time about grades, they call all the time and ask tons of questions. What if I let them down? Work is killing me, but I can't quit because I need the money. It takes up too much time though and my grades are hurting. Hmmm, I'm really stuck good. Maybe I could find a job on campus that was easier on me. What should I write now? Even little stuff stresses me out like I might sleep in and miss my early class and what if I get the flu? And I'm getting fat. I need exercise.

1.6 ACTIVITY

Select a topic you developed in Activity 1.1 or Activity 1.2. (Use a topic you have not already used for Activity 1.4 or Activity 1.5.) If you prefer, your topic can be "whether or not sports figures make suitable heroes." Then, on a separate sheet, freewrite for about 10 minutes on the topic you selected. When you are finished, underline the ideas that could be used to develop your topic. Then respond to the following:

1. List the ideas you underlined.

    _____

    _____

    _____

    _____

    _____

    _____

    _____

2. Did focused freewriting help you develop a topic? Why or why not?

    _____

    _____

    _____

Keeping a journal

A journal is a place to write for yourself. Your instructor may collect your journal and respond to some of what you have written, but he or she will not evaluate your writing, so you can write what you want in the way you want.

A journal is *not* a diary, because in it you do much more than record the events of your day. Instead, you can think things through in these ways:

1. You can explore ideas just to see where they take you.
2. You can react to the events of your day and write about how they affect you and others.

3. You can write to discover what you think about an issue or event.
4. You can write about your feelings and unleash emotions.
5. You can experiment with writing styles and drafts.

When you need writing ideas, check your journal entries.

To give you an idea of what a journal entry is like, here is a sample:

November 29, 2000

Today I saw a student in a wheelchair. Whenever I see someone in a wheelchair, I try not to make eye contact because I don't want the person to think I'm staring or feeling pity. It's my way of being courteous. Then I realized that lots of times I was making eye contact with people not in wheelchairs, and I was smiling at them. Now I wonder if people in wheelchairs feel like they're being ignored when people try to avoid looking at them. I think that by trying to be polite, I was being rude. From now on, when I see people in wheelchairs, I'm going to smile at them.

To keep a journal, do the following:

1. Buy a sturdy notebook about $8\frac{1}{2} \times 11$ inches. The best notebooks are sewn at the binding, but a spiral notebook will do.
2. Write in your journal each day for at least 10 or 15 minutes. Many writers like the discipline of writing at the same time each day.
3. Date each entry and begin each one on a new page. This makes rereading your journal easier.
4. Use a good-quality pen or a computer to avoid ink and pencil smears.
5. Do not worry about grammar, spelling, or how good your writing is. Just write the best you can in a way that satisfies *you*.

If you are ever stuck for a topic for a journal entry, review this list for ideas.

1. Record your feelings about something that happened to you or to someone else.
2. Explore the meaning of something that happened to you or to someone else.
3. Write about one of your hopes, fears, or anxieties.
4. Explain what you worry about and why.
5. Tell what you like best about yourself and why.
6. Tell what you like least about yourself and why.
7. Explain what you think is right with the world.
8. Explain what you think is wrong with the world.
9. Record a vivid childhood memory.
10. React to something you have read in a newspaper.
11. Describe the ideal friend.
12. Write about a person you admire, respect, like, or dislike. Try to determine why you feel as you do about the person.
13. Write about a change you would like to make in your surroundings.
14. Write about your goals for the next year.
15. Write about your goals for the next 10 years.
16. Write about how you think school is going.
17. Write about a movie you have seen or a book you have read.

CONNECT

Many successful students keep reading journals, where they record their reactions to their reading, how ideas they read connect to what they have learned in other classes, and how they can put to use the ideas they have read about.

18. Write about one of your classmates.

19. Describe a recent holiday celebration.

20. Describe a family relationship.

Write in a journal for three days in a row, and then answer the following question.
What do you think of the journal experience?

_____

_____

_____

_____

CONNECT

Before writing your answer to an essay examination question, write an informal outline that gives the main points to include in your answer. The outline will keep your answer organized and serve as a reminder in case you suddenly forget something you wanted to say.

STAGE 4: WRITING YOUR FIRST DRAFT

After discovering some ideas to develop your writing topic, you can begin your first draft. When you do, the following suggestions can help.

1. DEVELOP AN INFORMAL OUTLINE.   To guide your draft, list the ideas you plan to include, in the order you plan to write them. However, do not feel bound to this outline. You can change things as needed.

2. WRITE FAST AND DO NOT LOOK BACK.   Try to get your draft down in one sitting by expressing yourself the best way you can without worrying about anything. Just begin writing and keep pushing forward, no matter what, until you get to the end.

3. SKIP OVER THE TROUBLESOME SPOTS.   If you cannot think of a word, leave a blank and press on. If you are not sure how to express an idea, jot down anything you can and worry about it later. The key to drafting is focusing on what you *can* do without worrying about what you cannot do.

4. LET THE DRAFT BE ROUGH.   Your first draft is merely a first attempt to express yourself, so it is bound to have problems. Do not let this fact discourage you, because you can make all the changes you want later on.

5. DOUBLE- OR TRIPLE-SPACE.   This way you will have room to make changes later, when you revise.

6. RESPOND TO NEW IDEAS THAT OCCUR TO YOU.   You may think of a worthwhile idea to add, or you may decide to leave out an idea. That's fine. Go ahead and make the changes that occur to you.

7. TAKE ACTION IF YOU GET STUCK.   If you cannot make progress on your draft, try one of these strategies:

- Write the way you speak. Do not worry about expressing yourself in a "college style." Just write out your ideas the way you would speak them to a friend. You can rewrite later if necessary.

- Write your draft the way you would write a letter to a friend. This technique may help you relax and get your ideas down.

- Return to the techniques for discovering ideas. You may have thought you had enough material to begin drafting when you did not.

1.8 ACTIVITY

Select a topic, along with the ideas you discovered to develop that topic, from Activity 1.4, Activity 1.5, or Activity 1.6. On a separate sheet, write an informal outline by listing the ideas in the order you can write them in a first draft. (If you need more ideas, try one of the techniques for discovering ideas.) Next, write a first draft, and then answer these questions:

1. Which suggestions for writing a draft did you follow?

    _____

    _____

    _____

    _____

2. While you were writing your draft, did you feel comfortable (like you knew what you were doing)? Why or why not?

    _____

    _____

    _____

    _____

Save your draft; you will need it for Activity 1.9.

STAGE 5: REVISING YOUR DRAFT

Your first draft gives you raw material to shape into writing suitable for a reader. The process of shaping that raw material is **revising.** Revising is the heart of writing. It is *not* a simple matter of changing a few words, checking spellings, and adding a few commas. Instead, it is a time-consuming process that often involves a major overhaul of the first draft. In fact, it is not unusual for a writer to produce several more drafts in the course of revising.

When writers revise, they look at the following aspects of their drafts:

Content

Organization

Wording

When you revise, some of the following suggestions may help.

1.   LEAVE YOUR WORK FOR A DAY BEFORE YOU REVISE.   This way, you can clear your head and see your work more objectively.

2.   USE A REVISING CHECKLIST.   Rework your draft until you can answer "yes" to each of these questions:

*   Does my writing have a central point?
*   Does everything relate to that central point?
*   Are all my ideas backed up with explanatory details or proof (supporting details)?
*   Are all my points clear?
*   Is my opening interesting?

TIP

Think of revising as like sketching a tree over and over until you get it right, or as close as you can. Or think of it as like seasoning soup bit by bit until it tastes right.

- Does my closing tie things off smoothly?
- Are my ideas in a logical order and connected by transitions?
- Have I used specific words (such as "shouted" and *NYPD Blue)* instead of general words (such as "said" and "television show")?
- Is my word choice concise?

3. REVISE IN STAGES.   The first time through, make the easiest changes. Then go down the above checklist and work through it item by item. Take a break whenever you need to.

4. REVISE OVER A PERIOD OF DAYS.   Because revising is time-consuming, spread the work out over a period of days so you do not become tired. This also gives you time to rethink your writing and make changes.

5. READ YOUR DRAFT ALOUD.   Read to yourself or an audience. Or read into a tape recorder and play back the tape. Many times you will hear problems that you have not seen.

6. TYPE YOUR DRAFT IF YOU HAND WRITE IT FIRST.   Writers often spot problems in type that they overlook in their own handwriting. But remember, a typed draft at this stage is not a final product; you still have work to do.

7. BE MESSY.   You can cross things out, write in the margins, draw arrows, and generally mark up a draft.

8. WAIT TO CORRECT GRAMMAR AND USAGE.   You can check spelling, add commas, look for sentence fragments, and such later when you edit. If you do those things now, your attention will be diverted from content, organization, and wording.

Revising with the aid of reader response

You can get valuable revision advice if you ask someone with good judgment about writing to read and react to your draft. However, do not ask someone who hesitates to offer criticism. If your campus has a writing center, you can find a reliable reader there. Also, try to get two or three readers to react to your draft so you can look for consensus. If your readers disagree on a point and you cannot decide who is right, ask your instructor.

Here are two ways to get reader response.

POWER UP

To make it easier to give and receive reader response, form a writers' group with two or three classmates. Meet regularly to trade drafts, share ideas, and lend support.

METHOD 1

Give each of your readers an unmarked copy of your draft. If necessary, make photocopies or print additional copies from your computer. Give each reader a copy of the following instructions.

1. At the top of the page, write out the main idea of the writing.
2. Place an ! next to any point you find particularly strong.
3. Underline anything that you think is particularly well expressed.
4. Place a ? next to anything you do not understand.
5. Place a ^ anywhere that more information is needed.
6. Circle words or phrases that need to be improved.

METHOD 2

Give your readers a copy of this form and ask them to complete it.

1. What is the main point of the writing? _____

_____

2. What do you like best about the writing? _____

_____

_____

3. How does the writing hold your interest? If it does not, explain why. _____

_____

_____

4. Is there anything you do not understand? If so, what? _____

_____

_____

5. What information, if any, should be added to make the piece clearer?

_____

_____

6. Note any words, phrases, or sentences that are particularly strong. _____

_____

_____

7. Note any words, phrases, or sentences that should be revised. _____

_____

_____

8. What is the most important revision the writer should make? _____

_____

_____

TIP

You can also get reader response by reading your draft aloud over the phone, by e-mailing a draft to a friend, or by posting the draft on a message board if your course is online.

1.9 ACTIVITY

Reread the revising suggestions, and on a separate sheet revise the draft you wrote for Activity 1.8. Then answer these questions:

1. Which of the revising suggestions did you find the most helpful?

_____

_____

_____

2. Did you notice problems in your draft that you did not see at the time you wrote it? _____

_____

3. Do you like your revision better than your first draft? If so, in what way(s)?

_____

_____

_____

Save your revised draft; you will need it for Activity 1.10.

STAGE 6: EDITING YOUR REVISED DRAFT

Editing occurs after revising—after you have reworked content, organization, and wording. To edit, you study your revised draft to find and correct errors in grammar, usage, spelling, capitalization, and punctuation. Because errors distract and annoy a reader, eliminating them is important. The following procedures can help you edit.

1. LEAVE YOUR DRAFT FOR A DAY BEFORE YOU EDIT. Getting away will help you clear your head so you do not overlook errors.

2. EDIT SLOWLY. By the time you get to editing, you will be so familiar with your writing that you will tend to see what you *meant* to write rather than what you really *did* write. To compensate for this tendency, move *slowly*, lingering over each word and punctuation mark for a few seconds. To keep your speed down, edit one line at a time, placing a ruler under each line. Point to each word and punctuation mark as you go. Make sure your eyes are not looking beyond the word you are pointing to.

3. LOOK FOR THE MISTAKES YOU TYPICALLY MAKE. If you often misspell words, make a special effort to check spellings. If you have a tendency to write run-on sentences, edit carefully to find run-ons.

4. EDIT IN STAGES. The first time through, look for the mistakes you have a tendency to make. The second time, edit anything else that catches your eye. The next time through, study several sentences or a paragraph at a time. Always take a break when you are tired. If you typically make many mistakes, edit over a period of days so you can move as slowly as possible.

5. TRUST YOUR INSTINCTS. If you have a feeling that something is wrong, it probably is. Even if you do not know the name of the problem or how to solve it, assume that something is wrong. If you need help identifying and solving the problem, talk to your instructor or a writing center tutor.

6. READ YOUR DRAFT ALOUD. If something sounds "off," assume you have a problem.

7. LEARN THE RULES. You cannot edit confidently if you do not know the grammar, spelling, punctuation, and capitalization rules. This book can help you learn them.

1.10 ACTIVITY

Reread the editing suggestions. Then, on a separate sheet, edit the draft you revised for Activity 1.9. When you are finished, answer these questions:

1. Which of the editing suggestions did you find the most helpful?

_____

_____

_____

2. Approximately how many editing errors did you find?

STAGE 7: PROOFREADING YOUR FINAL COPY

After you edit your draft, you will type or copy it into its final form, the one you will submit to your reader. Because it is easy to make copying or typing mistakes, you should check for errors one last time. This last check for errors in the final copy is called **proofreading**. When you proofread, you should go very slowly, checking each word and punctuation mark.

Your instructor may ask you to proofread and submit the draft you edited for Activity 1.10.

WRITING AT THE COMPUTER

Many people enjoy composing their work at the computer because the machine makes many aspects of writing more efficient. For example, some programs underline possible misspelled words and highlight possible grammar and style problems. If you do not own your own computer, learn whether your campus has a computer lab available to you. Also, many public libraries have computers available for personal use.

Tips for writing at the computer

1. LEARN HOW THE COMPUTER AND WORD PROCESSING PROGRAM OPERATE. If you are an inexperienced computer user, get some instructions from the computer lab assistant. Also, many computers have helpful tutorials that walk you through the best way to use the machines and their word-processing programs, so you can take advantage of all of the convenient features to rearrange text, add and delete material, move material from one spot to another, find and replace words, and insert punctuation and capitalization.

2. IF YOU USE COMPUTERS ON CAMPUS, BEGIN YOUR WORK WELL AHEAD OF THE DUE DATE. A computer may not be available today just because your paper is due tomorrow.

3. LEARN TO TYPE, IF YOU CANNOT ALREADY DO SO. You can even use the computer to learn by purchasing a typing tutorial and practicing each day.

4. SAVE YOUR WORK OFTEN. Print onto paper or copy to a floppy disk at the end of each work session. That way, your writing is preserved in the event of a power failure or hard drive malfunction.

5. KEEP YOUR SCRAPS. As you generate ideas, draft, and revise, you will often write things and then decide to "scrap" them. Rather than hit the "delete" key, save those scraps in a separate "scrap file." You never know when you might change your mind and decide to use something after all. Or you may want to use one of your scraps in a later writing.

6. REMEMBER THAT WRITING GENERATED ON A COMPUTER CAN LOOK BETTER THAN IT REALLY IS. Because computer copy looks so much better than handwritten copy, you can be fooled into thinking your computer draft does not need much revision. Writing done at the computer needs just as much revision as writing done by hand.

7. GO ONLINE. These sites can be very helpful to writers:

WWWebster Dictionary: *http://www.m-w.com/mw/netdict.htm:* Provides free online access to Merriam-Webster's Collegiate Dictionary and Thesaurus.

Britannica.com: *http://www.britannica.com/:* Provides free online access to the *Encyclopaedia Britannica*, articles from magazines such as *Newsweek*, *Discover*, and *The Economist*, a guide to recommended websites, and more.

OWL: Online Writing Lab at Purdue University: *http://owl.english.purdue.edu/ lab/owl/index.html:* Offers a wealth of information for both students and teachers of writing, including handouts, tutorials, workshops, and hundreds of links to other writing resources across the World Wide Web. This site even offers (limited) online tutoring! Definitely worth checking out.

The McGraw-Hill Guide to Electronic Research: *http://www.mhhe.com/ socscience/english/compde/riger.html:* If you're new to computers—or if you're familiar with only one system—visit this site for some basic orientation.

Online Learning Center to Accompany Jumpstart! and Jumpstart! with Readings: *www.mhhe.com/jumpstart:* Provides additional exercises and support material.

Strategies for writing at the computer

As you compose at the computer, you may find some of the following strategies helpful.

To Discover Ideas

1. TRY BLINDFOLDED FREEWRITING.   Turn down the light on your computer screen until the screen is dark. Then freewrite for about 10 minutes. When time is up, print out your freewriting. You will be likely to have lots of typos, but many writers find that not seeing their work on the screen makes their thoughts flow more freely.

2. USE YOUR FAVORITE TECHNIQUES FOR DISCOVERING IDEAS.   You can use the computer to freewrite with the screen light on, ask yourself questions, and list.

To Draft

1. USE THE COPY/MOVE FUNCTIONS TO DEVELOP AN INFORMAL OUTLINE.   If you made a list to discover ideas, you can easily arrange the ideas on that list into the order you want to discuss them in your draft.

2. SPLIT YOUR SCREEN.   Most computers will allow you to place your outline or the ideas you discovered on one part of your screen to refer to as you write your draft on another part of the screen.

3. WRITE FAST AND DON'T LOOK BACK.   Many computer functions make it easy to change things, but your goal when you draft is to push forward. Avoid the temptation to revise as you draft.

To Revise

1. LEARN THE HELPFUL FEATURES OF YOUR WORD-PROCESSING PROGRAM.   They will help you copy, add, move, and delete text with ease.

2. AT LEAST ONCE, REVISE A PRINT COPY OF YOUR WRITING.   You may see things on paper that you overlook on the screen. If you want to revise directly on the paper copy, you can use the insert function to add spaces and give yourself plenty of room to write.

3. SAVE ALL VERSIONS OF YOUR WRITING.   You may want to return to something you did earlier.

4. IF YOUR PROGRAM HAS A THESAURUS, USE IT.   When you cannot think of the word you need, a **thesaurus** (a dictionary of synonyms) can help. However, do not use any word unless you are sure you understand its exact meaning.

5. SPLIT YOUR SCREEN.   Place the revising checklist on pages 12–13 on one part of the screen. You can easily refer to it as you revise the draft on the other part of your screen.

6. USE THE COMPUTER TO GET READER RESPONSE.   Some schools have their computers on a network, making it very easy for you to send your draft to others for revision suggestions. Otherwise, you can e-mail your draft to others by pasting it into the mail or sending it as a file attachment. Also send one of the forms on page 14, so you can get the information you are looking for.

7. USE THE BOLDFACE FUNCTION TO HIGHLIGHT PARTS YOU ARE UNSURE ABOUT.   Then print the draft and give it to two or more reliable readers, and ask them to react to the parts in boldface.

To Edit

1. USE A SPELL CHECKER.   If your computer program has a spell check, use it. Be careful, however, because they are not foolproof. For example, they do not distinguish between soundalikes (*know* and *no*) and they will not recognize when you have used an incorrect word that is spelled correctly (*fled* instead of *sled*).

2. USE GRAMMAR CHECKERS CAUTIOUSLY.   These programs are often not very reliable, so never automatically accept what they tell you. Check everything out yourself.

3. EDIT A PRINT COPY AT LEAST ONCE.   Sometimes you notice things on paper that you overlook on the screen.

4. USE YOUR COMPUTER'S SEARCH FUNCTION TO LOCATE TROUBLESPOTS.   For example, if you often misuse the semicolon, have your computer find every semicolon so you can check each one.

USING E-MAIL

E-mail is an important means of communication on many college campuses. Many instructors use e-mail to communicate with students, and they encourage students to use it to communicate with them. In addition, if you like to collaborate or have classmates react to your writing, you can e-mail copies of your work for review and have them e-mailed back to you with comments. E-mail is also an excellent way to ask questions of your instructor and classmates, confirm assignments, and test ideas. It is an important vehicle of communication in the business world, where it is often the primary form of communication. When you use e-mail, remember the following points.

1. NEVER WRITE ANYTHING YOU WOULDN'T PUT ON A POSTCARD. E-mail is *not* private.

2. WHEN YOU FORWARD A MESSAGE, DO NOT ALTER THE WORDING. If you want to shorten the message when you forward it, just quote the relevant part.

3. CAPITAL LETTERS ARE THE EQUIVALENT OF SHOUTING.   Do not write in all capitals.

4. SAVE EMOTICONS ("SMILEYS") FOR PERSONAL E-MAIL.   They are too informal for business and academic use.

5. FILL IN THE SUBJECT LINE.   Informing the recipient of the subject of your e-mail is an important courtesy.

6. DO NOT SEND CHAIN LETTERS OR JOKES.   They are inappropriate for business and academic e-mail.

7. AVOID HEAVY ABBREVIATIONS IF YOUR READER IS NOT SURE TO KNOW THEM.   Abbreviations such as LOL (laugh out loud) and BTW (by the way) will confuse a reader who does not know them.

8. DO NOT FORWARD E-MAIL WITHOUT PERMISSION.   The writer meant the message for you.

POWER UP

Describe your current writing process. What habits do you have? Where do you like to write? How do you come up with ideas? How do you decide what to change? How many drafts do you usually write?

RECHARGE

Remember that writing is a process involving many steps completed over time. The steps include

- Finding a writing topic.
- Considering audience and purpose.
- Discovering ideas to develop the topic.
- Writing a first draft.
- Revising the draft.
- Editing the revised draft.
- Proofreading.

This chapter describes a variety of ways to complete each aspect of the writing process. Your responsibility is to try a number of these techniques to discover the ones that work the best for you.

GETTING IN GEAR

thinking in writing: Make a list of your most vivid "writing memories," your best-remembered positive or negative experiences with writing in school, at home, or on the job. For example, you might list the time you wrote a love poem to your first grade teacher, had a school paper read in class, got a reaction to a letter you wrote, or experienced particularly difficult bout of writer's block.

writing from experience: Pick a writing memory from your list and write a paragraph that explains what happened. Write a second paragraph that tells how you were affected by the experience.

writing in context: How much writing will you have to do in other classes? What kinds of writing will you have to do? Talk to students who have taken courses you will have to take, and ask them these questions. Then write a paragraph that explains the amount and kind of writing you can expect to do in the coming years.

CHAPTER **2**

Writing a Paragraph

CHAPTER GOALS

By the end of this chapter, you will:

Know the parts of a paragraph.

Understand the characteristics of the paragraph parts.

Know how to write your own paragraphs.

THE PARTS OF A PARAGRAPH

A **paragraph** is a group of sentences working together to develop one main idea.

Generally, a paragraph has three parts: the *topic sentence*, the *supporting details*, and the *closing*.

- The main idea is expressed in the **topic sentence.**
- The main idea is developed in the **supporting details.**
- The paragraph is brought to a satisfying end in the **closing.**

To help you recognize the parts of a paragraph, here is a sample with the topic sentence, supporting details, and closing labeled.

Topic sentence expresses the main idea of the paragraph.

Supporting details develop the main idea mentioned in the topic sentence.

Closing brings the paragraph to a satisfying end.

Helping College Athletes Be Better Students

Colleges can do more to help their athletes succeed academically. The administration should make special tutors available to athletes to provide help as it is needed. In addition, because student athletes have such significant demands on their time, the school should offer workshops designed to teach them time-management techniques. Additional workshops that focus on study skills would also benefit athletes tremendously, as these skills are not always learned in the classroom, and student athletes need to work as efficiently as possible to make the most of their study time. Finally, coaches should receive weekly grade reports so if an athlete's grades slip, the problem can be caught early and solved. If colleges take these steps, student athletes will not be cheated out of an education.

2.1 ACTIVITY

Read the paragraph below and then answer the questions that follow it.

The oyster toadfish is a very strange animal. With flaps of slimy skin hanging from its face like melted candle wax, it looks like a creature from a monster movie. Unlike most fish, the toadfish is not afraid of people and will dart straight toward divers if they come too close. Most other fish would just swim away. Oyster toadfish are not only unusually aggressive; they are also surprisingly loud. Both males and females make loud grunting sounds, and during mating season, the male makes a sound like the blast of a foghorn. In fact, mating toadfish are so loud that people living near coasts have been kept awake all night by their loud noises. Certainly, the oyster toadfish is one of the most unusual fish in the sea.

1. What is the main idea of the paragraph? Which sentence best expresses the main idea?

   The oyster toadfish is strange.

   The first sentence expresses the main idea.

2. What name is given to the sentence that expresses the main idea?

   topic sentence

3. To develop the main idea, the supporting details give three reasons the oyster toadfish is strange. What are they?

   The fish looks like a creature from a monster movie.

   It does not fear people and is aggressive.

   It is loud.

4. What detail supports the idea that the fish looks like a creature from a monster movie?

   Flaps of slimy skin hang from its face.

5. What detail supports the idea that the fish does not fear people and is aggressive?

   It darts toward divers.

6. What details support the idea that the fish is loud?

   Males and females make loud, grunting sounds.

   During mating, the male sounds like a foghorn.

   Mating fish keep people awake.

7. What purpose does the last sentence serve?

   The last sentence brings the paragraph to a satisfying end.

THE TOPIC SENTENCE

The **topic sentence** presents the main idea to be developed or explained in the paragraph.

The topic sentence can appear anywhere in a paragraph; however, for now, place the topic sentence first. This way, you can easily refer to it and stay on course.

An effective topic sentence usually has two parts. One part mentions the topic, and the other mentions the writer's view of that topic.

Topic sentence:	*My brother expects too much of people.*
Topic:	*the writer's brother*
View:	*He expects too much of people.*
Topic sentence:	*Cultural anthropology was the most important course I took in college.*
Topic:	*cultural anthropology*
View:	*It was the writer's most important course.*

Topic sentence:	*All new cars should be required to have air bags on both the driver's side and the passenger's side.*
Topic:	*air bags*
View:	*They should be required on both the driver's and the passenger's sides on new cars.*

2.2 ACTIVITY

For the following topic sentences, draw one line under the words that give the topic and two lines under the words that give the writer's view of the topic.

EXAMPLES   More schools should adopt a twelve-month calendar.

Computers simplify our lives.

1. Traveling by train offers many advantages.
2. Billboards should be banned along scenic highways.
3. Of all my friends, Dana has the most ambition.
4. Nurses are not appreciated as much as they should be.
5. Pornography on the Internet should be regulated.
6. Being an only child is a lonely existence.
7. Many parents believe that rock videos encourage sexual experimentation.
8. Freedom of speech does not mean what many people think it does.

WRITING AN EFFECTIVE TOPIC SENTENCE

An effective topic sentence does not give the writer either too much or too little to say.

Statements of fact do not make good topic sentences because they leave the writer with nothing to say. The following sentences, for example, make poor topic sentences.

Students should study.
I own a 1993 Honda Accord.
Jimmy Juarez is a tutor.

These statements of fact can be reshaped as topic sentences that give the writer something to say.

The study technique I use can help many students.
The Honda Accord is the best car on the road today.
Because he uses humor to teach, Jimmy Juarez is an outstanding tutor.

Broad statements make poor topic sentences because they give the writer too much to say in one paragraph. These sentences, for example, take in too much territory to be suitable topic sentences.

The history of the United States is filled with contradictions.
  [The whole history in one paragraph?]
My childhood was a happy time. [All of the writer's childhood in one paragraph?]
Professional sports should be reformed. [All professional sports in one paragraph?]

Your topic sentence should not sound like an announcement.

No: *This paragraph will discuss my most embarrassing moment.*

Yes: *My most embarrassing moment occurred when I met my mother-in-law for the first time.*

No: *I will explain why high schools should require four years of a foreign language.*

Yes: *High schools should require four years of a foreign language.*

2.3 ACTIVITY

Five of the following topic sentences are acceptable. Three are unacceptable because they are statements of fact, and two are unacceptable because they are too broad. If the topic sentence is acceptable, write "acceptable" on the blank. If it is a statement of fact, write "fact." If it is too broad, write "broad."

EXAMPLE _____fact_____ I am a college freshman.

1. _____broad_____ Montana is a beautiful state.

2. _____fact_____ I attended the Browns-Dolphins football game.

3. _____acceptable_____ Taking a year off between high school and college is a good idea.

4. _____acceptable_____ Carla's practical jokes are more cruel than funny.

5. _____fact_____ The neighborhood watch program reduced crime in the city by 15 percent.

6. _____acceptable_____ In my family, Sunday evening is the best part of the week.

7. _____broad_____ Public education should be reformed in every way.

8. _____acceptable_____ Students can overcome exam anxiety if they follow these steps.

9. _____fact_____ Children need to be loved.

10. _____acceptable_____ Dr. Garcia is the best teacher I ever had.

2.4 ACTIVITY

For each subject area below, write an acceptable topic sentence. If you need ideas, try freewriting or asking questions (see page 4).

EXAMPLES friends:

Nothing comes between friends as fast as jealousy.

shopping:

To get the best bargains, shop outlet stores with caution.

1. a favorite movie or television show:

   Sesame Street teaches children to respect the differences among people.

2. a difficult decision:

   Deciding to quit the basketball team was the most difficult decision I ever made.

3. college life:

   To succeed in college, students must learn how to avoid distractions.

4. family life:

   Being the youngest of six children had its advantages.

5. the difference between two cities:

   Chicago's downtown has survived the growth of the suburbs, but downtown St. Louis feels like a ghost town.

6. sports:

   Karate increased my self-confidence.

7. adolescence:

   Teenagers should not work while they attend high school.

8. a funny experience:

   I will never forget the time Uncle Harry drove off in the wrong car.

2.5 INDIVIDUAL OR GROUP ACTIVITY

Alone or with a classmate or two, read the following paragraph, which lacks a topic sentence. Compose a suitable topic sentence, and write it in the blank.

The ozone layer must be protected. Because it blocks out harmful rays from the sun, there would be no life on earth without ozone. However, for years, human-made pollution has been destroying the ozone layer. As a result, the sun's harmful ultraviolet rays are reaching the earth. These ultraviolet rays can cause skin cancer in humans and other serious problems in plants and animals. Therefore, governments, industries, and scientists must do everything possible to prevent further damage to the ozone layer.

YOUR WRITING PROCESS

To come up with a main idea to focus your paragraph on, try one or more of the following:

- Freewrite for five to ten minutes (see page 4). If you need a starting point, write about something that angers you, excites, you, or makes you happy.
- Ask questions (see page 5).
- Review your journal for ideas (see page 9).
- Look through your local and campus newspaper for issues of interest.

SUPPORTING DETAILS

When you place your topic sentence first, the sentences that come after it are the **supporting details.** The function of the supporting details is to *develop* the topic sentence by explaining it or showing that it is true. For example, reread the paragraph in Activity 2.1 on page 20. The topic sentence is:

The oyster toadfish is a very strange animal.

Here is a list of the paragraph's supporting details, which explain or prove the topic sentence:

Flaps of slimy skin make it look like a monster.
It is not afraid of people and dives toward them.
It is very loud.
It makes a loud grunting sound.
The male sounds like a foghorn.
Mating toadfish keep people awake.

2.6 ACTIVITY

Reread "Helping College-Athletes Be Better Students" on page 20, and answer these questions.

1. What is the topic sentence?

    Colleges can do more to help their athletes succeed academically.

2. What four points form the supporting details because they explain or prove the topic sentence? List them below.

    A. Tutors should be available.

    B. Workshops should be given to teach time-management techniques.

    C. Workshops should be given to teach study skills.

CONNECT

As a study aid, you can rewrite your lecture notes in paragraphs. Put each main idea in a topic sentence. Make the relevant examples, definitions, and clarifying points the supporting details. For a closing, draw a conclusion from or state the importance of the information in the paragraph.

D. Coaches should get weekly grade reports.

_____

WRITING EFFECTIVE SUPPORTING DETAILS: SHOW; DON'T JUST TELL

A reader will not believe what you say just because you say it. That is, you cannot just *tell* your reader that something is true; you must also *show* that it is true with the right kind of **supporting details.** To show and not just tell, back up your statements with:

- Description
- Examples
- A story
- Reasons
- A combination of one or more of the above

1. DESCRIPTION.   Let's say that you have written this statement, maybe even as a topic sentence:

Julio's new girlfriend is eccentric.

To *show* that the girlfriend is eccentric, you can use description, like this:

Julio's new girlfriend is eccentric. When I met her, she wore red and white plaid pants. At the bottom, five safety pins held up the hem. Her green and orange polka-dot blouse was worn inside out. Her makeup was particularly strange because she wore black eyeshadow and black eyeliner. Believe it or not, below her nose pierced with a large ring, she wore black lipstick. Her hair was a normal brown, but she wore one side down to her shoulder and the other cut up above her ear. If this person is not eccentric, then she must be a member of a punk band.

Supporting details in a descriptive paragraph are often arranged in spatial order. **Spatial order** means that supporting details are arranged across space, say front to back, near to far, left to right, or top to bottom. Notice that in the sample paragraph above, the supporting details are arranged from bottom to top: pants to blouse to face makeup to hair.

By arranging details in a spatial or other logical order, you help your reader follow your ideas more easily. However, often you need to do more than arrange details logically. You must signal how ideas relate to each other by using connecting words and phrases called transitions. Some **transitions,** such as the ones listed below, signal a spatial order.

POWER UP

Look again at the newspaper or magazine article you examined for topic sentences in the previous Power Up. Focus now on supporting details. How many are provided in each of the five paragraphs you examined? Does each paragraph support its topic sentence adequately? Be wary of writing that lacks adequate support.

TRANSITIONS THAT SIGNAL SPATIAL ORDER			
above	in front	outside	on one side
below	surrounding	beyond	across from
to the right	inside	far away	alongside

Notice that in the sample paragraph above, these transitions signal a spatial relationship: *at the bottom* and *below her nose.*

2. EXAMPLES. Say you have written this statement, perhaps as a topic sentence:

As a teenager, I was painfully shy.

You can use examples to *show* your shyness, like this:

As a teenager, I was painfully shy. For example, I never joined any organizations at school because I was too shy to go to meetings where someone might try to engage me in conversation. To avoid all notice, I dressed in very plain clothes and wore my hair simply. If, by chance, a member of the opposite sex did notice me and speak, I instantly developed a stammer. Worst of all, I was unable to speak in front of the class. In junior high school, I got a C in English, my best subject, because I could not give an oral book report. As I get older, I become less shy, but I doubt I will ever be an outgoing person.

When supporting details include examples, those examples are often arranged in a **progressive order,** which means that the best or most telling example is saved for last.

When you use examples in a progressive order, transitions can signal how your ideas relate to each other. Below are some common transitions for signaling examples and for indicating progressive order.

TRANSITIONS THAT SIGNAL EXAMPLES			
for example	for instance	as an example	to illustrate

TRANSITIONS THAT SIGNAL PROGRESSIVE ORDER		
first	more/most important	furthermore
above all	more significant	equally important
worst of all	finally	moreover

Notice in the sample paragraph above, that the first example is introduced with the transition for example. The last example is shown to be the most telling because it is introduced with the transition worst of all.

3. A STORY. Say you have written this statement, perhaps as a topic sentence:

Coach Dennis McGregor did more than anyone to build my self-confidence.

To *show* that the coach built your self-confidence, you could tell a story, like this:

Coach Dennis McGregor did more than anyone to build my self-confidence. In eighth grade, I was an awkward boy who was the last one picked for teams in gym and the first one to make a stupid mistake. I felt worthless and unpopular. Then one day Coach McGregor asked me to stay after school. He asked me if I wanted to

CONNECT

Listen for transitions such as *for example, first,* and *furthermore* in your class lectures. They will help you organize your notes.

learn to kick a football. I told him I probably couldn't do it, but he insisted on teaching me anyway. He worked with me after school three days a week, and over the summer he coached me twice a week. Then came the shocker. In July before high school, he told me he expected me to try out for the high school football team as a field goal kicker. I was terrified, but Coach made me try because he said he knew I could do it. On the day of tryouts, he was there. When it was my turn to try out, I glanced at Coach and he gave me his famous thumbs-up sign. Suddenly, his confidence became my own, and I had a successful tryout. I became a second stringer, but just making the team did more for my confidence than anything since. I will always be grateful to Coach McGregor.

When you tell a story, your supporting details will probably be arranged in **chronological order,** which means that details are arranged over time, from what happened first, to what happened second, to what happened third, and so on. The story details in the previous sample paragraph are arranged in chronological order.

When you use chronological order, the following transitions can help you signal how your ideas relate to each other over time.

TRANSITIONS THAT SIGNAL TIME ORDER				
first	now	then	before	after
later	gradually	suddenly	finally	at the same time
afterward	soon	next	in the meantime	

The previous sample paragraph uses a number of transitions to signal time order, including these: *in eighth grade, then one day, then, in July before high school, suddenly.*

4. REASONS.   Say you have written this statement, perhaps as a topic sentence:

All incoming freshmen should be required to take a one-week study skills course prior to the start of classes.

To show that the required study skills course is a good idea, you could offer reasons, like this:

All incoming freshmen should be required to take a one-week study skills course prior to the start of classes. First of all, many new freshmen are returning to school after a long absence. These people probably need to brush up their study skills. A greater concern is the fact that 18-year-old freshmen have often never had a study skills course and need to learn how to study. Also, techniques that were used to study in high school may not be effective in college, particularly since students often take courses unlike anything they encountered in high school. Perhaps most important is the fact that colleges need to decrease the number of students who flunk out, so they can stay in business. A mandatory study skills course prior to the start of classes can help colleges achieve this goal.

POWER UP

Could this topic sentence have been supported using different details? If so, offer a few examples. Do the details the paragraph has now adequately support the topic sentence? Explain.

Like examples, reasons are often presented in progressive order (see page 27). Notice in the previous sample paragraph that the reasons are arranged from the least to the most important. This progressive order is signaled by introducing the first reason with "First of all," the second reason with the transition "a greater concern" and the last reason with the transition "perhaps most important."

5. A COMBINATION. To *show* and not just tell, you can often combine any two or more of the previous techniques. For example, to show that Julio's girlfriend is eccentric, you could first *describe* her eccentric appearance and then *give examples* of her eccentric behavior.

2.7 ACTIVITY

Pick six of the topic sentences you wrote in response to Activity 2.4. Indicate whether the supporting details are likely to be description, examples, a story, reasons, or a combination. If the details are likely to be a combination, state what the combination will be.

CONNECT

If you like to highlight points for study in your textbooks, look for topic sentences and main supporting details. You can highlight them in different colors. For a quick review, look only at topic sentences; for a more thorough review, read the main supporting details as well.

EXAMPLE   Topic sentence: *To get the best bargains, shop outlet stores with caution.*

Supporting details: *reasons to be cautious and examples of what happens when not cautious*

1. Topic sentence: _____

   _____

   Supporting details: _____

   _____

2. Topic sentence: _____

   _____

   Supporting details: _____

   _____

3. Topic sentence: _____

   _____

   Supporting details: _____

   _____

4. Topic sentence: _____

   _____

   Supporting details: _____

   _____

5. Topic sentence: _____

   _____

   Supporting details: _____

   _____

6. Topic sentence: _____

_____

Supporting details: _____

_____

2.8 ACTIVITY

Each of the sentences below *tells*. After each one, add a sentence that *shows*.

EXAMPLE   Americans are becoming more health-conscious. *For example,*
they are eating fewer fatty foods.

1. The history exam was very difficult. I was able to answer only half the
questions.

2. The storm caused much hardship. People were without electricity for
five days.

3. Gloria's apartment is filthy. Globs of dried food are stuck to the floor.

_____

4. Students who work while they attend school often have a difficult time.
They do not get enough sleep, so they are always tired.

5. College offers students many rewarding experiences. For example, I have
met people from five different countries.

2.9 INDIVIDUAL OR GROUP ACTIVITY

After each topic sentence below, list three supporting details that could be written to
show and not just tell. Work alone or with two classmates.

EXAMPLE   My sixteenth birthday was the best ever.

I was given a surprise party.

My sister bought me a leather coat.

My parents took me out to dinner.

1. The scene at Boltin Department Store's going-out-of-business sale was one of
complete chaos.

People were fighting each other to get to the sale racks.

Merchandise was scattered all over the floor.

Customers were yelling at salesclerks.

2. Advertising makes people want things they don't really need.

Women want expensive makeup.

Men want high-priced colognes.

Children want sugared cereals.

3. We would be better off if we threw out our television sets.

   We could get more exercise.

   We could talk to each other more.

   We could read more.

4. I'll never forget the time I got a traffic ticket.

   I was late for work.

   A police officer pulled me over.

   The officer yelled at me.

5. Laricia's is an excellent restaurant.

   The food is authentic Italian.

   Meals are priced under $15.

   The table servers are attentive.

2.10 ACTIVITY

The following paragraph could be improved with more details, so it would show and not just tell. On a separate sheet, rewrite the paragraph by adding the following:

A. A sentence or two after sentence 2 to show that the father drives too fast
B. A sentence or two after sentence 3 to show that he does not watch the road
C. A sentence or two after sentence 4 to show that he tries to get the best of other drivers

[1]If you drive with my father, you take your life in your hands. [2]For one thing, he
Even on city streets, he rarely goes below 50 mph.   He is always fiddling with the radio or
drives too fast. [3]He also does not watch the road the way he should. [4]Worst of all,
checking his hair in the mirror.
he is very aggressive when he gets behind the wheel, so he is always trying to get the
He tailgates, cuts people off, and races drivers to traffic lights.
best of other drivers. [5]He is so bad, in fact, that my mother and I now refuse to get

in the car with him unless one of us drives.

WRITING EFFECTIVE SUPPORTING DETAILS: STICK TO THE POINT

Supporting details should not stray from the topic and view presented in the topic sentence. This way, the paragraph has **unity**. For example, consider a paragraph with this topic sentence:

> Before beginning their job interviews, students should learn how to dress for success.

This topic sentence will allow you to discuss clothing style, but it will not allow you to discuss how to behave.

CONNECT

Sometimes students who are not sure of the correct response pad their answers to examination questions with detail not strictly related to the question. How do you think busy instructors react to answers that lack unity?

2.11 ACTIVITY

Cross out the one sentence in each paragraph below that does not stick to the point.

Elderly people should take special care to stay physically fit. They should avoid high-fat items and food high in sodium and be sure to take multivitamins, especially if their appetites are poor. At least three times a week, they should get an hour or so of aerobic exercises, perhaps by swimming or walking briskly. ~~The exercise does not have to be expensive to be effective.~~ If sleep is difficult, they should be sure to rest adequately during the day. If elderly people follow these commonsense guidelines, they can stay fit and healthy for many years to come.

Good teachers share several important characteristics. First, they plan classes carefully so information is clearly presented. Second, they welcome questions and take as much time as necessary to answer them. ~~Some teachers, unfortunately, consider questions an intrusion and become annoyed when they are asked.~~ Good teachers also stay abreast of developments in their fields by reading professional journals and attending conferences. Finally, good teachers grade work fairly and return it promptly.

YOUR WRITING PROCESS

To come up with supporting details for your paragraph, try the following:

- Listing (see page 7).
- Mapping (see page 8).
- Focused freewriting (see page 8).
- Talking to other people about your topic. They may have some ideas for you to consider.

After coming up with ideas, write your first draft with the strategies on page 11. If you experience writer's block and need more help than you find on page 11, try these ideas:

- Leave your work for a while. Take a walk, eat a snack, or listen to music. Afterward, you may be more ready to write.
- Do not worry about perfection. You may be blocked because you are expecting your writing to be too good too soon.
- Change your surroundings and tools. If you are in your bedroom, go to the library; if you are using a computer, try a pen and notebook paper.

WRITING EFFECTIVE SUPPORTING DETAILS: REVISE FOR CONCISE, SPECIFIC WORD CHOICE

What you say is very important. That is why you need to show and not just tell, stick to the point, and use transitions. However, *how* you say things is also important, which is why you must strive for concise, specific word choice. You do not need to worry about word choice during drafting. However, during revision you should make your word choices both specific and concise.

Concise word choice

To be **concise,** avoid using many words when you can express yourself equally well in a few words. To appreciate how a concise sentence can be more pleasing than a wordy one, read the following examples.

Wordy: *My physician, who happens to be an allergy specialist, tells me on a frequent basis that I should always be sure to avoid processed sugar.*

Concise: *My physician, an allergy specialist, frequently tells me to avoid processed sugar.*

One way to be concise is to reduce wordy phrases to a single word.

Wordy Phrase	Concise
at this point in time	now
on a frequent basis	frequently
in the event that	if
in society today	today
in today's modern world	today
has the ability to	can

Another way to be concise is to revise to eliminate repetitious phrases.

Repetitious	Concise
the color green/green in color	green
mix together	mix
the final conclusion	the conclusion
a true fact	a fact
the reason why	the reason
very necessary	necessary
very unique	unique

Specific word choice

Words can be general or specific. **General words** are vague and do not give the reader a very detailed idea. **Specific words** are more exact and give the reader a more detailed, precise idea. To appreciate how specific words convey a more detailed idea, consider these examples.

General: *The child ate a snack.*

Specific: *The two-year-old boy gleefully sucked on a cherry Popsicle.*

When you revise, substitute specific words for some of your general ones.

General	Specific
walk	stroll/wander/strut
feel good	elated/excited/optimistic
feel bad	depressed/apprehensive/nervous
nice	colorful/playful/spirited/
hat	red stocking cap
drink	slurp
meat	rare roast beef
book	*The Color Purple*

POWER UP

Choose a magazine or newspaper article that you find interesting. Count the number of specific words used in a single paragraph. Do you think the number has anything to do with your interest? Explain.

2.12 ACTIVITY

Revise each sentence to make it more concise.

EXAMPLE   At a point in time about 5,000 years ago, the Chinese discovered how to make the fabric silk.   *About 5,000 years ago, the Chinese discovered how to make silk.*

1. The Chinese as a people had the ability to make silk from silkworm cocoons.

   The Chinese could make silk from silkworm cocoons.

2. For about 3,000 years of time, the Chinese kept this discovery a secret to themselves.

   For about 3,000 years, the Chinese kept this discovery a secret.

3. Because of the fact that the poor people could not afford real silk cloth, they tried to make other cloth look silky.

   Because the poor could not afford real silk, they tried to make other cloth look silky.

4. Women would beat on cotton with sticks for the purpose of softening the fibers of cloth.

   Women would beat on cotton with sticks to soften the fibers.

5. Then they rubbed it against a big rock stone to make it shiny bright.

   Then they rubbed it against a big rock to make it shiny.

6. The shiny cotton was called by the name of "chintz."

   The shiny cotton was called "chintz."

7. Because chintz was a cheaper reproduction copy of silk, calling something "chintzy" means it is cheap in price and not a good quality.

   Because chintz was a cheaper copy of silk, calling something "chintzy" means it is cheap and not good quality.

2.13 ACTIVITY

Revise the following sentences to make the words more specific.

EXAMPLE   The food was terrible.   *The baked chicken tasted greasy and too salty.*

1. The noise bothered me.

   The shrill whistle made me shiver.

2. The view was beautiful.

   From the car, the rolling, green hills looked lush and peaceful.

3. Later on, the girl began to feel bad.

   By bedtime, five-year-old Rajá was weak and nauseated.

4. The room was a terrible mess.

   The kitchen was covered in red sauce because the pressure cooker exploded.

5. The kitchen smelled funny.

   Because the milk was left on the counter, the kitchen smelled sour.

6. The person who went down the street seemed happy.

   The letter carrier whistled cheerfully as he strolled down the sidewalk.

POWER UP

Think of a movie you saw or book you read that had an excellent beginning and middle but a bad ending. Now think of a dinner that ended with a disappointing dessert. How did you react to these unsatisfactory closings? What do they tell you about the importance of ending well? What does that suggest about the importance of paragraph closings?

THE CLOSING

Sometimes a paragraph needs a **closing sentence** to bring it to a satisfying finish, and sometimes it does not.

To decide if it needs a closing sentence, read your paragraph aloud. If it sounds like it finishes abruptly, add a closing sentence.

Many times an appropriate closing sentence will suggest itself to you. When it does not, try one of these approaches:

- Draw a conclusion from the supporting details. See "Helping College Athletes Be Better Students" on page 20 for an example of this approach.
- Repeat the idea in the topic sentence. See the paragraph in Activity 2.1 for an example of this approach.
- State what you think will happen in the future. See the paragraph developed with examples on page 27 for an example of this approach.

2.14 ACTIVITY

If you think either of the paragraphs below needs a closing sentence, add one. If you think it does not need a closing sentence, explain why.

The university administration must turn its attention to solving the parking problem on our campus. Although this is a commuter school, there are too few parking spaces for the faculty, staff, and students who drive here each day. As a result, students are often late to class because they have to drive around hunting for an empty parking space. Many of the lots that do exist are unpaved. It makes me angry to drive my new Chevy into a lot only to have gravel thrown up to chip the paint. Half the time I don't even know if my car will be there when I return because the university does not have enough parking attendants to go around. With no attendant on duty, my car could be stolen. In fact, three cars have been stolen in the last four months. _____

Something simply must be done about the parking problem.

_____

Before you consider drinking and driving, you should know about my friend, Jerry. Jerry graduated on a Friday morning. Following the ceremony, he kissed his mother and took off for a day of celebrating with his friends. His first stop was the lake for some swimming and sunbathing. Of course, there was beer to drink. That night was the party at Pam's. Everyone was there, and so was the booze. Jerry got behind the wheel to drive home at 2 A.M. He did not think he was drunk, but he was. The coroner's report proved it. Jerry was dead just 14 hours after graduation. _____

Last sentence provides sufficient closure.

_____

YOUR WRITING PROCESS

In addition to following the suggestions on pages 12–13, try some of the following strategies to revise your draft.

- Revise in stages. Rather than trying to do everything at once, revise for an hour at a time, taking breaks between each revision session.
- Trust your instincts. If something inside suggests you have a problem, do not ignore the feeling.
- Check each of your sentences against your topic sentence to be sure you are maintaining unity.
- Check each of your sentences to be sure it suits your audience and helps fulfill your purpose.
- If your draft is too long, try narrowing the scope of your topic sentence. For example, instead of a topic sentence that says, "High school was the best time of my life," write "In my senior year of high school, I learned about the importance of friendship."
- If your draft is too short, try describing a relevant person or scene, or try adding clarifying examples.

In addition to following the suggestions on page 15, try some of the following strategies to edit your draft.

- Edit last. If you edit too soon, you will take your attention away from the drafting and revising concerns. Also, you do not want to edit a sentence that you omit during the revision process.
- When in doubt, check it out. If you are unsure of something, do not let it pass. Consult this book, your instructor, or a writing center tutor for advice. Remember, though, the writing center is not an editing service. The tutors there will gladly read and respond to your work, and they will answer specific questions, but they will not fix your mistakes.

RECHARGE

The parts of a paragraph are the topic sentence, the supporting details, and the closing.

- The topic sentence
  Presents the main idea.
  Should not be a fact.
  Should not be too broad.
  Should not be an announcement.

- The supporting details
  Develop the topic sentence.
  Should show and not just tell.
  Should be expressed in concise, specific words.
  Should have transitions to connect ideas.
  Should have unity.

- The closing
  Brings the paragraph to a satisfying close.

2.15 CHAPTER REVIEW ACTIVITY

The following is the first draft of a paragraph that could be entertaining if it were revised effectively. Read it and diagnose the chief problems in the spaces that follow. Then, on a separate sheet, revise the paragraph to eliminate the problems you diagnosed.

How to Make a Rotten Impression on a Job Interview

This paragraph will tell you how to make a rotten impression on a job interview. Knowing how to make a rotten impression on a job interview is important because making a good impression could lead to a job offer, and then you would have to actually go to work. To make an immediate bad impression, dress like a slob. Also, as the interviewer is speaking to you, be sure to act distracted and uninterested. If you are halfway into the interview and you think there is even a remote chance you might be offered a position, try insulting the interviewer (or his or her parents).

1. Diagnosis of topic sentence:
   in the form of an announcement
   _____

2. Diagnosis of supporting details:
   tell without showing
   _____

3. Diagnosis of closing:
   abrupt; closing sentence needed
   _____

GETTING IN GEAR

thinking in writing: American educator and writer Bel Kaufman said, "Education is not a *product*: mark, diploma, job, money—in that order; it is a *process*, a never-ending one." In your journal or elsewhere, freewrite for 10 or 15 minutes, focusing on Kaufman's words.

writing from experience: Tell about a time when education, for you, was a process rather than a product.

writing in context: Assume you have been asked to address the college-bound graduating seniors at a local high school. Your purpose is to give these students an idea of what to expect when they get to college. In a paragraph, write a definition of *education* to open your remarks and remind students of what college is all about.

CHAPTER 3

Writing an Essay

CHAPTER GOALS

By the end of this chapter, you will:

Know the parts of an essay.

Understand the characteristics of each part.

An **essay** is a composition of several paragraphs that work together to develop one central idea. When your topic requires a fuller treatment than you can give in a single-paragraph writing, then you need to write an essay.

Like a paragraph, an essay has a beginning, a middle, and an end. The beginning is the *introduction*, the middle is the *body paragraphs*, and the end is the *conclusion*.

	PARAGRAPH	ESSAY
BEGINNING	Topic sentence	Introduction
MIDDLE	Supporting details	Body paragraphs
END	Closing	Conclusion

POWER UP

An introduction influences a reader's first impression of a writing. What happens if that impression is negative? In what other situations are first impressions important?

THE BEGINNING OF AN ESSAY: THE INTRODUCTION

You have learned that a paragraph opens with a topic sentence that presents the main idea to be developed or explained. In an essay, the first paragraph, which is the **introduction,** also presents the main idea—in a sentence called the **thesis.** In addition to giving the thesis, the introduction should create interest so the reader will want to read on.

THE MIDDLE OF AN ESSAY: THE BODY

After the topic sentence, a paragraph has supporting details that develop the topic sentence. In an essay, the supporting details appear in two or more **body paragraphs.** Each body paragraph develops a single point related to the thesis. Thus, if you want to present and explain two points, you will have two body paragraphs. Three points will mean three body paragraphs, and so on.

The structure of a body paragraph is the same structure you learned for a one-paragraph composition: topic sentence and supporting details.

THE END OF AN ESSAY: THE CONCLUSION

In a one-paragraph writing, the closing brings the piece to a satisfying close. In an essay, the final paragraph, which is the **conclusion,** serves the same purpose.

COMPARING A PARAGRAPH AND ESSAY

To help you see how an essay is put together and how its parts are similar to paragraph parts, here is an essay-length expansion of the paragraph on page 28.

A MANDATORY STUDY SKILLS COURSE

Paragraph 1 is the *introduction.* It creates interest by presenting a problem (poor study skills of students).

The underlined *thesis* presents the main idea of the essay, the proposed solution to the problem.

Paragraph 2 is a *body paragraph.* The underlined *topic sentence* presents the main idea of the paragraph—that many new students have been out of school for a long time—an idea that develops the thesis.

The rest of the paragraph is the *supporting details,* which develop the topic sentence.

Paragraph 3 is a *body paragraph.* The underlined *topic sentence* presents the main idea of the paragraph—that 18-year-old students never learned proper study skills—an idea that develops the thesis. The rest of the paragraph is *supporting details* to develop the topic sentence.

Paragraph 4 is a *body paragraph.* The underlined *topic sentence* presents the main idea of the paragraph—that a study skills course is in the best interest of colleges—an idea that develops the thesis. The rest of the paragraph is *supporting details* to develop the topic sentence.

Paragraph 5 is the *conclusion,* which brings the essay to a satisfying finish by gracefully restating the thesis and main points.

[1]Every fall with the new crop of freshmen, instructors complain that students do not know how to study. The problem is not just with new students, though. Many upper-classmen struggle with the best way to complete assignments and prepare for exams. There is a solution to this problem, and it is an easy one to implement. All incoming freshmen should be required to take a one-week study skills course prior to the start of classes.

[2]First of all, many first-year students are returning to school after a long absence. These people probably need to brush up their study skills. They may have forgotten such things as time management, critical reading, and efficient note-taking. Even if they still remember most of these things, they are often insecure and nervous because they have not used these skills for a long time. A study skills course would be a refresher that would help students reclaim lost skills and build the confidence that will help them succeed.

[3]A greater concern is the fact that 18-year-old students have often never had a study skills course and need to learn how to study. Let's face it, many students get through high school without ever cracking a book. It isn't until they get to college that they have to study, and then they do not know how. Also, for those who did crack a book, techniques that were used to study in high school may not be effective in college, particularly since students often take courses unlike anything they encountered in high school. For example, many students never had sociology, psychology, anthropology, political science, art appreciation, and education classes in high school, so they may not understand how to approach this new material.

[4]Perhaps most important is the fact that colleges need to decrease the number of students who flunk out, so they can stay in business. Whether we like to think so or not, a college is a business, and if it does not keep customers (students), it will have to close its doors. Here at this university, we have had to hire a professional marketing firm to advertise and attract students to make up for the ones we lose along the way. With a mandatory study skills course prior to the start of classes, we will lose fewer students and so need to worry less about attracting new ones.

[5]A mandatory study skills course prior the start of classes can better prepare freshmen so they get better grades. With better grades, fewer will flunk out, so colleges will worry less about enrollment. Everybody wins.

3.1 ACTIVITY

To answer these questions, compare "A Mandatory Study Skills Course" with the paragraph version on page 28.

1. Which sentence of the paragraph version expresses the main idea? What is that sentence called? The first sentence, the topic sentence, expresses the main idea.

2. Which sentence of the essay expresses the main idea? What is that sentence called? The last sentence of paragraph 1, the thesis, expresses the main idea.

3. What idea does paragraph 2 present to help support the thesis? In what sentence is that idea presented? What is that sentence called? Paragraph 2 presents the idea that many freshmen are returning to school after a long absence. The idea is presented in the first sentence, which is called the topic sentence.

4. List the four main supporting details that develop the main idea of paragraph 2.
    the need to brush up on study skills
    forgetting important skills
    feeling insecure and nervous
    the course as a refresher

5. Which three of the ideas in your answer to number 4 do not appear in the paragraph version?
    forgetting important skills
    feeling insecure and nervous
    the course as a refresher

6. What idea does paragraph 3 present to help support the thesis? In what sentence is that idea presented? What is that sentence called? The first sentence, the topic sentence, presents the idea that 18-year-olds need to learn how to study.

7. List the two main supporting details that develop the main idea of paragraph 3.
    Many never studied in high school.
    High school techniques may not be effective in college.

8. What example is used in paragraph 3? What transition introduces that example? Does that example appear in the paragraph version? The example, introduced with "for example," is of college courses that students may not have had in high school. The example does not appear in the paragraph version.

9. What idea does paragraph 4 present to help support the thesis? In what sentence is that idea presented? What is that sentence called? The idea, presented in the first sentence (the topic sentence), is that colleges need to decrease the number of students who flunk out.

10. List the three main supporting details that develop the main idea of paragraph 4.

    College is a business.

    Colleges must keep their students or close.

    A study skills course can help colleges keep students.

11. Which of the ideas in your answer to number 10 do not appear in the paragraph version? all of them

12. How does the conclusion bring the essay to a satisfying finish? The conclusion highlights the main points and ends with a dramatic statement.

YOUR WRITING PROCESS

The strategies for writing an essay are like those for writing a paragraph, most of which you read about in Chapters 1 and 2.

To Come Up with a Topic and Ideas to Develop the Topic

- Freewrite
- Ask questions
- List
- Map

To Write an Effective Thesis

- Follow the same guidelines you did for writing an effective topic sentence (see pages 22–23).
- Avoid statements of fact.
- Avoid broad statements.
- Avoid announcements.
- Make sure you are writing about something you know enough about.

To Draft

- Prepare an outline of your body paragraphs by placing each of your topic sentence ideas at the top of its own column on a page. Then list the ideas that will develop the topic sentence idea in the appropriate column.
- Be sure your draft has at least two body paragraphs.
- If you have trouble with your introduction, write it last.
- Follow the drafting suggestions on page 11.

POWER UP

Will you have to write essays on the job? If you do not know, speak to someone in the position you hope to have one day.

To Revise and Edit
- Check each topic sentence against your thesis to be sure you are sticking to the point.
- Check the details of each body paragraph against its topic sentence to be sure you are sticking to the point.
- Give your introduction to two people and ask them whether it creates interest.
- Ask a reliable reader to review your draft and answer these questions:
  Is there any place where I show without telling?
  Is there any place where a transition is needed?

For other reader-response suggestions, see page 13.

- Check your words to be sure you are being both specific and concise.
- For additional revision and editing suggestions, see page 13.

RECHARGE

An essay is made up of several paragraphs. These are

- The introduction
  Creates interest.
  Presents the thesis (main idea).
- The body paragraphs
  Develop points related to the thesis.
  Have topic sentence and supporting details.
- The conclusion
  Brings essay to a satisfying close.

The strategies for writing a paragraph and the qualities of effective writing that you learned in Chapters 1 and 2 also apply to writing an essay.

GETTING IN GEAR

thinking in writing: What would happen if teachers stopped giving grades? Make a list of the changes you think would occur.

writing from experience: Explain how your life has been affected by grades. You can support your points with examples and one or more stories.

writing in context: Educators are always looking for ways to improve the educational system. Assume the role of an educator and devise an alternative to traditional grading practices. Explain how your plan works and why it is a good one.

Understanding the Sentence

PART TWO

CHAPTER 4

Subjects and Verbs

CHAPTER GOALS

By the end of this chapter, you will:

Recognize the subject and verb of a sentence.

Understand the functions of the subject and verb.

Recognize the simple subject of a sentence.

Recognize action verbs.

Recognize linking verbs.

Recognize helping verbs.

THE SENTENCE

We often think of a sentence as a group of words beginning with a capital letter and ending with a period, but there is more to it than that. To be a sentence, a word group must be complete enough to stand independently. Most of the time, you can speak a word group out loud and hear whether it is complete enough to stand alone as a sentence. To appreciate this fact, read aloud these word groups and decide which one is complete enough to stand as a sentence:

> *the storm moved offshore*
> *as the storm moved offshore*

You probably recognized that the first word group is complete enough to stand as a sentence. In fact, if you add a capital letter and a period, you *do* have a sentence:

> *The storm moved offshore.*

However, try adding a capital letter and a period to the second word group:

> *As the stormed moved offshore.*

Here you do not have a sentence even with the capital letter and period because the necessary completeness is lacking; you are left feeling that something is missing.

GRAMMAR ALERT !

A word group can be complete enough to be a sentence, even if some information is unknown. Consider this sentence:

> *She yelled at him.*

Although we do not know the names of the person who yelled and the person who was yelled at, the word group is complete enough for sentence status.

4.1 ACTIVITY

If the word group is complete enough to be a sentence with the addition of a period and capital letter, write "yes" on the blank. If it is not complete enough for sentence status, write "no." If you are unsure, speak the word group aloud and listen for completeness.

1. <u>yes</u> every generation has its crazy fads
2. <u>yes</u> in the 1930s, dance contests were the rage
3. <u>yes</u> these contests were called marathons
4. <u>no</u> because people would see how long they could dance
5. <u>no</u> the winning couple dancing for the most hours straight

6. __yes__ the longest dance marathon was won by Mike Ritof and Edith Boudreauz
7. __no__ when they danced from August 29, 1930, through April 1, 1931
8. __yes__ in all, they danced for 216 days
9. __no__ although they were allowed to rest for twenty minutes every hour
10. __yes__ dancing must have cheered people up during this time of the Great Depression

THE FIRST NECESSARY COMPONENT: THE SUBJECT

Every sentence must have a subject. The **subject** is the word or words that answer one of these questions:

> Who or what does or did something?
> Who or what exists or existed in a particular way?

Here is an example:

> *Our soccer team won the state championship.*

Ask:	Who or what does or did something?
Answer:	*our soccer team*
Subject:	*our soccer team*

Let's look at another example:

> *My coat is too small.*

Ask:	Who or what exists or existed in a particular way?
Answer:	*my coat*
Subject:	*my coat*

4.2 ACTIVITY

The following sentences are incomplete because the subjects are missing. To complete each sentence, fill in the blank with any appropriate subject.

EXAMPLE   _The lost wallet_   is behind the sofa.

1. __The librarian__ explained how to use the computerized card catalog in the library reference room.

2. __Corn flakes__ and __wheat toast__ are my favorite breakfast foods.

3. __The magician__ was the best act in the talent show.

4. __My roommate's car__ needed expensive repairs.

5. __The sour milk__ should be thrown away.

THE COMPLETE SUBJECT AND THE SIMPLE SUBJECT

The **complete subject** is another name for the subject discussed in the preceding section. As you now understand, you can find the complete subject by asking, Who or what does or did something? or Who or what exists or existed in a particular way?

> *My elderly aunt is taking a psychology course in college.*

Ask: Who or what does or did something?

Answer: *my elderly aunt*

Complete subject: *my elderly aunt*

The Simple Subject

The **simple subject** is the most important part of the complete subject. The simple subject will usually be a **noun,** a word that names a person, a place, an object, an idea, or an emotion (like *father, Nashville, table, freedom,* or *fear*). Or it will be a **pronoun,** a word that substitutes for a noun (*I, you, he, she, it, we, they*).

Sentence: *The horror movie had a surprise ending.*

Complete subject: *the horror movie*

Simple subject: *movie*

Sentence: *My oldest and dearest friend is coming to town.*

Complete subject: *my oldest and dearest friend*

Simple subject: *friend*

CONNECT

Later you will learn that your ability to find simple subjects will help you choose verbs and pronouns correctly.

4.3 ACTIVITY

In the following sentences, the complete subjects are underlined. Circle the simple subjects.

EXAMPLE   The elegant dress costs too much money.

1. Our research papers are due at the end of the week.
2. My favorite actor is Matt Damon.
3. Most incoming freshmen register for a writing course.
4. This early spring is certainly chasing away my blues.
5. My youngest brother wants to join the FBI.

4.4 ACTIVITY

For each of the following sentences, write the complete subject in the first blank and the simple subject in the second blank.

EXAMPLE   The red leather shoes are on sale.

Complete subject: *the red leather shoes*

Simple subject: *shoes*

1. The home's previous owner had five children.

Complete subject: the home's previous owner

Simple subject: owner

2. Very young children can suffer from stress.

Complete subject: very young children

Simple subject: children

3. An old man sat on the park bench reading the paper.

Complete subject: ___an old man_____

Simple subject: ___man_____

4. The circus animals performed several amazing tricks.

Complete subject: ___the circus animals_____

Simple subject: ___animals_____

5. The new ad campaign was a huge success.

Complete subject: ___the new ad campaign_____

Simple subject: ___campaign_____

The Location of the Subject

You have probably noticed that the subject often comes near the beginning of a sentence. Sometimes, one or more words come before the subject, as in these examples:

Sentence:	*In the afternoon, Milana volunteers at the Senior Citizens Center.*
Ask:	Who or what does or did something?
Answer:	*Milana*
Subject:	*Milana*
Words before the subject:	*in the afternoon*
Sentence:	*For the time being, the labor union is experiencing a membership decline.*
Ask:	Who or what exists or existed in a particular way?
Answer:	*the labor union*
Subject:	*the labor union*
Words before the subject:	*for the time being*

TIP

To make sure you have a complete sentence when one or more words come before the subject, drop the words before the subject. What's left should still be a complete sentence.

4.5 ACTIVITY

Underline the complete subjects and circle the simple subjects. The first one is done as example.

1. Once in a while, a person will bite into an apple and find a worm. 2. These worms get into apples in a surprising way. 3. The little critters are born there. 4. In the middle of summer, small apples are growing on apple trees. 5. At that time, female flies lay their eggs inside some of the apples. 6. The eggs hatch into tiny worms called larvae. 7. These worms begin eating the apples. 8. If unpicked, the apples fall from the tree in autumn. 9. The larvae crawl out and bury themselves in the ground. 10. Then, a hard skin forms around each one. 11. The next summer, a fly emerges from the skin. 12. A person biting into an apple at the wrong time can find a worm.

Action-Word Subjects

The simple subject of a sentence can be a form of an action word. This form can end in *-ing* (a **gerund**) or begin with *to* (an **infinitive**), as in the following examples.

Running is an excellent activity for reducing stress.
Seeing you again is a pleasure. [The simple subject is *seeing*.]

To win is my only goal.

To win the game will take a miracle. [The simple subject is *to win*.]

The simple subjects in the following sentences are forms of action words. Underline the complete subjects and circle the simple subjects.

EXAMPLE [Eating] dinner at eight o'clock is very elegant.

1. [Changing] majors is not difficult.
2. [To earn] an A in this course requires dedication.
3. [Leaving] the maps at home was a big mistake.
4. Crash [dieting] poses a health risk.
5. [To apologize] to Sasha will take courage.

Subjects with Prepositional Phrases

Prepositions show the relationship of one thing to another.

The kitten sat in the corner.

In is a preposition that shows the relationship of the kitten to the corner: it was *in* the corner.

Here is a list of words often used as prepositions. Study it to familiarize yourself with these words.

about	before	in	toward
above	behind	into	under
across	beside	like	until
after	between	of	up
against	by	off	with
along	during	on	without
among	except	over	
around	for	through	
at	from	to	

TIP

Think of a ball and a box. Many words that can describe the relationship of the ball to the box are prepositions. For example, a ball can be in the box, near the box, or above the box, so *in, near,* and *above* are prepositions.

A **prepositional phrase** is a preposition and the words that go with it. The following are prepositional phrases. The prepositions are underlined as a study aid.

<u>among</u> the ruins	<u>by</u> day	<u>of</u> the people
<u>around</u> the corner	<u>for</u> me	<u>over</u> the hill
<u>between</u> us	<u>in</u> the night	<u>without</u> a doubt

A complete subject often includes a prepositional phrase, but the simple subject will *never* be a word in that prepositional phrase.

Sentence: *Six of the scouts earned merit badges.*

Complete subject: *six of the scouts*

Simple subject: *six* [*Scouts* is part of the prepositional phrase "of the scouts" and cannot be a simple subject.]

TIP

For a complete discussion of prepositions and prepositional phrases, see Chapter 17.

TIP

Learning how prepositions are used in English can be difficult. Reading and listening to how people speak can help. Listening to TV and radio can also be very instructive.

Sentence:	*Three members of the band are absent.*
Complete subject:	*three members of the band*
Simple subject:	*members* [*Band* is part of the prepositional phrase "of the band" and cannot be a simple subject.]

The complete subject can include more than one prepositional phrase, like this:

The car at the side of the road has stalled.

Complete subject:	*the car at the side of the road*
Prepositional phrases:	*at the side/of the road*
Simple subject:	*car*

4.7 ACTIVITY

In the sentences below, underline the prepositional phrases.

EXAMPLE   <u>Without you</u>, I am <u>in trouble</u>.

1. True pepper is made <u>from a pepper plant</u> <u>with the scientific name</u> of *Piper nigrum*. [*Hint:* This sentence contains three prepositional phrases.]
2. Other kinds <u>of pepper</u> are obtained <u>from plants</u> <u>of entirely different families</u>. [Hint: This sentence contains three prepositional phrases.]
3. Pepper is considered the most important spice <u>in the world</u>.
4. <u>In ancient times</u> and <u>during the middle ages</u>, only the rich could afford pepper.
5. It was carried <u>by caravan</u> <u>from the Far East</u>, which made it an item fit <u>for a king</u>. [Hint: This sentence contains three prepositional phrases.]
6. <u>Before modern times</u>, pepper was often used <u>like gold</u>.

4.8 ACTIVITY

Rewrite the sentences below, adding one or more prepositional phrases of your choice before or after the subject of each sentence.

EXAMPLE   The baby began crying for a bottle.
In the middle of the night, the baby began crying for a bottle.

1. The score was 12–14.

   The score of the game was 12–14.

2. Grandpa caught three large-mouth bass and some bluegills.

   At Willow Lake, Grandpa caught three large-mouth bass and some bluegills.

3. The audience began to leave in disgust.

   Before the end of the first act, the audience began to leave in disgust.

4. Delores accepted a basketball scholarship.

   In her senior year, Delores accepted a basketball scholarship.

5. All the children dressed in scary costumes.

   For Halloween, all the children dressed in scary costumes.

4.9 ACTIVITY

Underline the complete subject. Draw a line through any prepositional phrases that appear in the complete subject, and circle the simple subject.

EXAMPLE   The invention of the pop-top can illustrates that necessity is the mother of invention.

1. An engineer from Dayton, Ohio was on a picnic with his family in 1959.
2. The name of the engineer is Ermal Cleon Fraze.
3. The engineer by the name of Fraze became thirsty for a beer.
4. None of the utensils in the picnic basket included a can opener, however.
5. The bumper on his car provided Fraze with an idea.
6. His moment of insight led him to open the can on his bumper.
7. This act of desperation resulted in Fraze inventing the easy-open can.
8. The device in its earliest form pulled off the entire top of a can.
9. In this form, the device was patented in 1963.
10. An improvement on this invention came in 1965.
11. On the top of the can a ring of metal pulled a pre-punctured tab, to form the pop-top can.
12. The patent by Fraze of the "push in, fold-back" top occurred in 1965.
13. The rights to his invention were sold to Aluminum Company of America (Alcoa).
14. The royalties from the sale made Fraze a very rich man.
15. Each of the 150 billion cans of beer, soda, and juice sold every year in the United States earned Fraze a royalty payment.

Compound Subjects

A simple subject can be made up of two or more words. In this case, the sentence has a **compound subject**.

Sentence:	Louise and Ivan save $500 a year with grocery coupons.
Ask:	Who or what does or did something?
Answer:	Louise and Ivan
Compound simple subject:	Louise and Ivan

Sentence:	*Exercise and proper diet are important.*
Ask:	Who or what exists or existed in a particular way?
Answer:	*exercise and proper diet*
Complete subject:	*exercise and proper diet*
Compound simple subject:	*exercise and diet*

Sentence:	*The right attitude and a winning personality will get you the job.*
Ask:	Who or what does or did something?
Answer:	*the right attitude and a winning personality*
Complete subject:	*the right attitude and a winning personality*
Compound simple subject:	*attitude and personality*

4.10 ACTIVITY

Underline the complete subject and write the compound simple subject in the blank.

EXAMPLE   <u>The beginning and ending of the play</u> were funny.

beginning and ending

1. <u>The hammer and nails</u> are in the basement.

   hammer and nails

2. <u>The wind and hail</u> damaged the trees.

   wind and hail

3. <u>High wind and heavy rain</u> made driving difficult.

   wind and rain

4. <u>The eggs, cheese, and bread</u> are in the other grocery bag.

   eggs, cheese, and bread

5. <u>The police car and ambulance</u> arrived at the accident within minutes.

   car and ambulance

6. <u>The sturdy wood and the excellent craftmanship</u> make this chair an excellent buy.

   wood and craftsmanship

7. <u>A high salary and an on-site nursery</u> are the best features of this job.

   salary and nursery

8. <u>Tourism and fishing</u> are the chief sources of income for the coastal town.

   tourism and fishing

9. <u>Unhappy viewers and corporate sponsors</u> protested the content of the controversial television program.

     viewers and sponsors _____

10. <u>Newspaper reports and television accounts of the incident</u> contradict each other.

     reports and accounts _____

4.11 INDIVIDUAL OR GROUP ACTIVITY

Alone or with classmates, fill in the blanks in the following sentences with compound subjects.

EXAMPLE   _Businesspeople_ and _senior citizens_ were unhappy with the new tax law.

1. Both _Carlotta_ and _Phillip_ decided to change their majors to criminal justice.

2. _Good food_ and _friendly people_ are necessary for a successful party.

3. _A large engine_, _an attractive interior_, and _a reasonable price_ are the car's best features.

4. _Fans_ and _the press_ gathered outside the auditorium to await the arrival of the rock stars.

5. _Furniture_, _large appliances_, and _clothing_ are on sale this week at the mall.

4.12 ACTIVITY

Combine each pair of sentences into one sentence with a compound subject.

EXAMPLE   Two cups of sugar are needed for this recipe.
Three eggs are also needed.

      Two cups of sugar and three eggs are needed for

      this recipe.

1. Antonio drove to Pittsburgh for the Steelers game.
Karl drove with him.

      Antonio and Karl drove to Pittsburgh for the Steelers game. _____

      _____

2. This fall, three classroom buildings were closed for repairs.

Two dormitories were also closed for repairs.

      This fall, three classroom buildings and two dormitories were closed for repairs. _____

      _____

3. Apartment buildings will be constructed on that land.
   A small park will be constructed there too.

   Apartment buildings and a small park will be constructed on that land.

   _____

4. Damaging winds will accompany the storm.
   Hail will also accompany it.

   Damaging winds and hail will accompany the storm.

   _____

5. The movie's plot annoyed me.
   So did the background music.

   The movie's plot and background music annoyed me.

   _____

6. Your test scores are very good.
   Your recommendations are very good as well.

   Your test scores and recommendations are very good.

   _____

7. In this store, the prices are excellent.
   The selection of merchandise is excellent too. [*Hint:* Your verb will be *are*.]

   In this store, the prices and the selection of merchandise are excellent.

   _____

8. The president visited the flood-ravaged town along the Mississippi River.
   The vice president went with him.

   The president and vice president visited the flood-ravaged town along the

   Mississippi River.

9. For many parents, teenage hairstyles are a mystery.
   Teenage fashions are also a mystery to them.

   For many parents, teenage hairstyles and teenage fashions are a mystery.

   _____

10. Many movies are unsuitable for children.
    Some television programs are also unsuitable.

    Many movies and some television programs are unsuitable for children.

    _____

Unstated Subjects

When a sentence gives a command or makes a request, the subject is not always written out. Then, the subject is the unstated word *you.*

Command with unstated subject:	*Leave me alone!*
Unstated subject:	*you*
Command with stated subject:	*You leave me alone!*

TIP

Here's a test to try when you are unsure whether a word group is a command or request (and, therefore, a complete sentence): If you can rephrase the words as a question beginning with *Would you,* you have a command or request. "Leave me alone" becomes "Would you leave me alone?" so you have a sentence.

Request with unstated subject:	*Close the curtains, please.*
Unstated subject:	*you*
Request with stated subject:	*You close the curtains, please.*

4.13 ACTIVITY

Rewrite the following commands and requests so that the subject is stated.

EXAMPLE   Go to the store for me, please.

You go to the store for me, please.

1. Leave to pick Julio up at eight o'clock.

   You leave to pick Julio up at eight o'clock.

2. Answer me right now.

   You answer me right now.

3. Try to understand what I am telling you.

   You try to understand what I am telling you.

4. Call the police immediately!

   You call the police immediately!

5. Turn off the television and study.

   You turn off the television and study.

THE FUNCTION OF VERBS

Every sentence must include a **verb.** Sometimes the verb shows action.

James sings show tunes in the shower.

Subject:	*James*
Verb (shows action):	*sings*

Sometimes the verb links the subject to a word or words that either rename or describe that subject.

The train was 20 minutes early.

Subject:	*train*
Verb:	*was* [Links subject to descriptive words "20 minutes early."]

My sister is a professional dancer.

Subject:	*sister*
Verb:	*is* [Links subject to words that rename the subject—"professional dancer."]

GRAMMAR ALERT: !

Some words can be verbs in some sentences and subjects in others:

Subject:	*This drink is too sweet for me.*
Verb:	*I drink eight glasses of water a day.*

POWER UP

For each of the following words, write two sentences, one using the word as a subject and one using it as a verb: *love, breed, time.* What helps a reader determine how the word is used?

CONNECT

Pay attention to the action verbs in essay examination questions. Verbs such as *analyze, discuss, compare, define, explain,* and *demonstrate* direct the nature of your response.

Subject: *My morning run was refreshing.*

Verb: *I run every morning before breakfast.*

Action Verbs

Most verbs are action verbs.

As their name suggests, **action verbs** show activity or movement. They can also show some kind of process or thought.

Action verbs that show activity or movement:	*eat, run, go, hit, fall, sing, throw, jump, drive*
Action verbs that show thought:	*think, consider, reflect, desire*
Action verbs that show process:	*rest, review, try, enjoy, answer*

Some action verbs are made up of two words. Examples are:

burn up	look over	pick up	send out
drop in	look up	put on	take off
fill up	make up	quiet down	think over

4.14 INDIVIDUAL OR GROUP ACTIVITY

Alone or with two classmates, see how many action verbs you can list in 60 seconds. When time is up, sort your verbs into three categories: verbs that show activity or movement, verbs that show process, and verbs that show thought.

4.15 ACTIVITY

POWER UP

Action verbs usually make for the most vivid writing. Choose an editorial from your local newspaper. Count the number of action verbs and the number of verbs overall. What percentage are action verbs? Do you think they make a difference in the effectiveness of the piece?

Circle the action verbs in the following passage. A sentence may have more than one action verb. One sentence has a two-word verb.

1. We hear stories of dumb criminals all the time. 2. Many of these criminals fail because they do not think ahead. 3. For example, consider the two thieves who robbed a highway toll plaza in Atlanta. 4. They never considered just how much 2,000 quarters weigh. 5. The men should have brought something stronger than a trash bag for the quarters. 6. Although the men got away, the trash bag tore under the weight of the quarters. 7. The men put as much change as they could in the bag. 8. Then they ran. 9. However, most of the loot was dropped on the highway. 10. Police found another $70 worth of change in the car the crooks abandoned after the heist. 11. This story shows that if you plan a robbery make sure your container can hold the loot.

Linking Verbs

Although most verbs show action, some do not. Instead, these verbs link the subject to something that renames or describes the subject. For this reason, these verbs are called **linking verbs.** Here are four examples.

Chris is my oldest and closest friend.

Subject:	*Chris*
Linking verb:	*is*
Renames the subject:	*my oldest and closest friend*

Black olives <u>are</u> an essential ingredient in the salad.

Subject:	*Black olives*
Linking verb:	*are*
Renames the subject:	*essential ingredient*

The soup <u>seems</u> too hot to eat.

Subject:	*The soup*
Linking verb:	*seems*
Describes the subject:	*too hot*

The man <u>appears</u> confused.

Subject:	*The man*
Linking verb:	*appears*
Describes the subject:	*confused*

Study the following list of linking verbs, so you will recognize them easily in sentences.

TIP

Most linking verbs are forms of *be* or sensory verbs.

am	was	appear	taste
be	were	feel	smell
is	been	seem	look
are	being	sound	become

4.16 ACTIVITY

Circle each linking verb. Underline the subject and the words after the linking verb that rename or describe the subject.

EXAMPLE <u>Alison</u> was the <u>head majorette for three years.</u>

1. Shortly after dinner at the restaurant, <u>Mohan</u> became <u>ill</u>.
2. *<u>Hill Street Blues</u>* was the <u>best cop show on television.</u>
3. <u>Anna</u> seems <u>mature beyond her years.</u>
4. This <u>piano</u> sounds <u>out of tune to me.</u>
5. <u>Six of us</u> are always <u>late to our eight o'clock class.</u>
6. Without a doubt, <u>spring</u> is <u>my favorite time of year.</u>
7. Now that I have taken algebra, <u>I</u> am <u>confident about my math skills.</u>
8. Because of the traffic jam, <u>we</u> were <u>late for the play.</u>

4.17 ACTIVITY

In each sentence below, if the underlined verb is an action verb, write "AV" over it. If it is a linking verb, write "LV" over it.

EXAMPLE John <u>was</u>[LV] upset because the storm <u>ruined</u>[AV] his garden.

1. The growing deer population <u>causes</u>[AV] problems for area motorists.

2.   Nuha <u>studied</u> biology most of the evening, but now she <u>seems</u> ready for bed.

3.   Whenever injustice <u>surfaces</u>, Clark Kent <u>becomes</u> Superman.

4.   I <u>choked</u> on a piece of chicken, but Carla <u>used</u> the Heimlich maneuver and <u>dislodged</u> the meat.

5.   If I <u>am</u> absent, I always <u>borrow</u> someone's class notes.

Helping Verbs

The **complete verb** can be made up of more than one word. The action verb or the linking verb is the **main verb.** The other verb is the **helping verb.**

You <u>should ask</u> Dr. Brezinski that question.

Action verb:	*ask*
Helping verb:	*should*
Complete verb:	*should ask*

You <u>will be</u> the winner of the contest.

Linking verb:	*be*
Helping verb:	*will*
Complete verb:	*will be*

So you will recognize them easily, study this list of helping verbs.

am	were	might	should	has
be	been	can	do	had
is	being	could	did	shall
are	may	will	does	
was	must	would	have	

GRAMMAR ALERT !

Some of the helping verbs on this list (*am, is, are, was,* and *were,* for example) are also on the list of linking verbs on page 59. When these verbs appear alone, they are linking verbs. When they appear with action or other linking verbs, they are helping verbs.

The complete verb can include more than one helping verb.

Karen and Tony <u>have been studying</u> for hours.

Action verb:	*studying*
Helping verbs:	*have been*

GRAMMAR ALERT !

The descriptive words *not, just, never, only, already,* and *always* often appear with helping verbs, but they are not verbs themselves.

I <u>will</u> never <u>agree</u> to that plan.

Descriptive word:	*never*
Complete verb:	*will agree*

I do not understand you.

Descriptive word: *not*

Complete verb: *do understand*

Underline the complete verbs and circle the helping verbs. Remember, the complete verb can include more than one helping verb, and descriptive words are not verbs.

EXAMPLE   Our daily newspaper [is] now <u>experiencing</u> financial problems.

1. The city's only art theater [will] <u>close</u> next week.
2. You [may] not <u>come</u> with us to the beach.
3. Because of the winter storm, many activities [have been] <u>canceled</u>.
4. Robin Williams [is] <u>known</u> as a brilliant comedian.
5. I [have] <u>looked</u> everywhere for my car keys.
6. Our star quarterback [may have] <u>broken</u> his ankle.
7. All cars [should] <u>include</u> air bags on both the driver and the passenger sides.
8. Too much sun [can] <u>cause</u> skin cancer.
9. Angela [has been] <u>volunteering</u> at the hospital for years.
10. All new employees [must] <u>take</u> a drug test.
11. I [will] never <u>understand</u> you.
12. Many children in kindergarten [are] already <u>reading</u>.
13. The firefighters [are] <u>hosting</u> a pancake and sausage breakfast.
14. Once again, Aaron [has] <u>left</u> the supper dishes on the counter.
15. In the back of the refrigerator, some very strange things [are] <u>growing</u>.

Compound Verbs

A sentence can have two or more verbs for the same subject. In this case, the sentence is said to have a **compound verb.** Here is an example:

The untrained puppy <u>chewed</u> the rug and <u>ruined</u> the sofa.

Simple subject: *puppy*

Ask: What about the puppy?

Answer: *It chewed and ruined.*

Compound verb: *chewed; ruined*

A linking verb can be one or more parts of a compound verb.

I <u>was</u> ill and <u>stayed</u> home. [*Was* is a linking verb, and *stayed* is an action verb.]

Cobina <u>appears</u> happy and <u>looks</u> fit. [Both *appears* and *looks* are linking verbs.]

A helping verb can appear in one or more parts of a compound verb.

Airlines <u>are cutting</u> costs and <u>increasing</u> fares. [*Are* is a helping verb, *cutting* and *increasing* are action verbs.]

GRAMMAR ALERT !

A verb that follows *to* is not part of the complete verb. It is a special form known as an **infinitive**.

The child wants to go with his mother. [The complete verb is *wants*, not *go*, which follows *to*.]

4.19 ACTIVITY

The following sentences have compound verbs. Underline those verbs. Remember, a verb that follows *to* (an infinitive) is not part of the complete verb.

EXAMPLE   I <u>am going</u> with you and <u>driving</u> the car.

1. The snow <u>fell</u> throughout the night and <u>blanketed</u> the area.
2. The general public <u>does</u> not <u>recognize</u> the popularity of rap music and <u>appreciate</u> its message.
3. You <u>should leave</u> at six o'clock and <u>arrive</u> by midnight.
4. I <u>have watched</u> this movie four times and still <u>consider</u> it to be a classic.
5. The restaurant's veal special <u>tastes</u> good and <u>costs</u> little.
6. I <u>feel</u> healthy and <u>am</u> at my best in the mountains.

4.20 ACTIVITY

Combine each pair of sentences into one sentence with a compound verb. To do so, eliminate the subject of the second sentence. (Item 4 requires you to combine three sentences into one.)

EXAMPLE   A low-fat diet prevents heart disease.
It also causes weight loss.

A low-fat diet prevents heart disease and causes weight
loss.

1. The newspaper advertisement misrepresented the product.
   The advertisement created confusion.

   The newspaper advertisement misrepresented the product and created confusion.

   _____

2. The judge heard the attorney's closing arguments.
   He made his decision.

   The judge heard the attorney's closing arguments and made his decision.

   _____

3. My morning run begins promptly at seven o'clock.
   It ends at eight-fifteen.

   My morning run begins promptly at seven o'clock and ends at eight-fifteen.

   _____

4. Before our guests arrive, we must shop.
   We must cook the meal.

We must clean the house.

Before our guests arrive, we must shop, cook the meal, and clean the house.

5. The supermarket melons smell sweet.
They look ripe.

The supermarket melons smell sweet and look ripe.

6. The salesperson explained the car's features.
She offered us a test drive.

The salesperson explained the car's features and offered us a test drive.

7. Janet studied her biology text.
She read over her class notes.

Janet studied her biology text and read over her class notes.

8. I studied the map for 10 minutes.
I found the fastest route to Omaha.

I studied the map for 10 minutes and found the fastest route to Omaha.

9. Mario went to summer school for six weeks.
Then he worked as a lifeguard at the city pool.

Mario went to summer school for six weeks and then worked as a lifeguard at the

city pool.

10. Carefully, I selected the most beautiful plant.
I presented it to Grandmother for her eightieth birthday.

Carefully, I selected the most beautiful plant and presented it to Grandmother for her

eightieth birthday.

4.21 ACTIVITY

POWER UP

Select a newspaper or magazine article and circle the first 15 complete verbs. Label each action verb, linking verb, or helping verb.

Circle the complete verbs in the following paragraph. Remember, descriptive words are not verbs, and verbs that follow *to* (infinitives) are not part of the complete verb.

Nevada resident Gary Murray's dog was hurt in a car accident. As a result, Murray invented the Love Belt, a seat belt for dogs. The Love Belt comes in three sizes—small, medium, and large. In case of an accident, it restrains the dog to minimize injury. A dog owner can even use the Love Belt as a leash outside the car. Thousands of dogs are hurt or killed every year in car accidents. However, the Love Belt reduces the risk of serious injury and provides valuable protection for beloved pets.

IF ENGLISH IS YOUR SECOND LANGUAGE

1. Remember that helping verbs come *before* action verbs.

   HV AV
   Marco will go with us.

   A word can come between the helping verb and the action verb.

   HV   AV
   Marco will [not] *go with us.*

   HV   AV
   Marco will [always] *go with us.*

2. These verbs are helping verbs; they appear with action verbs or linking verbs:

can	might	should
could	must	will
may	shall	would

   With action verb: *Joe can play the piano.*
   With linking verb: *Jackie can be annoying.*

   Note: Can can be an action verb, as in this example:

   I can tomatoes every summer.

3. The forms of *do (do, does,* and *did)* and the forms of *have (have, has,* and *had)* can be either action verbs or helping verbs.

   Action verb: *The dog had puppies.* [*Had* means "gave birth to."]
   Helping verb: *Connie had spoken first.*
   Action verb: *Alejandro did all the work.*
   Helping verb: *You did help me.*

4. As helping verbs, *do, does,* and *did* can be used three ways: (A) with *not* or *never* to express a negative, (B) to ask a question, (C) to emphasize the action verb.

   A. *I do not know the answer. I never did see that.*
   B. *Where do you live?*
   C. *They do drive very fast.*

5. The forms of *be (am, is, are, was,* and *were)* can be either helping verbs or linking verbs.

   Helping verb:
   HV AV
   Traffic is moving slowly.

   Linking verb:
   LV
   This shirt is too tight.

6. A number of English verbs are made up of two words. Some of these two-word verbs can be separated, and some cannot be separated. For example, *give in* cannot be separated, but *put off* can be separated. However, verbs that *can* be separated do not always *have* to be separated.

   Separable: *I must put that appointment off until next week.*
                    I must put off that appointment until next week.
   Inseparable: *The police will not give in to the protestors' demands.*

   If you are unsure which verbs are separable and which are not, consult the list that follows. Example sentences appear with the first nine verbs in each list.

TIP

Listen and learn! Some people leave talk radio on when they are doing things like washing dishes, just to gain practice recognizing the rhythms and idioms of English.

Separable Two-Word Verbs

ask out:	*I will ask her out.*
burn down:	*We must burn the tree down.*
	We must burn down the tree.
burn up:	*The fire burned the papers up.*
	The fire burned up the papers.
bring up:	*Bring the issue up at the next meeting.*
	Bring up the issue at the next meeting.
call off:	*The umpire called the game off when the rain began.*
	The umpire called off the game when the rain began.
call up:	*Call the porter up to get our bags.*
	Call up the porter to get our bags.
clean up:	*You should clean this mess up yourself.*
	You should clean up this mess yourself.
cut up:	*The butcher cut the meat up into chops.*
	The butcher cut up the meat into chops.
drop off:	*I dropped Marcel off at school this morning.*
	I dropped off Marcel at school this morning.

fill out	help out	point out	take out
fill up	leave out	put away	think over
give away	look over	put off	throw away
give back	look up	put on	try on
hand in	make up	put together	wake up
hand out	pick out	shut off	wrap up
hang up	pick up	take off	

Inseparable Two-Word Verbs

come across:	*I came across old letters in the attic.*
drop in (on someone):	*My neighbor drops in every day to visit.*
get along (with someone):	*My sister and I never got along.*
get away (with something):	*Students rarely get away with cheating.*
get up:	*Get up at six o'clock if you want to leave with me.*
give in:	*The parents gave in to the crying child.*
give up:	*The robber gave up and put down his gun.*
go out (with someone):	*Jean and I go out every Saturday.*
go over (something):	*Let's go over the notes together.*

grow up	run out (of something)
play around	
quiet down	speak up
run across (someone or something)	stay away from
	take care of
run into (someone or something)	wake up

RECHARGE

Sentences must have both a subject and a verb.

1. The **complete subject** says who or what does or did something or who or what exists or existed in a particular way.
2. The **simple subject**
   - Is the most important part of the complete subject.
   - Is a **noun** or **pronoun**.
   - Can be a form of an action word.
   - Will **never** be a word in a **prepositional phrase**.
   - Is **compound** when it is made up of two or more words.
   - Can be unstated when the sentence gives a command or makes a request.
3. The **complete verb**
   - Is an **action verb** if it shows activity, thought, or a process.
   - Is a **linking verb** if it connects the subject to something that renames or describes that subject.
   - Can be made up of an action verb or a linking verb with a **helping verb**.
   - Is **compound** when two or more verbs appear for the same subject.

4.22 CHAPTER REVIEW ACTIVITY

Underline the complete subject in each sentence. Then write the simple subject on the first blank and the complete verb on the second blank.

EXAMPLE The average American household buys and wraps 30 Christmas gifts each year.

Simple subject: _household_

Complete verb: _buys; wraps_

1. The grandparents of most people spend an average of $82 per grandchild for a holiday gift.

   Simple subject: grandparents

   Complete verb: spend

2. People like to send Christmas cards in addition to gifts.

   Simple subject: People

   Complete verb: like

3. The first Christmas card was created in England on December 9, 1842.

   Simple subject: card

   Complete verb: was created

4. <u>More than three billion Christmas cards</u> are sent annually in the United States alone.

   Simple subject: cards

   Complete verb: are sent

5. <u>A greater number of diamonds</u> are typically purchased at Christmas than at any other time.

   Simple subject: number

   Complete verb: are purchased

6. <u>Many people</u> also like to sing Christmas carols as part of their holiday celebration.

   Simple subject: people

   Complete verb: like

7. <u>The tradition of Christmas caroling</u> began as an old English custom.

   Simple subject: tradition

   Complete verb: began

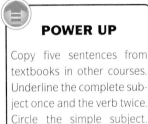

POWER UP

Copy five sentences from textbooks in other courses. Underline the complete subject once and the verb twice. Circle the simple subject. Describe the subjects and verbs: Are they compound? Are there prepositional phrases or action-word subjects? Are the verbs action, helping, or linking?

8. <u>This custom</u> was called Wassailing and toasted neighbors to wish them a long life.

   Simple subject: custom

   Complete verb: was called; toasted

9. <u>Christmas trees</u>, for many, are also an important part of the holiday tradition.

   Simple subject: trees

   Complete verb: are

10. <u>People in the United States</u> buy and put up 37.1 million real Christmas trees each year.

    Simple subject: people

    Complete verb: buy; put up

4.23 CHAPTER REVIEW ACTIVITY

Draw one line under each simple subject and two lines under each complete verb.

[1]<u>Pieces</u> of junk <u>are traveling</u> in space around our planet. [2]This space <u>junk will travel</u> in orbit around earth for many years. [3]Five thousand <u>pieces</u> of the space junk <u>are</u> the size of baseballs. [4]Almost 40,000 <u>pieces</u> <u>are</u> the size of golf balls or smaller. [5] Each <u>piece</u> of junk <u>orbits</u> earth once every hour. [6]At that speed, peanut-sized <u>metal</u> and <u>plastic</u> <u>could wreck</u> a spaceship. [7]The <u>junk</u> <u>will</u> also <u>pose</u> a threat to future space stations.

[8]The <u>junk</u> <u>got</u> into space in different ways. [9]Some <u>pieces</u> <u>slipped</u> through the fingers of astronauts or <u>broke</u> off old satellites. [10]For safety's sake,

astronauts <u>may have</u> to collect the space junk.[11] The <u>cost</u> of such an operation <u>could be</u> enormous. [12]In addition, <u>spaceships</u> <u>may need</u> covers to protect them from the pieces. [13]<u>Engineers</u> <u>will have</u> to design these covers. [14]Of course, their efforts <u>will create</u> another expense. [15]The <u>problem</u> <u>is</u> a serious one and <u>must be solved</u>.

GETTING IN GEAR

thinking in writing: List 10 experiences in your life that are memorable for some reason—because they were exciting, frightening, surprising, embarrassing, particularly happy, or particularly sad. Then pick one of those experiences and answer all of the following questions that are relevant:

- Who was involved?
- What happened?
- Where did it happen?
- When did it happen?
- Why did it happen?
- How did it happen?

writing from experience: Tell the story of one of your memorable experiences, being sure to answer the relevant *who, what, when, where, why,* and *how* questions given above.

writing in context: Reader's Digest often includes articles about the significant experiences that people have. These experiences are not ones that change the course of the world; they are often significant because they teach valuable lessons. Assume you are writing for *Reader's Digest;* tell the story of one of your memorable experiences. Be sure to explain the lesson to be learned from that experience.

CHAPTER 5

Coordination

CHAPTER GOALS

By the end of this chapter, you will:

Recognize independent clauses.

Know three ways to join independent clauses in one sentence.

In Chapter 4, you learned that a sentence has a subject, a verb, and enough completeness to stand alone. Now let's add another piece of information: Any word group that can stand as a sentence is an **independent clause**.

Independent clause:	*the photographer checked the lighting*
Sentence:	*The photographer checked the lighting.*
Independent clause:	*the phone company raised its rates*
Sentence:	*The phone company raised its rates.*

A sentence can be made up of just one independent clause, like this:

The child has a slight fever.

A sentence can also be made up of two or more independent clauses. The proper joining of two or more independent clauses in one sentence is called **coordination**, and the sentence created is a **compound sentence**.

Sentence:	*The child has a slight fever, and she is coughing.*
Independent clause:	*the child has a slight fever*
Independent clause:	*she is coughing*
Sentence:	*Five cross-country skiers left at dawn, but they had to turn back.*
Independent clause:	*five cross-country skiers left at dawn*
Independent clause:	*they had to turn back*

GRAMMAR ALERT !

Sentences with compound subjects or compound verbs, or both, are not necessarily made up of more than one independent clause.

The <u>daffodils</u> and the <u>crocuses</u> are already in bloom. [One independent clause with a compound subject]

The police officers <u>cleared</u> the area and <u>closed</u> the street. [One independent clause with a compound verb]

TIP

For more information on compound subjects and compound verbs, see pages 53 and 61.

5.1 ACTIVITY

In the sentences below, place brackets around each independent clause. In the blank before each sentence, write the number of independent clauses in the sentence. (Some of the sentences have only one independent clause.)

EXAMPLE _____2_____ [Honeymoons are commonplace,] but [most newlyweds do not know the origin of this common tradition.]

1. _____1_____ [In very ancient times, a bridegroom had to "capture" his bride.]

2. _____2_____ [He would capture her,] and [then he would hide her.]

3. _____2_____ [The bride's relatives looked for her,] or [the whole tribe tried to find her.]

4. _____2_____ [This custom seems crude now,] but [the modern honeymoon developed from it.]

5. _____2_____ [Some people today do not have honeymoons,] but [many people still do.]

6. _____1_____ [Other people get married and postpone the honeymoon for months after the marriage.]

7. _____2_____ [These people wait,] and [they save money for their honeymoon trip.]

8. _____1_____ [Both weddings and honeymoons are often less traditional these days.]

9. _____2_____ [Still, many people go on honeymoons,] for [it is the traditional thing to do.]

10. _____1_____ [The new bride and groom see the honeymoon as a holiday and a chance to relax after the wedding.]

COORDINATION—METHOD 1

You can join independent clauses in the same sentence with one of the following:

, and	, nor	, so
, but	, for	, yet
, or		

The words in the above list are **coordinating conjunctions.** Coordinating conjunctions can be used with commas to join independent clauses.

Independent clause: *the band stopped playing at eleven*
Independent clause: *we danced until midnight*
Coordination: *The band stopped playing at eleven* ⟨ *, but* ⟩ *we danced until midnight.*

Be sure you use the coordinating conjunction that expresses the meaning you are after.

1. Use **, and** to show addition:

   The mechanic changed the oil ⟨ *, and* ⟩ *he rotated the tires.*

2. Use **, but** or **, yet** to show contrast:

   The bus was late ⟨ *, but* ⟩ *I made it to work on time.*
   The bus was late ⟨ *, yet* ⟩ *I made it to work on time.*

TIP

To remember the coordinating conjunctions, think of "boyfans": *but, or, yet, for, and, nor, so.*

71   CHAPTER 5   COORDINATION

POWER UP

Look through a magazine, newspaper, or book and find five sentences that use a comma and a coordinating conjunction to join independent clauses. Think about why the particular conjunction was chosen.

3. Use **, or** to show an alternative:

   You can come with me [*, or*] *you can wait here.*

4. Use **, nor** to give a negative alternative:

   The children may not see this movie [*, nor*] *may they watch cartoons.*

5. Use **, for** to mean "because":

   The southern town was paralyzed by the snowfall [*, for*] *it owned no snowplows.*

6. Use **, so** to mean "as a result":

   Class was canceled [*, so*] *I went to the library.*

GRAMMAR AND PUNCTUATION ALERT

A comma by itself *cannot* join independent clauses. A coordinating conjunction must be used with the comma.

No: *The cars collided, there was no damage.*

Yes: *The cars collided, but there was no damage.*

5.2 ACTIVITY

Using a comma and logical coordinating conjunction, join each of the pairs of sentences to make one sentence.

EXAMPLE   Rowdy parents and coaches have too long disrupted children's athletic events.
It is past time that something was done.

Rowdy parents and coaches have too long disrupted children's athletic events, so (and) it is past time that something was done.

1. The people on the sidelines were silent one Sunday.
   Thousands of parents had to obey a one-day noise ban instituted by the Northern Ohio Girls Soccer League.

   The people on the sidelines were silent one Sunday, for thousands of parents had to obey a one-day noise ban instituted by the Northern Ohio Girls Soccer League.

2. Parents had to keep mum.
   Coaches had to keep quiet as well.

   Parents had to keep mum, and coaches had to keep quiet as well.

3. Parents sucked hard on lollipops.
   Some even put duct tape over their mouths.

   Parents sucked hard on lollipops, and some even put duct tape over their mouths.

4. Except for an occasional spontaneous cheer, most parents kept quiet.
   They were still able to communicate their enthusiasm.

   Except for an occasional spontaneous cheer, most parents kept quiet, but (yet) they were still able to communicate their enthusiasm.

Copyright © 2002, The McGraw-Hill Companies, Inc.

5. Parents let their homemade signs encourage the players.
   They used hand and arm gestures to convey their emotion.

   <u>Parents let their homemade signs encourage the players, or (and) they used hand and arm</u>

   <u>gestures to convey their emotion.</u>

6. The players were allowed to encourage each other vocally.
   No one else was permitted to do so.

   <u>The players were allowed to encourage each other vocally, but (yet) no one else was</u>

   <u>permitted to do so.</u>

7. The players had a great time.
   They could make decisions on their own without being questioned or yelled at.

   <u>The players had a great time, for they could make decisions on their own without being</u>

   <u>questioned or yelled at.</u>

8. The ban was a national first.
   It is unknown how popular it can be on a larger scale.

   <u>The ban was a national first, and (so/but/yet) it is unknown how popular it can be on a</u>

   <u>larger scale.</u>

9. League officials do not plan to make silence a permanent policy.
   They are considering another day of silent games for 3,800 girls, aged 8 to 14.

   <u>League officials do not plan to make silence a permanent policy, but (yet) they are</u>

   <u>considering another day of silent games for 3,800 girls, aged 8 to 14.</u>

10. Parents either love the ban.
    They dislike it intensely.

    <u>Parents either love the ban, or they dislike it intensely.</u>

    _____

5.3 INDIVIDUAL OR GROUP ACTIVITY

Alone or with two classmates, fill in the blanks with independent clauses. Be sure your additions are complete enough that they can stand alone as sentences.

EXAMPLE I left in plenty of time, but *<u>I arrived late for the</u>*
<u>concert.</u>

1. I carefully opened the closet door, and <u>all my books fell off the shelf.</u>

   _____

2. Chris tried backing into the parking space, but <u>it was too narrow.</u>

   _____

3. We can go to the movie at the Metro, or <u>we can rent a video.</u>

   _____

4.   Waldeen can no longer play tennis, for <u>she sprained her ankle.</u>

   _____

5.   Dr. Shaheen explained the assignment carefully, so <u>we would know exactly</u>

   <u>what to do.</u>

6.   The program was funny, yet <u>many critics did not like it.</u>

   _____

5.4 ACTIVITY

On a separate sheet, compose five sentences, each with a different coordinating conjunction (*and, but, or, nor, for, so,* or *yet*). Be sure the conjunctions join independent clauses, and remember to use a comma before each conjunction.

COORDINATION—METHOD 2

You can join independent clauses in the same sentence with one of the following:

; consequently,	; meanwhile,	; otherwise,
; furthermore,	; moreover,	; therefore,
; however,	; nevertheless,	; thus,
; instead,	; nonetheless,	

The words in this list are **conjunctive adverbs.** Conjunctive adverbs can be used with semicolons and commas to join independent clauses.

TIP

The words in the conjunctive adverb list are only "conjunctive" when they are positioned between two independent clauses. In that case, they are used with the semicolon and comma. Other times, the words are ordinary adverbs and used without semicolons.

Independent clause:	*we ordered a pepperoni pizza*
Independent clause:	*meatball sandwiches were delivered*
Coordination:	*We ordered a pepperoni pizza; however, meatball sandwiches were delivered.*

Notice that the semicolon comes first, the conjunctive adverb comes second, and the comma comes third, to form this pattern:

   ; conjunctive adverb,
   ; therefore,
   My back aches; therefore, I cannot lift anything.

Be sure you use the conjunctive adverb that expresses the meaning you are after.

1.   Use ; however, ;nevertheless, or ; nonetheless, to show a contrast, as follows:

   The Civil War is over ⌐*; however,*⌐ *some people will not forget it.*
   The Civil War is over ⌐*; nevertheless,*⌐ *some people will not forget it.*
   The Civil War is over ⌐*; nonetheless,*⌐ *some people will not forget it.*

2.   Use ; furthermore, or ; moreover, to mean "in addition."

   This car dealership offers a variety of models ⌐*; furthermore,*⌐ *it offers an excellent buyer-protection plan.*
   This car dealership offers a variety of models ⌐*; moreover,*⌐ *it offers an excellent buyer-protection plan.*

POWER UP

To test the importance of co-ordination, choose a para-graph or two from a newspa-per or magazine and remove all coordination, converting all the compound sentences to simple sentences. How has the quality of the writing changed? Why do you think the writer originally used coordination?

3. Use <u>; therefore,</u> <u>; thus,</u> <u>; consequently,</u> to mean "as a result."

    Daylight savings time begins tonight <u>; therefore,</u> *we lose an hour of sleep.*

    Daylight savings time begins tonight <u>; thus,</u> *we lose an hour of sleep.*

    Daylight savings time begins tonight <u>; consequently,</u> *we lose an hour of sleep.*

4. Use <u>; meanwhile,</u> to mean "at the same time."

    I left for Virginia at noon <u>; meanwhile,</u> *Alice was on her way to Ohio.*

5. Use <u>; otherwise,</u> to indicate an alternative.

    You must study your history notes <u>; otherwise,</u> *you will not pass the test.*

6. Use <u>; instead,</u> to mean "in place of."

    I did not sleep last night <u>; instead,</u> *I thought about all my problems.*

PUNCTUATION ALERT

Be sure to use a semicolon before and a comma after any conjunctive adverb that joins independent clauses.

No:	*I gave Charlie the book, however, he had already read it.*
No:	*I gave Charlie the book however he had already read it.*
No:	*I gave Charlie the book however, he had already read it.*
Yes:	*I gave Charlie the book; however, he had already read it.*

5.5 ACTIVITY

Use a semicolon, logical conjunctive adverb, and a comma to join each pair of sentences below into one sentence.

EXAMPLE   I got a C on my algebra midterm.
All my other grades are A's and B's.

I got a C on my algebra midterm; nonetheless, all my other grades are A's and B's.

1. The cat was whining to be fed.
    She had a dish full of cat food.

    The cat was whining to be fed; however, she had a dish full of cat food.

2. Louie's band was invited to play for the homecoming dance.
    They were asked to play at Jake's Roadhouse.

    Louie's band was invited to play for the homecoming dance; furthermore, they were asked to play at Jake's Roadhouse.

3. Carmen often waits until the last minute to write her papers.
   She does not do her best work.

   Carmen often waits until the last minute to write her papers; consequently, she does not

   do her best work.

4. The villain was sneaking up on the defenseless victim.
   Superman was racing to the rescue.

   The villain was sneaking up on the defenseless victim; meanwhile, Superman was racing

   to the rescue.

5. I expected the dentist to pull my tooth.
   She performed a root canal.

   I expected the dentist to pull my tooth; instead, she performed a root canal.

6. These tires have never been rotated.
   They are wearing unevenly.

   These tires have never been rotated; thus, they are wearing unevenly.

7. Many schools no longer group students by ability.
   They do not group students by age.

   Many schools no longer group students by ability; moreover, they no do not group students

   by age.

8. High-impact aerobics is no longer considered safe.
   Most aerobics classes are now low-impact workouts.

   High-impact aerobics is no longer considered safe; instead, most aerobics classes are now

   low-impact workouts.

9. The road department repaired the potholes last month.
   The streets are again filled with treacherous holes.

   The road department repaired the potholes last month; nonetheless, the streets are again

   filled with treacherous holes.

10. Gary lent me his history notes.
    He shared his chapter outlines with me.

    Gary lent me his history notes; furthermore, he shared his chapter outlines with me.

11. You must return the library books by Friday.
    You will pay a fine.

    You must return the library books by Friday; otherwise, you will pay a fine.

12. The shingles on this house are old and worn.
    The roof is leaking.

    The shingles on this house are old and worn; furthermore, the roof is leaking.

5.6 INDIVIDUAL OR GROUP ACTIVITY

Alone or with two classmates, fill in the blanks with independent clauses. Be sure your additions have enough completeness that they could stand as sentences.

EXAMPLE   Michael developed a stress fracture; therefore, *he was forced to quit the track team.*

1. The stray dog looked harmless; however, I never trust unfamiliar animals.

2. My new car gets excellent gas mileage; nevertheless, I cannot afford its upkeep.

3. You must turn off the electricity before installing the new ceiling fan; otherwise, you may get a shock.

4. Trash collectors remain on strike for the second week; meanwhile, garbage is piling up everywhere.

5. Clifford has the highest grade point average in the class; furthermore, he is an award-winning artist.

6. More than half of the student body has the flu; therefore, classes have been canceled for the rest of the week.

7. The spring rains have flooded the main roads; thus, travel is difficult.

8. Lee's car was damaged in an accident on Main Street; consequently, he must take the bus to work.

9. Americans are becoming more concerned about what they eat; moreover, they are learning the importance of exercise.

10. You should not take Route 5; instead, you should take the turnpike.

5.7 ACTIVITY

On a separate sheet, write five sentences that use a semicolon, a conjunctive adverb, and a comma to join independent clauses. Try to use a different conjunctive adverb (*however, nevertheless, nonetheless, meanwhile, furthermore, therefore, thus, otherwise, consequently, moreover,* or *instead*) in each sentence.

COORDINATION—METHOD 3

You can use a semicolon to join closely related independent clauses in the same sentence.

Independent clause:	*some people like convertibles*
Independent clause:	*other people hate them*
Coordination:	*Some people like convertibles; other people hate them.*

PUNCTUATION ALERT

When you use a semicolon, be sure you have an independent clause on *both* sides.

No:	*The sun brightened my day; and raised my spirits.*
Explanation:	An independent clause appears before the semicolon but not after it.
Yes:	*The sun brightened my day and raised my spirits.*
Yes:	*The sun brightened my day; it raised my spirits.*

POWER UP

Go through your lecture notes for another class and find two ideas that can be expressed in a sentence using coordination. Does writing the ideas this way help you understand and learn them? Explain.

5.8 ACTIVITY

Add semicolons where they are needed to join two independent clauses. Remember, an independent clause must appear on both sides of the semicolon. (Two sentences do not need a semicolon, because they are correct as they are.)

EXAMPLE I looked everywhere for your wallet; I couldn't find it, though.

1. People try many crazy things to make money in the stock market; most of them never work out.
2. I thought I had heard everything; then I read about an investing yucca plant.
3. The plant is an investor on the Stockholm stock exchange; it issues buy and sell orders on 16 of the most active stocks.
4. Swedish artist Ola Pehrson attached electrodes to the plant; sensors connect the plant to a computer.
5. The sensors chart the plant's growth; the computer links the growth to stock market performance.
6. When the yucca's stock recommendations perform better than the general stock index, the plant is given water and light.
7. Sometimes the plant fails to deliver profits; then it stays dry and in the dark.
8. The yucca is part of an exhibition by seven Swedish artists and not a serious investment scheme.

5.9 ACTIVITY

In each item below, follow the independent clause with a semicolon and another independent clause. Be sure the words you add have enough completeness that they could stand alone as a sentence.

EXAMPLE I do not like to eat beef *; Margery does not like to eat chicken.*

1. I turned on the hot water *; only a trickle came out of the tap.*

2. Some people have trouble telling the truth *; they even believe their own lies.*

3. We waited over an hour for Dave *; then we left without him.*

4. The electricity went out at noon *; it was not restored until after midnight.*

5. The presidential candidate promised to bring jobs to our area *; he also promised to lower taxes.*

6. The house needed a new roof *; everything else was in good shape.*

5.10 INDIVIDUAL OR GROUP ACTIVITY

In each of the following sets, only two word groups are independent clauses. Alone or with two classmates, decide which word groups are independent clauses. Circle those word groups, and then write a sentence using the circled independent clauses joined by a semicolon.

EXAMPLE when the sun came up
the sun came up
I left for my favorite fishing spot
when I left for my favorite fishing spot.

The sun came up; I left for my favorite fishing spot.

1. air bags can save lives
because air bags can save lives
all cars should have them
since all cars should have them

Air bags can save lives; all cars should have them.

2. seven thousand medicines come from the rain forest
   although seven thousand medicines come from the rain forest
   whereas we do not do enough to protect this ecology
   we do not do enough to protect this ecology

   Seven thousand medicines come from the rain forest; we do not do enough to protect

   this ecology.

3. although the spring rains were heavy
   the spring rains were heavy
   though the crop was not ruined
   the crop was not ruined

   The spring rains were heavy; the crop was not ruined.

4. while I set the table
   I will set the table
   you can heat the stew
   if you heat the stew

   I will set the table; you can heat the stew.

5. the bride and groom entered the hall
   as the bride and groom entered the hall
   when the band began to play
   the band began to play

   The bride and groom entered the hall; the band began to play.

6. after the curtain came up
   the curtain came up
   the first act of the play began
   as the first act of the play began

   The curtain came up; the first act of the play began.

 IF ENGLISH IS YOUR SECOND LANGUAGE

1. The relationship between independent clauses is spelled out by the coordinating
   conjunction or conjunctive adverb you choose. To be sure you convey the desired
   relationship, consult the following chart of frequently used coordinating
   conjunctions and conjunctive adverbs.

Meaning	Coordinating Conjunction	Conjunctive Adverb
addition	, and	; furthermore,
		; moreover,
contrast	, but	; however,
	, yet	; nevertheless,
		; nonetheless,

Meaning	Coordinating Conjunction	Conjunctive Adverb
alternative	, or	; instead,
	, nor [negative]	; otherwise,
result	, so	; therefore,
		; consequently,
		; thus,

2. When *nor* connects independent clauses, the verb comes before the subject in the second clause.

$$\text{V \ S}$$
I cannot go, nor do I want to.

$$\text{V \qquad\qquad S}$$
The stove does not work, nor does the refrigerator.

RECHARGE

Coordination is the correct joining of two or more **independent clauses** in the same sentence. There are three methods of coordination. Each is illustrated with these independent clauses:

Independent clause: Congress passed a trade bill

Independent clause: the president vetoed it

1. Join the independent clauses with a comma and **coordinating conjunction.**

Coordination: *Congress passed a trade bill, but the president vetoed it.*

2. Join the independent clauses with a semicolon, **conjunctive adverb,** and comma.

Coordination: *Congress passed a trade bill; however, the president vetoed it.*

3. Join the independent clauses with a semicolon.

Coordination: *Congress passed a trade bill; the president vetoed it.*

5.11 CHAPTER REVIEW ACTIVITY

In each item in this exercise, join the two sentences into one, using the method of co-ordination indicated.

EXAMPLE　　Use a comma and a coordinating conjunction:
The yard is covered with leaves.
We will have them raked up by sundown.

The yard is covered with leaves, but we will have them raked up by sundown.

1. Use a comma and a coordinating conjunction:
Gregor passed his CPR test.
He took a first aid course.

Gregor passed his CPR test, and he took a first aid course.

2. Use a semicolon, a conjunctive adverb, and a comma:
Paul Harvey is my favorite radio commentator.
No local station carries his broadcasts.

Paul Harvey is my favorite radio commentator; however, no local station carries his

broadcasts.

3. Use a semicolon:
Karl worked five hours of overtime.
Then he went home to sleep before class.

Karl worked five hours of overtime; then he went home to sleep before class.

4. Use a comma and a coordinating conjunction:
You can buy these shoes on sale across town.
You can pay full price in this store.

You can buy these shoes on sale across town, or you can pay full price in this store.

5. Use a semicolon:
These pants no longer fit.
I need to go on a diet immediately.

These pants no longer fit; I need to go on a diet immediately.

6. Use a semicolon, a conjunctive adverb, and a comma:
The storm knocked out the power.
We have no electricity for cooking supper.

The storm knocked out the power; thus, we have no electricity for cooking supper.

7. Use a comma and a coordinating conjunction:
Nicolas Cage is a brilliant actor.
Critics do not like his most recent movie.

Nicolas Cage is a brilliant actor, but critics do not like his most recent movie.

8. Use a semicolon:
Every fall, the networks offer many new programs.
By December, most of them are off the air.

Every fall, the networks offer many new programs; by December, most of them are

off the air.

9. Use a comma and a coordinating conjunction:
My in-laws are coming to visit this weekend.
I must clean every inch of the house.

My in-laws are coming to visit this weekend, so I must clean every inch of the house.

10. Use a semicolon, a conjunctive adverb, and a comma:
   Carol got a raise for her hard work.
   She received a letter of appreciation from her boss.

Carol got a raise for her hard work; furthermore, she received a letter of appreciation from

her boss.

5.12 CHAPTER REVIEW ACTIVITY

Read aloud the paragraph below, and you will notice how choppy it sounds. To eliminate this choppiness with coordination, rewrite the entire paragraph according to the directions given. Then read the revision and notice the improvement the coordination makes.

A. Join sentences 1 and 2 with a comma and "but."

B. Join sentences 3 and 4 with a comma and "and."

C. Join sentences 5 and 6 with a semicolon.

D. Join sentences 7 and 8 with a semicolon, "furthermore," and a comma.

E. Join sentences 10 and 11 with a comma and "for."

F. Join sentences 12 and 13 with a comma and "yet."

Most people know that the breakfast drink Tang resulted from space research,
[1] Most people know that the breakfast drink Tang resulted from space research.
but few people know about other discoveries and inventions that came from space-related
[2] Few people know about other discoveries and inventions that came from
research. The Dustbuster got its start when Black and Decker was asked to develop
space-related research. [3] The Dustbuster got its start when Black and Decker
cordless tools for sampling lunar soil, and the heart-rate monitors on exercise machines
was asked to develop cordless tools for sampling lunar soil. [4] The heart-rate
were developed to keep track of astronauts' exertion levels. A particular kind of solar
monitors on exercise machines were developed to keep track of astronauts'
cell powers the $1.5 billion Hubble space telescope; it is the same kind of cell that
exertion levels. [5] A particular kind of solar cell powers the $1.5 billion Hubble
powers a five-dollar calculator. The fabric used for Apollo space suits now covers the
space telescope. [6] It is the same kind of cell that powers a five-dollar calculator.
Georgia Dome in Atlanta; furthermore, it covers airport terminals in Denver.
[7] The fabric used for Apollo space suits now covers the Georgia Dome in

Atlanta. [8] It covers airport terminals in Denver. [9] Also, the Golden Gate Bridge

and the Statue of Liberty are protected from corrosion by the same coatings
The coating developed to protect plastic spacecraft parts has
that protect launch pads. [10] The coating developed to protect plastic spacecraft
another application as well, for it is used as the scratch-resistant coating for plastic
parts has another application as well. [11] It is used as the scratch-resistant
eyeglass lenses. Some people think that the space program has no practical applications, yet
coating for plastic eyeglass lenses. [12] Some people think that the space program
that is just not the case.
has no practical applications. [13] That is just not the case.

thinking in writing: Make a list of your most important personal and professional goals, the ones you hope to meet in the next five or so years.

writing from experience: Explain why you attend college, focusing on how you expect your college education will help you meet your personal and professional goals.

writing in context: An institution's mission statement lays out the purposes that the institution should serve. For example, some schools have the goal of helping local public school teachers keep their certifications current. Other schools might define one of their purposes as developing distance learning to reach people who cannot get to campus. Assume your school is revising its mission statement and has asked for input from students. Identify and explain a specific goal your school should have in its mission statement and why that goal should be there.

CHAPTER 6

Subordination

CHAPTER GOALS

By the end of this chapter, you will:

Recognize dependent clauses.

Know two ways to join dependent clauses to independent clauses.

DEPENDENT CLAUSES

You learned in Chapter 5 that an *independent clause* can stand as a sentence.

Independent clause: *the parking lot was full of potholes*

Sentence: *The parking lot was full of potholes.*

Now it is time to learn about another kind of clause: the dependent clause. The **dependent clause** has a subject and verb, but it cannot stand as a sentence because it is not complete. If you read a dependent clause aloud, you can often hear that it lacks completeness. Try reading these dependent clauses aloud to notice this.

Dependent clause: *when the whistle blew*

Dependent clause: *after the music stopped*

Dependent clause: *since my leg hurts*

Do you find yourself asking What? or What then? That's because the word group is incomplete.

6.1 ACTIVITY

All the following word groups are clauses because they have subjects and verbs. If the word group is an independent clause because it can stand as a sentence, write "IC" on the blank. If it is a dependent clause because it lacks the completeness to stand as a sentence, write "DC" on the blank. If you are unsure, read the clause aloud to listen for completeness.

EXAMPLES   *IC*   Cherrapunji, in India, holds the record for the most rain in one month.

   DC   When it got 30.5 feet of rain in July 1861.

1.   IC   Cherrapunji also had the most rain in one year.
2.   DC   When it received an astounding 86.8 feet in 1861.
3.   IC   Cherrapunji earned the title of the wettest place on earth.
4.   DC   Although Mount Wai-'ale-' in Hawaii has the most rainy days a year, a whopping 350.
5.   IC   On the other hand, the Atacama Desert in northern Chile is considered the driest place on earth.
6.   DC   Since it holds the record for going the longest without rainfall.
7.   IC   In 1971, the first rain for 400 years fell on the Atacama desert.

8. __IC__   The hottest place on earth is Al'Aziziyah in the Sahara Desert.
9. __DC__   Where a shade temperature of 58 degrees centigrade is recorded.
10. __DC__   Even though Death Valley, here in the United States, has come close to that temperature.

SUBORDINATING CONJUNCTIONS

Dependent clauses begin with one of the following words, which are called **subordinating conjunctions.**

after	because	until
although	before	when
as	even though	whenever
as if	if	where
as long as	since	wherever
as soon as	though	whether
as though	unless	while

Dependent clause:	*before you go*
Subordinating conjunction:	*before*
Dependent clause:	*whenever the humidity is high*
Subordinating conjunction:	*whenever*
Dependent clause:	*as soon as dinner is over*
Subordinating conjunction:	*as soon as*

GRAMMAR ALERT

Some words can be subordinating conjunctions in some sentences and prepositions (words that show how things relate in time or space) in other sentences. (For a complete discussion of prepositions, see Chapter 19.)

Subordinating conjunction:	*I never understood Shakespeare's language until I read it aloud.*
Preposition:	*The new supermarket will not open until Tuesday.*

You can make an independent clause a dependent clause if you add a subordinating conjunction.

Independent clause:	*my back hurts*
Dependent clause:	*because my back hurts*
Subordinating conjunction:	*because*
Independent clause:	*the rain finally stopped*
Dependent clause:	*after the rain finally stopped*
Subordinating conjunction:	*after*
Independent clause:	*Charlie sings the blues*
Dependent clause:	*whenever Charlie sings the blues*
Subordinating conjunction:	*whenever*

GRAMMAR ALERT:
Dependent clauses cannot stand as sentences.

Dependent clause:	*before you go to sleep at eleven*
No:	*Before you go to sleep at eleven.*
Independent clause:	*you go to sleep at eleven*
Yes:	*You go to sleep at eleven.*

6.2 ACTIVITY

Fill in the blank in each sentence with a logical subordinating conjunction. (See the list of subordinating conjunctions on page 85 for possibilities.) Then underline each independent clause and place brackets around each dependent clause.

EXAMPLE   *[When* _____ Harvard's football team played Carlisle Institute's team in 1908,*]* the coaches of both teams used sneaky tactics.

1. The coach of Harvard was Percy Haughton, [while _____ the coach of Carlisle was "Pop" Warner.]

2. Warner had used a sneaky trick [when _____ he played Syracuse the week before.]

3. [Because _____ he wanted to outsmart Syracuse] Warner had pads sewn into his players' jerseys.

4. [Since _____ the pads were the same size, shape, and color as a football,] the opposing team had trouble determining which player had the ball.

5. Warner got away with his scheme [because _____ the pads were not against the rules.]

6. [Since _____ he knew Warner would try the trick again,] Coach Haughton devised his own strategy.

7. [As _____ Warner and Haughton met on the field to pick the game football,] Warner reached into his bag and pulled one out.

8. He had dyed all the footballs red, to match his team's jerseys

   [before _____ the game was to begin.]

9. [Unless _____ they had remarkable vision or supernatural powers,] Carlisle's players would not be able to tell who had the ball.

10. [Although _____ it was not against the rules,] the red balls gave Harvard an unfair advantage, allowing them to win.

SUBORDINATION—METHOD 1

Subordination is the joining of an independent clause and a dependent clause in the same sentence to create what is known as a **complex sentence**.

In subordination, the dependent clause can come either before or after the independent clause:

Independent clause:	*we could not sleep*
Dependent clause:	*because the radio was blaring*

Subordination:	*We could not sleep because the radio was blaring.*
Subordination:	*Because the radio was blaring, we could not sleep.*
Independent clause:	*Jan gets a headache*
Dependent clause:	*when the humidity is high*
Subordination:	*Jan gets a headache when the humidity is high.*
Subordination:	*When the humidity is high, Jan gets a headache.*

PUNCTUATION ALERT

Place a comma after a dependent clause that comes at the beginning of a sentence.

Comma:	*If I were you, I would go.*
Explanation:	The comma comes after the opening dependent clause.
No comma:	*I would go if I were you.*
Explanation:	Because the dependent clause comes at the end of the sentence, no comma is used.

6.3 ACTIVITY

The following sentences are made up of one independent clause and one dependent clause. Sometimes the dependent clause comes first, and sometimes the independent clause comes first.

A. Underline the independent clause once.
B. Underline the dependent clause twice.
C. Circle the subordinating conjunction that begins the dependent clause.
D. Notice that opening dependent clauses are followed by commas.

POWER UP

Find five sentences with subordination in newspapers, magazines, or textbooks. Copy the sentences and underline the independent clause once and the dependent clause twice. Then circle the subordinating conjunction. Would it be possible to express the same thoughts without using dependent clauses? If so, what changes would have to be made?

EXAMPLE   Before you leave, I want to ask you a question.

1. Since we are experiencing a drought, we cannot water our grass.
2. Although I need a vacation, I cannot get away this summer.
3. Katrina cannot eat caramels because she wears braces on her teeth.
4. The university is becoming barrier-free in order to accommodate students who use wheelchairs.
5. While I understand your point, I do not agree with it.
6. I plan to see *Rent* when I visit New York this summer.
7. As dinner came to an end, Andre proposed to Josette.
8. Marcel plans to visit Africa as soon as he graduates next year.
9. Even though the superintendent has made many changes in the school system, more needs to be done.
10. Joey will be back on the basketball team if he gets his leg in shape for the first practice.

6.4 ACTIVITY

Join each pair of sentences into one sentence by changing one of the independent clauses to a dependent clause beginning with a subordinating conjunction (see the list on page 85). First write the sentence with the dependent clause placed first. Next, rewrite the sentence with the dependent clause placed last. Remember to use a comma after an opening dependent clause.

EXAMPLE   Most of the world drives on the right side of the road.
A quarter of the world's countries drive on the left.

Although a quarter of the world's countries drive on the left,

most of the world drives on the right side of the road.

Most of the world drives on the right side of the road, although

a quarter of the world's countries drive on the left.

1. So many countries still drive on the left.
There must be a logical explanation for the practice.

Because so many countries still drive on the left, there must be a logical explanation for

the practice.

There must be a logical explanation for the practice because so many countries still drive

on the left.

2. Up to the late 1700s, everybody traveled on the left.
It was the sensible option for feudal, violent societies.

Because it was the sensible option for feudal, violent societies, up to the late 1700s,

everybody traveled on the left.

Up to the late 1700s, everybody traveled on the left because it was the sensible option for

feudal, violent societies.

3. Most people are right-handed.
Jousting knights with their lances under their right arms naturally passed on
each other's right.

Since most people are right-handed, jousting knights with their lances under their right

arms naturally passed on each other's right.

Jousting knights with their lances under their right arms naturally passed on each other's

right since most people are right-handed.

4. You passed a stranger on the road.
You walked on the left to ensure that your protective sword arm was between
yourself and that person.

When you passed a stranger on the road, you walked on the left to ensure that your

protective sword arm was between yourself and that person.

You walked on the left to ensure that your protective sword arm was between yourself and

that person when you passed a stranger on the road.

5. The drive-on-the-right policy was adopted by the United States.
It was eager to cast off all ties with its British colonial past.

When the drive-on-the-right policy was adopted by the United States, it was eager to cast

off all ties with its British colonial past.

It was eager to cast off all ties with its British colonial past when the drive-on-the-right

policy was adopted by the United States.

6. Americans began driving on the right.
Left-sided driving fell out of favor.

As soon as Americans began driving on the right, left-sided driving fell out of favor.

Left-sided driving fell out of favor as soon as Americans began driving on the right.

TIP

Read your writing out loud. If it sounds choppy or singsong, try adding some sentences with subordination and some with coordination to achieve a more pleasing style.

7. People began driving on the right.
America was once the only reliable manufacturer of cars.

When people began driving on the right, America was the only reliable manufacturer of cars.

America was the only reliable manufacturer of cars when people began driving on the right.

8. It seems strange that people of different countries drive on different sides of the road.
You understand there are historical reasons for the difference.

Until you understand there are historical reasons for the difference, it seems strange that people of different countries drive on different sides of the road.

It seems strange that people of different countries drive on different sides of the road until you understand there are historical reasons for the difference.

6.5 ACTIVITY

On a separate sheet, write six sentences that join dependent and independent clauses. Three of the sentences should have the dependent clause at the beginning, and three should have the dependent clause at the end. Remember to place a comma after an opening dependent clause.

SUBORDINATION—METHOD 2

A particular kind of dependent clause begins with one of the following words, which are called **relative pronouns.**

who   whose   which   that

A dependent clause that begins with one of these relative pronouns is called a **relative clause.**

Relative clauses can be joined with independent clauses to form sentences:

Sentence: *Anita, who is my best friend, got the highest grade on the algebra test.*

Independent clause: *Anita got the highest grade on the algebra test*

Relative clause: *who is my best friend*

Relative pronoun: *who*

Sentence: *The man whose car is stalled has called the automobile club.*

Independent clause: *the man has called the automobile club*

Relative clause:	*whose car is stalled*
Relative pronoun:	*whose*
Sentence:	*The question, which I do not understand, is worth 10 points.*
Independent clause:	*the question is worth 10 points*
Relative clause:	*which I do not understand*
Relative pronoun:	*which*
Sentence:	*The sweater that I gave you is all wool.*
Independent clause:	*the sweater is all wool*
Relative clause:	*that I gave you*
Relative pronoun:	*that*

GRAMMAR ALERT

Who and *whose* refer to people. *Which* refers to things and animals. *That* refers to people and things.

No:	*He is the person <u>which</u> gave me the letter.*
Yes:	*He is the person <u>who</u> gave me the letter.*

A relative clause can appear in the middle of or at the end of the independent clause.

Relative clause in the middle:	*The woman <u>who is running for mayor</u> is currently a teacher.*
Relative clause at the end:	*This is the painting <u>that I want to buy.</u>*

There are two kinds of relative clauses. The first kind is necessary for identifying who or what is referred to:

The child who lives across the street is adorable. [Who *lives across the street* is necessary for identifying which child is adorable. Without the clause, we do not know which child is being referred to.]

The second kind of relative clause is <u>not</u> necessary for identifying who or what is referred to:

Kelly O'Hara, who lives across the street, is adorable. [The person is identified by her name, so *who lives across the street* is not necessary for identifying who is being referred to.]

PUNCTUATION ALERT

How you punctuate a relative clause depends on whether or not the clause is necessary for identifying who or what is referred to. If the clause is *not* necessary for identification, set it off with commas. If it *is* necessary for identification, do not use commas.

Necessary for identification:	*The person who studies hard will get good grades.*
Unnecessary for identification:	*My roommate, who studies hard, will get good grades.*

TIP

To check whether a clause is necessary or not, try dropping it out of the sentence. What's lost? Is the person or thing referred to still clearly identified?

TIP

For a related discussion, see page 141 on subject-verb agreement.

6.6 ACTIVITY

Underline the relative clause in each of the following sentences, and circle the relative pronoun.

EXAMPLE   This is the dog ⟨that⟩ bit Mohan yesterday.

1. I spoke to Frank, ⟨who⟩ helped me solve the problem.
2. This side of town, ⟨which⟩ is very old, is being restored.
3. Gregory, ⟨who⟩ hurt his back, had to give up track.
4. Carlotta, ⟨whose⟩ poetry has been published in local anthologies, is very talented.
5. The board of education voted to close South High School, ⟨which⟩ is the oldest high school in the city.
6. This is the store ⟨that⟩ has so many good bargains.
7. The child ⟨whose⟩ dog was lost cried all night.
8. The person ⟨who⟩ gave me directions was very polite.
9. A restaurant ⟨that⟩ has high prices will not survive in a college town.
10. I am the one ⟨who⟩ told you the truth.

6.7 ACTIVITY

Join each pair of sentences into one sentence by changing the second sentence to a relative clause beginning with *who*, *whose*, *which*, or *that*. You will need to eliminate one or more words in the second sentence. Remember that *who* and *whose* refer to people, *which* refers to things and animals, and *that* refers to people and things. Also remember that clauses not necessary for identification are set off with commas.

POWER UP

Choose two pairs of sentences from Activity 6.7 and connect them in a different way, with either coordination or another means of subordination.

EXAMPLE   The CD player is broken.
Henry got the CD player for his birthday.

The CD player that Henry got for his birthday is broken.

1. Roberto is sure to win an art scholarship.
Roberto is a talented portrait artist.

Roberto, who is a talented portrait artist, is sure to win an art scholarship.

2. The medicine is very expensive.
Aunt Helen needs the medicine.

The medicine that Aunt Helen needs is very expensive.

3. The blue jays will attack anyone in the yard.
The blue jays are very territorial.

The blue jays, which are very territorial, will attack anyone in the yard.

4. This blazer is the wrong color for you.
   The blazer is inexpensive.

   This blazer, which is inexpensive, is the wrong color for you.

5. Marni wants to be a graphic artist.
   Marni is Gregory's best friend.

   Marni, who is Gregory's best friend, wants to be a graphic artist.

6. The ambulance weaved through traffic.
   The traffic had come to a halt.

   The ambulance weaved through traffic, which had come to a halt.

7. The baseball smashed through the living room window.
   The window had just been replaced.

   The baseball smashed through the living room window, which had just been replaced.

8. Daylight savings time means I lose an hour of sleep.
   Daylight savings time is meant to save energy.

   Daylight savings time, which is meant to save energy, means I lose an hour of sleep.

9. Professor Yoshida is an excellent chemistry teacher.
   Professor Yoshida's lectures are never boring.

   Professor Yoshida, whose lectures are never boring, is an excellent chemistry teacher.

10. This is the Terry McMillan book.
    It is the book I want you to read.

    This is the Terry McMillan book that I want you to read.

11. Dave Barry is my favorite humorist.
    Dave Barry writes for the *Miami Herald*.

    Dave Barry, who writes for the *Miami Herald*, is my favorite humorist.

12. I lost my grandmother's watch.
    My grandmother received the watch at her retirement party.

    I lost my grandmother's watch, which she received at her retirement party.

13. The man looks suspicious to me.
    The man is sitting on the park bench.

    The man who is sitting on the park bench looks suspicious to me.

14. I am very proud of the sweater.
    I knitted the sweater myself.

    I am very proud of the sweater that I knitted myself.

15. Corey and Madeline bought a car.
    The car has every available option.

    Corey and Madeline bought a car that has every available option.

6.8 INDIVIDUAL OR GROUP ACTIVITY

Alone or with two or three classmates, complete each of the following sentences with a relative clause. Remember, *who* and *whose* refer to people; *which* refers to things and animals; *that* refers to people and things.

EXAMPLE   Inez, who _____loves milk_____ , is allergic to dairy products.

1. This is the restaurant that features vegetarian dishes.

2. Cigarette smoking, which causes heart and lung disease
   _____ , is now banned in all city buildings.

3. Joseph, whose short stories appear in the school newspaper
   _____ , is motivated to succeed.

4. Lillian, who has a wacky sense of humor _____ ,
   can always cheer me up.

5. Officer Stein is the police officer who rescued two people from a
   burning car.

6.9 ACTIVITY

On a separate sheet, write five of your own sentences with relative clauses. Remember to use commas to set off clauses unnecessary for identifying who or what is referred to.

IF ENGLISH IS YOUR SECOND LANGUAGE

If you speak English as a second language, review the following tips.

1. The relationship between an independent clause and a dependent clause is made clear by the subordinating conjunction you choose. To be sure you convey the desired relationship, consult the following chart of frequently used subordinating conjunctions.

Relationship	Subordinating Conjunction
time	after, as soon as, before, until, when, whenever, while
cause	as, because, since
condition	if, unless, as long as
contrast	although, even though, though
location	where, wherever
choice	whether

Notice how the underlined subordinating conjunction changes the relationship between the clauses in the following examples:

When I am on a diet, I cannot eat sugar. [Time]
Because I am on a diet, I cannot eat sugar. [Cause]
If I am on a diet, I cannot eat sugar. [Condition]

2. When a relative clause comes in the middle of the sentence, do not use a pronoun to repeat the subject of the independent clause.

No: *My sister, who is getting married this weekend, she is very nervous.*
Yes: *My sister, who is getting married this weekend, is very nervous.*

RECHARGE

1. **Subordination** is the correct joining of an **independent clause** and a **dependent clause** in the same sentence.

Independent clause:	*we will not have our grades until next week*
Dependent clause:	*because the computer is down*
Subordination:	*We will not have our grades until next week because the computer is down.*
Subordination:	*Because the computer is down, we will not have our grades until next week.*

2. In the first method of subordination, the dependent clause begins with a subordinating conjunction.

When the crocuses bloom, I know it is spring.
Asbestos must be removed from the structure before renovations begin.

Place a comma after a dependent clause that comes at the beginning of a sentence.

If you leave on vacation, you should unplug the appliances.

3. In the second method of subordination, a dependent clause called a **relative clause** begins with a **relative pronoun** (*who, whose, which, that*) and is joined with an independent clause.

> *The car, which has a hundred thousand miles on it, needs new tires.*

If the relative clause is necessary for identifying who or what is referred to, do not set it off with commas.

> *The firefighter who saved the child was honored by the press.*

If the relative clause is not necessary for identifying who or what is referred to, set it off with commas.

> *The captain of the firefighters, who saved the child, was honored by the press.*

6.10 CHAPTER REVIEW ACTIVITY

Join each pair of sentences into one sentence, according to the directions given.

EXAMPLE   Make the second sentence a dependent clause and place it at the end of the first sentence:

Insects have been present for about 350 million years.
Humans have been around for only 10,000 years.

Insects have been present for about 350 million years, while

humans have been around for only 10,000 years.

1. Make the first sentence a dependent clause and place it at the beginning of the second sentence:
   Ants are small.
   They can lift and carry more than 50 times their own weight.

   Although ants are small, they can lift and carry more than 50 times their own weight.

2. Make the first sentence a dependent clause and place it at the beginning of the second sentence:
   Monarch butterflies are very light.
   It takes about 100 of them to weigh an ounce.

   Because Monarch butterflies are very light, it takes about 100 of them to weigh an ounce.

3. Make the second sentence a relative clause and join it to the first sentence:
   Houseflies find sugar with their feet.
   Their feet are 10 million times more sensitive than human tongues.

   Houseflies find sugar with their feet, which are 10 million times more sensitive than

   human tongues.

4. Make the second sentence a relative clause and join it to the first sentence:
   To survive the cold of winter months, many insects replace their body water with a chemical called glycerol.
   Glycerol acts as an antifreeze.

   To survive the cold of winter months, many insects replace their body water with a chemical

   called glycerol, which acts as an antifreeze.

5. Make the first sentence a dependent clause and place it before the second sentence:

   The droppings of millions of cattle started ruining the land in Australia.
   Dung beetles were imported to reduce the problem.

   When the droppings of millions of cattle started ruining the land in Australia, dung beetles

   were imported to reduce the problem.

6. Make the second sentence a relative clause and join it to the first sentence after "mosquitoes":

   Male mosquitoes do not bite humans.
   Male mosquitoes live on plant juices and other natural liquids.

   Male mosquitoes, which live on plant juices and other natural liquids, do not bite humans.

7. Make the first sentence a dependent clause and place it after the second sentence:

   A newly married couple was provided with enough honey wine to last for a month.
   The term *honeymoon* comes from the Middle Ages.

   The term *honeymoon* comes from the Middle Ages, when a newly married couple was

   provided with enough honey wine to last for a month.

8. Make the second sentence a relative clause and join it to the first sentence after "Wasps":

   Wasps have been known to get "drunk" and pass out.
   Wasps feed on fermenting juice.

   Wasps, which feed on fermenting juice, have been known to get "drunk" and pass out.

9. Make the first sentence a dependent clause and place it at the beginning of the second sentence:

   Honeybees make about 10 million trips to collect enough nectar for production of one pound of honey.
   They can be considered a very determined species.

   Because honeybees make about 10 million trips to collect enough nectar for the production

   of one pound of honey, they can be considered a very determined species.

10. Make the second sentence a relative clause and join it to the first sentence after "beans":

    Mexican jumping beans actually have a caterpillar of a bean moth inside.
    Mexican jumping beans are sometimes sold commercially.

    Mexican jumping beans, which are sometimes sold commercially, actually have a caterpillar

    of a bean moth inside.

6.11 CHAPTER REVIEW ACTIVITY

Read aloud the paragraph below and notice how choppy it often sounds. To eliminate this choppiness with subordination, rewrite the paragraph according to the directions given. Then read the revision and notice the improvement that subordination makes. Remember to use commas after opening dependent clauses and to set off relative clauses unnecessary for identification.

A. Make sentence 2 a relative clause and join it to sentence 1, after "Drew."
B. Make sentence 4 a dependent clause beginning with "where," and join it to the end of sentence 3.
C. Make sentence 6 a dependent clause beginning with "until," and join it to the end of sentence 5.
D. Make sentence 8 a dependent clause beginning with "after," and join it to the beginning of sentence 9.
E. Make sentence 12 a relative clause and join it to sentence 13 after "Drew."
F. Make sentence 15 a dependent clause beginning with "where," and join it to the end of sentence 14.

[1]Charles Drew grew up in a poor family in a Washington, DC, ghetto. [2]He discovered the modern processes for preserving blood for transfusions. [3]His intelligence and athletic skill won him a scholarship to Amherst College. [4]He was captain of the track team, starting halfback on the football team, and an honors student. [5]After graduation, Drew taught and coached at Morgan College in Baltimore. [6]He earned enough money to go to the medical school at McGill University in Montreal. [7]There he became increasingly interested in the general field of medical research and in the specific problems of blood transfusion. [8]He graduated from McGill in 1932. [9]He eventually joined the faculty of Howard University and was appointed the head of surgery. [10]During World War II, he was appointed head of the National Blood Bank program. [11]At the time, the official government policy mandated that whites' and African Americans' blood be given only to members of their respective races. [12]Drew became furious with the official government policy. [13]Drew resigned from his post and returned to Howard University. [14]In 1944, he became chief of surgery at Freedman's Hospital, in Washington, DC. [15]His presence encouraged young African Americans to enter medicine. [16]Sadly, Drew died in a car crash in 1950.

Handwritten annotations:

Charles Drew, who discovered the modern processes for preserving blood transfusions, grew up in a poor family in a Washington, DC, ghetto. His intelligence and athletic skill won him a scholarship to Amherst College where he was captain of the track team, starting halfback on the football team, and an honors student. After graduation, Drew taught and coached at Morgan College in Baltimore until he earned enough money to go to medical school at McGill University in Montreal.

After he graduated from McGill in 1932, he eventually joined the faculty of Howard University and was appointed the head of surgery.

Drew, who became furious with the official government policy, resigned from his post and returned to Howard University. In 1944, he became chief of surgery at Freedman's Hospital, in Washington, DC, where his presence encouraged young African Americans to enter medicine.

GETTING IN GEAR

thinking in writing: Take two sheets of paper and label one "personal" and the other "professional." On the first sheet, list things or characteristics you want to have in five years. Do the same on the second sheet.

writing from experience: Explain what you would like your life to be like one year after graduation from college. You can describe your job, your living arrangements, your personal life, and anything else you care to write about. Then go on to explain how your college experiences will help you achieve your goals.

writing in context: Viennese poet Franz Grillparzer (1791–1872) once said, "The cradle of the future is the grave of the past." Agree or disagree with that statement, using one or more examples to support your view.

CHAPTER **7**

Sentence Fragments

CONNECT

Fragments are common in advertising and classified ads ("Car available. In good condition.") Why do you think this is? Remember, though, that in college, business, and formal writing, fragments are not acceptable.

DEFINITION OF A SENTENCE FRAGMENT

You can put a football player in ballet slippers and tights, but that won't make him a dancer. Similarly, you can begin a word group with a capital letter and end it with a period, but that won't always make it a sentence. To be a sentence, a word group must have three things:

- A subject
- A complete verb
- The completeness to stand independently

A word group missing one or more of these sentence elements is a **sentence fragment.**

Fragment:	*Eats pizza every day for lunch.* [Who eats pizza? The subject is missing.]
Sentence:	*Hans eats pizza every day for lunch.*
Fragment:	*Students registering for summer school on Monday.* [Part of the verb is missing.]
Sentence:	*Students are registering for summer school on Monday.*
Fragment:	*When the interstate is complete.* [What will happen when the interstate is complete? Information necessary for completeness is missing.]
Sentence:	*When the interstate is complete, business will expand in our area.*

7.1 ACTIVITY

Each word group below looks like a sentence because it has a period and a capital letter. However, five of the word groups are really sentence fragments because one of the sentence elements is missing (the subject, all or part of the verb, or information necessary for completeness). Read each word group aloud and listen to determine whether something is missing. If the word group is a sentence, write "S" on the blank; if it is a fragment, write an "F."

1. _____S_____ The British painter Joseph Turner lived from 1775 to 1851.
2. _____F_____ Renowned for his landscape paintings.
3. _____S_____ His paintings have spectacular color effects.
4. _____F_____ That capture the play of light on a scene.
5. _____F_____ For example, a sunset or a storm of dramatic intensity.

Just for practice, try turning the fragments here into sentences. Then try to put sentences 1–10 together in a paragraph, using subordination and coordination for a pleasing style. (Review Chapters 5 and 6 if necessary.)

6. ___F___ Turner wanting to see what a storm at sea looked like.

7. ___S___ He had himself tied to the mast of a ship.

8. ___S___ The ship was sailing through a storm.

9. ___S___ People often do unusual things.

10. ___F___ When they are passionate about their art.

ELIMINATING FRAGMENTS THAT RESULT FROM MISSING SUBJECTS OR MISSING SUBJECTS AND VERBS

Because fragments can confuse or annoy a careful reader, you must eliminate them from your writing.

To eliminate a fragment that results from a missing subject, you have two choices:

- Add the missing subject.
- Join the fragment to a sentence.

Sentence and fragment:	*I needed to be awake by six o'clock. But forgot to set the alarm.*
Add the missing subject:	*I needed to be awake by six o'clock. But I forgot to set the alarm.*
Join the fragment to a sentence:	*I needed to be awake by six o'clock but forgot to set the alarm.*

To eliminate a fragment that results from a missing subject and verb, you have two choices:

- Add the missing subject and verb.
- Join the fragment to a sentence.

Sentence and fragment:	*Marcus bought a new suit. With wide lapels and baggy pants.*
Add the missing subject and verb:	*Marcus bought a new suit. It had wide lapels and baggy pants.*
Join the fragment to a sentence:	*Marcus bought a new suit with wide lapels and baggy pants.*

7.2 ACTIVITY

All but one of the pairs of word groups below consist of one fragment and one sentence. The fragments have missing subjects or missing subjects and verbs. First, underline the fragment. Then eliminate it, using the correction method of your choice. Remember, one pair of word groups is already correct.

EXAMPLE   Clarence Birdseye made cooking easier. And freed women from a great deal of cooking drudgery.

Clarence Birdseye made cooking easier and freed women from a great deal of cooking drudgery.

or

Clarence Birdseye made cooking easier. He freed women from a great deal of cooking drudgery.

1. Clarence Birdseye was a naturalist and fur trader. <u>Traveling in Labrador in 1916.</u>

   Clarence Birdseye was a naturalist and fur trader, traveling in Labrador in 1916.

2. <u>With his keen scientific mind.</u> He understood Inuit fish-freezing techniques.

   With his keen scientific mind, he understood Inuit fish-freezing techniques.

3. He recognized that speed was the key. <u>And could revolutionize the food industry.</u>

   He recognized that speed was the key. It could revolutionize the food industry.

4. Slow freezing is a problem. Large ice crystals will form within and outside the cells.

   correct

5. During the thawing period, the large crystals cause damage. <u>In the cell walls of plants and the membranes in animals.</u>

   During the thawing period, the large crystals cause damage in the cell walls of plants and

   the membranes of animals.

6. <u>Damaged to a significant extent.</u> Vegetables become mushy and meat becomes tough.

   Damaged to a significant extent, vegetables become mushy and meat becomes tough.

7. However, the Inuits laid freshly caught fish on the ice. <u>To freeze quickly.</u>

   However, the Inuits laid freshly caught fish on the ice to freeze quickly.

8. Their fish had the flavor and texture of the fresh catch. <u>And did not suffer from the freezing process.</u>

   Their fish had the flavor and texture of the fresh catch. It did not suffer from the freezing

   process.

9. Birdseye returned home. <u>Then established Birdseye Seafoods.</u>

   Birdseye returned home. Then he established Birdseye Seafoods.

10. Later he expanded his business to include meats, fruits, and vegetables. <u>Making frozen foods the forerunner of convenience foods.</u>

    Later he expanded his business to include meats, fruits, and vegetables, making frozen

    foods the forerunner of convenience foods.

ELIMINATING FRAGMENTS THAT RESULT FROM INCOMPLETE VERBS

Some verb forms cannot appear alone; they must appear with other verbs called **helping verbs.** Here are two examples:

> helping verb
> The party [is] ending now.

> helping verb
> The runner [has] broken the school record.

If a necessary helping verb is left out, a sentence fragment results.

Fragment: *The party ending now.*

Fragment: *The runner broken the school record.*

> **TIP**
>
> The **helping verbs** are *am, be, is, are, was, were, been, being, may, must, might, can, could, would, will, should, do, did, does, have, has, had,* and *shall.* They are discussed on page 60.

GRAMMAR ALERT !

Words ending in *-ing* cannot be complete verbs by themselves; they must appear with helping verbs.

Fragment: *The storm slowing rush hour traffic.*

Sentence: *The storm is slowing rush hour traffic.*

Fragment: *Judd considering three job offers.*

Sentence: *Judd was considering three job offers.*

To eliminate a fragment that results from an incomplete verb, you have two possibilities:

- Add the missing helping verb.
- Change the verb form.

Add the Missing Helping Verb

Sentence and fragment: *We raced down the pier. However, the ferry gone by the time we arrived.*

Correction: *We raced down the pier. However, the ferry was gone by the time we arrived.*

Change the Verb Form

Sentence and fragment: *Arina enjoys early morning exercise. At six a.m. she jogging down neighborhood streets.*

Correction: *Arina enjoys early morning exercise. At six a.m. she jogs down neighborhood streets.*

7.3 ACTIVITY

In the items below, underline the fragments that result from incomplete verbs and rewrite to eliminate them. One is already correct.

EXAMPLE   The marching band is presenting an excellent halftime show. It moving in intricate steps across the field.

> *The marching band is presenting an excellent halftime show. It is moving in intricate steps across the field.*

or

The marching band is presenting an excellent halftime show. It

moves in intricate steps across the field.

1. Uncle Miquel was surprised when he saw his nephew. <u>He grown four inches over the summer.</u>

   Uncle Miquel was surprised when he saw his nephew. He grew four inches over the

   summer.

2. Eddie Murphy is a popular comedian. <u>He also proving himself as an actor.</u>

   Eddie Murphy is a popular comedian. He also is proving himself as an actor.

3. Jonah was forced to chair the fund-raising committee by himself. <u>No one else offering to help.</u>

   Jonah was forced to chair the fund-raising committee by himself. No one else offered

   to help.

CONNECT

Like the writers of classified ads, you may find yourself using fragments in informal writing situations, particularly when speed is an issue. You may write them in casual e-mail to friends, in lecture notes, in shopping lists, and the like. Remember, though, that in formal business, academic, and personal writing, you should edit to eliminate fragments.

4. Larry drove through a stop sign. <u>He distracted by thoughts of a problem at work.</u>

   Larry drove through a stop sign. He was distracted by thoughts of a problem at work.

5. The character of professional tennis has changed over the years. <u>Top players being younger than ever before.</u>

   The character of professional tennis has changed over the years. Top players are younger

   than ever before.

6. Father and Mother's anniversary will be special this year. We are planning a surprise party at their favorite restaurant.

   correct

7. Football used to be much more physical than basketball. <u>Now basketball seeming just as physical.</u>

   Football used to be much more physical than basketball. Now basketball seems just as

   physical.

8. <u>The economy improving gradually.</u> There is a new optimism in the country.

   The economy is improving gradually. There is a new optimism in the country.

9. I tried to call you before I left. <u>Your phone ringing busy for two hours.</u>

   I tried to call you before I left. Your phone rang busy for two hours.

10. <u>The students working late in the library.</u> They are preparing for final exams.

   <u>The students are working late in the library. They are preparing for final exams.</u>

ELIMINATING FRAGMENTS THAT RESULT FROM LACK OF COMPLETENESS

A word group can have a subject and verb but still not be a sentence because it is not complete. The following word groups have subjects and verbs; however, read them aloud, and you will hear that they are not complete and cannot stand as sentences.

Fragment: *Before our company arrives.*

Fragment: *When the last hamburger is cooked.*

Fragment: *Although we disagree with each other.*

In Chapter 6 (see page 84), you learned that a **dependent clause** has a subject and verb but is still not a complete sentence. Word groups that have a subject and a verb but are still incomplete can be called *dependent clause fragments.*

To eliminate a dependent clause fragment that results from lack of completeness, join the fragment to a sentence.

Fragment and sentence: <u>*Because you left so early.*</u> *You missed the best part of the party.*

Correction: *Because you left so early, you missed the best part of the party.*

Sentence and fragment: *Harriet is a talented dancer.* <u>*Who plans to study in New York.*</u>

Correction: *Harriet is a talented dancer, who plans to study in New York.*

GRAMMAR ALERT ❗

Missing information does not always create a fragment. A word group can be a complete sentence even if some information is unknown.

Sentence: *We offered them a ride.* [The word group is complete and is a sentence, even though we do not know who "we" and "them" are.]

Copyright © 2002, The McGraw-Hill Companies, Inc.

> ### TIP
>
> Dependent clauses begin with one of the following words, known as subordinating conjunctions: *after, although, as, as if, as long as, as soon as, as though, because, before, even though, if, since, though, unless, until, when, whenever, where, whatever, whether,* and *while.* See page 85 for more information.

7.4 ACTIVITY

In each pair, underline the fragment that results from lack of completeness, and then rewrite to eliminate the fragment. One pair is already correct.

EXAMPLE   Whenever I read about dumb criminals. I marvel at their stupidity.

   Whenever I read about dumb criminals, I marvel at their

   stupidity.

1. <u>Even though I thought I had heard it all.</u> A recent news report surprised me.

   <u>Even though I thought I had heard it all, a recent news report surprised me.</u>

2. Convenience store robbers often wear ski masks. <u>Since they want to hide their faces.</u>

   Convenience store robbers often wear ski masks since they want to hide their faces.

3. <u>Because one criminal was not thinking ahead.</u> He made a serious error.

   Because one criminal was not thinking ahead, he made a serious error.

4. <u>When he held up a convenience store.</u> He used a clear plastic bag instead of a ski mask.

   When he held up a convenience store, he used a clear plastic bag instead of a ski mask.

5. <u>Since he did not have a disguise.</u> Upon entering the store, he grabbed a transparent garbage bag.

   Since he did not have a disguise, upon entering the store he grabbed a transparent garbage bag.

6. <u>Before he really thought things through.</u> He put the bag over his head.

   Before he really thought things through, he put the bag over his head.

7. <u>After putting the bag over his head.</u> The thief robbed the store of less than a hundred dollars.

   After putting the bag over his head, the thief robbed the store of less than a hundred dollars.

8. <u>When he tried to break into a house later.</u> The police arrested him.

   When he tried to break into a house later, the police arrested him.

9. The garbage bag bandit told police he was a crack addict. <u>As soon as they arrested him.</u>

   The garbage bag bandit told police he was a crack addict as soon as they arrested him.

10. Prosecution should not be too difficult. Because the store robbery was recorded on the security camera, the evidence against the man is strong.

    correct

TIPS FOR FINDING FRAGMENTS

1. You can easily overlook fragments if you simply read over your draft. A better way is to study each sentence for five to ten seconds, checking for subjects, verbs, and completeness.

2. Try slowly reading your draft backward, from last sentence to first. Listen for lack of completeness.

3. Be sure that every sentence with an *-ing* form for the main verb (*eating, sleeping, driving,* etc.) also includes a helping verb (*is eating, was sleeping, were driving,* etc.).

4. Read aloud word groups beginning with *because, when, while, unless, if, especially, although,* and *since* to be sure they are complete to be sentences.

5. Fragments cannot be made into questions, so if you are unsure whether a word group is a fragment, try changing it to a question. If it cannot be done, you have found a fragment.

6. If you compose at the computer, reformat your paper into a list of sentences. (You can either do this manually or find and replace every sequence of two spaces with an "enter" symbol.) With your work in list form, you may find it easier to detect fragments. When finished, reformat your paper into its original form.

7.5 ACTIVITY

The following paragraph has six sentence fragments. First underline the fragments. Then make corrections above the line to eliminate the fragments.

Although females are taught at an early age to protect themselves against crime. Women [correction: crime, women]
receive mixed messages about what they should do. For example, women are trained to
be polite. If a stranger asks for directions or a date asks a woman to come inside his
apartment. Her first instinct is to comply to avoid being rude. Thus placing herself in [correction: apartment, her; she places]
jeopardy. When criminals look for potential victims. They look for meekness. Women [correction: victims, they]
are not trained to be aggressive, so they often present the appearance of vulnerability. [correction: vulnerability,]
Making themselves targets of an attack. The best advice for women who want to [correction: making]
protect themselves is to take a self-defense course. Which may be offered by the local [correction: course, which]
police department. Such a course instructs women in how to avoid dangerous
situations and what to do if threatened or attacked.

7.6 ACTIVITY

The following paragraphs contain eight sentence fragments. First underline the fragments. Then make corrections above the line to eliminate the fragments.

Lyme disease is a perplexing illness. Caused by the bite of a bloodsucking tick the [correction: illness. It is caused]
size of a pencil point. The tick is so small that a child playing in the woods might
not notice its bite. Or its presence on his or her body. [correction: bite or]

Lyme disease usually attacks the skin, heart, nervous system, and joints. The
symptoms are usually triggered by a red ~~rash. That~~ ^{rash that} appears near the site of a tick
bite. The rash may appear from 1 to 32 days after the ~~bite. And~~ ^{bite and} last from two
months to a year.

Since early detection and treatment of this mysterious disease usually prevent
major ~~complications. It~~ ^{complications, it} is important to be alert to the symptoms of Lyme disease. If
untreated, it can cause chronic arthritis, heart problems, blindness, and even death.
As with most bacterial ~~infections. Lyme~~ ^{infections, Lyme} disease is usually treated with antibiotics.
Most children recover quickly. However, pregnant women must be particularly
~~careful. Because~~ ^{careful because} Lyme disease causes birth defects. Still, there is no reason to
~~panic. Since~~ ^{panic, since} the ticks that carry Lyme disease are relatively rare.

IF ENGLISH IS YOUR SECOND LANGUAGE

1. In some languages, a sentence does not require a subject. However, this is not
    the case in English. A sentence must have a subject; a word group that does
    not have a subject is a fragment.

2. In some languages, a sentence does not have a verb. However, this is not the
    case in English. A sentence must have a verb; a word group that does not have
    a verb is a fragment.

3. Sometimes a verb form that needs a helping verb is spelled the same way as the
    verb form that does not need a helping verb. This can cause confusion and lead
    to sentence fragments. Just remember that if the subject performs the action of
    the verb, then a helping verb is *not* required. However, if the subject receives
    the action of the verb, then a helping verb *is* required.

    Sentence: *The fire burned my finger.* [The subject performs the action.]
    Fragment: *My finger burned by the fire.* [The subject receives the action.]
    Sentence: *My finger was burned by the fire.* [The subject receives the action.]

RECHARGE

1. In order to be a **sentence**, a word group must have

    • A subject
    • A complete verb
    • Sufficient completeness to stand independently

    A word group lacking one of these elements is a **sentence fragment**, even
    if it begins with a capital letter and ends with a period.

2. To eliminate a fragment that results from a missing subject, add the
    subject or join the fragment to a sentence.

    Fragment: *I put the pasta on a high heat. And forgot about it for an hour.*
    Sentence: *I put the pasta on a high heat. I forgot about it for an hour.*
    Sentence: *I put the pasta on a high heat and forgot about it for an hour.*

3. To eliminate a fragment that results from an incomplete verb, add a missing helping verb or change the verb form.

Fragment: *The expensive vase broken.*

Sentence: *The expensive vase is broken.*

Sentence: *The expensive vase broke.*

4. To eliminate a dependent clause fragment, join the fragment to a sentence.

Fragment: *Although the traffic is heavy. Everyone is traveling the speed limit.*

Sentence: *Although the traffic is heavy, everyone is traveling the speed limit.*

7.7 CHAPTER REVIEW ACTIVITY

The following paragraph has seven fragments. First underline the fragments. Then make corrections above the line to eliminate the fragments.

Even babies enjoy friendships. By the time they are one. Most children enjoy [one, most] peekaboo and simple games with their peers. They enjoy social situations and sustained interaction. Many children even showing [show] a clear preference for certain children. Two-year-old friends fighting [fight] over toys, but also playing [play] cooperatively with each other. By the time they are three, children use their friendships as bargaining tools. If they don't get what they want. They [want, they] shout, "You're not my friend anymore." The age of three can be a stormy period for peer relationships. By five, children recognize that friendship means more than playing together. Children at this age solve problems and make plans together. By eight, choice of friends depending [depends] on common interests and compatibility. Girls are likely to have one or two friends. Whereas [friends, whereas] boys are more likely to play in groups. In addition, girls and boys resolve conflicts differently. Boys argue about the rules. However, they usually resolve the conflict. And [conflict and] go on playing. Girls tend to end the game. By the time they are preteens, both sexes have developed skills for settling conflicts with a minimum of fuss. As teenagers, however, young people enter a new period of turbulence. As a result, friendships and alliances can shift.

7.8 CHAPTER REVIEW ACTIVITY

Find and correct the seven fragments in the following passage.

The names of most states have some kind of meaning. But [meaning, but] not so for Idaho. The name really is a form of gibberish. The name *Idaho* was first popularized by mine ~~owners. Who~~ *owners, who* thought it would be a good name for the Pikes Peak mining country. The mine owners claimed that the word was Apache for "Comanche," who were the dominant tribe in the area. The story was believed, and Congress was set to approve the ~~name. When~~ *name when* it was discovered that *Idaho* meant nothing in Apache or any other language. It was a hoax. As a result, the area was named Colorado at the last minute.

However, the name *Idaho* ~~refusing~~ *refused* to die. That same year the name began cropping up in the Pacific Northwest. Now it was said to derive from the Shoshone ~~phrase. Meaning~~ *phrase meaning* "Behold the sun coming down on the mountains." Others claimed it meant "gem of the ~~mountains." While~~ *mountains," while* still others said it meant "salmon eaters." Despite the conflicting reports, a county in Washington Territory was officially named Idaho. In 1863, one of the senators who had blocked the use of the name two years earlier now supported it. Congress then ~~going~~ *went* along with the name and ~~dubbing~~ *dubbed* the territory Idaho.

GETTING IN GEAR

thinking in writing: List 10 things you like best about your school. Then list 10 things you like least.

writing from experience: Write about the best or worst feature of your college or university, being sure to explain why this feature is so good or bad. Try to make your reader feel the same way you do about the feature.

writing in context: Assume that you have been named a student member of your college or university's board of trustees. In your official capacity, write a report for the board that argues for a specific change to improve your school.

CHAPTER **8**

Run-On Sentences and Comma Splices

TIP

For a more detailed discussion of independent clauses, see page 69.

RECOGNIZING RUN-ON SENTENCES AND COMMA SPLICES

A word group that can stand as a sentence is an **independent clause.**

Independent clause:	*your library books are overdue*
Sentence:	*Your library books are overdue.*
Independent clause:	*you must pay $2*
Sentence:	*You must pay $2.*

A **run-on sentence** is a problem that occurs when two independent clauses are not separated. (Remember, an *independent clause* is a word group that can be a sentence.)

Independent clause:	*your library books are overdue*
Independent clause:	*you must pay $2*
Run-on:	*Your library books are overdue you must pay $2.*
Independent clause:	*a truck overturned on the turnpike*
Independent clause:	*the right lane is closed for 10 miles*
Run-on:	*A truck overturned on the turnpike the right lane is closed for 10 miles.*

A **comma splice** is a problem that occurs when independent clauses are separated only by a comma.

Independent clause:	*your library books are overdue*
Independent clause:	*you must pay $2*
Comma splice:	*Your library books are overdue, you must pay $2.*

[A comma separates the independent clauses.]

Independent clause:	*a truck overturned on the turnpike*
Independent clause:	*the right lane is closed for 10 miles*
Comma splice:	*A truck overturned on the turnpike, the right lane is closed for 10 miles.*

8.1 ACTIVITY

If the word group is a run-on sentence because there is no separation between independent clauses, write "RO" on the blank; if it is a comma splice because only a comma separates the independent clauses, write "CS" on the blank; if it is correct, write "C" on the blank.

TIP

Do not think in terms of long and short. Something very short can be a run-on or comma splice: "We left they didn't." Something long can be correct: "Peter, one of the most dynamic characters in the novel, demonstrates his complexity in the way he handles power and in the surprising way he expresses compassion at unexpected moments."

1. __CS_____ The duck-billed platypus is about 180 million years old, it lives in Australia.

2. __RO_____ The platypus spends most of its time in the water that is where it feeds.

3. __C_____ It dives under the water to feed on crayfish, snails, and fish.

4. __RO_____ The platypus swims with its eyes, ears, and nose tightly shut special sensors in its bill guide it.

5. __CS_____ The platypus has adapted to many environments over the years, that is why it has lasted so long.

6. __C_____ The duck-billed platypus teaches us the importance of adaptability in the face of change.

THREE WAYS TO ELIMINATE RUN-ONS AND COMMA SPLICES

1. Use a period and a capital letter to make each independent clause its own sentence.

TIP

For more on coordinating conjunctions, see page 70.

Run-on:	*Bilal was a camp counselor last summer he enjoyed working with young children.*
Correction:	*Bilal was a camp counselor last summer. He enjoyed working with young children.*
Comma splice:	*Alligators are not picky eaters, they eat turtles with the shells on.*
Correction:	*Alligators are not picky eaters. They eat turtles with the shells on.*

2. Separate independent clauses with a comma and one of the following words, which are called **coordinating conjunctions.**

and	for	or	yet
but	nor	so	

Run-on:	*The secretary put me on hold she forgot to get back to me.*
Correction:	*The secretary put me on hold* [, but] *she forgot to get back to me.*
Comma splice:	*First whip the cream into stiff peaks, then fold it into the chocolate mixture.*
Correction:	*First whip the cream into stiff peaks* [, and] *then fold it into the chocolate mixture.*

PUNCTUATION ALERT ❗

And, but, or, nor, for, so, and *yet* are the only conjunctions that can be used with just a comma to separate independent clauses. Words and phrases like *however, therefore, for example,* and *thus* must be used with a semicolon to separate independent clauses.

No (comma splice):	*I enjoy math, however, Joey does not.*
Yes:	*I enjoy math* $\boxed{\text{, but}}$ *Joey does not.*
Yes:	*I enjoy math* $\boxed{\text{; however,}}$ *Joey does not.*

GRAMMAR ALERT !

A comma by itself cannot separate independent clauses. The commas must appear with *and, but, or, nor, for, so,* or *yet.*

No (comma splice):	*The Kennywood Tigers won the Little League tournament, their coach took them for ice cream.*
Yes:	*The Kennywood Tigers won the Little League tournament* $\boxed{\text{, so}}$ *their coach took them for ice cream.*

3. Change one of the independent clauses to a **dependent clause** (a word group that has both a subject and verb but still cannot stand as a sentence) and connect it to the remaining independent clause. To turn the independent clause into a dependent clause, add one of these **subordinating conjunctions** to the appropriate independent clause:

after	as soon as	even though	unless	where
although	as though	if	until	wherever
as	because	since	when	whether
as if	before	though	whenever	while
as long as				

Run-on:	*Hurricane Floyd threatened the East Coast state governors ordered the largest evacuation in peacetime history.*
	subordinating conj. *dependent clause*
Correction:	$\boxed{\text{When}}$ *Hurricane Floyd threatened the East Coast, state governors ordered the largest evacuation in peacetime history.*
Comma splice:	*Traffic jams occurred from Florida to Virginia, too many people were on the highways at the same time.*
	subordinating conj.
Correction:	*Traffic jams occurred from Florida to Virginia* $\boxed{\text{because}}$
	dependent clause
	too many people were on the highways at the same time.

CONNECT

Why would run-ons and comma splices be a problem in newspaper articles, business letters, and textbooks?

GRAMMAR ALERT !

Do not place a period after the new dependent clause, or you will create a problem called a **sentence fragment.** See page 98.

8.2 ACTIVITY

Combine the independent clauses according to the directions given.

EXAMPLE   Use a subordinating conjunction to change one independent clause to a dependent clause:
a blind contestant recently appeared on the television game show "Jeopardy!"
producers had to make only a few changes

When a blind contestant recently appeared on the television game show "Jeopardy!" producers had to make only a few changes.

A. Use a period and capital letter:

1. Eddie Timanus of Reston, Virginia, is totally blind
   he is a sportswriter for *USA Today*

   Eddie Timanus of Reston, Virginia, is totally blind. He is a sportswriter for *USA Today*.

2. Timanus appeared October 20, 1999
   he won $14,400

   Timanus appeared October 20, 1999. He won $14,400.

3. the show agreed to make a few changes to accommodate Timanus
   all the changes were minor.

   The show agreed to make a few changes to accommodate Timanus. All the changes
   were minor.

B. Use a comma and coordinating conjunction:

4. the producers of the show eliminated video daily doubles
   they also eliminated video-based clues

   The producers of the show eliminated video daily doubles, and they also eliminated
   video-based clues.

5. these minor adjustments were made
   no other changes to content occurred

   These minor adjustments were made, but no other changes to content occurred.

6. the blind player was also given a braille card with the category names
   he received a computer keyboard

   The blind player was also given a braille card with the category names, and he received
   a computer keyboard.

C. Use a subordinating conjunction to change one of the independent clauses to a
   dependent clause:

7. the computer keyboard was a necessary accommodation
   Timanus needed to type his wagers and Final Jeopardy answer

   The computer keyboard was a necessary accommodation because Timanus needed to
   type his wagers and Final Jeopardy answer.

8. Timanus's appearance is noteworthy
   he is not the first of his family to appear on the show

   Although Timanus's appearance is noteworthy, he is not the first of his family to appear
   on the show.

9. his mother was a contestant in 1991
she became the first of the family to make an appearance on "Jeopardy!"

When his mother was a contestant in 1991, she became the first of the family to make

an appearance on "Jeopardy!"

Alone or with two classmates, compose another independent clause to follow each independent clause given here. Separate the clauses with periods and capital letters or with commas and coordinating conjunctions.

EXAMPLES   The steak was overcooked *, but the vegetables were crisp*

and tasty.

The fog has grounded all airplanes *. I'm not sure how I'll get*

home.

1. I can't find my credit card anywhere *. I will have to call the credit card*

company.

2. Some people are excellent public speakers *, but others are terrified to speak in*

public.

3. The examination was very long *, for it covered eight chapters.*

4. At two A.M., I was still awake *. I decided to get out of bed and clean the bedroom.*

5. The speeding car did not stop for the red light *. As a result, a pedestrian was*

nearly run over.

6. Jill has studied karate for three years *, but now she wants to study judo.*

7. The book was a little confusing at first *. However, by the third chapter I*

understood it.

8. The service in this restaurant is excellent *, and the prices are surprisingly low.*

> **POWER UP**
>
> Write a seven- or eight-sentence paragraph about friendship. Then rewrite it without periods and capital letters marking sentence boundaries. Give the altered paragraph to a classmate and ask that person to evaluate how difficult it is to read. Then have your classmate rewrite the paragraph to eliminate the run-ons.

TIPS FOR FINDING RUN-ONS AND COMMA SPLICES

1. Look individually at everything you are calling a sentence to determine how many independent clauses you have. If you have more than one, be sure they are properly separated.

2. Check your commas. If you have independent clauses on *both* sides of a comma, be sure to include a coordinating conjunction (*and, but, or, nor, for, so,* or *yet*).

TIP

See page 73 on using words like *however* and *therefore* to separate independent clauses.

3. Pay special attention to the following words. You can use your computer's "find" function to locate them.

as a result	for example	however	then
consequently	furthermore	moreover	therefore
finally	hence	nevertheless	thus

If independent clauses appear on *both* sides of these words, be sure the clauses are separated by a period and a capital letter or by a semicolon; a comma won't do the job.

8.4 ACTIVITY

POWER UP

For extra practice, correct the run-ons and comma splices in Activity 8.1.

Make corrections above the line to eliminate the two run-ons and two comma splices.

There is much to learn about ~~thunderstorms, however,~~ thunderstorms. However, we do know some things. First, as a thunderstorm moves along, the front part has the most powerful flashes of lightning. This knowledge allows meteorologists to warn people where the most dangerous part of a storm will hit. The most powerful thunderstorms have very high ~~clouds the~~ clouds, while the front part often has very strong winds. These winds can cause the tops of clouds to tilt toward the ground. When the clouds tilt far enough, powerful flashes of lightning streak between the clouds and the ground.

Thunderstorms form when the air becomes hot and damp. They can reach a height of ten ~~miles, they~~ miles, and they can stretch ten to fifteen miles across. These storms can hold millions of gallons of ~~water upper~~ water. Upper parts of the storm have tiny drops of ice.

8.5 ACTIVITY

Make corrections above the line to eliminate one run-on and four comma splices.

The amount of sleep a person needs is related to age. Babies sleep about 20 hours a ~~day, kids~~ day. Kids need 10 or 11 hours a night up to their teenage years. Most adults sleep seven or eight ~~hours many~~ hours, but many people over 50 sleep even less.

Some people can get by with very little ~~sleep, for~~ sleep. For example, high school student Randy Gardner didn't sleep for 264 hours as part of a science fair project. On the last night, he was alert enough to play 100 games on a baseball machine in a penny arcade. When Randy finally went to bed, he needed less than 15 hours of sleep to catch up. He felt fine after the ~~experiment, however,~~ experiment. However, he is unusual. In similar experiments, people who stayed awake began to hallucinate.

No one knows for sure what sleep ~~does, some~~ does. Some researchers think that sleeping and dreaming help the brain to develop.

8.6 ACTIVITY

Make corrections above the line to eliminate the run-ons and comma splices in the following passage.

Researchers from the University of Washington have made a controversial ~~claim,~~ ^{claim.} ~~according~~ ^{According} to them, a three-minute heated discussion between spouses reveals whether a marriage will fail. Their findings are based on videotapes of couples arguing. The researchers studied 124 couples for six ~~years each~~ ^{years. Each} couple had been married under nine months when the study began.

Researchers began discussions on such hot topics as communication, money, or in-law ~~problems, then~~ ^{problems, and then} they asked the couples to resolve the problems on their own. The videotaped discussions were later classified according to facial expressions, voice tone, and speech content. Seventeen couples later divorced. The researchers realized something interesting about these couples. The spouses related to each other in a particular way. In both happy and unhappy marriages, women began the discussions. However, women in unhappy marriages began with criticism and character ~~attacks, happier~~ ^{attacks, while happier} couples minimized their problems. The husband's response was very important. Husbands in happy marriages asked for clarification of the ~~problem, however,~~ ^{problem. However,} they did not necessarily take blame for the problem.

The point of the study is not diagnosing couples in three ~~minutes it is~~ ^{minutes. It is} more significant than that. Couples need to learn to disagree in ways that do not jeopardize their marriages. They can do that if they ask themselves an important question during disagreements: "Does the marriage win, or do I win?"

IF ENGLISH IS YOUR SECOND LANGUAGE

In many languages, commas can legitimately separate independent clauses. If you speak one of these languages—like Spanish or Vietnamese—double-check everything you write in English to be sure that your main clauses are separated by a period and a capital letter, or by a comma used with a coordinating conjunction.

RECHARGE

1. A **run-on sentence** occurs when two **independent clauses** (word groups that can be sentences) are not separated. A **comma splice** occurs when two **independent clauses** are separated by nothing more than a comma.

   Independent clause: *the airlines began a fare war*
   Independent clause: *ticket prices have dropped dramatically*

Run-on:	*The airlines began a fare war ticket prices have dropped dramatically.*
Comma splice:	*The airlines began a fare war, ticket prices have dropped dramatically.*

2. You can correct run-ons and comma splices in the following three ways:

- Use a period and capital letter to make each independent clause a sentence.

  The airlines began a fare war. Ticket prices have dropped dramatically.

- Separate the independent clauses with a comma and **coordinating conjunction** (*and, but, or, nor, for, so, yet*).

  The airlines began a fare war, so ticket prices have dropped dramatically.

- Change one of the independent clauses to a **dependent clause** (word group with a subject and verb that *cannot* stand as a sentence) and join it to the remaining independent clause.

  Because the airlines began a fare war, ticket prices have dropped dramatically.

8.7 CHAPTER REVIEW ACTIVITY

Make corrections above the line to eliminate the two run-ons and three comma splices.

Egypt's pyramids are the oldest stone buildings in the world, they [world. They] were built about 5000 years ago. These ancient tombs are also among the world's largest structures. The biggest is taller than a 40-story building, furthermore, [building. Furthermore,] it covers an area greater than that of 10 football fields. The average weight of one pyramid stone is two and a half tons that's [tons. That's] the weight of two midsize cars. To complete one of these giant structures, 100,000 people worked for 20 seasons.

More than 80 pyramids still stand today. Inside their limestone surfaces there are secret passageways, hidden rooms, ramps, bridges, and shafts, most [shafts. Most] have concealed entrances and false doors. Each pyramid housed a pharaoh's preserved body it [body, and it] also held the goods needed to live well in the next life.

The pyramids were monuments to the pharaoh's power, but today they stand as reminders of a creative ancient civilization.

8.8 CHAPTER REVIEW ACTIVITY

Make corrections above the line to eliminate the run-ons and comma splices.

When it comes to inventions and discoveries, people do not often think of the food industry, but they should. Many foods we take for granted were

discoveries at one time. Consider margarine, for example. Napoleon was
upset, for the
~~upset, the~~ butter his soldiers carried on long trips always spoiled. In 1869, he

held a contest to see if anyone could make a butter substitute, something that
challenge. He
would last longer. Hippolyte Mege-Mouries responded to the ~~challenge, he~~
oleomargarine, and he
mixed beef fat, water, and milk. The result was ~~oleomargarine he~~ won the prize.

The first person to think of the ice cream cone may have been Ernest
Fair. It
Hamwi. Hamwi was selling waffle-like pastry at the 1904 World's ~~Fair it~~ was

called *zalabia*. Next to him was a man selling dishes of ice cream. Business
idea. He
was good, and the man soon ran out of dishes. Hamwi got an ~~idea he~~ would

roll zalabia into cones and put ice cream inside. The cones were an instant

success.

The story of chewing gum is also interesting. *Chicle* is a kind of dried tree
sap. It
~~sap, it~~ is also the stuff the first gum was made from. Thomas Adams brought

some chicle to the United States in 1872. He wanted to use it as a cheap

substitute for rubber. Fooling around one day, Adams put some chicle in his
When he
mouth. ~~He~~ convinced others that chewing the stuff was pleasant, chewing gum

was born.

GETTING IN GEAR

thinking in writing: Figuring out the right thing to do is not always easy, and doing the right thing is not always easy, either. Students sometimes cheat, politicians sometimes lie, merchants sometimes overcharge, physicians sometimes engage in Medicare fraud—and the list could go on. Drawing on your own experience, what you have observed, and what you have read in the papers, write out as many examples as you can think of that illustrate "doing the wrong thing."

writing from experience: Tell about a time you had difficulty "doing the right thing." Explain why you had trouble and what you ultimately did.

writing in context: Assume you are a guest at someone's house. During the very expensive, elaborately prepared dinner, your host tells an offensive joke that reflects a prejudice against an ethnic group. Although everyone laughs, you are bothered by the joke. What, if anything, should you do? Explain how you think you would behave and defend your behavior.

PART TWO REVIEW

Activity: Coordination and Subordination

Read the paragraphs and notice how choppy they sound because they lack coordination and subordination. Next, revise the paragraphs by adding the needed coordination and subordination. (You do not have to change every sentence, and you can take out and add words.) Read your revision and notice the improvement coordination and subordination make in the flow.

Harriet ~~Tubman was~~ [Tubman, who was] called the Moses of her ~~people. She~~ [people,] was a conductor on the Underground Railroad. She became a legend in her own ~~time. She~~ [time because she] led approximately 300 slaves to freedom in 10 years. She had no real childhood or formal education. She labored in physically demanding jobs as a woodcutter and field hand. ~~She~~ [Although she] had heard that some masters were ~~kind. She~~ [kind, she] never experienced any. She decided to escape ~~slavery. She~~ [slavery when she] was 29. She set out with only the north star to guide ~~her. She~~ [her, and she] made her way to freedom in Pennsylvania. She returned to Baltimore a year later to rescue her sister. She then began guiding others to ~~freedom. The~~ [freedom, although the] Fugitive Slave Law was passed, making her travels more difficult. Rewards offered by slaveowners for her capture totaled ~~$40,000. She~~ [$40,000, but she] was still not deterred.

Tubman's heroism was highlighted between 1862 and 1865. She was sent to the South as a spy and scout for the Union army. Her knowledge of geography and sense of direction were an ~~asset. She~~ [asset, so she] explored the countryside in search of Confederate fortifications. ~~She~~ [Although she] received official commendation from Union ~~officers. She~~ [officers, she] was never paid for her services. ~~The war ended. She~~ [When the war ended, she] established a home for poor, elderly blacks. She became involved in a number of causes, including women's suffrage. Her death brought ~~obituaries. They~~ [obituaries that] showed her fame throughout the United States and Europe. She was buried with military rites.

Activity: Sentence Fragments, Run-On Sentences, and Comma Splices

Revise to eliminate the fragments, run-ons, and comma splices.

Many phrases that we speak and hear often have interesting ~~histories, for~~ [histories; for] example, you may have used or heard the phrase "to be in the ~~doldrums." Which~~ [doldrums," which] means to be depressed or in low spirits. The phrase has an interesting origin. The doldrums is a name given by early sailors to a zone at the equator. At this site, winds are often ~~light, their~~ [light, and their] direction is uncertain. As a result, sailing ships were often becalmed. For sailors in sailing ships, the doldrums were a great contrast to the trade winds, which blow steadily in the zone between the Tropics and the equator.

The northeast and southeast trade winds converge on the ~~equator. Where~~ _{equator, where} pressure

is low and the air rises. Because the air rises at the ~~equator. There~~ _{equator, there} is plenty of rain.

Sudden squalls and thunderstorms occur frequently. Sailing in such conditions is

~~difficult~~ _{difficult, for} the ship is not carried along in any particular direction. The exact location

of the doldrums moves with the seasons. In June, they are about 5 degrees north of

the ~~equator, in~~ _{equator, and in} December they are about 5 degrees south.

Another expression that you may have used or heard is "spitting image."

There are many stories about the origin of this phrase. Most of ~~them related~~ _{them are related} to

literal spitting. In some cultures, spit was associated with conception, so a woman

who wanted to have a child would drink water containing her husband's saliva. In

the 1600s, children in England who resembled a parent were said to look like they

had been "spit out of" that parent's mouth. Over the years, the phrase appeared as

"spit and ~~image," this~~ _{image." This} probably happened because it sounds so much like "spitting

image." Today, however, "spitting image" ~~being~~ _{is} the most common form of the

phrase.

Understanding
Verbs

PART THREE

CHAPTER 9

The Present Tense/Subject-Verb Agreement

A verb in the **present tense** shows that something is happening *now*. It can also show that something happens *regularly*. Here are two examples:

Something happening now: *The basement is flooded.*

Something that happens regularly: *The spring rains arrive in early May.*

SUBJECT-VERB AGREEMENT

Sometimes a present tense verb ends in *-s* or *-es*, and sometimes it does not.

Present tense with *-s*: *This shoe feels tight.*

Present tense without *-s*: *These shoes feel tight.*

Present tense with *-es*: *Dad always watches the sunset.*

Present tense without *-es*: *Mom and Dad always watch the sunset.*

The subject of the sentence determines whether or not a present tense verb takes an *-s* or *-es* ending. When you match the correct verb form to the subject, you have **subject-verb agreement.**

To achieve subject-verb agreement, add an *-s* or *-es* ending when the subject is *he, she, it,* or a *singular noun.* A **singular noun** names one person, place, object, idea, or emotion.

He sleeps until noon every Saturday.

She watches too much television.

It appears to be broken.

The hospital employs two thousand people.

Leave off the *-s* or *-es* ending when the subject is *I, we, they, you,* or a *plural noun.* A **plural noun** names more than one person, place, object, idea, or emotion.

I expect a raise next month.

We celebrate Thanksgiving in an untraditional way.

They join me in thanking you for your help.

You <u>hold</u> this end of the rope.

Firefighters <u>deserve</u> our respect.

POWER UP

Look up the word *agreement* in a collegiate or unabridged dictionary. How does its grammatical meaning compare and contrast with its other meanings?

WITH THESE WORDS	USE THESE FORMS	EXAMPLE
he	add *-s* or *-es*	He watches.
she	add *-s* or *-es*	She eats.
it	add *-s* or *-es*	It stops.
singular noun	add *-s* or *-es*	A baby sleeps.
I	omit *-s* or *-es*	I run.
we	omit *-s* or *-es*	We watch.
they	omit *-s* or *-es*	They talk.
you	omit *-s* or *-es*	You study.
plural noun	omit *-s* or *-es*	Birds fly.

9.1 ACTIVITY

Rewrite the sentences, changing the underlined past tense verbs to the present tense.

EXAMPLE   It <u>started</u> with your breath.

It starts with your breath.

1. As you <u>exhaled,</u> a trail of carbon dioxide <u>wafted</u> away from you like a ribbon.

   As you exhale, a trail of carbon dioxide wafts away from you like a ribbon.

2. A lucky mosquito <u>stumbled</u> across it, <u>zigzagged</u> back and forth, and <u>moved</u> in on it.

   A lucky mosquito stumbles across it, zigzags back and forth, and moves in on it.

3. As the mosquito <u>maneuvered</u> closer, she <u>picked</u> up on other clues, such as a warm, sweaty body.

   As the mosquito maneuvers closer, she picks up on other clues, such as a warm, sweaty body.

4. If she <u>considered</u> the clues appealing, the insect <u>landed,</u> and you <u>turned</u> into dinner.

   If she considers the clues appealing, the insect lands, and you turn into dinner.

5. Experiments <u>showed</u> that mosquitoes <u>liked</u> people on the basis of body chemistry and body temperature.

   Experiments show that mosquitoes like people on the basis of body chemistry and body temperature.

6. In a group of ten people exposed to mosquitoes, three <u>tended</u> to be bitten many times, four <u>faced</u> being bitten only once or twice, and three <u>escaped</u> being bitten at all.

   In a group of ten people exposed to mosquitoes, three tend to be bitten many times, four

   face being bitten only once or twice, and three escape being bitten at all.

CONNECT

You will use the present tense often in college writing. For example, you would use the present tense in a paper for a political science class that compares the campaign styles of two candidates.

7. Thus, people <u>attracted</u> mosquitoes on the basis of uncontrollable factors.

   Thus, people attract mosquitoes on the basis of uncontrollable factors.

8. I <u>appreciated</u> knowing this because it <u>explained</u> why I <u>attracted</u> mosquitoes, and my husband <u>repelled</u> them.

   I appreciate knowing this because it explains why I attract mosquitoes, and my husband

   repels them.

9. I <u>wondered</u> why I always <u>scratched</u> my way through camping trips, but he <u>suffered</u> no such problem.

   I wonder why I always scratch my way through camping trips, but he suffers no such

   problem.

10. We <u>realized</u> that something <u>marked</u> us as different and <u>recognized</u> what it is: I <u>smelled</u> better to bugs.

    We realize that something marks us as different and recognize what it is: I smell better

    to bugs.

9.2 INDIVIDUAL OR GROUP ACTIVITY

Working alone or with two classmates, write a sentence using each of the present tense verb forms given below. Choose your subjects from this list (you will not use all the subjects):

I	we
he	she
they	you
the young child	the growing teenager
the young children	the growing teenagers

EXAMPLE   like   *The young children like ice cream.*

1. likes   He likes to spend his weekends fishing at the lake.

2. eat   The growing teenagers eat three sandwiches for lunch.

3.   eats   The young child eats too much candy.

_____

4.   give   We give our old magazines to the Senior Center.

_____

5.   gives   Once a month she gives art lessons to hospitalized children.

_____

6.   see   Every summer they see my parents at Cape May.

_____

7.   sees   The growing teenager sees himself as a basketball star.

_____

AM/IS/ARE (FORMS OF TO BE)

The verb **to be** has three present tense forms: **am, is,** and **are.**
  Use *am* with *I.*

I am late for work.

Use *is* with *he, she, it,* and *singular nouns.* **Singular nouns** name one person, place, object, emotion, or idea.

He is not here.
She is the top salesperson.
It is too early for dinner.
The decision is final.

Use *are* with *you, we, they,* and *plural nouns.* **Plural nouns** name more than one person, place, object, emotion, or idea.

You are my best friend.
We are almost home.
They are an hour early.
These boys are hospital volunteers.

Am, are, and *is* are often helping verbs. That is, they are often used with other verbs to form the complete verb.

I ⟨am⟩ going with you.
You ⟨are⟩ sitting in my chair.
Jan ⟨is⟩ expecting an A in history.

Is and *are* can be combined with *not* to make shortened forms called **contractions.**

is + not = isn't
are + not = aren't

TIP

Helping verbs are discussed on page 60.

Notice that an apostrophe replaces the *o* in *not.*

Mickey <u>isn't</u> afraid of failure.
The leaves <u>aren't</u> changing color yet.

When you are unsure whether to use *am, is,* or *are,* consult the following list:

I	am (am not)
he, she, it, the child	is (isn't)
we, you, they, the children	are (aren't)

GRAMMAR ALERT

Be is often heard in place of *are* and *am.* This usage should be avoided in college and business writing.

No:	*You be late.*	No:	*I be late.*
Yes:	*You are late.*	Yes:	*I am late.*
No:	*They be late.*	No:	*He/she/it be late.*
Yes:	*They are late.*	Yes:	*He/she/it is late.*
No:	*We be late.*	No:	*Donna be late.*
Yes:	*We are late.*	Yes:	*Donna is late.*
No:	*The guests be late.*		
Yes:	*The guests are late.*		

9.3 ACTIVITY

Fill in the blanks with the correct present tense form: *am, is,* or *are.*

EXAMPLE   Heavy rains _____*are*_____ a problem this time of year.

1. A good dictionary __is_____ an important tool for a writer.

2. The students __are_____ angry because tuition has been increased again.

3. If she __is_____ late again, she __is_____ in trouble.

4. Because of the snow, we __are_____ unable to leave for work.

5. I __am_____ certain he __is_____ the best person for the job.

6. Believe it or not, you __are_____ my favorite cousin.

7. Of course, it __is_____ a matter of opinion, but I __am_____ sure that this restaurant __is_____ the best in town.

8. We __are_____ going with you if you __are_____ willing to have some company on the trip.

9.4 ACTIVITY

Rewrite the sentences below, changing the underlined past tense forms of *to be* to present tense forms. You will choose among *am*, *is*, and *are*.

CONNECT

When writing about the creators of literature and art, use the present tense, even though the author or artist is long dead. For example, write, "Hemingway often *examines* (not *examined*) death in his novels." This use of the present is called the **historical present**.

EXAMPLE   Marcel <u>was</u> annoyed with me because I <u>was</u> so forgetful.

Marcel is annoyed with me because I am so forgetful.

1. Leslie <u>was</u> the leader of the Community Action Council.

     Leslie is the leader of the Community Action Council.

2. They <u>were</u> discussing their problems in the living room.

     They are discussing their problems in the living room.

3. Because you <u>were</u> the oldest, you <u>were</u> responsible for the children's behavior.

     Because you are the oldest, you are responsible for the children's behavior.

4. Carlotta's new job <u>was</u> becoming more difficult than her old one.

     Carlotta's new job is becoming more difficult than her old one.

5. After their accident, the children <u>were</u> afraid to ride their bikes, so they <u>were</u> forced to walk everywhere.

     After their accident, the children are afraid to ride their bikes, so they are forced to walk
     everywhere.

6. I <u>was</u> sure we should turn left, but you <u>were</u> sure we should turn right.

     I am sure we should turn left, but you are sure we should turn right.

7. We <u>were</u> surprised by your decision, but they <u>were</u> not.

     We are surprised by your decision, but they are not.

8. In the outfield, the players <u>weren't</u> bored because the batters <u>were</u> hitting long balls.

     In the outfield, the players aren't bored because the batters are hitting long balls.

9.5 ACTIVITY

On a separate sheet, write two sentences using *isn't* and two sentences using *aren't*.

HAVE/HAS

The verb **to have** has two present tense forms: **has** and **have**.

Use *has* with *he, she, it,* and *singular nouns*. **Singular nouns** name one person, place, object, emotion, or idea.

> He *has* a new job.
> She *has* enough money for the trip.
> It *has* to be eight o'clock by now.
> Carla *has* the flu.

Use *have* with *I, you, we, they,* and *plural nouns*. **Plural nouns** name more than one person, place, object, emotion, or idea.

> I *have* two dogs and a cat.
> You *have* the nicest lawn on the street.
> We *have* your best interests in mind.
> They *have* a good idea.
> The scouts *have* a new summer camp.

Have and *has* can be helping verbs. That is, they can appear with other verbs to form the complete verb.

> He [has] left for the semester.
> The tomatoes [have] shriveled on the vine.

Have and *has* can be combined with *not* to make shortened forms called **contractions.**

> have + not = haven't
> has + not = hasn't

Notice that an apostrophe replaces the *o* in *not*.

> I *haven't* selected a major.
> The bus *hasn't* left yet.

When you are unsure whether to use *have* or *has*, consult the following list:

I, you, we, they, the children	have (haven't)
he, she, it, the child	has (hasn't)

TIP

Helping verbs are discussed in more detail on page 60.

9.6 ACTIVITY

In the sentences below, fill in the blanks with the correct present tense form: *have* or *has*.

EXAMPLE   This restaurant _____*has*_____ excellent pizza.

1. The dean's office __has_____ the information you need.

2. You __have_____ understood my point very well.

3. Before leaving, I __have_____ something to say.

4. We <u>have</u> the food, and you have the drinks.

5. Many people <u>have</u> complained about poor service in this store.

6. They <u>have</u> almost convinced me, but I still <u>have</u> one or two doubts.

7. He <u>has</u> an excellent point, but Mary <u>has</u> a good point as well.

8. Unfortunately, the boat <u>has</u> sailed, so we <u>have</u> been stranded.

9.7 ACTIVITY

Rewrite the sentences below, changing the underlined past tense forms of *to have* to present tense forms. You will choose either *have* or *has*.

POWER UP

Explain the difference in meaning between each sentence in one pair of sentences in Activity 9.7.

EXAMPLE   I <u>had</u> a present for your birthday.

I have a present for your birthday.

1. I <u>had</u> the department chair's permission to take that course.

   I have the department chair's permission to take that course.

   _____

2. You <u>had</u> the worst case of the flu I <u>had</u> ever seen.

   You have the worse case of the flu I have ever seen.

   _____

3. Every year, the Spanish Club <u>had</u> a car wash to help raise money for a trip to Mexico.

   Every year, the Spanish Club has a car wash to help raise money for a trip to Mexico.

   _____

4. To end the hostilities, the countries <u>had</u> agreed to peace talks.

   To end the hostilities, the countries have agreed to peace talks.

   _____

5. We <u>had</u> plans for the evening, so we <u>had</u> to refuse your invitation.

   We have plans for the evening, so we have to refuse your invitation.

   _____

6. You <u>had</u> to drive because Jan <u>had</u> an appointment, but she <u>had</u> no car.

   You have to drive because Jan has an appointment, but she has no car.

   _____

9.8 ACTIVITY

On a separate sheet, write two sentences using *haven't* and two sentences using *hasn't*.

DO/DOES

The verb **to do** has two present tense forms: **do** and **does.**

Use *do* with *I, you, we, they,* and *plural nouns.* **Plural nouns** name more than one person, place, object, emotion, or idea.

I *do* a hundred situps a day.

You *do* beautiful work.

We *do* whatever we can.

They *do* more than enough.

Teachers *do* their jobs for little pay.

Use *does* with *he, she, it,* and *singular nouns.* **Singular nouns** name one person, place, thing, emotion, or idea.

He always *does* the right thing.

She *does* the work of two people.

It *does* not make sense.

The machine *does* the job quickly.

Do and *does* can be helping verbs. That is, they can appear with other verbs to form the complete verb.

I do believe your explanation.

Lilly does enjoy Mexican food.

Do and *does* can be combined with *not* to make shortened forms called **contractions.**

do + not = don't

does + not = doesn't

Notice that an apostrophe replaces the *o* in *not.*

Many people *don't* agree with you.

This problem *doesn't* have a solution.

When you are unsure whether to use *do* or *does,* consult the following list:

I, you, we, they, the children	do (don't)
he, she, it, the child	does (doesn't)

> **TIP**
>
> Helping verbs are discussed in more detail on page 60.

9.9 ACTIVITY

In the sentences below, fill in the blanks with the correct present tense form: *do* or *does.*

EXAMPLE   Living in an apartment _____*does*_____ have its advantages.

1. I <u>do</u> expect you to clean the garage today.

2. You <u>do</u> what you think is right, and you will be fine.

3. This car <u>does</u> get better gas mileage, but it <u>does</u> cost more.

4. We <u>do</u> understand your problem, but it <u>does</u> not excuse your behavior.

5. In this resort town, service people <u>do</u> expect tourists to tip 20 percent of the bill.

6. She <u>does</u> realize that she must learn to be more assertive.

7. If the students <u>do</u> what their instructor suggests, they will <u>do</u> a good job on the research paper.

8. It <u>does</u> not matter what he <u>does.</u>

9.10 ACTIVITY

Rewrite the sentences below, changing the underlined past tense forms of *to do* to present tense forms. You will choose either *do* or *does*.

EXAMPLE   They <u>did</u> go to Myrtle Beach every year.

They do go to Myrtle Beach every year.

1. The fire department <u>did</u> inspect houses to check for faulty wiring.

   The fire department does inspect houses to check for faulty wiring.

2. The children <u>did</u> love to play Nintendo for hours at a time.

   The children do love to play Nintendo for hours at a time.

3. On vacation, we <u>did</u> expect to gain at least five pounds.

   On vacation, we do expect to gain at least five pounds.

4. I <u>did</u> all the baking for the annual family reunion.

   I do all the baking for the annual family reunion.

5. You <u>did</u> well on math portions of standardized tests, and Marco <u>did</u> well on the verbal portions.

   You do well on math portions of standardized tests, and Marco does well on the verbal portions.

6. He <u>did</u> hope to win a scholarship for his senior year.

   He does hope to win a scholarship for his senior year. _____

   _____

7. We <u>didn't</u> invite him to concerts because he <u>didn't</u> like crowds.

   We don't invite him to concerts because he doesn't like crowds. _____

   _____

9.11 REVIEW ACTIVITY

Fill in the blanks in the passage below with the correct present tense forms. Make your selections by choosing a verb for the first blank from number 1 in the list, a verb for the second blank from number 2, and so forth. The first blank is filled in as an example.

POWER UP

Find a newspaper account of a crime or activity written in the past tense. Rewrite the article in the present tense. If necessary, change or omit words like "last week" so the passage makes sense in the present tense.

1. am/is/are	6. take/takes	11. am/is/are
2. offer/offers	7. have/has	12. bring/brings
3. begin/begins	8. start/starts	13. draw/draws
4. close/closes	9. have/has	14. am/is/are
5. am/is/are	10. doesn't/don't	15. do/does

Florida's Daytona International Speedway ____1 _is_ ____ a year-round attraction. It ____2 offers ____ world-class racing events throughout the year. The races ____3 begin ____ in early February with the Busch Clash and Sun Bank 24 Hour race. They ____4 close ____ in February with the Super Bowl of Stock Car Racing, the Daytona 500. Several races ____5 are ____ scheduled in between.

Many races ____6 take ____ place in March, but the highlight ____7 has ____ been the Annual Daytona 200 Formula 1 Championship Race. In July, the Independence Day celebration ____8 starts ____ early with the S.C.C.A. Paul Revere 250. This race ____9 has ____ Camaros, Corvettes, and other Trans Am Series cars racing at night. However, the biggest event ____10 doesn't ____ come until Independence Day itself. This event ____11 is ____ the Firecracker 400, a Nascar Grand National Stock Car Race. November ____12 brings ____ the Pro-Am Superbike Finals, and December brings the World Enduro Championship. This December race ____13 draws ____ over 1000 entries in classes of racing go-carts. It ____14 is ____ the biggest meeting of its kind in the world. The race can be fast because the quickest carts ____15 do ____ go over 130 mph.

9.12 INDIVIDUAL OR GROUP REVIEW ACTIVITY

Alone or with two classmates, complete each sentence by supplying a present tense verb and any other words you want to add. You can use a verb from the list or one of your own.

EXAMPLE   This television program *is very popular with teenagers.*

is	think	nap	have
are	thinks	naps	has
does	study	walk	believe
do	studies	walks	believes

1. Many movie fans think the PG-13 rating is applied inconsistently.

2. My best friend studies very early in the morning before her eight o'clock class.

3. In the afternoon, he walks his dog through the park.

4. Every summer, they have a college student from abroad live with them.

5. An elderly woman has considerable wisdom to share with a young woman.

6. You are responsible for paying your own expenses on this trip.

7. To get better grades, we study an extra hour every day.

8. In my opinion, she does not have the qualifications to be the student council president.

SUBJECTS WITH PHRASES

A **phrase** is a group of words that does not have both a subject and a verb.
Phrases like the following often appear in the subject:

at first	in the evening	next to
beside me	of the cake	toward the hall
by the lake	on top of	with a friend
for a while	near the door	under the couch

When deciding which present tense verb to use, rule out any phrases that appear in the subject.

TIP

When you have a noun subject with a phrase, you may find it easier to check agreement by changing the noun to a pronoun. "The box near the shelves is empty" becomes "It is empty."

Which is it?   *A pile of papers __is__ in the corner.*

or

A pile of papers __are__ in the corner.

Rule out the phrase: *of papers*

TIP

A full discussion of subjects with phrases begins on page 51. Now is a good time to review that discussion.

Now which is it?   *A pile is in the corner.*

or

A pile are in the corner.

Correct verb: *is*

Correct sentence: *A pile of papers is in the corner.*

9.13 ACTIVITY

Cross out the phrase in the subject of each of the following sentences, and then write the correct verb in the blank.

EXAMPLE   (hang/hangs) A shirt ~~with three missing buttons~~

_____*hangs*_____ in the closet.

1. (have/has) Six members ~~of the team~~ _have_____ knee injuries.

2. (am/is/are) A friend ~~from my high school days~~ _is_____ visiting me next week.

3. (cost/costs) The houses ~~on this street~~ _cost_____ over $100,000.

4. (travel/travels) The students ~~with their teacher~~ _travel_____ to Scotland next week.

5. (am/is/are) This collection ~~of old books~~ _is_____ rare and valuable.

6. (do/does) The children ~~in the park~~ _do_____ play well together.

7. (have/has) One ~~of my back molars~~ _has_____ a cavity.

8. (read/reads) The first 100 pages ~~of this novel~~ _read_____ very slowly.

9. (do/does) The best stores ~~in the mall~~ _do_____ have their merchandise on sale today.

10. (make/makes) Trips ~~to the doctor~~ always _make_____ me nervous.

9.14 ACTIVITY

Complete each of the following sentences with the correct present tense verb and any other words you want to add.

EXAMPLE   (am/is/are) Your points of view _are always carefully_____

_thought out._____

1. (concern/concerns) The first of my problems _concerns how to find a_____

_part-time job._____

2. (have/has) The yellow sweater in the pile of old clothes _has a coffee stain on the_ _sleeve._

3. (am/is/are) Three professors at this college _are known for their genetic research._

4. (cost/costs) These clothes on the sale table _cost less than half of the original price._

5. (play/plays) One of my brothers _plays bass guitar in a local rock band._

6. (sway/sways) The trees in the front of my house _sway gracefully in the summer_ _breeze._

7. (am/is/are) The reaction to the current new movies _is not very enthusiastic._

8. (cause/causes) The trash along the roads _causes the entire area to look bad._

9. (do/does) The words of this song _do have a special meaning to me._

10. (taste/tastes) The apples in the basket _taste particularly tart._

COMPOUND SUBJECTS

TIP

Compound subjects are explained in more detail on page 53.

A **compound subject** is made up of two or more subjects joined by *and* or *or*, like this:

Dad and Mom are moving to Nebraska.
The train or the bus can take you into town.

Subjects joined by *and* are considered plural. Therefore, use the same present tense form you would use for *they* or *we*.

              [They   are]
The mayonnaise and the eggs [are] _spoiled._

        [We   love]
My parents and I [love] _dogs._

With subjects joined by *or*, use the present tense form that works with the subject that is closer to the verb.

The necklace or the bracelet [is] _a good gift for Jenny._

Either the juice or the oranges [are] _a good source of vitamin C._

To avoid an unnatural-sounding sentence when one subject is singular and the other is plural, place the plural word second.

Correct but unnatural sounding: *The musicians or the manager <u>checks</u> the sound equipment.*

Better: *The manager or the musicians <u>check</u> the sound equipment.*

9.15 ACTIVITY

Fill in each blank below with the correct present tense form of the verb in parentheses.

EXAMPLE   (am/is/are) Cigarettes and alcohol _____*are*_____ not as heavily taxed as they could be.

1. (monitor/monitors) The principal or the English teachers __*monitor*_____ the students taking the test.

2. (perform/performs) The cheerleaders and their captain __*perform*_____ a dance routine at halftime.

3. (have/has) Either the wind or the hail __*has*_____ brought the power lines down.

4. (make/makes) Apple cider and fresh corn __*make*_____ the perfect accompaniment to a fall dinner.

5. (drive/drives) Juan or his parents __*drive*_____ the elderly neighbors to the store once a week.

6. (know/knows) Vanessa or Leonid __*knows*_____ the directions to the hotel.

7. (plan/plans) The football coach or his assistants __*plan*_____ defensive strategy.

8. (make/makes) The book or the scarf __*makes*_____ a suitable gift.

9. (visit/visits) Either Carla or her brother __*visits*_____ Grandma every day.

COLLECTIVE NOUN SUBJECTS

Collective nouns name a group of people or things. They are words such as these:

band	crew	group	mob
class	crowd	herd	orchestra
committee	flock	jury	team

   Most often, the sense of a collective noun is that all the people or things function as one unit. Then the collective noun is singular and appears with the same present tense forms any other singular noun uses.

The band <u>plays</u> spirited marches.

The committee <u>determines</u> the membership fee.

The jury <u>decides</u> the defendant's fate.

POWER UP

Many groups of animals are called by special collective nouns. Which animals are referred to by the following: gaggle, herd, pride, flock, school? If you are unsure, check a dictionary.

9.16 ACTIVITY

For each item below, write a sentence using the collective noun subject and the correct present tense form of the verb in parentheses.

TIP

If you are unsure about using collective nouns, place "the members of the" before the collective noun and use a plural verb. Instead of "The family vacations in Maine," you can write "The members of the family vacation in Maine."

EXAMPLE   (to spend) The family *spends every summer at*
                Cape May.

1. (to pray) At the end of the service, the congregation prays silently.

2. (to play) For concerts, the orchestra plays a mix of popular and classical music.

3. (to enjoy) The audience enjoys the opening act as much as the headliner.

4. (to rehearse) The dance company rehearses a new ballet once a year.

5. (to march) The army marches 10 miles each day, regardless of the weather.

6. (to practice) Every Saturday, the team practices for three hours.

INDEFINITE PRONOUN SUBJECTS

Words such as those in the following list are called **indefinite pronouns,** because they do not refer to a definite person, place, object, emotion, or idea.

anybody	everybody	some
anyone	everything	somebody
each	one	someone

The indefinite pronouns listed below are always singular, so they are used with the same present tense verb forms as singular nouns.

-body words:		*-one* words:	
	anybody		anyone
	everybody		everyone
	nobody		no one
	somebody		one
			someone
-thing words:	anything	other words:	each
	everything		either
	nothing		neither
	something		

Everybody knows who you are.
Something is better than nothing.

TIP

To decide whether to use a singular or plural verb with indefinite pronouns that can be either singular or plural, substitute a pronoun and then decide. "All of the pain is/are gone" becomes "*It is* gone." "All of the answers is/are correct" becomes "*They are* correct."

Nothing <u>succeeds</u> like success.
No one <u>believes</u> you.

These indefinite pronouns can be either singular or plural, depending on the meaning of the sentence.

all	few	more	some
any	many	most	

Some of the manuscript <u>is</u> missing.
Some of the cookies <u>are</u> missing.

GRAMMAR ALERT !

Remember that the subject will not be part of a prepositional phrase, so the correct sentence is "One of the pages *is* torn," not "One of the pages *are* torn." See page 51 for more on subjects and phrases.

9.17 ACTIVITY

Fill in each of the following blanks with the correct present tense form of the verb in parentheses.

EXAMPLE   (am/is/are) Everybody _____*is*_____ expected to help clean up.

1. (understand/understands; ask/asks) No one __understands__ the question, so somebody __asks__ Dr. Garcia to repeat it.

2. (appear/appears; seem/seems) Nothing __appears__ out of place in the living room, but something __seems__ wrong in the kitchen.

3. (believe/believes) Everyone __believes__ you can succeed, but no one __believes__ it more than I do.

4. (tell/tells; have/has) Something __tells__ me that someone __has__ been using my tape player.

5. (feel/feels) Nothing __feels__ better than an all-cotton sweater.

6. (is/are) Some of my fears __are__ rational.

7. (is/are) Some of the hem __is__ torn.

VERBS BEFORE SUBJECTS

You have probably noticed that the subject of a sentence usually comes before the verb. This is **normal order.**

         S   V
My <u>father</u> <u>collects</u> coins and stamps.

Sometimes the verb comes before the subject. This is **inverted order.** With inverted order, you must know how to choose the correct present tense form.

When a sentence begins with *there is*, *there are*, *here is*, or *here are*, look for the subject *after* the verb before deciding whether to use *is* or *are*.

$$\overset{V}{There\ \underline{is}}\ \underset{S}{\underline{a\ storm\ warning}}\ for\ this\ afternoon.$$

$$\overset{V}{There\ \underline{are}}\ \underset{S}{\underline{two\ answers}}\ to\ that\ question.$$

$$\overset{V}{Here\ \underline{is}}\ \underset{S}{\underline{your\ book}}.$$

$$\overset{V}{Here\ \underline{are}}\ \underset{S}{\underline{the\ lost\ keys}}.$$

When you ask a question, the verb often comes before the subject.

$$\overset{V}{\underline{Are}}\ \overset{S}{they}\ your\ friends?$$

$$Where\ \overset{V}{\underline{is}}\ \underset{S}{\underline{the\ newspaper}}?$$

Sometimes the subject is between the parts of the verb.

$$\overset{V}{\underline{Has}}\ \overset{S}{\underline{the\ mail}}\ \overset{V}{\underline{arrived}}?$$

$$\overset{V}{\underline{Will}}\ \overset{S}{\underline{you}}\ \overset{V}{\underline{be\ going}}\ with\ me?$$

> **TIP**
>
> To check for the correct present tense verb, rearrange a sentence with inverted order so that it has normal order. "Here is/are your mail" becomes "Your mail is here." Rearrange a question to make a statement. "Has/have you eaten?" becomes "You have eaten."

9.18 ACTIVITY

Complete the following to form sentences.

1. There is __a parking space just around the corner.__ _____

2. There are __chocolate chip cookies on the kitchen counter.__ _____

3. Here is __a book about how to find the perfect job.__ _____

4. Here are __the keys to the house and the car.__ _____

9.19 ACTIVITY

Fill in each blank below with the correct present tense form of the verb in parentheses.

1. (am/is/are) __Are_____ you leaving for work early today?

2. (have/has) Where __have_____ Eduardo and Todd gone now?

3. (do/does) Why __do_____ the birds sing so sweetly in spring?

4. (do/does) How __does_____ Michael keep his room so neat?

5. (have/has) How __has_____ your aunt been feeling?

6. (am/is/are) What __is_____ the meaning of that remark?

7. (have/has) __Have_____ all the doors and windows been locked?

8. (am/is/are) __Am_____ I the only one working the afternoon shift?

WHO/WHICH/THAT

Who, which, and **that** are *relative pronouns*. A **relative pronoun** refers to another word in the sentence.

My sister is a person who reads constantly. [*Who* refers to *person.*]

Cotton pants, which shrink in hot water, are cool and comfortable.
  [*Which* refers to *pants.*]

This is the coat that fits me. [*That* refers to *coat.*]

Relative pronouns often function with present tense verbs. The form of the verb is determined by the word the relative pronoun refers to.
  In the following sentence, which is correct—*is* or *are?*

My cousins, who _____ twins, visit me every summer.

Who refers to *cousins.* It is "cousins are" (not "cousins is"). Therefore, the correct version is:

My cousins, who <u>are</u> twins, visit me every summer.

> **TIP**
>
> For another discussion of relative pronouns and a related discussion of dependent clauses, see page 89.

9.20 ACTIVITY

In each sentence below, circle the relative pronoun and draw an arrow to the word it refers to. Then fill in the blank with the correct present tense form of the verb in parentheses.

EXAMPLE   (am/is/are) I prefer food [that] _____*is*_____ not heavily seasoned.

1. (laugh/laughs) Eric is a person [who] __laughs_____ easily.

2. (hope/hopes) These are the people [who] __hope_____ to buy my parents' house.

3. (remember/remembers) Chris is an individual [who] __remembers_____ everybody's name.

4. (have/has) I am the person [who] __has_____ to solve all the problems around here.

5. (am/is/are) These are the items [that] __are_____ priced for the garage sale.

6. (contain/contains) These boxes, [which] __contain_____ usable clothing, can be taken to the women's shelter.

7. (am/is/are) This plan, [which] __is_____ the best I can come up with, should solve your problem.

8. (do/does) The campus parking problem, which <u>does</u> seem to be getting worse, will be addressed by student government.

9. (make/makes) Igor is someone who <u>makes</u> things more difficult than necessary.

10. (have/has) These are the volunteers who <u>have</u> offered to organize the charity dance.

IF ENGLISH IS YOUR SECOND LANGUAGE

1. When the complete verb is made up of two or more verbs, do not add -*s* or -*es* to the last verb.

> No: *The child does sings well.*
> Yes: *The child does sing well.*

2. Use *am* between *I* and an -*ing* verb.

> No: *I be leaving soon.*
> No: *I is leaving soon.*
> Yes: *I am leaving soon.*

3. Use *have* or *has* before *been*.

> No: *The lazy employee been fired.*
> Yes: *The lazy employee has been fired.*
> No: *The lazy employees been fired.*
> Yes: *The lazy employees have been fired.*

4. Use a singular verb with noncount nouns. **Noncount nouns** name things that are not normally counted. They are words that cannot appear with a number in front of them—words such as these:

air	food	homework	oil
baggage	furniture	honesty	sugar
fear	health	luggage	water

> No: *The baggage are still on the airplane.*
> Yes: *The baggage is still on the airplane.*

Noncount nouns are also discussed on page 236.

RECHARGE

1. To achieve **subject-verb agreement**, singular subjects must be used with singular present tense verbs, and plural subjects must be used with plural present tense verbs.

- Add an -*s* or -*es* ending with these subjects: *he, she, it, singular nouns.*

It always rains on my vacations.

- Omit the -s or -es with these subjects: *I, we, they, you, plural nouns.*

  Five students expect an A on the exam.
- The verb *to be* has three present tense forms: *am, is, are.*
- The verb *to have* has two present tense forms: *has, have.*
- The verb *to do* has two present tense forms: *does, do.*

2. To decide on whether to use a singular or plural verb, rule out phrases that appear with the subject.

   My collection of antique vases is valuable.

3. A **compound subject** is two or more subjects joined by *and* or *or.*

   - Use a plural verb with subjects joined by *and.*

     My dog and my cat play well together.
   - With subjects joined by *or,* use the verb that agrees with the closer subject.

     The pasta or the potatoes provide carbohydrates.

     The potatoes or the pasta provides carbohydrates.

4. A **collective noun** names a group of people or things. Use a singular verb when the people or things function as one unit.

   The committee makes its decision.

5. An **indefinite pronoun** does not refer to a specific person, place, object, emotion, or idea. Some indefinite pronouns are always singular and take singular verbs; some are always plural and take plural verbs; some can be either singular or plural, depending on the meaning of the sentence.

6. When a sentence has **inverted order**, the verb comes before the subject.

   Where are the necessary forms?

7. With the **relative pronouns** *who, which,* and *that* choose the verb that agrees with the word the relative pronoun refers to.

   Chris is a person who believes in superstition.

9.21 CHAPTER REVIEW ACTIVITY

Rewrite the sentences, using the correct present tense forms of the underlined verbs with the subjects given. In some cases, you will have to change the form of the underlined verb.

EXAMPLE   Writing center tutors <u>help</u> many people.

   A. The writing center tutor *helps many people.*

   B. They *help many people.*

1. The teachers <u>plan</u> to review the material before the exam.

   A. The teacher *plans to review the material before the exam.*

    B. I <u>plan to review the material before the exam.</u>

2. We <u>do</u> understand your need to be alone.

    A. He <u>does understand your need to be alone.</u>

    B. Jane and I <u>do understand your need to be alone.</u>

3. We <u>have</u> collected a number of interesting books you can borrow.

    A. She <u>has collected a number of interesting books you can borrow.</u>

    B. They <u>have collected a number of interesting books you can borrow.</u>

4. The children <u>are</u> hoping for a surprise treat.

    A. The child <u>is hoping for a surprise treat.</u>

    B. You <u>are hoping for a surprise treat.</u>

5. We <u>aren't</u> sure which route is the fastest way to St. Louis.

    A. Karl <u>isn't sure which route is the fastest way to St. Louis.</u>

    B. She <u>isn't sure which route is the fastest way to St. Louis.</u>

6. These boxes of papers <u>are</u> a fire hazard.

    A. That box of papers <u>is a fire hazard.</u>

    B. It <u>is a fire hazard.</u>

7. My collections of video and audio tapes <u>take</u> up 10 shelves in my bedroom.

    A. My collection of video and audio tapes <u>takes up 10 shelves in my bedroom.</u>

    B. It <u>takes up 10 shelves in my bedroom.</u>

8. Marie and Ed <u>have</u> helped with the charity auction every year.

    A. Marie or Ed <u>has helped with the charity auction every year.</u>

B. I have helped with the charity auction every year.

9. Several people <u>plan</u> homecoming activities that will appeal to as many students as possible.

A. A committee plans homecoming activities that will appeal to as many students as possible.

B. You plan homecoming activities that will appeal to as many students as possible.

10. These are the people who <u>live</u> across the street.

A. This is the person who lives across the street.

B. There are the people who live across the street.

11. Here <u>is</u> the letter you have been looking for all week.

A. Here are the letters you have been looking for all week. [Fill in the blank with *is* or *are*.]

B. Where is the letter you have been looking for all week? [Fill in the blank with *is* or *are*.]

9.22 CHAPTER REVIEW ACTIVITY

On a separate sheet, rewrite the following paragraphs, changing the underlined past tense verb forms to present tense forms.

A team of scientists <u>was</u> [is] interested in what makes people laugh. They <u>were</u> [are] interested because they <u>realized</u> [realize] that laughter <u>had</u> [has] medicinal value. In their studies, they learned that laughter <u>did</u> [does] help sick people feel better and heal faster. It also <u>helped</u> [helps] people overcome mild forms of depression. The scientists who <u>were</u> [are] involved in the research <u>did</u> [do] not agree on the reason for laughter's benefits. While some researchers <u>believed</u> [believe] laughter <u>stimulated</u> [stimulates] the immune system, other researchers <u>had</u> [have] offered another view. They <u>suggested</u> [suggest] that laughter <u>jolted</u> [jolts] the body into producing pain-blocking chemicals. Some scientists <u>didn't</u> [don't] accept either explanation.

One doctor who <u>studied</u> [studies] laughter <u>noted</u> [notes] something interesting. We <u>didn't</u> [don't] have to be sick to benefit from laughter. This doctor <u>explained</u> [explains] that laughter <u>was</u> [is] good exercise. There <u>were</u> [are] 15 different muscles exercised in just a little smile. A giggle or bigger laugh <u>tightened</u> [tightens] and then <u>relaxed</u> [relaxes] muscles all over the body. <u>Did</u> [Does] he really think that laughter <u>qualified</u> [qualifies] as a mini-workout?

9.23 CHAPTER REVIEW ACTIVITY

Edit the passage to eliminate the nine errors in subject-verb agreement.

The police ~~has~~ [have] used polygraphs (lie detectors) since 1924 to help determine the guilt or innocence of suspected criminals. These machines measure blood pressure, pulse rate, and respiration simultaneously by means of a pneumograph tube around the subject's chest and a pulse cuff around the arm. Impulses from the subject ~~is~~ [are] picked up and traced on graph paper. The theory is that respiration, blood pressure, and pulse ~~be~~ [are] affected by the person's emotional state. Fluctuations from the norm ~~signifies~~ [signify] emotional tumult—and, hence, a lie. These tests are not mistake-proof, however. Their accuracy depends, in part, upon the expertise and sound judgment of the person who ~~administer~~ [administers] the test.

The test requires the administrator to ask a series of control questions. These are questions like, "What is your name?" and "Did you ever steal anything in your entire life?" If the subject ~~answer~~ [answers] no to the latter question, he or she likely ~~be~~ [is] lying, and a change in pulse or breathing will be observed. Then when the key question about a crime is asked, chances ~~is~~ [are] good that the administrator can tell if the truth is being told. This is done by comparing the degree of change in the line on the graph with the lines corresponding to the answers to the control questions.

Because the outcome of lie detector tests ~~depend~~ [depends] on the skill of the test giver, polygraphs are forbidden in court and can not be used as testimony. Psychologists are not convinced of the validity of polygraphs, but the police consider them an invaluable aid.

GETTING IN GEAR

thinking in writing: Go to a spot on campus—either indoors or outdoors. Observe the spot for about an hour. As you do so, list the chief characteristics of the spot. For example, if you observe the lake in the middle of campus, your list might include the green, wooden benches on the hill overlooking the lake, and the students at the edge of the water studying on blankets.

writing from experience: Write a description of the spot you visited that conveys one of the prevailing characteristics of the place. For example, if you decide that the place is peaceful, convey what is peaceful about the place; if it is hectic or cluttered or beautiful, describe what makes the spot hectic, cluttered, or beautiful. If necessary, return to the spot to observe and list some more.

writing in context: Assume you are a student intern in your campus's publications office, and you have been asked to write a description of an appealing spot on campus to include in a recruitment brochure to be mailed to area high schools. Describe a spot on campus for the brochure. Be sure your description will appeal to prospective 18-year-old students.

CHAPTER 10

The Past Tense

A verb in the **past tense** shows that something took place before now. Here are two examples.

> *Last spring, Jeffrey <u>celebrated</u> his graduation with a party for his closest friends.* [Jeffrey celebrated before now, so the verb is in the past tense.]
>
> *The streets <u>flooded</u> after the heavy spring rains.* [The streets flooded before now, so the verb is in the past tense.]

FORMING THE PAST TENSE OF REGULAR VERBS

A large group of verbs, called **regular verbs,** form the past tense by adding *-d* or *-ed* to the base form. Here are some examples.

REPRESENTATIVE REGULAR VERBS— PAST TENSE FORMS		
Base Form	**Past Tense**	**Example**
bake	baked	*Yesterday I <u>baked</u> cookies.*
climb	climbed	*Yesterday I <u>climbed</u> a tree.*
help	helped	*Yesterday I <u>helped</u> you.*
jump	jumped	*Yesterday I <u>jumped</u> over a fence.*
slap	slapped	*Yesterday I <u>slapped</u> him.*
walk	walked	*Yesterday I <u>walked</u> five miles.*

TIP

In speech, you do not hear the *-d* or *-ed* ending when it comes before a *-t.* Thus, "I *used* to own a dog" sounds like "I *use* to own a dog," and "I was *supposed* to go" sounds like "I was *suppose* to go." Remember that you must write *used* and *supposed*—the *-ed* or *-d* must appear in the past tense.

SPELLING ALERT !

In some verbs ending in a vowel-consonant (like *slap* in the above list), the last letter is doubled before the *-ed* is added. When you are unsure, see pages 299 and 301 for the rule on when to double or consult a dictionary to check spelling.

The same past tense form is used, regardless of the subject.

I <u>needed</u> something.	*We <u>needed</u> something.*
You <u>needed</u> something.	*They <u>needed</u> something.*
He <u>needed</u> something.	*The child <u>needed</u> something.*
She <u>needed</u> something.	*The children <u>needed</u> something.*
It <u>needed</u> something.	

10.1 ACTIVITY

Rewrite the sentences, changing the underlined present tense verbs to past tense verbs.

EXAMPLE   I <u>answer</u> the questions you <u>ask</u>.

I answered the questions you asked.

CONNECT

You will use the past tense often in your college writing. For example, a history paper about the events that caused World War I will rely on the past tense. Name two other times you are likely to use the past tense in college writing.

1. The children <u>want</u> the toys advertised on their favorite cartoon shows.

   The children wanted the toys advertised on their favorite cartoon shows.

2. Marina and Rico <u>love</u> pasta, so they <u>cook</u> it every night for supper.

   Marina and Rico loved pasta, so they cooked it every night for supper.

3. On the way to South Carolina, we <u>pass</u> the beautiful Virginia mountains.

   On the way to South Carolina, we passed the beautiful Virginia mountains.

4. You <u>follow</u> the road to the left, and he <u>scouts</u> the trail on the right.

   You followed the road to the left, and he scouted the trail on the right.

5. She <u>returns</u> from work in time to cook dinner for her family.

   She returned from work in time to cook dinner for her family.

6. They <u>fill</u> the garbage bags and <u>drag</u> them out to the curb for the weekly trash pickup.

   They filled the garbage bags and dragged them out to the curb for the weekly trash pickup.

7. Your comment <u>reminds</u> me of the time we went fishing together.

   Your comment reminded me of the time we went fishing together.

8. The river <u>flows</u> south to Columbus, and then it <u>turns</u> east.

   The river flowed south to Columbus, and then it turned east.

10.2 ACTIVITY

Fill in the blanks in the following sentences with the correct past tense forms of the regular verbs in parentheses.

1. (to maintain)   Football coach Earl Blaik of Army always __maintained__ strict discipline.

2. (to play)   Once Army __played__ against an inexperienced team.

3. (to score; to cause)   Army __scored__ so many points that they __caused__ the other team to feel humiliated.

4. (to order)   Coach Blaik __ordered__ his players to take it easy on the team.

5. (to try; to turn)   The team __tried__ to follow their coach's orders, but fate __turned__ the tables.

6. (to fumble)   The opposition __fumbled__ the ball.

7. (to scoop; to remember)   A West Point player __scooped__ up the loose ball, but then he __remembered__ the coach's orders.

8. (to stop; to look)   The player __stopped__ in his tracks and __looked__ fearfully at Coach Blaik on the sidelines.

9. (to place)   Then he __placed__ the ball down on the one-yard line.

10.3 ACTIVITY

On a separate sheet, write sentences using the past tense forms of the regular verbs given.

1. (to play)
2. (to graduate)
3. (to discuss)
4. (to lift)
5. (to wonder)
6. (to hope)

FORMING THE PAST TENSE OF IRREGULAR VERBS

A group of verbs, called **irregular verbs,** do not form the past tense by adding -d or -ed. Instead, they form the past tense in a variety of ways, as the following examples show.

Yesterday I _was_ late.   Yesterday I _drew_ a map.
Yesterday I _broke_ my arm.   Yesterday I _dove_ in the pool.

The same past tense form is used, regardless of the subject.

I _fell_ down.   We _fell_ down.
You _fell_ down.   They _fell_ down.
He _fell_ down.   The child _fell_ down.
She _fell_ down.   The children _fell_ down.
It _fell_ down.

You already know the past tense forms of many irregular verbs. You can check the forms you do not know in the dictionary. Different dictionaries list verb forms in different ways, but typically the second form given is the past tense. Thus, if you look up _fly,_ you will see these forms: _fly, flew, flown._ The second form (_flew_) is the past tense. Sometimes the -ing form (flying) is also given. If no verb forms are given, the verb is regular and forms its past tense by adding -d or -ed, as explained on page 147.

You can also check the past tense form of many irregular verbs by consulting the chart on this page.

POWER UP

Select an article from a news magazine and circle five irregular verbs.

REPRESENTATIVE IRREGULAR VERBS—PAST TENSE FORMS.

Base Form	Past Tense	Base Form	Past Tense
be	was; were	hear	heard
become	became	hide	hid
begin	began	hold	held
blow	blew	hurt	hurt
break	broke	keep	kept
bring	brought	know	knew
build	built	lay (meaning "place")	laid
buy	bought		
catch	caught	lead	led
choose	chose	leave	left
come	came	lend	lent
cut	cut	let	let
dive	dove	lie (meaning "rest")	lay
do	did		
draw	drew	lose	lost
drink	drank	make	made
drive	drove	mean	meant
eat	ate	meet	met
fall	fell	pay	paid
feed	fed	put	put
feel	felt	quit	quit
fight	fought	read	read
find	found	ride	rode
fly	flew	ring	rang
forbid	forbad (or forbade)	rise	rose
		run	ran
forget	forgot	say	said
forgive	forgave	see	saw
freeze	froze	sell	sold
get	got	send	sent
give	gave	set	set
go	went	shake	shook
grow	grew	shine (meaning "give light")	shone
hang (a picture)	hung		
hang (meaning "execute")	hanged	shine (meaning "polish")	shined
have	had	sing	sang

REPRESENTATIVE IRREGULAR VERBS— PAST TENSE FORMS, *(CONTINUED)*			
Base Form	Past Tense	Base Form	Past Tense
sit	sat	throw	threw
stand	stood	understand	understood
steal	stole	wake	woke
swim	swam	wear	wore
take	took	win	won
teach	taught	wind	wound
tell	told	write	wrote
think	thought		

10.4 ACTIVITY

Rewrite the sentences, changing the underlined present tense verbs to past tense verbs. Consult previous list or a dictionary if you are unsure of the correct form.

CONNECT

Documentaries often use the present tense to discuss their subjects. Consider, for example, a documentary about San Francisco. Could the present tense sentences in Activity 10.4 be used?

EXAMPLE   The Beatles' last concert <u>takes</u> place in San Francisco in 1966.

The Beatles' last concert took place in San Francisco
in 1966.

1.   On August 29, 1966, the Beatles <u>have</u> their last performance before 25,000 people in San Francisco's Candlestick Park.

   On August 29, 1966, the Beatles had their last performance before 25,000 people in

   San Francisco's Candlestick Park.

2.   Although they still <u>come</u> together to record until 1970, they <u>do</u> not play live in concert after 1966.

   Although they still came together to record until 1970, they did not play live in

   concert after 1966.

3.   San Francisco also <u>gives</u> rise to the United Nations in 1945; however, because many Europeans <u>think</u> the city too far to travel to, officials <u>choose</u> to move the site to New York.

   San Francisco also gave rise to the United Nations in 1945; however, because many

   Europeans thought the city too far to travel to, officials chose to move the site to New York.

4.   Interestingly, the term "sandlot baseball" also <u>begins</u> in San Francisco.

   Interestingly, the term "sandlot baseball" also began in San Francisco.

5.   The term comes from the 1860s, when a cemetery <u>stands</u> where the Civic Center sits.

   The term comes from the 1860s, when a cemetery stood where the Civic Center sits.

6. City leaders <u>take</u> the cemetery and <u>rebuild</u> it into a park, leveling a sand hill when they <u>do</u> so.

   City leaders took the cemetery and rebuilt it into a park, leveling a sand hill when they

   did so.

7. As a result, the 17-acre park <u>becomes</u> known as the "sandlots."

   As a result, the 17-acre park became known as the "sandlots."

10.5 ACTIVITY

Fill in the blanks with the correct past tense forms of the irregular verbs in parentheses. If you are unsure of the correct forms, check the list beginning on page 150 or your dictionary.

EXAMPLE (to give; to find) Georges de Mestral _____*gave*_____ us an

alternative to zippers and buttons when he _____*found*_____ a new way to fasten things.

1. (to go; to see)   One day in 1948, de Mestral __went_____ into the

   woods to walk with his dog, and he __saw_____ the way burrs fastened themselves to his dog's coat and his own clothing.

2. (to put; to take)   Curious, de Mestral __put_____ a bit of burr under

   a microscope and __took_____ a close look.

3. (to seek)   Looking closely at the burr, he __sought_____ to understand how it worked.

4. (to understand; to have)   He __understood_____ that the burr

   __had_____ barbed, hooklike seed pods that meshed perfectly with the looped fibers in the clothes.

5. (to think; to stand)   De Mestral then __thought_____ that the discovery

   could lead to a fastening system that __stood_____ a chance of competing with the zipper.

6. (to come; to give)   He __came_____ up with a way to reproduce the

   hooks and loops in woven nylon and __gave_____ the invention the name Velcro, from the French words *velours* and *crochet*.

10.6 ACTIVITY

Refer to the chart of irregular verbs beginning on page 150, and select five verbs whose past tense forms you are unsure about. On a separate sheet, compose sentences using the past tense forms of the five verbs.

10.7 ACTIVITY

Fill in the blanks with the correct past tense forms of the irregular verbs in parentheses. Consult the list beginning on page 150 or your dictionary if you are unsure of the correct forms.

POWER UP

Pair up with a classmate and quiz each other on the past tense forms of the irregular verbs beginning on page 150. Make a list of any forms you miss and study the list regularly.

A native of South Carolina (to tell) __told__ me this popular coastal myth about Alice Belin Flagg. It all (to begin) __began__ in 1849 on a beautiful plantation in Murrells Inlet, South Carolina. Alice (to come) __came__ to live there with her widowed mother and overprotective brother, Dr. Flagg. While attending school in Charleston, Alice (to fall) __fell__ in love with a wealthy young man, who (to give) __gave__ her a beautiful engagement ring. When she (to let) __let__ her brother see the ring, he (to become) __became__ enraged and (to forbid) __forbade (forbad)__ her to wear it. He (to feel) __felt__ the man was beneath Alice and (to give) __gave__ her orders never to see him. Heartbroken, Alice secretly (to wear) __wore__ the ring on a ribbon around her neck.

A few days before the May Ball of 1849, Alice (to grow) __grew__ ill with a fever. When Dr. Flagg (to make) __made__ his medical examination of his sister, he (to find) __found__ the ring and (to throw) __threw__ it into the waters of Murrells Inlet. Soon after that, Alice died, crying out for her ring. According to legend, Alice still roams the halls of the plantation, searching for her ring. Recent and past visitors there (to say) __said__ they (to see) __saw__ her and (to feel) __felt__ her pull on their wedding bands as she looked for her own. Long after they (to leave) __left__ the island, many of these visitors (to think) __thought__ they (to hear) __heard__ Alice sobbing quietly.

WAS/WERE

To be is the only verb with more than one past tense form. Its forms are **was** and **were**.

Use *was* with *I, he, she, it,* and *singular nouns.* **Singular nouns** name one person, place, object, emotion, or idea.

I *was* late for work yesterday.

He *was* the first person here.

She *was* angry with you.

It *was* hot upstairs.

The dinner *was* excellent.

Use *were* with *you, we, they,* and *plural nouns.* **Plural nouns** name more than one person, place, object, emotion, or idea.

You were right about me.

We were late for lunch.

They were tired after their trip.

The flowers were beautiful.

TIP

Helping verbs are discussed in more detail on page 60.

Was and *were* are often **helping verbs.** That is, they are often used with another verb to form a complete verb.

I [was] studying all afternoon.

The clothes [were] drying on the line.

Was and *were* can be combined with *not* to make shortened forms called **contractions.**

was + not = wasn't

were + not = weren't

SPELLING ALERT

Notice that an apostrophe replaces the *o* in *not.*

The bus wasn't crowded.

We weren't impressed with the band.

When you are unsure whether to use *was* or *were,* consult this list:

I, he, she, it, the child	was (wasn't)
you, we, they, the children	were (weren't)

GRAMMAR ALERT

Many frequently heard forms should be avoided in college and business writing.

No:	*You was late.*	No:	*We was late.*
Yes:	*You were late.*	Yes:	*We were late.*
No:	*They was late.*	No:	*The band members was late.*
Yes:	*They were late.*	Yes:	*The band members were late.*
No:	*He/she/it weren't late.*		
Yes:	*He/she/it wasn't late.*		

10.8 ACTIVITY

Rewrite the following sentences, changing the underlined present tense forms of *to be* to past tense forms. (Use *was* or *were.*)

EXAMPLE   The storm <u>is</u> moving inland.

The storm was moving inland.

1. Area theaters <u>are</u> raising their ticket prices because their operating expenses <u>are</u> increasing.

Area theaters were raising their ticket prices because their operating expenses were

increasing.

2. Mr. Tong <u>is</u> worried because his job <u>is</u> in jeopardy.

Mr. Tong was worried because his job was in jeopardy.

3. Red and orange <u>aren't</u> Keisha's favorite colors.

Red and orange weren't Keisha's favorite colors.

4. The problem <u>isn't</u> the expense of golf; it <u>is</u> the time involved.

The problem wasn't the expense of golf; it was the time involved.

5. You <u>are</u> right about Carlo; he <u>is</u> the best person for the job.

You were right about Carlo; he was the best person for the job.

6. He <u>is</u> the person they <u>are</u> talking about.

He was the person they were talking about.

7. I <u>am</u> uncomfortable because my shoes <u>are</u> too tight.

I was uncomfortable because my shoes were too tight.

8. The couple <u>is</u> planning a small wedding because the bride and groom <u>are</u> saving their money for tuition.

The couple was planning a small wedding because the bride and groom were saving their money for tuition.

9. We <u>are</u> working while they <u>are</u> on vacation.

We were working while they were on vacation.

10. The employees <u>aren't</u> very courteous, so the store <u>is</u> losing business.

The employees weren't very courteous, so the store was losing business.

10.9 ACTIVITY

Write sentences by following each subject with *was* or *were* and any other words that make a logical sentence.

EXAMPLE   At midnight, I *was hungry for a turkey sandwich.*

1.   The faded curtains were torn and shabby.

2. My new car was the only possession I cared about.

3. He was 21 on Thursday.

4. It was a day to remember.

5. After dinner, they were leaving for the theater.

6. Last week, I was the only one to get an A for class participation.

7. In my opinion, you were wrong to accuse me of lying.

IF ENGLISH IS YOUR SECOND LANGUAGE

1. The past tense is used for actions that began and ended in the past. Time expressions are often used with the past tense; these are expressions such as *last week, a year ago, yesterday,* and *in May.*

    Last week, I _adopted_ a stray cat.
    Louisa _lost_ her driver's license yesterday.

2. Do not add a *-d* or *-ed* ending to the past tense form of an irregular verb.

    no: The choir _sanged_ all our favorite hymns.
    yes: The choir _sang_ all our favorite hymns.

RECHARGE

1. **A past tense verb** indicates that something took place before the present time.

2. **A regular verb** forms the past tense by adding *-d* or *-ed.*

    Phyllis _asked_ three questions in class.

3. **An irregular verb** forms the past tense a variety of ways. Correct past tense forms can be checked in a dictionary or in the list on page 150.

    The swimmers _dove_ into the cold lake.

4. **The verb to be** has two past tense forms: *was, were.*

    The teacher _was_ proud of her class.
    The teachers _were_ proud of their classes.

10.10 CHAPTER REVIEW ACTIVITY

Fill in the blanks in the following passage with the correct past tense forms of the verbs in parentheses. Some of the verbs are regular, and some are irregular.

Frederic Remington (1861–1909) (to paint) _painted_ the rugged life he (to see) _saw_ in the West, although he (to come) _came_ from the East. Born in Canton, New York, Remington (to study) _studied_ art at Yale University and at the Art Students League in New York City. In 1880, when he (to be) _was_ 19, he (to move) _moved_ to the West, where he (to begin) _began_ to paint the life around him. Remington (to have) _had_ contact with the U.S. Cavalry, which (to bring) _brought_ him near battles between the North American Indians and U.S. soldiers. He (to paint) _painted_ many of these battles. In his work, Remington also (to depict) _depicted_ what he (to feel) _felt_ and (to see) _saw_ : men relaxing by the warmth of a campfire, the alert expression of an Indian scout, the sweat of a racing horse rider. Thus, the Wild West lives on in Remington's painting.

10.11 CHAPTER REVIEW ACTIVITY

On a separate sheet, rewrite the following passage by changing the verbs from present tense to past tense. Some of the verbs are regular, and some are irregular.

In 1879, when Ivory soap ~~is~~ [was] developed by Procter and Gamble, it ~~sinks~~ [sank] just like any other brand. The soap's "floatability" ~~comes~~ [came] about by accident.

One day, a worker ~~goes~~ [went] to lunch, and ~~leaves~~ [left] the machine on that ~~mixes~~ [mixed] the solution of soap. When he ~~returns~~ [returned], he ~~discovers~~ [discovered] a curious frothy mixture.

Several workers ~~examine~~ [examined] the mixture and ~~decide~~ [decided] it ~~is~~ [was] still usable. Soon, the soap ~~hits~~ [hit] the market, and the manufacturer ~~gets~~ [got] letters from excited consumers who ~~want~~ [wanted] more "floating soap."

The company ~~traces~~ [traced] the soap to the frothy solution and ~~realizes~~ [realized] that if they ~~beat~~ [beat] air into the mixture as it ~~is~~ [was] being made, the soap ~~becomes~~ [became] lighter than water. That ~~is~~ [was] what they ~~do~~ [did], and as a result, the soap ~~floats.~~ [floated].

GETTING IN GEAR

thinking in writing: Silent film actress Mary Pickford said, "If you have made mistakes, even serious ones, there is always another chance for you. What we call failure is not the falling down, but the staying down." In a page or so of freewriting, explain what you think Mary Pickford meant.

writing from experience: Tell about a time when you failed at something. Explain what you learned from the experience.

writing in context: Most schools use grades to indicate whether students succeed or fail. Do you think grades are an accurate measure of success and failure? Explain your view.

CHAPTER 11

The Perfect Tenses and Active and Passive Voice

THE PAST PARTICIPLE

When you studied the present tense in Chapter 9 and the past tense in Chapter 10, you learned about the base and past tense forms of verbs. Now it is time to learn about a third verb form—the *past participle*.

The **past participle** form is important because it is used to form the two verb tenses you will learn about later in this chapter.

For regular verbs, the past participle form is the same as the past tense form. It is made by adding *-d* or *-ed* to the base form. Examples are shown in the following list.

REPRESENTATIVE REGULAR VERBS—PAST TENSE AND PAST PARTICIPLE FORMS		
Base Form	Past Tense	Past Participle
dance	danced	danced
move	moved	moved
plant	planted	planted
want	wanted	wanted

Regular verbs are also discussed on page 147.

Irregular verbs do not form the past participle by adding *-d* or *-ed*. Instead, they form the past participle in a variety of ways, as the examples in the following list of representative irregular verbs show.

REPRESENTATIVE IRREGULAR VERBS—PAST TENSE AND PAST PARTICIPLE FORMS

POWER UP

Identify five irregular verbs whose principal parts you are unsure of. Write out the principal parts of these verbs, and study them until you feel confident you know them.

Base Form	Past	Past Participle
be	was; were	been
become	became	become
begin	began	begun
blow	blew	blown
break	broke	broken
bring	brought	brought
build	built	built
buy	bought	bought
catch	caught	caught
choose	chose	chosen
come	came	come
cut	cut	cut
dive	dove	dived
do	did	done
draw	drew	drawn
drink	drank	drunk
drive	drove	driven
eat	ate	eaten
fall	fell	fallen
feed	fed	fed
feel	felt	felt
fight	fought	fought
find	found	found
fly	flew	flown
forbid	forbad; forbade	forbidden
forget	forgot	forgotten
forgive	forgave	forgiven
freeze	froze	frozen
get	got	gotten (got)
give	gave	given
go	went	gone
grow	grew	grown
hang (a picture)	hung	hung
hang (meaning "execute")	hanged	hanged
have	had	had
hear	heard	heard
hide	hid	hidden
hold	held	held
hurt	hurt	hurt
keep	kept	kept
know	knew	known

Base Form	Past Tense	Past Participle
lay (meaning "place")	laid	laid
lead	led	led
leave	left	left
lend	lent	lent
let	let	let
lie (meaning "rest")	lay	lain
lose	lost	lost
make	made	made
mean	meant	meant
meet	met	met
pay	paid	paid
put	put	put
quit	quit	quit
read	read	read
ride	rode	ridden
ring	rang	rung
rise	rose	risen
run	ran	run
say	said	said
see	saw	seen
sell	sold	sold
send	sent	sent
set (on a table)	set	set
shake	shook	shaken
shine (meaning "give light")	shone	shone
shine (meaning "polish")	shined	shined
sing	sang	sung
sit (in a chair)	sat	sat
stand	stood	stood
steal	stole	stolen
swim	swam	swum
take	took	taken
teach	taught	taught
tell	told	told
think	thought	thought
throw	threw	thrown
understand	understood	understood
wake	woke	woken (or waked)
wear	wore	worn
win	won	won
wind	wound	wound
write	wrote	written

You already know the past participle forms of many irregular verbs. You can check the forms you do not know in the previous list or in a dictionary. Different dictionaries list verb forms in different ways, but typically the last form given is the past participle. Thus, if you look up *fly*, and find *fly, flew, flown*, you know that *flown* is the past participle. If no verb forms are given, the verb is regular and makes its past participle by adding *-d* or *-ed* to the base form.

THE PRINCIPAL PARTS OF VERBS

The base, past, and past participle forms you have been studying are known as the **principal parts** of verbs. Learning the principal parts is important because all verb tenses are formed from them. The present tense is formed from the base. The past tense is formed from the past. The perfect tenses (which you will learn about later in this chapter) are formed from the past participle. The following list shows how principal parts are used.

Base	Past	Past Participle
Makes the present tense.	Makes the past tense.	Makes the present perfect and past perfect tenses with helping verbs.
Be	**Was; Were**	**Been**
I am late. [present]	*I was late.* [past]	*I have been late.* [present perfect]
	We were late. [past]	*I had been late.* [past perfect]
Cook	**Cooked**	**Cooked**
I cook dinner. [present]	*I cooked dinner.* [past]	*I have cooked dinner.* [present perfect]
		I had cooked dinner. [past perfect]
Do	**Did**	**Done**
I do it. [present]	*I did it.* [past]	*I have done it.* [present perfect]
		I had done it. [past perfect]

Remember, the past and past participle forms of *regular verbs* look alike. They are made by adding *-d* or *-ed* to the base form. (See *cook* in the above list.) You can find the past and past participle forms of *irregular verbs* by checking the list on pages 160–161 or by consulting a dictionary.

11.1 ACTIVITY

Fill in the following blanks with the principal parts of the verbs given. Some of the verbs are regular, and some are irregular. If you need help with the irregular verbs, consult the list beginning on page 160 or your dictionary.

EXAMPLES	Verb	Base	Past	Past Participle
	to eat	*eat*	*ate*	*eaten*
	to dance	*dance*	*danced*	*danced*

Verb	Base	Past	Past Participle
1. to bake	bake	baked	baked
2. to try	try	tried	tried
3. to teach	teach	taught	taught
4. to type	type	typed	typed
5. to bring	bring	brought	brought
6. to stand	stand	stood	stood
7. to steal	steal	stole	stolen
8. to drink	drink	drank	drunk
9. to enjoy	enjoy	enjoyed	enjoyed
10. to help	help	helped	helped

THE PRESENT PERFECT TENSE

The **present perfect tense** has three uses:

1. To show that something began in the past and continues into the present time.

   Already we have studied an hour.

2. To show that something began in the past and just recently ended.

   The hospital has completed its new wing.

3. To show that something occurred at an unspecified time in the past.

   I have eaten chocolate covered ants before.

11.2 ACTIVITY

In each pair of sentences below, one sentence has a verb in the present perfect tense, and one does not. Place a check mark next to the sentence with the verb in the present perfect tense.

EXAMPLE   _____ I cooked chicken for supper.

   ✓ I have cooked chicken for supper.

1. ✓ The bands have warmed up for an hour.
   _____ The bands will warm up for an hour.

2. ✓ Greg has read three novels this summer.
   _____ Greg read three novels this summer.

3. _____ Caroline enjoys the summer band concerts in the park.
   ✓ Caroline has enjoyed the summer band concerts in the park.

4. ✓ The movie has begun ten minutes early.
   _____ The movie began ten minutes early.

5. _____ The union members will vote on the new contract.
   ✓ The union members have voted on the new contract.

CONNECT

You will have many opportunities to use the present perfect tense in your classes. For example, you would use it in an economics class to discuss a trend that began in the past and continues into the present: "The unemployment rate *has declined* steadily for the last five years."

6. ___✓___ The road crew has resurfaced the highway.

_____ The road crew resurfaces the highway.

7. _____ Carlotta lived in California all her life.

___✓___ Carlotta has lived in California all her life.

8. ___✓___ The flooding has destroyed the corn crop.

_____ The flooding destroyed the corn crop.

Forming the Present Perfect Tense

The **present perfect tense** is a two-word verb form. It is made by combining *have* or *has* with the past participle.

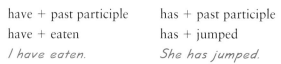

have + past participle	has + past participle
have + eaten	has + jumped
I have eaten.	*She has jumped.*

The past participle form does not change; *have* or *has* is used according to the subject.

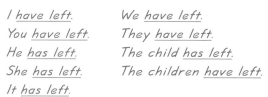

I have left.	*We have left.*
You have left.	*They have left.*
He has left.	*The child has left.*
She has left.	*The children have left.*
It has left.	

For an explanation of when to use *have* and when to use *has*, see page 129.

TIP

The present perfect tense sometimes includes a time indicator such as "since," "recently," "already," and "for the past few days." Here is an example: "*For the past three days,* I have been ill."

GRAMMAR ALERT ⚡

Be sure to use *have* or *has* with the past participle.

No: *We gone with you every year.*

Yes: *We have gone with you every year.*

Remember to use the *-d* or *-ed* ending with the past participle forms of regular verbs.

No: *We have enjoy ourselves.*

Yes: *We have enjoyed ourselves.*

Be sure you are using the past participle form and not the past tense form.

No: *We have went with you every year.*

Yes: *We have gone with you every year.*

11.3 ACTIVITY

Complete the present perfect by filling in each of the following blanks with the past participle form of the verb in parentheses. If you need help with the forms for irregular verbs, consult the list beginning on page 160 or your dictionary.

EXAMPLE   (to settle) The dust has _____*settled*_____ on the tables.

1. (to change) Computers have _changed_____ the way writing classes are conducted.

2. (to learn) Students have _learned_____ to generate ideas at the computer.

3. (to become) They have also _become_ comfortable drafting and revising at the computer keyboard.

4. (to take) Collaboration has _taken_ on new dimensions as students and teachers sit at each other's screens and suggest revisions.

5. (to evolve) Although writing instruction has _evolved_ now that computers are in the classroom, some students still prefer their typewriters or favorite pens.

6. (to alter) Still, computers have _altered_ writing instruction, and there is no turning back.

Complete the present perfect tenses by filling in the blanks in the following sentences with *have* or *has*. If you need help, see page 164.

EXAMPLE The workers _have_ stopped to eat lunch.

1. I _have_ explained my point of view before.

2. Some players _have_ walked off the field in protest.

3. The doctor _has_ told you what you should do to improve your cardiovascular fitness.

4. Because you _have_ been honest with me, I will be honest with you.

5. This airline company _has_ increased its fares by 15 percent.

6. It _has_ snowed all night, so schools are closed.

7. We _have_ prepared the guest room for your arrival.

8. She _has_ decided to apply to graduate school.

In each pair of sentences below, one verb should be a past tense form and the other should be a present perfect tense form. Using meaning as your guide, fill in each blank with either the past tense or the present perfect tense of the verb in parentheses.

POWER UP

How does the meaning differ for each sentence in the pairs in Activity 11.5?

EXAMPLE (to practice) The team _practiced_ foul shots last week.
Since early this morning, the team _has practiced_ foul shots.

1. (to be) Since 1989, James _has been_ your best friend.
Until 1989, James _was_ your best friend.

2. (to enter) Last week, George _entered_ his terrier in the dog show.
Every year since I've known him, George _has entered_ his terrier in the dog show.

3. (to eat) I <u>have eaten</u> lunch in this restaurant almost every day since it opened.

   I <u>ate</u> lunch in this restaurant almost every day until it closed.

4. (to wear) Marcus is easily recognized by his handlebar mustache; he <u>has worn</u> it for years.

   Marcus was easily recognized by his handlebar mustache; he <u>wore</u> it for years.

11.6 ACTIVITY

Fill in the blanks with the correct past tense or present perfect tense of the verb in parentheses, whichever is appropriate.

EXAMPLE (to be) Tea <u>*has been*</u> popular for a long time.

From the time you have been old enough to drink caffeine, you probably (to enjoy) <u>have enjoyed</u> tea many times, but you probably (to think) <u>have thought</u> little about its origins. The Chinese (to discover) <u>discovered</u> tea around 2700 B.C. By the 1400s, the tea ceremony (to be) <u>was</u> part of the culture of Japan, but tea (to be) <u>has been</u> available in the West only since the 1600s.

In today's dollars, the tea of the 1600s (to sell) <u>sold</u> for $100 a pound. It (to be) <u>was</u> so expensive that the teapots made in the seventeenth and eighteenth centuries (to be) <u>were</u> small. Each pot (to hold) <u>held</u> about two cups of tea, and tea was kept in a locked tea caddy. Sugar and milk (to be) <u>have been</u> added ingredients only since around 1665. Interestingly, people (to drink) <u>have drunk</u> iced tea only since the 1880s, and they (to enjoy) <u>have enjoyed</u> the convenience of tea bags since the first one was made in New York City in 1908.

The custom of serving afternoon tea (to start) <u>started</u> in the late 1600s, and (to remain) <u>has remained</u> popular in many countries to this day. Now in many places, tea parties (to become) <u>have become</u> fashionable once again.

THE PAST PERFECT TENSE

The **past perfect tense** shows that one thing occurred in the past before another thing occurred in the past. Thus, when you are writing in the past tense, you can use the past perfect to show that something occurred in the *more distant* past. Here are two examples.

CONNECT

The past perfect tense often comes in handy when you are telling a story, and the order of events is critical: "The clock *had struck* midnight before the lights went out."

       past   *more distant past*

I [*believed*] *you* [*had made*] *a mistake.*

       past   *more distant past*

She [*said*] *that Michael* [*had left*].

To form the past perfect tense, use *had* with the past participle.

had + past participle
had + fallen

I had fallen.	*We had fallen.*
You had fallen.	*They had fallen.*
He had fallen.	*The child had fallen.*
She had fallen.	*The children had fallen.*
It had fallen.	

If you are unsure of the past participle form for an irregular verb, consult the list beginning on page 160 or your dictionary.

GRAMMAR ALERT !

Remember to use the past participle with *had*.

No: *The children eaten their lunch.*

Yes: *The children had eaten their lunch.*

Be sure to use the *-d* or *-ed* ending with the past participle of regular verbs.

No: *They had play all day.*

Yes: *They had played all day.*

Be sure to use the past participle form and not the past tense form with *had*.

No: *I had began at noon.*

Yes: *I had begun at noon.*

Knowing when to use the present perfect tense and when to use the past perfect tense can be tricky when a single sentence has more than one verb in more than one tense. In general, use the present perfect tense with the present tense and the past perfect tense with the past tense.

      present perfect   *present*

After I *have finished* *a book, I* *lend* *it to someone.*

           past perfect   *past*

Because my boss *had given* *me several assignments, I* *was* *busy.*

11.7 ACTIVITY

Each of the following sentences has a part that refers to the past and a part that refers to the more distant past. Draw one line under the part that refers to the past and two lines under the part that refers to the more distant past.

EXAMPLE   After I had eaten, I became ill.

1. Molly had applied four times before she entered the police academy.
2. When I went to sleep last night, I had decided to quit my job.
3. After Benjamin had explained his problem, his adviser helped him.

Active voice emphasizes the *performer* of the action; passive voice emphasizes the *receiver* of the action. Ordinarily, you should use active voice to give sentences more energy. However, when you do not know who performed an action or when the performer is unimportant, use passive voice.

Weak passive voice (who did the scolding?):	The children were scolded for being late.
Active voice (the subject identifies the person who did the scolding):	The principal scolded the children for being late.

11.10 ACTIVITY

For each sentence, first underline the verb. Then write an "A" if the sentence is in the active voice and "P" if it is in the passive voice.

EXAMPLE   _A_   The Iditarod, an 1,150-mile dog sled race, <u>occurs</u> once a year.

1. _P_   Once, the Iditarod <u>was called</u> "The Last Great Race on Earth."
2. _A_   Each team of 12 to 16 dogs and their mushers <u>race</u> from Anchorage, Alaska, to Nome in 10 to 17 days.
3. _P_   The races <u>are run</u> over the roughest, most beautiful terrain in the state, perhaps in the world.
4. _A_   The course <u>includes</u> jagged mountain ranges, a frozen river, dense forest, desolate tundra, and miles of windswept coast.
5. _A_   In addition, temperatures <u>fall</u> far below zero.
6. _P_   Often, a complete loss of visibility <u>is caused</u> by high winds.
7. _A_   Finally, long hours of darkness and treacherous hills <u>add</u> to the difficulty.
8. _A_   This <u>is</u> not just a dog sled race.
9. _P_   It <u>is</u> best <u>described</u> as a challenge to the stamina and conditioning of well-trained humans.
10. _A_   Mushers <u>enter</u> from all walks of life.
11. _A_   Fishers, lawyers, doctors, miners, artists—both male and female— <u>have</u> their own reasons to take the challenge.

11.11 ACTIVITY

Three sentences in the paragraph are in the passive voice. Identify them and rewrite them to be in the active voice.

The Iditarod is now a National Historic Trail. This trail began as a mail and supply route from the coastal towns of Seward and Knik to the interior mining camps and beyond to the west coast. Mail and supplies were brought in by dog sleds. On the return trip, gold was taken out by them. In 1925, part of the Iditarod Trail became a life-saving highway. Diphtheria threatened to devastate the population. Serum was needed by the victims. Again, intrepid dog mushers and

Dog sleds brought in mail and supplies.
On the return trip, they took out gold.
The victims needed serum.

their faithful hard-driving dogs saved the day because they got the necessary medicine to the region. Today's Iditarod race is a commemoration of this past—a past Alaskans view with understandable pride.

IF ENGLISH IS YOUR SECOND LANGUAGE

1. Certain words are often used with the present perfect tense to show that something began in the past and continues into the present. These words are *since, for, until now, so far, now,* and *these days.*

   Eduardo <u>has been</u> a boy scout leader <u>since</u> 1985.
   Katie <u>has worked</u> for a professional photographer <u>for</u> 10 years.
   No one <u>has done</u> that job <u>until now</u>.
   <u>These days</u> the pollen count <u>has been</u> high.

2. Certain other words are often used with the present perfect tense to show that something just recently ended. These words are *just, already,* and *recently.*

   The movie <u>has just ended</u>.
   The instructor <u>has already passed out</u> the test papers.
   A new project director <u>has recently joined</u> the firm.

3. In many languages, particularly Asian languages, the present, past, and perfect tenses do not exist. If you speak one of these languages, be patient with yourself until you get a feel for the perfect tenses. You are more likely to see these tenses in writing than to hear them spoken, so be sure to study the forms when you see the perfect tenses in your English reading.

RECHARGE

1. The **past participle** form of a regular verb is identical to the past tense form; it is made by adding *-d* or *-ed* to the base form (*talk + -ed = talked*). The **past participle** of an irregular verb is formed in a variety of ways (*become, begun, known*).

2. Use the past participle with *has* or *have* to form the **present perfect tense**. The present perfect tense shows that something began in the past and continues into the present (The play *has run* for 49 weeks), that something began in the past and recently ended (The workers *have negotiated* a new contract), or that something occurred at an unspecified time in the past (The rabbits *have eaten* the vegetables in the garden).

3. Use the past participle with *had* to show that one thing occurred in the past before another thing occurred in the past: We realized that you *had eaten* already.

4. **Active voice** means that the sentence subject performs the action; **passive voice** means that the sentence subject is acted upon. To form the passive, use the past participle with *am, is, are, was,* or *were.*

   Active voice: The dog hid the bone.
   Passive voice: The bone was hidden by the dog.

11.12 CHAPTER REVIEW ACTIVITY

Fill in the blanks with the correct present perfect or past perfect forms of the verbs in parentheses.

After I looked over my essay, I no longer liked what I (to write) _had written_ . Whenever I am unsure about my writing, I ask Luis to read it because in the past he (to give) _has given_ me excellent advice. This time was no exception. He told me I (to rush) _had rushed_ through the supporting details. As a result, I (to develop) _had developed_ my points inadequately. For the better part of today, I added examples to support my points. I thought I (to provide) _had provided_ enough details, but now I see that I had not. I feel much better about the piece now that I (to illustrate) _have illustrated_ my points. I (to work) _have worked_ harder on this essay than any other one this term.

11.13 CHAPTER REVIEW ACTIVITY

Correct the errors with present perfect tense, past perfect tense, and passive voice by crossing out and writing above the line. The first correction is made as an example.

In the United States, some of our wilder television programs are adaptations of shows from other countries. For example, in 1999 in the Netherlands, people were ~~glue~~ *glued* to their television sets to watch a wildly popular program called *Big Brother*. For the show, every minute of the participants' days was videotaped and played live on television and the Internet. The show lasted a hundred days before it ~~cancelled~~ *was cancelled*.

The show, which was ~~name~~ *named* for the "Big Brother" in George Orwell's classic novel *1984*, simulated the ever-present Big Brother of the book with the 24 cameras and 59 microphones that were ~~place~~ *placed* throughout the house—even in the bathroom. Before the 100-day run of the show ended, millions of viewers ~~have~~ *had* followed the real-life soap opera on television and the program's website. They watched as participants engaged in conversation, conducted their affairs, made tea, took out the garbage, and so forth.

At regular intervals, viewers were ~~gave~~ *given* the opportunity to vote on their favorite participants. The last to leave the show were men named Bart, Ruud, and Willem. By the time they were ~~finish~~ *finished* with the show, the three had been rocketed to stardom. At the end of the run, viewers had the final say on their favorite character, with the $120,000 top prize going to Bart, 23. Participants' surnames were not ~~maked~~ *made* public.

Just when I think I ~~had~~ have heard it all, a story like this comes along to prove

me wrong. However, the program was not too outlandish for American

television, for a version of it appeared in the United States.

thinking in writing: Has college been what you expected it to be? To begin answering this question, do some mapping. In the center of a page, write "college expectations," and draw a circle around it. Branch off from that circle by following the mapping instructions on page 8.

writing from experience: Write about one or more ways college has or has not met your expectations. You can draw upon your mapping for ideas or consider the following: classes, workload, teachers, other students, living conditions, social life, tests, and extracurricular activities.

writing in context: Write a letter to an incoming college freshman to help that person form realistic expectations for the first year of college. First decide what kind of student you are writing to: a student-athlete, an adult learner, a part-time student, a student who will work while attending school, or an international student. Try to give that person an accurate sense of what to expect at the same time you foster enthusiasm for what lies ahead.

CHAPTER **12**

The Progressive Tenses

CHAPTER GOALS

By the end of this chapter, you will:

Understand the present participle form.

Recognize the present and past progressive tenses.

Use the present and past progressive tenses correctly.

THE PRESENT PARTICIPLE

The **present participle** is the *-ing* form of a verb.

Base Form	Present Participle
do	doing
love	loving
sing	singing
swim	swimming

The present participle is important because it is used to make two verb tenses you will learn about in this chapter.

SPELLING ALERT !

Sometimes the last letter is doubled before *-ing* is added (*swim* becomes *swimming*), and sometimes the last letter is dropped before adding *-ing* (*love* becomes *loving*). These rules are discussed on pages 298 and 301. If you are unsure of the spelling of a present participle, check your dictionary.

THE PRESENT PROGRESSIVE TENSE

The **present progressive tense** shows that an action is in progress *right now*. Here are two examples:

> *Janet is sleeping late.*
> *The leaves are changing color.*

Unlike the simple present, the present progressive always shows that something is occurring at the time the sentence is being spoken or written.

Present Progressive	Simple Present
Janet is sleeping late	*Janet sleeps late.*
The leaves are changing color.	*The leaves change color.*

The present progressive can also show that something will take place in the future.

> *Tomorrow I am leaving for Maine.*
> *Soon you are going home.*

CONNECT

The present progressive tense is often used by sportscasters describing the ongoing action of an event, like this: "Tiger Woods *is approaching* the green." What effect does this tense have on the audience?

TIP

For an explanation of when to use *am*, *is*, and *are*, see page 126.

To form the present progressive, use *am*, *is*, or *are* with the present participle.

am + present participle	is + present participle	are + present participle
am + eating	is + eating	are + eating

I am eating.

He is eating.
She is eating.
It is eating.
The child is eating.

You are eating.
We are eating.
They are eating.
The children are eating.

GRAMMAR ALERT !

Be sure to use *am*, *is*, or *are* with the *-ing* form to make the present progressive.

No: *I going to the store now.*
Yes: *I am going to the store now.*

No: *My mother going to the store now.*
Yes: *My mother is going to the store now.*

No: *We going to the store now.*
Yes: *We are going to the store now.*

12.1 ACTIVITY

Rewrite the sentences, changing the underlined present tense verbs to present progressive forms.

EXAMPLE   Joyce <u>hopes</u> to join your softball team.

Joyce is hoping to join your softball team.

1. The firefighters <u>battle</u> the three-alarm blaze.

   The firefighters are battling the three-alarm blaze.

2. Ilya <u>hopes</u> to win a scholarship for his sophomore year.

   Ilya is hoping to win a scholarship for his sophomore year.

3. For extra protein, we <u>eat</u> turkey sandwiches for lunch.

   For extra protein, we are eating turkey sandwiches for lunch.

4. Because of the excessive heat, I <u>drink</u> extra fluids.

   Because of the excessive heat, I am drinking extra fluids.

POWER UP

How does the meaning change when the tenses in the sentences in Activity 12.1 are altered from present to present progressive tense?

5. You <u>spend</u> too much time on unimportant matters.

   You are spending too much time on unimportant matters.

6. At this time, he <u>works</u> out in the gym for two hours.

   At this time, he is working out in the gym for two hours.

7. All the neighbors <u>complain</u> because the children <u>play</u> the radio very loudly.

   All the neighbors are complaining because the children are playing the radio very loudly.

8. When you leave for school, I <u>plan</u> to rent your room.

   When you leave for school, I am planning to rent your room.

9. If it <u>rains,</u> she wants to work this afternoon.

   If it is raining, she wants to work this afternoon.

10. She <u>explains</u> the problem, but she also <u>offers</u> a solution.

    She is explaining the problem, but she is also offering a solution.

THE PAST PROGRESSIVE TENSE

The **past progressive tense** is used to show that something was ongoing in the past. Here are two examples:

> The telephone <u>was ringing</u>.
> I <u>was hoping</u> to go to Florida.

The difference between the simple past and the past progressive is this: the simple past shows that something began and ended in the past, but the past progressive stresses that an action was continuing across past time.

Past Progressive	Simple Past
The dog <u>was barking</u> all night.	The dog <u>barked</u> all night.
I <u>was working</u> in the library.	I <u>worked</u> in the library.
We <u>were telling</u> you the truth.	We <u>told</u> you the truth.

The past progressive is often used to show that one thing was going on *before* another thing happened, *at the same time* another thing happened, or *after* another thing happened.

Here is an example of one thing going on before another thing happened.

> This happened second.   This happened first.
> Before my dinner guests arrived, I <u>was searching</u> for extra napkins.

In this example, one thing was going on at the same time another thing happened.

Both events happened at the same time.

The performer took a bow while the audience was clapping.

Here, one thing was going on after another thing happened.

This happened first.   *This happened second.*

After the storm ended, the children were splashing in the puddles left in the street.

To form the past progressive, use *was* or *were* with the present participle.

was + present participle	were + present participle
was + going	were + going
Helen was going home.	*We were going home.*
I was going.	*We were going.*
The child was going.	*They were going.*
He was going.	*You were going.*
She was going.	*The children were going.*
It was going.	

GRAMMAR ALERT ❗

Be sure to use *was* or *were* with the *-ing* form of a verb to make the past progressive.

No: *Mark leaving early.*

Yes: *Mark was leaving early.*

No: *They leaving early.*

Yes: *They were leaving early.*

12.2 ACTIVITY

Rewrite the sentences, changing the underlined past tense forms to past progressive forms.

EXAMPLE Dr. Munroe explained the answer.

Dr. Munroe was explaining the answer.

1. We studied our history before we went to dinner.

   We were studying our history before we went to dinner.

2. I practiced my speech in front of the mirror after my roommate left for the evening.

   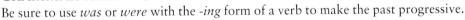
   I was practicing my speech in front of the mirror after my roommate left for the evening.

3. Before her plans changed, Juanita hoped to leave by five o'clock.
   Before her plans changed, Juanita was hoping to leave by five o'clock.

4. The storm clouds <u>gathered</u> all day.

The storm clouds were gathering all day.

5. Colleen <u>taught</u> fifth grade when she decided to return to school to become a physical therapist.

Colleen was teaching fifth grade when she decided to return to school to become a physical therapist.

6. Because you <u>sat</u> in the last row, you could not see the movie very well.

Because you were sitting in the last row, you could not see the movie very well.

7. The football team and the band <u>traveled</u> to Houston before fall semester began.

The football team and the band were traveling to Houston before fall semester began.

8. Wanda <u>felt</u> ill while she <u>ran</u> the 800-meter race.

Wanda was feeling ill while she was running the 800-meter race.

9. Your dog <u>barked</u> all night long.

Your dog was barking all night long.

10. The children <u>tried</u> to earn money by selling lemonade on the street corner.

The children were trying to earn money by selling lemonade on the street corner.

POWER UP

Verb tenses convey meaning. Explain the difference in meaning between these two sentences:
A. Emil sings in the choir.
B. Emil is singing in the choir.
Now explain the difference in meaning between these two sentences:
A. Alana ate her lunch.
B. Alana was eating her lunch.

IF ENGLISH IS YOUR SECOND LANGUAGE

1. The following verbs are rarely used in a progressive tense.

appreciate	hate	mind	recognize
be	know	need	understand
believe	like	prefer	want
dislike			

No: *I am appreciating your help.*
Yes: *I appreciate your help.*

2. The following verbs rarely appear in a progressive tense, unless they are describing a specific action, or they are part of certain expressions.

| appear | look | seem | sound |
| hear | see | smell | taste |

I am hearing something in the distance. [A specific action]
I hear the church bells.
Your plan is sounding better all the time. [An expression]

3. The following verbs almost never appear in a progressive tense.

belong to   own
cost   possess

No: *As a teenager, I was owning a dog.*
Yes: *As a teenager, I owned a dog.*

4. The progressive form of *have* is used with a form of *be* to mean "be experiencing" or "be eating" or "be drinking."

I am having trouble with my English homework.
Dana is having soup for lunch.
We are having wine with dinner.

5. In a progressive tense, *think* refers to a mental process. In a simple tense, it refers to a conclusion or opinion that has been reached.

I was thinking of changing my major. [A mental process]
I think we should leave now. [A conclusion]

RECHARGE

1. The **present participle** is the *-ing* form of the verb (*dancing, walking, thinking*).
2. Use the present participle with *am, is,* or *are* to form the **present progressive tense.** The present progressive shows that something is occurring at the time the sentence is being spoken or written (The concert *is running* late) or that something will take place in the future (Next week, I *am moving* to a new apartment).
3. Use the present participle with *was* or *were* to form the **past progressive tense.** The past progressive shows that something was ongoing in the past (They *were expecting* company for dinner). It also can show that one thing was going on before another (Before I hit the telephone pole, I *was trying* to change the radio station) or that something was going on at the same time another thing happened (The performers danced while they *were singing* the song).

12.3 CHAPTER REVIEW ACTIVITY

In each of the following pairs of sentences, place a check mark next to the sentence with the correct tense.

EXAMPLE _____ At the moment, Darla eats supper.
             _✔_ At the moment, Darla is eating supper.

POWER UP

Write three sentences that you hear or read today that use a progressive tense.

1. ___✓___ Most of the time, we shop at the corner market.
   _____ Most of the time, we are shopping at the corner market.

2. ___✓___ When we visited Toronto, we enjoyed the zoo.
   _____ When we visited Toronto, we were enjoying the zoo.

3. _____ By the time I am graduating, I will have two minors.
   ___✓___ By the time I graduate, I will have two minors.

4. _____ Chris leaves Boston to work in Chicago.
   ___✓___ Chris is leaving Boston to work in Chicago.

5. _____ You ate dinner when the phone rang.
   ___✓___ You were eating dinner when the phone rang.

6. _____ Laura explained her point when you interrupted her.
   ___✓___ Laura was explaining her point when you interrupted her.

7. _____ Finally, we take control of our lives.
   ___✓___ Finally, we are taking control of our lives.

8. ___✓___ Dr. Moritz always answers any questions we ask.
   _____ Dr. Moritz is always answering any questions we ask.

9. _____ They sleep late this morning.
   ___✓___ They are sleeping late this morning.

10. _____ She worked on her computer when the electricity went off.
    ___✓___ She was working on her computer when the electricity went off.

12.4 CHAPTER REVIEW ACTIVITY

On a separate sheet, rewrite the following passage, changing the underlined past and present tense verbs to the corresponding progressive forms.

Georgie <u>has</u> [is having] trouble deciding what he wants to do. At first, he <u>considered</u> [was considering] traveling across the country. Then he <u>thought</u> [was thinking] about joining the navy. Now he <u>wonders</u> [is wondering] whether he should quit school. If he does not decide what he wants soon, he will turn 30 with no sense of direction. I hope he <u>considers</u> [is considering] seeing a counselor because he needs to speak to someone who can help him set goals and direct his life.

GETTING IN GEAR

thinking in writing: Everyone has problems; they are a part of life. List the problems you are currently wrestling with.

writing from experience: Write about a problem in your life. It can be a personal problem (like fear of heights), a bad habit (like smoking), a family problem (like a parent losing a job), a school difficulty (like not knowing what to major in). You can write about how the problem affects you or how you deal with (or plan to deal with) the problem.

writing in context: Author and teacher of Eastern psychology Shakti Gawain says that "problems are messages." Explain what you think he means and agree or disagree, citing reasons for your view.

CHAPTER 13

Tense Shifts

CHAPTER GOALS

By the end of this chapter, you will:

Recognize confusing tense shifts.

Be able to eliminate confusing tense shifts from your writing.

As you know from Chapters 9 through 12, verbs have different forms—called **tenses**—to show present and past times.

> Past: *Kerry <u>played</u> guitar in a local band.*
> Present: *Kerry <u>plays</u> guitar in a local band.*

TENSE SHIFT

Sometimes writers must legitimately move from one tense to another to show a change in time.

> Move from past to present: *Last year, I <u>worked</u> at Hamburger Heaven,* (past)
>
> *but now I <u>am tutoring</u> in the math lab.* (present)

If you move from one tense to another without a valid reason, you create a problem called **tense shift.** An inappropriate tense shift is a problem because it confuses the time frame of your writing.

> Confusing tense shift: *After I <u>stepped</u> on the gas pedal, the light* (past)
> *<u>turns</u> red.* (present)
>
> Correction: *After I <u>stepped</u> on the gas pedal, the light* (past)
> *<u>turned</u> red.* (past)
>
> Confusing tense shift: *Lee <u>is cooking</u> cabbage for dinner. The smell* (present)
> *<u>was making</u> me ill.* (past)
>
> Correction: *Lee <u>is cooking</u> cabbage for dinner. The smell* (present)
> *<u>is making</u> me ill.* (present)

CONNECT

When you take notes in class, be careful to keep your tenses straight. Inappropriate shifts can create problems. For example, you do not want to write, "Sonnets *are* very popular" when your instructor said, "Sonnets *were* very popular."

GRAMMAR ALERT !

Watch out for confusing tense shifts when you are telling a story. Here is an example.

Confusing tense shift:

past   *past*
I *walked* into my morning class and *found* a seat.
             past   *past*
The instructor *began* lecturing, so I *took* notes.
   present   *present*
Then I *realize* that I *am* in the wrong class.

Correction:

past   *past*
I *walked* into my morning class and *found* a seat.
             past   *past*
The instructor *began* lecturing, so I *took* notes.
       past   *past*
Then I *realized* that I *was* in the wrong class.

GRAMMAR ALERT ❗

Will and *can* are used with the present tense. *Would* and *could* are used with the past tense.

Confusing tense shift:	When I *get* my paycheck, I *would* buy CDs.
Correction 1:	When I *get* my paycheck, I *will* buy CDs.
Correction 2:	When I *got* my paycheck, I *would* buy CDs.
Confusing tense shift:	When Lisa *graduates*, she *could* get a job.
Correction 1:	When Lisa *graduates*, she *can* get a job.
Correction 2:	When Lisa *graduated*, she *could* get a job.

13.1 ACTIVITY

Circle the verbs in the following sentences. Then write "TS" in the blank if there is a confusing tense shift. If there is no tense shift, or if the shift is appropriate to show a time change, write "OK" in the blank.

EXAMPLE _____TS_____ Megen [answered] the phone, and then she [sits] down for a long conversation.

1. __TS__ I [mixed] the flour, water, and eggs into a dough, which I [shaped] into a loaf. Then I [bake] it at 350 degrees.

2. __OK__ The mechanic [explained] to Gary that the car [needed] a new radiator.

3. __OK__ The soccer team [hopes] that next season they [can win] more games.

4. __OK__ Last week I [wanted] my own apartment, but now I [am] happy in a dormitory.

5. __TS__ The sky [darkened] as huge storm clouds [rolled] in. Then the lightning [begins].

6. __TS__ After lunch, the children [play] in the schoolyard. When the bell [rings], they [returned] to their classrooms.

7. __OK__ Douglas [was] certain that he [would make] the Dean's List this term.

POWER UP

Imagine a newspaper account of a bank robbery wherein the reporter shifted tenses inappropriately several times. What effect would the tense shifts have on the reader?

8. ___TS___ Before I |leave| on vacation, I |checked| the map and I |fill| my gas tank.

9. ___TS___ When I |buy| a new car, I |could take| you to work.

10. ___OK___ Because my key |was| bent, I |could| not |get| into my house.

13.2 ACTIVITY

Fill in each blank in the passage below with the verb form from the following list that does not create a confusing tense shift. Be prepared to explain your choices.

1. is/was	5. can/could	9. look/looked
2. is/was	6. will/would	10. am/was
3. feel/felt	7. find/found	11. can/could
4. do/did	8. am/was	

When I walked into my exercise class for the first time, I was depressed. Everyone __was__¹ in excellent shape, except me. The instructor, a young woman in her twenties, __was__² enthusiastic and amazingly fit. I __felt__³ as if I __did__⁴ not belong. For weeks I __could__⁵ not keep up, so I __would__⁶ drop out halfway through the class. Eventually, however, I __found__⁷ that I __was__⁸ getting stronger and that I __looked__⁹ better. Now I __am__¹⁰ no longer depressed in class because I __can__¹¹ work out with the best of them.

13.3 ACTIVITY

The following passage contains a number of tense shifts, but only seven of them are inappropriate. Cross out the incorrect verbs and write the correct ones above them.

Cell phones mean fast communication from almost any location. Those little
devices in our briefcases, pockets, and purses mean we ~~could~~ *can* conduct business while
shopping at the mall, arrange a dinner date while waiting in the dentist's office, and
make an airline reservation while pushing a shopping cart through the grocery
store. More important, the phones offer a new measure of safety. For example, a
flat tire on a deserted highway is less alarming with a cell phone on the front seat.

However, despite the safety and convenience they provide, cell phones can be
very annoying. Diners in restaurants ~~complained~~ *complain* regularly because their dinners are
disturbed by cell phone chats at the next table. Often we are talking face-to-face
with someone, only to have the conversation interrupted by the ring of the person's
cell phone. Worst of all is the inability to escape cell phone interruptions. Because
the phones are portable, they ~~interrupted~~ *interrupt* us everywhere—on the beach, in our cars,

on the tennis court—few places are unreachable by cell phone. Yet, no cell phone

interruption is more incredible than one that ~~occurs~~ [occurred] in a Hong Kong hospital.

A patient complained that a surgeon ~~uses~~ [used] a cell phone during an operation.

Taxi driver Chung Chi-cheong ~~says~~ [said] he heard the phone conversation while he ~~is~~ [was]

under local anesthetic for surgery to remove a polyp in his intestine. "During the op-

eration, I found the doctor talking. I was surprised because the conversation had

nothing to do with my medical condition," Chung said. "The conversation was about

buying a car and how much the car cost." Clearly, technology can be taken too far.

 IF ENGLISH IS YOUR SECOND LANGUAGE

When you write a direct quotation, a shift in tenses is often appropriate.

                                past   present

Appropriate tense shift: *Jamal <u>said</u>, "I <u>enjoy</u> winter sports."*

RECHARGE

1. A **tense shift** is an inappropriate move from one verb tense to another.

    First I <u>called</u> 911, and then I <u>go</u> to see if I can be of help.

2. To avoid a tense shift, use *will* and *can* with the present tense and *would* and *could* with the past tense.

13.4 CHAPTER REVIEW ACTIVITY

The following passage has eight confusing tense shifts. Cross out the incorrect verbs and write the correct forms above them.

On August 13, 1959, in a baseball game against the Giants, Los Angeles

Dodger Sandy Koufax struck out 18 batters. This ~~sets~~ [set] a National League

record that equaled the great Bob Feller's Major League triumph. In the game

before, Koufax had struck out 13 Philadelphia Phillies batters. His strikeouts

for the two games ~~total~~ [totaled] 31, which ~~creates~~ [created] a Major League record.

However, Koufax's greatest day came two years later. On May 29, 1961,

in a night game against the St. Louis Cardinals, Sandy Koufax ~~strikes~~ [struck] out 13

batters and ~~becomes~~ [became] the first National League player to win six games and to

lead the league in strikeouts.

By the middle of the 1961 season, Koufax had struck out 128 batters in

119 innings. Even more amazing is the fact that in only seven seasons he

_{struck}
~~strikes~~ out 811 players in 811 innings, to average one strikeout for every

inning he played. By the end of 1961, Koufax again ^{tied} ~~ties~~ Bob Feller's record by

striking out 18 batters in one game. In 1962, Koufax's earned run average of

2.54 ^{led} ~~leads~~ the National League. Truly, Sandy Koufax was one of baseball's

greatest players.

GETTING IN GEAR

thinking in writing: Freewrite about one of your friends. Try to fill about two pages.

writing from experience: Write a true story about a friend or friendship. You can tell a story about meeting or losing a friend, something you did with a friend, how you learned the meaning of friendship, loyalty among friends, or some other aspect of friendship.

writing in context: Write a definition of friendship appropriate for publication in an advice column. Explain and illustrate one or more of its chief characteristics by drawing on your own experience or observation.

PART THREE REVIEW

Activity: Verbs

The following passage has five subject-verb agreement errors, three tense shifts, two unnecessary passive voices, and two incorrect verb forms. Cross out the errors and write the corrections above the line.

In 1958, Bank of America introduced the first credit card and ~~creates~~ [created] the modern consumer. The availability of credit has ~~transform~~ [transformed] how Americans shop and budget their finances. In fact, the average American consumer ~~hold~~ [holds] more than $2,000 in credit.

"Charge cards" predated Bank of America's Bank Americard, but they were store-specific and offered credit only at a particular chain of gas stations or department stores. ~~Consumers themselves were provided credit by Bank of America's innovation.~~ [Bank of America's innovation provided consumers themselves with credit.] ~~Also, the retailer was given assurance of bill payment by it.~~ [Also, it gave the retailer assurance of bill payment.] At first, the Bank Americard (which later ~~becomes~~ [became] VISA) was available in California only. However, by 1970 it and MasterCharge (which later ~~becomes~~ [became] MasterCard) ~~was~~ [were] issuing cards across the country.

Credit cards can be a real convenience, but they can also create problems. In particular, one group of people at risk ~~are~~ [is] college students. Credit card companies send students unsolicited cards. Lured by the "buy-now-pay-later" philosophy, students run up big bills and later discover they ~~be~~ [are] unable to pay. Often, by the time these users of a credit card ~~discovers~~ [discover] they have a problem, they are so far in debt that it takes years for them to recover. Even worse, their credit rating can be ruined, creating a problem that ~~plague~~ [plagues] them for life.

Activity: Verbs

The following passage has five subject-verb agreement errors, three tense shifts, two incorrect verb forms, and one unnecessary passive voice. Cross out the errors and write the corrections above the line.

Long ago, there ~~was~~ [were] no regular firefighters. If a house caught fire, everybody ~~becomes~~ [became] a firefighter. People formed bucket brigades to fight fires. That changed in 1666, when London had a fire that burned down 13,000 buildings, including St. Paul's Cathedral. The English then ~~begin~~ [began] to develop hand-operated pumps, so firefighters could spray water through a hose. Citizens ~~begun~~ [began] to join together in volunteer companies. They promised to drop everything and rush to a fire whenever it ~~breaked~~ [broke] out.

In Philadelphia, Benjamin Franklin founded the first department of volunteer firefighters in the United States. It replaced the bucket brigades that had existed up to then. In 1835, ~~the first paid fire patrol was established by New York City.~~ There

> New York City established the first paid fire patrol.

were four members who ~~was~~ paid $250 a year. The following year, there were

> were

40 members, who ~~was~~ known as the Fire Police. Then in 1855, New York City

> were

~~organizes~~ the first firehouse.

> organized

   Today, in the United States, there ~~is~~ about 1,000 fire departments staffed by

> are

fully paid professional firefighters. In addition, more than 15,000 other

departments include both paid and volunteer firefighters. The proud group of paid

firefighters ~~include~~ over 80,000 people. The ranks of volunteers number over

> includes

800,000.

Understanding Pronouns

CHAPTER 14

Pronouns

To achieve the goals of this chapter, you must understand *nouns*, *pronouns*, and *antecedents*.

A **noun** names a person, a place, an object, an emotion, or an idea. Nouns are words such as these:

Person	Place	Object	Emotion	Idea
cousin	city	car	anger	belief
Delores	lake	Chevy	fear	concept
man	Memphis	foot	joy	democracy
teacher	world	hat	love	freedom

A **pronoun** is a word that substitutes for a noun. Pronouns help writers and speakers avoid unpleasant repetition.

> Unpleasant repetition: *Harry asked where <u>Harry's</u> coat was.*
> Better: *Harry asked where <u>his</u> coat was.*

The following words are pronouns and can therefore substitute for nouns.

I	me	my	mine
you	your	yours	
he	him	his	
she	her	hers	
it	its		
we	us	our	ours
they	them	their	theirs

The noun a pronoun substitutes for is called the **antecedent.**

Kimberly made her decision.

> Pronoun: *her*
> Antecedent: *Kimberly*

The teachers wrote their lesson plans.

> Pronoun: *their*
> Antecedent: *teachers*

Bev and Raul said that they enjoy sociology.

> Pronoun: *they*
> Antecedents: *Bev, Raul*

TIP

For a discussion of sentence subjects, see page 48.

USING PRONOUNS AS SUBJECTS

A pronoun often functions as the subject of a sentence, as in these examples:

> *They gave the cab driver a generous tip.*
> *He is my best friend.*

These pronouns are used as subjects: *I, you, he, she, it, we, they.*

USING PRONOUNS AS OBJECTS

TIP

The object of a verb is also called a **direct object**, and the object of *to* or *for* is also called the **indirect object**.

TIP

For a complete discussion of prepositions, see Chapter 19.

A pronoun can also function as the *object of the verb* or the *object of a preposition.*

When a pronoun receives a verb's action, it is the **object of the verb.** To find the object of a verb, ask "who or what?" after the verb, like this:

> *Chris threw it across the room.*

Verb:	*threw*
Ask:	Threw who or what?
Answer:	*it*
Object of verb:	*it*

A pronoun can come after a preposition (a word such as *in, on, to, of, near, at, for,* or *by*). In this case, the pronoun is the **object of a preposition.**

In the following examples, the preposition is circled and the pronoun is underlined.

> *Uri lives [near] me.*
> *Olivia has faith [in] you.*
> *The cat sleeps [beside] him.*

Sometimes the preposition is not written out. Instead, it is the unstated *to* or *for.* Here are two examples.

Unstated *to:*	*Chris gave her bad advice.* [Chris gave bad advice to her.]
Unstated *for:*	*Chester bought them a wedding gift.* [Chester bought a wedding gift for them.]

These pronouns are used as objects: *me, you, him, her, it, us, them.*

USING PRONOUNS AS POSSESSIVES

Pronouns can show possession (ownership), like this:

> *The students handed in their essays.* (The essays belong to the students.)
> *The woman caught her hem on the heel of her shoe.* (The hem and the shoe belong to the woman.)

These pronouns are used as possessives: *his, her, hers, its, our, ours, your, yours, their, theirs.*

GRAMMAR ALERT !

The possessive pronoun is *it*s, not *it*'s, which is the contraction form for "it is" or "it has."

Possessive:	The floor has lost its shine.
Contraction:	It's too early to call Judy.

A List of Subject, Object, and Possessive Pronouns

If you are ever unsure about which pronouns are used as subjects and which are used as objects, consult this list.

Subject Pronouns	Object Pronouns	Possessive Pronouns
Use as the subject of a sentence.	Use as the object of a verb or as the object of a preposition.	Use to show ownership.
Singular	*Singular*	*Singular*
I — *I like pizza.*	me — *Give the book to me.*	my — *I lost my keys.*
you — *You are a good friend.*	you — *Juanita likes you.*	mine — *These books are mine.*
he — *He is late.*	him — *Louis told him to leave.*	your — *Your ideas are important.*
she — *She dances well.*	her — *Ask her that question.*	yours — *The job is yours.*
it — *It does not work.*	it — *Karl will leave it here.*	his — *His car is stalled.*
		her — *Her temper is short.*
		hers — *This idea was hers.*
		its — *The idea has its advantages.*
Plural	*Plural*	*Plural*
we — *We cannot go.*	us — *Doris lent us the notes.*	our — *Our vacation was canceled.*
you — *You all should leave.*	you — *I like all of you.*	ours — *These problems are ours to solve.*
they — *They understand calculus.*	them — *Dad bought a car for them.*	your — *You students must do your homework.*
		yours — *Students, these handouts are yours to keep.*
		their — *Their anger is understandable.*
		theirs — *The fault is theirs.*

Note: You and *it* are used as both subjects and objects. *You, your,* and *yours* are both singular and plural.

14.1 ACTIVITY

POWER UP

Rewrite a seven- to ten-sentence passage from a newspaper or magazine, replacing every pronoun with a noun. Then read the result. What can you conclude about the use of pronouns?

Rewrite the sentences, changing the underlined nouns to pronouns. Be sure to use subject, object, and possessive pronouns correctly. Then label each pronoun you use "S" for subject, "O" for object, or "P" for possessive. Check the list above if you are unsure.

EXAMPLE   Some prisoners do not like soft jailers.
                              S   O
                They do not like them.

1. Some English criminals find a private prison too soft.
      S   O
      They find it too soft.

2. <u>These criminals</u> believe <u>the criminals'</u> guards treat <u>the criminals</u> too nicely.
    S   P   O
    They believe their guards treat them too nicely.

3. <u>The guards</u> treated <u>the prisoners</u> as fellow human beings.
    S   O
    They treated them as fellow human beings.

4. <u>This treatment</u> came as a shock to <u>the criminals</u>.
    S   O
    It came as a shock to them.

5. <u>Chief Inspector of Prisons Sir David Ramsbotham</u> reported <u>the phenomenon</u> in a report.
    S   O
    He reported it in a report.

6. According to <u>Ramsbotham</u>, <u>prisoners</u> were on a first-name basis with <u>the prisoners'</u> guards and shared meals with <u>the guards</u>.
                       O   S   P
    According to him, they were on a first-name basis with their guards and shared meals
                                                                          O
    with them.

7. <u>Prisoners</u> experienced "culture shock" at the prison because the jail did not offer <u>the prisoners</u> a sufficiently threatening environment.
    S   O
    They experienced "culture shock" at the prison because the jail did not offer them a

    sufficiently threatening environment.

8. To <u>the criminals</u>, <u>a jail</u> was not comfortable if <u>the jail</u> was too comfortable.
          O   S   S
    To them, it was not comfortable if it was too comfortable.

CHOOSING SUBJECT AND OBJECT PRONOUNS IN COMPOUNDS

POWER UP

Select something you have written recently—even a journal entry—and circle the first five pronouns. Then draw an arrow from each pronoun to its antecedent.

And or *or* can join a pronoun with a noun to form a **compound,** like one of these:

Lionel and I	my dog and me	Phyllis or she
the boy and him	my friend or he	the child and her

To decide whether a subject or object pronoun is needed in a compound, rule out everything in the compound except the pronoun. Here are two examples.
Which is correct?

My friend and I left early.

or

My friend and me left early.

Rule out everything in the compound except the pronoun.

~~My friend and~~ I left early.

~~My friend and~~ me left early.

Now you can tell that the correct pronoun is *I*.

I left early.

Therefore, the correct compound is this:

My friend and I left early.

Which is correct?

Lesley invited Antonio and I.

or

Lesley invited Antonio and me.

Rule out everything in the compound except the pronoun.

Lesley invited ~~Antonio and~~ I.

Lesley invited ~~Antonio and~~ me.

Now you can tell that the correct sentence is this:

Lesley invited Antonio and me.

GRAMMAR ALERT

In a compound, the pronoun is placed *after* the noun.

No: *Dr. Huang gave the answer to me and Jeff.*

Yes: *Dr. Huang gave the answer to Jeff and me.*

14.2 ACTIVITY

In each of the following pairs of sentences, rule out everything in the compound except the pronoun. Then place a check mark next to the correct sentence.

EXAMPLE   _____✓_____ ~~Harry and~~ I lost our library books.

_____ ~~Harry and~~ me lost our library books.

1. _____ Louisa asked ~~the boys or~~ he to stay.
   ___✓___ Louisa asked ~~the boys or~~ him to stay.

2. _____ The track coach showed ~~Frankie and~~ I the proper way to stretch.
   ___✓___ The track coach showed ~~Frankie and~~ me the proper way to stretch.

3. ___✓___ For our anniversary, my parents gave ~~Jack and~~ me a beautiful tablecloth.
   _____ For our anniversary, my parents gave ~~Jack and~~ I a beautiful tablecloth.

4. ___✓___ In the morning, ~~my brothers and~~ I will leave for Chicago.
   _____ In the morning, ~~my brothers and~~ me will leave for Chicago.

5. ___✓___ ~~The lab assistant or~~ she will conduct the experiment.
   _____ ~~The lab assistant or~~ her will conduct the experiment.

6. _____ Stavros gave the directions to ~~Lee and~~ he.
   ___✓___ Stavros gave the directions to ~~Lee and~~ him.

POWER UP

Identify each pronoun you circled in the previous Power Up activity as a subject, object, or possessive pronoun.

7. _____ Dr. Hernandez asked ~~Sheila and~~ they to look up the answer.

   __√____ Dr. Hernandez asked ~~Sheila and~~ them to look up the answer.

8. _____ ~~The governor and~~ them studied the legislation.

   __√____ ~~The governor and~~ they studied the legislation.

14.3 ACTIVITY

On a separate sheet, write sentences using each of the following compounds correctly.

1. Bob or us	4. my friends and I
2. Katrina and them	5. the teacher and her
3. my family and me	6. Angelo or he

CHOOSING SUBJECT AND OBJECT PRONOUNS IN COMPARISONS

Than and *as* can be used to show **comparisons,** like this:

> *Sanjeen runs faster <u>than</u> Mike.* [Compares the running ability of Sanjeen and Mike]
>
> *Lynette is <u>as</u> talented <u>as</u> Joan.* [Compares the talent of Lynette and Joan]

When *than* and *as* are used to compare, some words are unstated.

> *Sanjeen runs faster than Mike [runs].*
> *Lynette is as talented as Joan [is].*

CONNECT

Just as pronouns substitute for nouns, in math and science formulas with numbers substitute for formulas with words. This means that as a study aid in math and science, you can write formulas out in words to test your understanding and help remember them.

To choose the correct subject or object pronoun, mentally add the missing words. Which is it?

> *Darlene studies more than me.*

or

> *Darlene studies more than I.*

To decide, add the missing words:

> *Darlene studies more than me study.*
> *Darlene studies more than I study.*

Now you can tell that the correct sentence is this:

> *Darlene studies more than I.*

Which is it?

> *The teacher praised Dale as much as me.*

or

> *The teacher praised Dale as much as I.*

Add the missing words:

> *The teacher praised Dale as much as he praised me.*
> *The teacher praised Dale as much as he praised I.*

Now you can tell that the correct sentence is this:

> *The teacher praised Dale as much as me.*

GRAMMAR ALERT !

Sometimes pronoun choice affects meaning. Consider the following sentences, for example.

I like surfing more than he. [This sentence means that I like surfing more than he does.]

I like surfing more than him. [This sentence means that I like surfing more than I like him.]

14.4 ACTIVITY

Rewrite each sentence, adding the unstated words. Then write the correct subject or object pronoun in the blank.

TIP

In informal speech, you often hear an object pronoun after a form of *to be (am, is, are, was, were)*. For example, people often say on the telephone, "This is her," and you often hear, "It's me." In formal situations, however, use a subject pronoun after *to be*: "This is she." While we hardly ever hear "It is I" anymore, in the strictest, most formal contexts, it is still correct.

EXAMPLES   (I, me) Hugh enjoys stock car racing more than _____*I*_____ .

Hugh enjoys stock car racing more than I do.

(I, me) The honor belongs to Julio as much as _____*me*_____ .

The honor belongs to Julio as much as it belongs

_to me._

1. (I, me)   Nick is as good a carpenter as _I_ .

   Nick is as good a carpenter as I am.

2. (he, him)   Spicy food bothers Helen as much as _him_ .

   Spicy food bothers Helen as much as it bothers him.

3. (she, her)   Santha began working in the library later than _she_ .

   Santha began working in the library later than she did.

4. (we, us)   Learning languages is easier for Brett than _us_ .

   Learning languages is easier for Brett than it is for us.

5. (they, them)   No one is happier for you than _they_ .

   No one is happier for you than they are.

6. (they, them)   Taking risks is less stressful for Jonathan than _them_ .

   Taking risks is less stressful for Jonathan than it is for them.

7. (I, me)   This plan should help you as much as _me_ .

   This plan should help you as much as it helps me.

8. (we, us)   Lonnie always felt they were stronger swimmers than ___we___ .

   Lonnie always felt they were stronger swimmers than we were.
   _____

CHOOSING SUBJECT AND OBJECT PRONOUNS WHEN THE ANTECEDENT IMMEDIATELY FOLLOWS

Sometimes a pronoun is followed immediately by its **antecedent,** as in the following examples.

We students support the tuition increase.

   Pronoun: *we*
   Antecedent: *students*

The police officer told us pedestrians to cross the street.

   Pronoun: *us*
   Antecedent: *pedestrians*

To decide whether a subject or object pronoun is needed, rule out the antecedent. Which is it?

We freshmen must stick together.

or

Us freshmen must stick together.

Rule out the antecedent.

We ~~freshmen~~ must stick together.
Us ~~freshmen~~ must stick together.

Now you can tell that the correct choice is this:

We freshmen must stick together.

14.5 ACTIVITY

Combine each pair of sentences below into one sentence by following the correct pronoun with its antecedent.

EXAMPLE   Many of the seniors live in apartments.
               We are the seniors.

               Many of us seniors live in apartments.

1. We are required to take a writing course.
   We are new freshmen.

   We new freshmen are required to take a writing course.
   _____

2. All of the volunteer firefighters have had extensive training.
   We are the volunteer firefighters.

   All of us volunteer firefighters have had extensive training.
   _____

3. The university does not allow students to have cars on campus.
We are the students.

The university does not allow us students to have cars on campus.

4. The volunteers decided to raise money for the food bank.
We are the volunteers.

We volunteers decided to raise money for the food bank.

5. Cross-country skiers need considerable upper body strength.
We are cross-country skiers.

We cross-country skiers need considerable upper body strength.

6. None of the students knew that answer.
We are the students.

None of us students knew that answer.

USING REFLEXIVE AND INTENSIVE PRONOUNS

Reflexive pronouns and **intensive pronouns** end in *-self* in the singular and *-selves* in the plural. The reflexive and intensive pronouns are given in the following list.

REFLEXIVE AND INTENSIVE PRONOUNS	
Singular	**Plural**
myself	ourselves
yourself	yourselves
himself	themselves
herself	
itself	

Reflexive pronouns often indicate that the subject of the sentence did something to or for itself.

Janie helped herself to another cookie.

The child taught himself to ride a bike.

Reflexive pronouns can also express the idea of being alone or doing something without help.

We did our algebra homework ourselves.

Liam prefers to sit by himself.

Intensive pronouns can emphasize the words they refer to.

I myself never eat sugar.

The doctors themselves did not know what to do.

GRAMMAR ALERT

Never use *hisself* and *theirselves*.

No: *The boy locked hisself out of the house.*
Yes: *The boy locked himself out of the house.*

No: *They asked theirselves the same question.*
Yes: *They asked themselves the same question.*

GRAMMAR ALERT

Do not use a reflexive pronoun without a word it can refer to.

No: *Jerri and myself left early.*
Yes: *Jerri and I left early.*

14.6 ACTIVITY

On a separate sheet, write four sentences using reflexive pronouns and four using intensive pronouns. Three of your sentences should indicate the subject did something itself, three should emphasize, and two should express being alone or doing something without help.

IF ENGLISH IS YOUR SECOND LANGUAGE

1. Two different sentence patterns can be used to express the same idea, one with *to* or *for* written out, and one with *to* or *for* unstated. (Notice that the order of the pronouns is reversed when *to* or *for* is omitted.)

    Karen lent it to him yesterday.
    Karen lent him it yesterday.

    Luis made it for her already.
    Luis made her it already.

2. Remember that *yourself* is a singular form and *yourselves* is a plural form.

    You yourself know the answer. [One person knows.]
    You yourselves know the answer. [More than one person knows.]

RECHARGE

1. A **pronoun** substitutes for a **noun** (a word that names a person, place, object, emotion, or idea). The noun a pronoun substitutes for is the **antecedent**.

2. **Subject pronouns** can function as sentence subjects; **object pronouns** can function as objects of verbs or objects of prepositions; and **possessive pronouns** can show ownership.

- To choose the correct pronoun in a compound, rule out everything except the pronoun.
- To choose the correct pronoun in a comparison, add the unstated words.
- To choose the correct pronoun when its antecedent follows immediately, rule out the antecedent.

4. **Reflexive pronouns** indicate that sentence subjects did something to or for themselves. They also express the idea of being or acting alone.

5. **Intensive pronouns** emphasize the words they refer to.

14.7 CHAPTER REVIEW ACTIVITY

The following passage has nine errors in pronoun usage. Cross out the incorrect pronouns and write the correct ones above them.

More and more families are taking cruises together, and now that I have cruised with my family, I understand why. There is something for everyone on a cruise. Us [We] adults could relax all we wanted, while the children could amuse theirselves [themselves] with a wide range of activities, including Ping-Pong, treasure hunts, dances, swimming, and arcade games. My husband and me [I] particularly appreciated the adult entertainment provided by the casino, Las Vegas–style shows, and bingo. We never worried about the children because they were enjoying themselves as much as us [we]. In fact, my son told me hisself [himself] that he wants to cruise again with his father, brother, and I [me].

Perhaps the best part of a cruise is it's [its] food. My husband and me [I] gained 5 pounds on six-course meals served six times a day. Of course, cabin service is available 24 hours a day. The food is truly elegant. In fact, my children, husband, and I ate food we had only heard of before, including escargots.

I recommend a cruise to all families. It is surprisingly affordable, and I don't think any other vacationing family had as much fun as us [we] on our cruise.

GETTING IN GEAR

thinking in writing: Pick two holidays that you enjoy. For each one, make a list of the elements that make for an enjoyable celebration of that holiday.

writing from experience: Write about the best or worst holiday or birthday celebration you have experienced. Describe the event, being sure to explain what made it so good or bad.

writing in context: Assume you are a feature writer for either *Glamour* or *GQ* magazine. As such, write an article about how to create the perfect celebration for a particular holiday (you choose which one). Keep the typical readers of the magazine in mind when you write your piece.

CHAPTER GOALS

By the end of this chapter, you will:

Know when to use singular and when to use plural pronouns.

Know how to refer to people in general.

Know how to avoid sexist pronouns.

CHAPTER 15

Pronoun-Antecedent Agreement

When nouns name only one person, place, object, emotion, or idea, they are **singular.** When nouns name two or more people, places, objects, emotions, or ideas, they are **plural.** Here are some examples.

	Singular		Plural
one	doctor	two or more	doctors
	dog		dogs
	feeling		feelings
	lake		lakes
	religion		religions
	toy		toys

Some pronouns are *singular* because they substitute for singular nouns. Some pronouns are *plural* because they substitute for plural nouns.

TIP

The noun a pronoun replaces is called an **antecedent.** Antecedents are explained on page 191.

Singular Pronouns	Plural Pronouns
I	we
me	us
my, mine	our, ours
he, she, it	they
him, her	them
his, hers, its	their, theirs
Pronouns That Are Both Singular and Plural	
you	
your, yours	

PRONOUN-ANTECEDENT AGREEMENT

To achieve **pronoun-antecedent agreement,** you must use singular pronouns to substitute for singular noun antecedents and plural pronouns to substitute for plural noun antecedents. Here are some examples.

Singular pronoun and antecedent: *Dinah lost her car keys.*

Plural pronoun and antecedent: *The students opened their test booklets.*

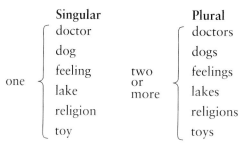

15.1 ACTIVITY

Above each underlined pronoun in the following passage, write the pronoun's noun antecedent. Also, write an "S" if the pronoun and antecedent are singular and a "P" if the pronoun and antecedent are plural. The first one is done as an example.

Large, round, flat stones were the first money. Because these stones were hard
stones-P   *stone-S*
to find, they were valuable. The larger the stone, the more valuable it was. A

smaller stone, which was the size of a dinner plate, might buy a fish or vegetables.
                                                    stones-P   *slaves-P*
Because the larger stones were so heavy, slaves carried them when their masters
                                                        people-P stones-P
went shopping. The richest people had stones too big to carry, so they left them in
        people-P   *people-P*
front of their houses to show everyone how rich they were.
                                                        people-P
People on the coasts used red, black, and white shells for their money. The
                                                            shells-P
woman in a household broke the shells into little pieces, polished them, and strung
shells-P   *woman-S*
them on strings. She could use one string to buy food and a hundred strings to

buy a cow.

Some people made bricks out of salt to use as money. Salt money was not heavy,
                                                    salt money-S
like stone, or hard to find, like shells. However, during a rain shower, it melted.
                                                metal money-S
Eventually, people began using metal money. It is better than most everything
                    metal money-S
else that has been tried, but it is heavy and takes up a lot of space, which explains

why people also use paper money.

PHRASES AFTER THE ANTECEDENT

Do not let a phrase after the antecedent trick you into choosing the wrong pronoun. To be sure that you choose correctly, eliminate the phrase. Here is an example.

Which is it?

A packet of letters is missing from its folder.

or

A packet of letters is missing from their folder.

Eliminate the phrase: *of letters*

Now which is it?

A packet is missing from its folder.

or

A packet is missing from their folder.

Correct pronoun: *its* [Singular pronoun to substitute for singular *packet*]

Correct sentence: *A packet of letters is missing from its folder.*

TIP

Remember that *its* is a possessive pronoun, so it shows ownership. *It's* is a contraction, meaning "it is" or "it has." When tempted to use *it's*, try replacing it with "it is" or "it has." If the substitution does not make sense, you want *its*, as at the right.

TIP

For more on phrases, see page 51.

15.2 ACTIVITY

In each sentence below, cross out the phrase after the antecedent, circle the antecedent, and then fill in the blank with the correct pronoun. Choose your pronoun from this list: *its, his, her, their.*

EXAMPLE   The proud father of the puppies wagged _____*his*_____ tail.

1. Six scouts in the troop lost ___*their*___ leader.

2. The members of the football team improved ___*their*___ grades this semester.

3. The workers in the union wanted ___*their*___ contract improved.

4. The box of souvenirs fell off ___*its*___ shelf in the closet.

5. One of the mothers took ___*her*___ child to a play group each day.

6. The can of vegetables has passed ___*its*___ expiration date.

7. A large bottle of pills sat on ___*its*___ side on the bathroom counter.

8. Police officers at the scene gave ___*their*___ account of the accident.

9. A government of the people gets ___*its*___ support from an informed electorate.

10. The opinions of the mayor have lost ___*their*___ influence with the city council.

COMPOUND ANTECEDENTS

A two-part antecedent is called a **compound antecedent.** Here is an example.

Francis and Alphonso lost their way on Route 80.

Pronoun:	*their*
Compound antecedent:	*Francis, Alphonso*

If the antecedents are joined by *and*, use a plural pronoun.

The young girl and her older brother played catch in their backyard.

If the antecedents are joined by *or*, choose the pronoun that agrees with the antecedent closer to it.

Singular: *Either Helene or Nikki will bring her tape recorder.* [*Nikki* is closer.]

Plural: *The teacher or the students will bring their tape recorder.* [*Students* is closer.]

For a more natural-sounding sentence, place the plural part of a compound antecedent second.

Correct: *Either the pillows or the sofa lost some of its stuffing.*

Correct but more natural sounding: *Either the sofa or the pillows lost some of their stuffing.*

Following the directions given, combine each pair of sentences below to form one sentence with a compound antecedent and correct pronoun.

EXAMPLE   Combine using *and*:
Henry cannot try his in-line skates yet.
Pablo cannot try his in-line skates yet.

Henry and Pablo cannot try their in-line skates yet.

1. Combine using *and*:
Lionel brought his dogs to the concert in the park.
Dimitri brought his dogs to the concert in the park.

    Lionel and Dimitri brought their dogs to the concert in the park.

2. Combine using *or*:
Chloe will win the award for her design.
My brothers will win the award for their design.

    Chloe or my brothers will win the award for their design.

3. Combine using *and*:
My car keys may not be in their usual place.
My wallet may not be in its usual place.

    My car keys and my wallet may not be in their usual places.

4. Combine using *or*:
The band director will compose her own music for the concert.
The assistant director will compose her own music for the concert.

    The band director or the assistant director will compose her own music for the concert.

5. Combine using *or*:
Jerry will lend Barry his biology notes.
Terry will lend Barry his biology notes.

    Jerry or Terry will lend Barry his biology notes.

6. Combine using *and*:
Evelyn left her gloves in the car.
Leo left his gloves in the car.

    Evelyn and Leo left their gloves in the car.

COLLECTIVE NOUN ANTECEDENTS

Collective nouns name a group of people or objects. They are words such as these:

audience	committee	group	mob
band	flock	jury	team

Usually a collective noun is singular because all the people or objects function as *one* unit. Thus, a collective noun usually takes a *singular* pronoun.

The crowd made its displeasure known.

Sometimes a collective noun is plural because the people or objects act *individually*. Then, the collective noun takes a *plural* pronoun.

The jury argued their opinions about the case.

Sometimes the collective noun can be either singular or plural, depending on the speaker or writer's viewpoint.

The steering committee announced its plans.

The steering committee announced their plans.

CONNECT

Think about your major, your career field, or subjects you are taking this term. What collective nouns are commonly used? Are they usually singular, plural, or either? For example, in math, *set* is common, as in "set of numbers," and is always singular. In law, *jury* is used, and it can be either singular or plural.

15.4 ACTIVITY

Circle the collective noun antecedents in the following sentences, and fill in the blanks with the correct singular or plural pronouns.

EXAMPLE   The [committee] reached _____*its*_____ decision by noon.

1. The [family] could not agree on where to take _its_____ vacation.

2. Our [society] has _its_____ share of problems.

3. The [orchestra] spent 10 minutes tuning _their_____ instruments.

4. Before the monthly meeting, the [school board] published _its_____ agenda.

5. The instructor told the [class] to write _their_____ names on _their_____ papers.

6. The [group] of protestors carried _their_____ signs to the front of City Hall.

15.5 ACTIVITY

Underline the collective noun and circle the pronoun that refers to it. If the pronoun is correct, do nothing. If it is incorrect, cross it out and write the correct pronoun above the line.

EXAMPLE   The sheep <u>herd</u> is losing [~~their~~] *its* grazing land.

1. The Student Services <u>staff</u> spent the afternoon planning [its] annual holiday party.
2. The <u>family</u> of rabbits lost [~~their~~] *its* home when the lawn mower ran across it. *its*
3. On the first Wednesday of every month, the membership <u>committee</u> has [~~their~~] *its* meeting.
4. After taking a final curtain call, the <u>cast</u> of the play retired to [their] dressing rooms.
5. The <u>trio</u> is known for [~~their~~] *its* folk songs and intricate musical arrangements.
6. The governor's <u>staff</u> could not make up [its] *their* minds about the best legislative initiative. [their is also correct]
7. The <u>audience</u> shouted [its] approval to the speaker.

INDEFINITE PRONOUN ANTECEDENTS

Indefinite pronouns do not refer to specific persons, places, objects, emotions, or ideas. They are words such as these:

anybody	everybody	some
anyone	everything	somebody
each	one	someone

Indefinite pronouns can be antecedents for other pronouns.

Everything has fallen from its shelf.

Antecedent: *everything*

Pronoun: *its*

The following indefinite pronouns are always singular, so they are used with singular pronouns.

-*body* words	**-*one* words**	**-*thing* words**	**other words**
anybody	anyone	anything	each
everybody	everyone	everything	either
nobody	no one	nothing	every
somebody	someone	something	neither
	one		

Nothing is in its place.

Somebody left her purse on the table.

Each of the priests took his vows.

The following indefinite pronouns will be either singular or plural, depending on the meaning expressed.

all   any   most   some

When singular in meaning, they are used with singular pronouns. When plural in meaning, they are used with plural pronouns.

Singular in meaning: *Some of the book is ripped from its binding.*

Plural in meaning: *Some of the students have quit their jobs.*

CONNECT

Indefinite pronouns are common in business writing. A memo to personnel from the human resources department might say, "*Anyone* who submits a sick leave form. . . ." A marketing report might state, "*Everyone* who responded to the survey. . . ."

CONNECT

People often use *they* or *their* to refer to singular indefinite pronouns. ("Nobody has their book in class today.") However, in college and business writing, use singular pronouns to refer to singular indefinite pronouns.

Avoiding Sexist Pronouns

In earlier times, writers routinely used masculine pronouns to refer to singular indefinite pronouns.

Everybody should receive his registration materials by Monday.

This usage is still grammatically correct. However, writers are now more aware that when the indefinite pronoun antecedent can refer to both males and females, other options are available, as described below.

Use both a male and a female pronoun.

Everybody should receive his or her registration materials by Monday.

Make both the antecedent and the pronoun plural.

All students should receive their registration materials by Monday.

Eliminate the gendered pronoun, if possible.

Everybody should receive registration materials by Monday.

> ☞ **TIP**
>
> Frequent use of "he or she" can be cumbersome, so whenever possible use the plural: "When *people* eat too little fat, *they* can have health problems."

Referring to People in General

When you refer to people in general, you have several choices. Here are some examples.

When people hurry, they make mistakes.
When a person hurries, he or she makes mistakes.
When we hurry, we make mistakes.
When someone hurries, he or she makes mistakes.
When anybody hurries, he or she makes mistakes.

Be sure to match the pronoun to the word you use to mean "people in general."

No: *If a person eats too much fat, they may get heart disease.* ["Person" is singular, and "they" is plural.]

Yes: *If a person eats too much fat, he or she may get heart disease.* ["Person" and "he or she" are both singular.]

Yes: *If people eat too much fat, they may get heart disease.* [Both "people" and "they" are plural.]

No: *When someone asks for help, we must give it to them.* ["Someone" is singular, but "them" is plural.]

Yes: *When someone asks for help, we must give it to him or her.* ["Someone" and "him or her" are both singular.]

15.6 ACTIVITY

Fill in the blank with the correct pronoun: *he or she, its,* or *their.*

EXAMPLE   Anybody can wallpaper a room if _____*he or she*_____ has patience and the right tools.

1. Most of the group jumped to _*their*_____ feet to applaud the orchestra's performance.

2. The travel instructions explained that everyone who crosses the border must

   have _*his or her*_____ passport.

3. I'm not sure what is it, but something in this room is not in

    __its_____ proper place.

4. Before time was up, all of them had answered __their_____ exam questions.

5. The police officer said that no one was leaving the scene of the accident

    without showing __his or her_____ driver's license.

15.7 ACTIVITY

The following sentences refer to people in general. Cross out the incorrect pronouns, and write the correct ones above them. Two sentences are correct.

POWER UP

Alone or with a classmate, compose sentences that begin with the following: *anyone, something, somebody, nothing, each girl, every person, some of the clothes.* Be sure that each sentence also includes a pronoun that substitutes for the indefinite pronoun.

EXAMPLE Before a person buys a used car, ~~they~~ *he or she* should have a mechanic check it out.

1. A working person often relies on ~~their~~ *his or her* baby-sitters.
2. A person who exercises regularly is better able to manage ~~their~~ *his or her* stress.
3. People who play basketball need to be light on their feet.
4. When someone does something foolish, ~~they~~ *he or she* can embarrass everyone.
5. A person who works as a police officer never knows when ~~they~~ *he or she* will face danger.
6. A person who always tells the truth may lose his or her friends.
7. If a person tries to be upbeat and pleasant, ~~they~~ *he or she* will be well liked.
8. When someone loves you, ~~they~~ *he or she* will overlook your faults.

IF ENGLISH IS YOUR SECOND LANGUAGE

The indefinite pronouns *some* and *any* are used in a generic sense.

Do you have any paper? [No specific kind of paper is asked for.]
Do you have my paper? [Specific paper is asked for.]

Juan needs some help. [The help can come from anyone.]
Juan needs your help. [The help must come from a specific person.]

RECHARGE

1. To achieve **pronoun-antecedent agreement**, use **singular pronouns** to refer to **singular nouns** (nouns that name one person, place, object, emotion, or idea) and **plural pronouns** to refer to **plural nouns** (nouns that name more than one person, place, object, emotion, or idea). Remember the following for correct pronoun-antecedent agreement:

    • Rule out phrases after the antecedent.
    • Use a plural pronoun with antecedents joined by *and.*

> • When antecedents are joined by *or,* use the pronoun that agrees with the closer antecedent.
> • Use a singular pronoun with a singular **collective noun** antecedent and a plural pronoun with a plural collective noun antecedent.
> • **Indefinite pronouns** can be antecedents. Some indefinite pronouns are singular, some are plural, and some are either singular or plural, depending on the meaning.
>
> **2.** Avoid sexist pronoun usage.

15.8 CHAPTER REVIEW ACTIVITY

Cross out incorrect or sexist pronouns, and write the correction above the line. If the sentence is correct, do nothing.

POWER UP

How do you think boys and girls were affected in earlier times when people did not try to avoid sexist pronouns? Consider, for example, that they always heard *doctor* used with *he,* and *secretary* used with *she.* Do you think it is important to avoid sexist usages? Explain.

1. Every teacher has ~~their~~ *his or her* own specialty.
2. A three-part series on local corruption won ~~their~~ *its* author a journalism award.
3. The child and her mother lost their way in the park.
4. Each employee should bring ~~his~~ *his or her* health records.
5. Someone put ~~their~~ *his or her* car in my parking space.
6. The cooperation by area labor leaders proved its effectiveness when unemployment dropped in the region.
7. The class was pleased to learn that ~~their~~ *its* assignment was postponed for a week.
8. Every lawyer hopes that his or her future holds a big, splashy case that makes the headlines.
9. Everyone has ~~his~~ *his or her* reasons for going to college.
10. Either Nicholas or my brothers will bring ~~his~~ *their* ladder.
11. The restaurant's offer of free french fries served its purpose because business improved.
12. Everybody agreed that ~~their~~ *his or her* time was well spent.
13. Anyone who wants ~~his~~ *his or her* car inspected should report to the police station on Saturday.
14. My file of financial records is missing from ~~their~~ *its* drawer.

15.9 CHAPTER REVIEW ACTIVITY

Fill in the blanks in the following passage with the correct pronouns, and circle their antecedents.

Elephants are very interesting animals. Both the African ⌐elephant¬ and the Asiatic ⌐elephant¬ can run with amazing speed when __they__ want to: up to 24 miles an hour. Surprisingly, the heaviest ⌐animal¬ of all land animals actually walks on __its__ toes, which is possible because large toe pads act as cushions. The trunk of an elephant is the longest nose of any living animal. It has 40,000 muscles and tendons. They make the trunk flexible and strong so it can pluck a single flower or lift a heavy log. Big tusks help elephants find their food. An elephant can plow up the ground with its tusks to find roots, or It can pry open tree trunks to get the soft wood inside. When water is scarce, the tusks of an elephant can drill into dry riverbeds to dig up water.

Elephants are very social and stay together in herds. A herd of elephants chooses its leader from among the old females. Female elephants in the herd are affectionate; they nuzzle each other frequently. Male elephants, however, are unpredictable—gentle and friendly one minute and violent and dangerous the next. Everybody who works in a zoo makes sure he or she is careful when working with the males.

Elephants have been subject to attack for a long time, but today a herd of elephants may be facing its greatest danger. Illegal hunters are killing these animals for their ivory tusks. Also, population increases limit the amount of land elephants can feed on, leading to starvation. Each local government or conservation group must use its influence to save these magnificent beasts.

GETTING IN GEAR

thinking in writing: Freewrite for about ten minutes on mistakes you have made and what you have learned from them. (See page 4 on how to freewrite.)

writing from experience: Tell about a time you made a mistake that taught you something important.

writing in context: American poet Nikki Giovanni has said, "Mistakes are a fact of life. It is the response to error that counts." Explain what she means and go on to agree or disagree with her.

CHAPTER 16

Other Pronoun Challenges

CHAPTER GOALS

By the end of this chapter, you will:

Avoid person shifts.

Use *this, that, these,* and *those* correctly.

Avoid unnecessary pronouns.

Avoid unclear pronoun reference.

Avoid unstated pronoun reference.

TIP

You can avoid person shift problems by remembering that *I, we,* and *you* do not substitute for nouns. *I* and *we* refer to the speaker/writer, and *you* refers to the listener/reader.

PERSON SHIFT

Use *you, your,* and *yours* only when you want to address your reader or listener directly, like this:

> *You always were a patient person.*
> *I understand your point.*
> *These books are yours.*

If you use *I, we,* or a noun, do not shift to *you,* or you will create a problem called **person shift.**

Shift from *I* to *you:*	*I prefer to study on the top floor of the library. You can really concentrate there.*
Correction:	*I prefer to study on the top floor of the library. I can really concentrate there.*
Shift from *we* to *you:*	*We have found hypnosis to be a helpful relaxation technique. You can also use it for self-improvement.*
Correction:	*We have found hypnosis to be a helpful relaxation technique. We can also use it for self-improvement.*
Shift from a noun to *you:*	*Seniors should visit the campus career center. You can learn about a variety of job options there.*
Correction:	*Seniors should visit the campus career center. They can learn about a variety of job options there.*

16.1 ACTIVITY

The passage includes eight person shifts. To eliminate the shifts, cross out each *you* that is used incorrectly, and write the correct pronoun above it.

Most colleges have many support services available to students. If students need help with a particular subject, they can visit the writing center, the reading lab, or the math lab. In addition, ~~you~~ they can go to the tutoring center for help in other subjects. Colleges offer other services as well. Students who are unsure about what to major in can visit the career services office, where ~~you~~ they can learn about marketable majors.

                                                             They
~~You~~ can also see a counselor in the counseling center and take some interest and

                                            they
aptitude tests to learn what ~~you~~ would be good at. In fact, I have an appointment there

                                 I   myself   my
this week because ~~you~~ want to learn something about ~~yourself~~ and ~~your~~ interests.

        One of the most valuable resources for students is the academic adviser, who can

          them
help ~~you~~ with difficult decisions. Thus, students are not alone. They have many

people and many resources waiting to help them.

THIS, THAT, THESE, THOSE

This, that, these, and *those* are **demonstrative pronouns,** used to point out specific people, places, objects, emotions, or ideas. Use *this* and *these* for something nearby and *that* and *those* for something farther away. In the examples below, notice that the antecedent comes *after* the verb.

TIP

For a related discussion, see page 224 on demonstrative adjectives.

Singular
Nearby: this

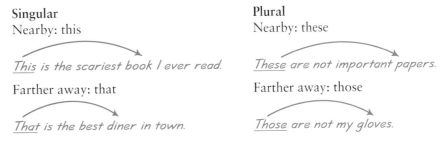

This is the scariest book I ever read.

Farther away: that

That is the best diner in town.

Plural
Nearby: these

These are not important papers.

Farther away: those

Those are not my gloves.

POWER UP

Why do you think *this, that, these,* and *those* are called *demonstrative?* If you are unsure, check a dictionary to learn the meaning and origin of the word *demonstrative.*

GRAMMAR ALERT !

Do not use *here* or *there* with a demonstrative pronoun.

No: *This here is my car.*

Yes: *This is my car.*

No: *That there is an expensive store.*

Yes: *That is an expensive store.*

Also, do not use *them* as a demonstrative pronoun.

No: *Them are the shoes I want.*

Yes: *Those [These] are the shoes I want.*

16.2 ACTIVITY

Correct the sentences by crossing out the incorrect word and writing the correct demonstrative pronoun above the line, if necessary. (In one case, more than one correction is possible.) If the sentence is correct, do nothing.

EXAMPLE
                        This
                ~~That~~ [nearby] is the car I want to buy.

          These [those]
1.   ~~Them~~ are the children who collected clothes for the homeless.
          These
2.   ~~Those~~ [near] are the shoes that hurt my feet, so I am returning them.

3.   If you ask me, these ~~here~~ are the more difficult math problems, not those ~~there.~~

4.   These [near] are the sweaters that are on sale. correct

5.   Those [far away] are beautiful flowers on the hill. correct

6. This [near] is the algebra problem we must complete for homework. correct
7. ~~That~~ This [nearby] is the person I want you to meet.

UNNECESSARY PRONOUNS

It is unnecessary (and incorrect) to use a pronoun immediately after its antecedent. Instead, use either the pronoun *or* the antecedent—not both.

No: *My <u>mother, she</u> told me to be careful.*

Yes: *My mother told me to be careful.*

Yes: *She told me to be careful.*

Notice that the comma between the antecedent and the pronoun is eliminated.

16.3 ACTIVITY

Cross out the unnecessary pronouns in the following passage.

Our government, ~~it~~ spends so much money that we are accustomed to hearing that billions of dollars are being spent on something. We are so accustomed, in fact, that we may not realize just how much a billion ~~it~~ really is. To help you appreciate the magnitude of a billion, consider this. If you wanted to count a billion dollars, one dollar at time, it would take you 32 years if you counted one dollar every second, day and night, without stopping. We know that because 32 years ~~it~~ is composed of one billion seconds. We should publish this information in the newspaper so people ~~they~~ would have a true appreciation for how much money a billion dollars is. Then, maybe citizens like us~~, we~~ would be more interested in how our legislators spend money.

CONNECT

Unclear reference can cause serious problems in business writing. For example, consider the confusion these sentences would cause in a report: "The district manager favors consolidating the sales force, and the marketing manager does not. She has good reasons for her view." Who has good reasons, the district manager or the marketing manager?

UNCLEAR REFERENCE

Unclear reference occurs when a reader cannot tell which of two antecedents a pronoun refers to. To solve the problem, change one of the pronouns to a noun. Here are two examples.

Cal was talking to Raul when he noticed the missing wallet. [Who noticed the missing wallet, Cal or Raul?]

Correction 1:   *Cal was talking to Raul when Raul noticed the missing wallet.*

Correction 2:   *Cal was talking to Raul when Cal noticed the missing wallet.*

When I placed the bowl on the glass shelf, it broke. [What broke, the shelf or the bowl?]

Correction 1:   *When I placed the bowl on the glass shelf, the bowl broke.*

Correction 2:   *When I placed the bowl on the glass shelf, the shelf broke.*

16.4 ACTIVITY

Rewrite the following sentences to solve problems of unclear reference. You will have to decide which word you want to be the antecedent. There is more than one correct answer.

215 CHAPTER 16 OTHER PRONOUN CHALLENGES

EXAMPLE   When Tom told Greg the truth, he became very angry.

When Tom told Greg the truth, Greg became very

angry.

1. Mother told Aunt Sue that her opinion was carefully thought out.

    Mother told Aunt Sue that Aunt Sue's opinion was carefully thought out.

2. Julia wanted to borrow Eleni's skirt and sweater, but she couldn't because it was at the cleaners.

    Julia wanted to borrow Eleni's skirt and sweater, but she couldn't because the skirt was

    at the cleaners.

3. When Daria saw Lizette across the math class, she smiled.

    When Daria saw Lizette across the math class, Daria smiled.

4. Senator Rodriguez introduced a fair trade bill and an education reform bill, but it had little chance of getting out of committee.

    Senator Rodriguez introduced a fair trade bill and an education reform bill, but the trade

    bill had little chance of getting out of committee.

5. The doctor urged Dad to quit smoking, but he did not think the lecture would work.

    The doctor urged Dad to quit smoking, but the doctor did not think the lecture would

    work.

6. The exterminators removed all the furniture from the attic and sprayed it to kill the fleas.

    The exterminator removed all the furniture from the attic and sprayed the attic to kill the

    fleas.

UNSTATED REFERENCE

A pronoun's antecedent must be written out, or a problem called **unstated reference** occurs.

Unstated reference occurs when *they* or *it* appears without a stated antecedent. To solve the problem, substitute a noun for the pronoun.

> *When I went to the Admissions Office, they said that the new catalogs were not ready yet.*

Who are *they*? Without an antecedent, we do not know, so we have a problem of *unstated reference*. To correct the problem, substitute a noun for the pronoun.

Correction: *When I went to the Admissions Office, the secretary said that the new catalogs were not ready yet.*

On the lid of my washer, it says not to overload the machine.

POWER UP

Unstated reference is more of a problem in writing than in speech. Why do you think this is so?

Copyright © 2002, The McGraw-Hill Companies, Inc.

What is *it?* Without an antecedent, we do not know, so we have a problem of *unstated reference.* To correct the problem, substitute a noun for the pronoun.

Correction: *On the lid of my washer, <u>the warning</u> says not to overload the machine.*

Unstated reference also occurs when the antecedent is a *form* of the intended word but is not the word itself. To correct the problem, substitute the intended form for the pronoun.

Jerry is highly motivated. <u>It</u> will help him succeed.

The intended antecedent is *motivation,* but this word does not appear; *motivated* does. To correct the problem, substitute *motivation* for the pronoun.

Correction: *Jerry is highly motivated. <u>His motivation</u> will help him succeed.*

In Hemingway's novels, <u>he</u> writes about death.

The intended antecedent is *Hemingway,* but this word does not appear; *Hemingway's* does. To correct the problem, rewrite the sentence with an antecedent that is not a possessive noun.

Correction: *In his novels, Hemingway writes about death.*

16.5 ACTIVITY

Rewrite the following sentences to correct problems with unstated reference.

EXAMPLE   Jason was very angry. It caused him to say things he did not mean.

Jason was very angry. His anger caused him to say things he did not mean.

1. Juanita has always been ambitious. It is the reason she is so competitive.

    Juanita has always been ambitious. Her ambition is the reason she is so competitive.

2. When I visited the homeless shelter, they explained that many homeless people were once part of the middle class.

    When I visited the homeless shelter, the volunteer explained that many homeless people were once part of the middle class.

3. In Billy Joel's new CD, he plays less piano than usual.

    In his new CD, Billy Joel plays less piano than usual.

4. In the restaurant, it says that no smoking is allowed.

    In the restaurant, a sign says that no smoking is allowed.

POWER UP

In speech, people often use *they* or *it* without a stated antecedent. Pay attention to the speech of others for a day or two, and record two or three examples of *they* or *it* used without a stated antecedent. Was the speaker's meaning clear? Why or why not?

5. Because exams begin next week, all my friends are tense. It is causing us to argue with each other.

    Because exams begin next week, all my friends are tense. The tension is causing us to

    argue with each other.

6. When I went to the health center, they advised me to get a flu shot.

    When I went to the health center, the nurse advised me to get a flu shot.

IF ENGLISH IS YOUR SECOND LANGUAGE

Sometimes, the use of *this*, *that*, *these*, and *those* depends on whether you are speaking in the present or the past tense.

Present tense:	*I believe <u>this</u> is important.*
Past tense:	*I believed <u>that</u> was important.*
Present tense:	*I understand <u>these</u> math problems.*
Past tense:	*I understood <u>those</u> math problems.*

RECHARGE

1. A **person shift** occurs when you refer to a noun with *I*, *we*, or *you*.

Shift:	*Skiers must have strong ankles, or <u>you</u> could hurt <u>yourself.</u>*
Correction:	*Skiers must have strong ankles, or <u>they</u> could hurt <u>themselves.</u>*

2. The **demonstrative pronouns** are *this*, *that*, *these*, and *those*.
3. Avoid using a pronoun immediately after its antecedent.

No:	*The firefighters, they deserve a pay increase.*
Yes:	*The firefighters deserve a pay increase.*

4. To avoid **unclear reference**, be sure a pronoun's antecedent is obvious.

No:	*The children asked their parents whether <u>they</u> were leaving.*
Yes:	*The children asked their parents whether <u>the parents</u> were leaving.*

5. To avoid **unstated reference**, be sure a pronoun's antecedent is written out.

No:	*I called the customer service department, and <u>they</u> said I could get a refund.*
Yes:	*I called the customer service department, and <u>a representative</u> said I could get a refund.*

GETTING IN GEAR

thinking in writing: Read an article that appears on the front page of your local or campus newspaper. Then write a page or two in your journal in response to that article.

writing from experience: Select one of the main points in the newspaper article you read and write out your reaction to that point. Try to explain why you react the way you do.

writing in context: Write a letter to the editor of the newspaper that ran the article you read. Your letter should argue a point related to the article or make an important statement about the article.

PART 4 REVIEW

Activity: Pronouns

The following passage has one incorrect possessive pronoun form, one incorrect pronoun used with a renaming word, one incorrect reflexive form, three errors in pronoun-antecedent agreement, two person shifts, two problems with demonstrative pronouns, and one unclear reference. Cross out the errors, and write the corrections above the line. (Changing the pronoun will require changing the verb in one case.)

Everyone in the United States says, "hello" when ~~they answer~~ ^{he or she answers} the telephone. In fact, this ~~here~~ greeting is so common that most people assume it has always been used. ~~You~~ ^{They} would be surprised to learn that the greeting is newer than ~~you~~ ^{they} think. The use of "hello" as a telephone greeting has ~~their~~ ^{its} first recorded use in 1883. Even then, it was not a shoo-in for the greeting. It competed with other options. Alexander Graham Bell ~~hisself~~ ^{himself} favored "ahoy."

The term "hello" has ~~it's~~ ^{its} origins in the form "hallo," which dates to 1840 and is a cry of surprise. "Hallo," in turn, is related to "halloo," a cry to urge on hunting dogs. ~~Us~~ ^{We} frequent users of hello may be interested in the fact that "halloo" dates to about 1700, but a variant, "aloo," appears in Shakespeare's *King Lear* a century earlier than that. ~~It~~ ^{"Haloo"} has an earlier variant—in 1588, Shakespeare used "hollo" in *Titus Andronicus*. The word group that predates "hello" also has ~~their~~ ^{its} cognates in Germanic languages, and ~~them~~ ^{those} may be words that also form part of the history of "hello."

The next time you greet someone on the phone, think about the history of the word you use to do so.

Activity: Pronouns

The following passage has one pronoun used incorrectly in a comparison, six errors in pronoun-antecedent agreement, one sexist pronoun, one incorrect demonstrative pronoun, one unnecessary pronoun, and one problem with unstated reference. Cross out the errors and make the corrections above the line. (Twice, changing the pronoun requires changing the verb.)

Perhaps you know more about state laws than ~~me~~ ^I, but if not, you will be surprised to learn some of the wacky laws on the books. For example, in Vermont, everyone must take one bath a week—on Saturday night (whether ~~they need~~ ^{he or she needs} it or not). Furthermore, people~~, they~~ cannot whistle underwater. In Michigan, a woman is not allowed to cut ~~their~~ ^{her} own hair without ~~their~~ ^{her} husband's permission. Also, any person over the age of 12 may own a handgun as long as ~~he~~ ^{he or she} has not been convicted of a felony. In Alaska, ~~they~~ ^{people} may not view moose from an airplane or push a live moose from a plane. In California, women in housecoats may not drive ~~her~~ ^{their} cars, nor may any vehicles without a driver have their speed exceed 60 miles per hour. In North Carolina, neither men nor women can plow ~~his or her~~ their fields with elephants or sing off key. A woman with a sweet tooth may want to move to Idaho, where a man may not give ~~their~~ his sweetheart a box of candy under 50 pounds. ~~This is~~ These are some bizarre laws, I must say.

Understanding Modifiers and Prepositions

PART FIVE

CHAPTER **17**

Adjectives, Adverbs, and Articles

CHAPTER GOALS

By the end of this chapter, you will:

Use adjectives and adverbs correctly.

Use demonstrative adjectives correctly.

Use *good* and *well* correctly.

Use *a, an,* and *the* correctly.

Avoid double negatives.

Use comparative and superlative forms correctly.

ADJECTIVES

Adjectives describe nouns and pronouns.

Spicy chili is my favorite food. [Spicy is an adjective because it describes the noun *chili*. *Favorite* is an adjective because it describes the noun *food*.]

He is hot and thirsty. [Both *hot* and *thirsty* are adjectives because they describe the pronoun *he*.]

Linking verbs (see page 58) cannot be described. Therefore, *hot* and *thirsty* must describe *he*.

17.1 ACTIVITY

CONNECT

Adjectives can be critical on the job. For example, when social workers and psychologists write case studies and notes about clients, descriptive words add precision. A psychologist might refer to "*agitated* behavior," and a social worker might note an "*impoverished* background." Police officers also choose words carefully when writing up incident reports: Was the behavior of the accused "violent" or "unruly"? It makes a difference.

Fill in each blank in the following sentences with an adjective. Then draw an arrow to the noun or pronoun it describes.

EXAMPLE   The _____*green*_____ car belongs to Chris.

1. That ___chipped_____ vase has been in our family for five generations.

2. My ___older_____ brother attends school in Michigan.

3. Carla gave David a(n) ___wool_____ sweater for his birthday.

4. You are very ___patient._____

5. I cooked a(n) ___excellent_____ dinner that included ___baked_____ chicken and ___mashed_____ potatoes.

17.2 INDIVIDUAL OR GROUP ACTIVITY

Alone or with two classmates list on a separate sheet every word you can think of to describe *child* (words such as *young, happy,* and *crying*). The words in your list will be adjectives.

DEMONSTRATIVE ADJECTIVES

When they describe nouns, *this, that, these,* and *those* are **demonstrative adjectives.** *This* and *that* are used with singular nouns, and *these* and *those* are used with plural nouns. Use **this** and **these** for people and objects that are nearby. Use **that** and **those** for people and objects that are farther away.

Singular	Plural
Nearby: *this*	Nearby: *these*
Farther away: *that*	Farther away: *those*

Singular: *This coat* [nearby]*is too small, but that coat* [farther away]*is fine.*

Plural: *These crackers* [nearby]*are fresh, but those cookies* [farther away]*are stale.*

GRAMMAR ALERT !

Them does not substitute for *this, that, these,* or *those.*

No: *Them shoes are an unusual color.*

Yes: *These shoes are an unusual color.*

Yes: *Those shoes are an unusual color.*

17.3 ACTIVITY

Write a sentence combining *this, that, these,* or *those* with the word given. Use *this, that, these,* and *those* one time each.

EXAMPLE tree *This tree offers excellent shade.*

1. child This child may have chicken pox.

2. houses The real estate agent hopes to sell those houses before summer.

3. movie That movie was too violent for Erica.

4. people These people have opened a coffeehouse near campus.

ADVERBS

Adverbs describe verbs, adjectives, or other adverbs. Adverbs often end in *-ly.*

CONNECT

Adverbs are important components of sports writing, in phrases such as these: "Won *handily,*" "beat *soundly,*" and "ran *brilliantly.*"

An adverb describing a verb: *You sing beautifully.*
An adverb describing an adjective: *Your suit is extremely attractive.*
An adverb describing another adverb: *Sheila speaks very loudly.*

Adverbs often tell *how, when,* or *where.*

An adverb telling *how:* *Your dress is very short.* [*Very* tells how short.]
An adverb telling *when:* *Jack arrived late.* [*Late* tells when Jack arrived.]
An adverb telling *where:* *I fell down.* [*Down* tells where I fell.]

17.4 INDIVIDUAL OR GROUP ACTIVITY

Alone or with two classmates, list on a separate sheet every word you can think of to describe *walking* (words such as *slowly, briskly,* and *clumsily*). These words will be adverbs.

17.5 ACTIVITY

Circle each adverb in the following sentences, and draw an arrow to the verb, adjective, or adverb it describes. Then, in the blank, write whether the adverb tells *how, when,* or *where.*

EXAMPLE   The lecturer spoke slowly. _____*how*_____

1. The car is traveling quickly. _how_____

2. These shoes are very old. _how_____

3. The teacher happily answered my questions. _how_____

4. Alex rotated my tires yesterday. _when_____

5. Please leave my books here. _where_____

17.6 ACTIVITY

Circle the descriptive words in the following sentences and draw arrows to the words they describe. Above each descriptive word, write "ADJ" if the word is an adjective or "ADV" if the word is an adverb.

EXAMPLE   *ADJ* Loud thunder frightens me *ADV* badly.

1. *ADJ* Happy children are playing *ADV* outside.

2. *ADJ* Rare books were discovered *ADV* yesterday.

3. You are *ADV* extremely *ADJ* talented.

4. Someone is playing music *ADV* too *ADV* loudly.

5. She politely asks very difficult questions.
   ADV   ADV   ADJ

6. Excellent grades earned you valuable scholarships.
   ADJ   ADJ

-Ly Adverbs

Many descriptive words have both an adjective form and an adverb form. The adverb form ends in *-ly*.

Adjective—Describes Nouns and Pronouns	**Adverb**—Describes Verbs, Adjectives, and Adverbs
slow: *The slow dance ended.*	slowly: *We walked slowly.*
happy: *She is a happy girl.*	happily: *He smiled happily.*
angry: *The father was angry.*	angrily: *I motioned angrily.*
quick: *Let's make a quick stop.*	quickly: *She ran quickly.*
loud: *Turn down the loud music.*	loudly: *You speak loudly.*

GRAMMAR ALERT !

Be sure to use the adverb (*-ly*) form to describe verbs.

No: *Jan drove careful down the icy road.*

Yes: *Jan drove carefully down the icy road.*

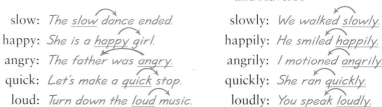

> **POWER UP**
>
> Choose a paragraph from the sports pages, strike out all the adjectives and adverbs, and read it back without them. What do adjectives and adverbs contribute to writing?

17.7 ACTIVITY

If a noun or pronoun is described, fill in the blank with the first form in parentheses, which is an adjective. If a verb, an adjective, or an adverb is described, fill in the blank with the *-ly* form, which is an adverb. Then draw an arrow to the word described.

EXAMPLE   (slow, slowly)   The _____*slow*_____ music relaxed me.

1. (eager, eagerly)   The little boy _eagerly_____ jumped on Santa Claus's lap.

2. (quick, quickly)   I drove _quickly_____ to the store to get the aspirin for Bryna's headache.

3. (fearful, fearfully)   During the storm, Henry was _fearful_____ that lightning would strike the old oak tree.

4. (extreme, extremely)   Please be careful with that pitcher because it is _extremely_____ old.

5. (thoughtful, thoughtfully)   Henri gazed _thoughtfully_____ at his essay as he considered his revision.

6. (silent, silently)   The _silent_____ congregation listened to the minister's sermon.

7. (graceful, gracefully)   The _graceful_____ dancer twirled effortlessly.

8. (comfortable, comfortably)   In the middle of the sofa, Carmen

sat _comfortably_ .

9. (quiet, quietly)   At midnight, I tiptoed through the

quiet house.

10. (real, really)   After working all day, Julio was _really_ tired.

On a separate sheet, write sentences using the given adjectives and adverbs correctly.

1. loud   4. seriously
2. loudly   5. painful
3. serious   6. painfully

GOOD AND WELL

Many writers confuse *good* and *well*.

Good is an adjective, so it usually describes nouns.

Salvadore is a good writer. [*Good* describes the noun *writer*.]

A good friend is a treasure. [*Good* describes the noun *friend*.]

Good is often used as an adjective after the words *taste*, *feel*, and *look*.

This chicken tastes good. [*Good* describes the noun *chicken*.]

A cotton sweater always feels good. [*Good* describes the noun *sweater*.]

Jake looks good today. [*Good* describes the noun *Jake*.]

Well is an adverb, so it usually describes verbs.

Janice explains things well. [*Well* describes the verb *explains* by telling how.]

I am sure I did well on the examination. [*Well* describes the verb *did* by telling how.]

Well is also an adjective, but only when it means "healthy."

I do not feel well today.   *Harry felt well enough to join us.*

Fill in the blanks in the following sentences with *good* or *well*.

EXAMPLE   After years of practice, I play piano _____*well*_____ .

1. The children behaved very _well_ at the museum.

2. You look very _good_ in that color.

3. The stew tastes _good_ now that you have added salt.

4. Julia speaks Spanish _well_ enough to use it on her trip to Mexico.

5. After his fourth piece of fudge, Uri did not feel __well__ .

6. Zachary looks __good__ even though he has been sick.

7. How __well__ did you understand this morning's psychology lecture?

8. This is a __good__ opportunity to visit Uncle Ike.

9. These new shoes feel __good__ on my tired feet.

10. Sandy gets along __well__ with all kinds of people.

ARTICLES—A AND AN

A and **an** are special adjectives called **articles.**

   Use *a* and *an* to mean *one*. Use *an* before a word that begins with a vowel sound (*a, e, i, o,* and *u*). Use *a* before a word that does not begin with a vowel sound. Here are some examples.

Vowel Sound	No Vowel Sound
an orange	a bat
an apple	a deer
an eagle	a pizza
an old scar	a new umbrella

Sometimes the letter *u* has a vowel sound, and sometimes it does not have one. Use *a* and *an* accordingly.

Vowel Sound	No Vowel Sound
an umpire	a unicorn
an uncle	a union
an understanding	a unit

Use *a* when the letter *h* is pronounced, and *an* when it is silent.

Vowel Sound	No Vowel Sound
an honor	a heart
an hour	a helmet

17.10 ACTIVITY

Place *a* or *an* (whichever is correct) in front of each of the following words or phrases, and use the phrase in a sentence.

EXAMPLE   ___an___ island *Most people know that Manhattan is an island.*

1. __an__ ironing board Why is there an ironing board in the middle of the living room?

2. __a__ book I bought Grandma Martinez a book for her birthday.

3. an uncertain future <u>If you drop out of school, you will have an uncertain future.</u>

4. an honest person <u>An honest person would return that wallet.</u>

5. a unique experience <u>Traveling across the country with Leo is a unique experience.</u>

6. an ugly coat <u>Why did you pay so much money for such an ugly coat?</u>

7. a hard problem <u>You have a hard problem, and I do not know how to help you.</u>

8. an honor <u>It is an honor to meet such a distinguished faculty member.</u>

DOUBLE NEGATIVES

The following words are **negatives** because they communicate the idea of *no.*

no	none	hardly
not	nowhere	scarcely
no one	nobody	
never	nothing	

Contractions often include the negative *not.*

can't = cannot	don't = do not
won't = will not	wouldn't = would not
shouldn't = should not	couldn't = could not

Use only *one* negative to express a negative idea.

No (two negatives):   *You <u>can't</u> bring <u>no</u> friend.*
 Yes (one negative):   *You <u>can't</u> bring a friend.*

No (two negatives):   *I <u>won't</u> do <u>nothing</u>.*
 Yes (one negative):   *I <u>won't</u> do anything.*
 Yes (one negative):   *I will do <u>nothing</u>.*

No (two negatives):   *He <u>doesn't</u> go <u>nowhere</u>.*
 Yes (one negative):   *He <u>doesn't</u> go anywhere.*
 Yes (one negative):   *He goes <u>nowhere</u>.*

GRAMMAR ALERT

Remember that *hardly* and *scarcely* are negatives.

 No (two negatives):   *I <u>can't hardly</u> hear you.*
 Yes (one negative):   *I can <u>hardly</u> hear you.*
 Yes (one negative):   *I can<u>not</u> hear you.*

No (two negatives):	*I can't scarcely believe it.*
Yes (one negative):	*I can't believe it.*
Yes (one negative):	*I can scarcely believe it.*

17.11 ACTIVITY

Rewrite the following sentences to eliminate the double negatives.

EXAMPLE I won't do no work now.

I won't do any work now.

1. I asked a question, but I didn't get no answer.

    I asked a question, but I didn't get an answer.

2. These people will not never do what we ask.

    These people will never do what we ask.

3. The audience in the balcony couldn't hardly see the stage.

    The audience in the balcony could hardly see the stage.

4. You can't go nowhere without me.

    You can't go anywhere without me.

5. Since Catherine moved, I scarcely never see her anymore.

    Since Catherine moved, I scarcely see her anymore.

6. I don't know nothing about fixing cars.

    I know nothing about fixing cars.

COMPARING TWO THINGS—COMPARATIVE FORMS

Adjectives and adverbs describe.

Paul runs fast. [*Fast* describes *runs*.]
Nuha is young. [*Young* describes *Nuha*.]

However, adjectives and adverbs let writers and speakers do more than describe. They also have forms that let us show how two things compare to each other. These forms are called the **comparative**. Here are two examples.

Paul runs faster than Nigel. [The speeds of Paul and Nigel are compared.]
Nuha is younger than Sue. [The ages of Nuha and Sue are compared.]

To form the comparative of one-syllable adjectives and adverbs, add *-er*.

Adjective or Adverb	Comparative
slow	slower
tall	taller
weak	weaker

SPELLING ALERT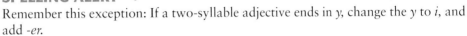

Sometimes the last letter is doubled before the *-er* is added. Thus, the comparative form of *thin* is *thinner*. If you are unsure of a spelling, check your dictionary or Chapter 23.

Use *more* to form the comparative of most adjectives and adverbs with two or more syllables.

Adjective or Adverb	Comparative
important	more important
slowly	more slowly
usual	more usual

SPELLING ALERT

Remember this exception: If a two-syllable adjective ends in *y*, change the *y* to *i*, and add *-er*.

Adjective	Comparative
easy	easier
friendly	friendlier
happy	happier

GRAMMAR ALERT

Never use the *-er* comparative form with *more*.

No: *I am more hungrier than a bear.*

Yes: *I am hungrier than a bear.*

No: *Be more carefuler next time.*

Yes: *Be more careful next time.*

17.12 ACTIVITY

Next to each adjective or adverb below, write the correct comparative form. If you are unsure about the spelling, check a dictionary.

EXAMPLES lonely _____lonelier_____   important _____more important_____

1. slow   slower
2. annoyed   more annoyed
3. big   bigger
4. angry   angrier
5. foolish   more foolish
6. lucky   luckier

7. young   younger
8. quickly   more quickly
9. beautiful more beautiful
10. careful more careful
11. fat   fatter
12. valuable more valuable

17.13 ACTIVITY

Fill in each blank in the following sentences with the correct comparative form of the adjective or adverb in parentheses.

EXAMPLE   (handsome)   Lionel gets ___*more handsome*___ every time I see him.

1. (fancy)   Chez Henri's is a _fancier_____ restaurant than Armando's.

2. (wide)   We will never get the box through the door because the box is
   _wider_____ than I thought.

3. (interesting)   The senior class play is _more interesting_____ than anyone thought it would be.

4. (rapidly)   We arrived early because we traveled _more rapidly_____ than anticipated.

5. (lucky)   Joel has purchased two winning lottery tickets in the last year; no one is _luckier_____ than he is.

6. (focused)   Dorothy's grades improved this semester because she is
   _more focused_____ on her studies than she was last semester.

7. (funny)   This comedian is _funnier_____ than the one we heard at the comedy club last Saturday.

COMPARING MORE THAN TWO THINGS— SUPERLATIVE FORMS

Adjectives and adverbs have forms that are used to compare more than two things. These forms are called the **superlative.** Here are two examples.

Paul is the fastest runner on the team. [The speeds of more than two runners are compared.]

Nuha is the youngest of three children. [The ages of three children are compared.]

To form the superlative of one-syllable adjectives and adverbs, add *-est.*

Adjective or Adverb	Superlative
hard	hardest
loud	loudest
slow	slowest

SPELLING ALERT

Sometimes the last letter is doubled before the *-est* is added. Thus, the superlative form of *thin* is *thinnest.* If you are unsure of a spelling, check a dictionary or Chapter 23.

Use *most* to form the superlative of most adjectives and adverbs with two or more syllables.

Adjective or Adverb	Superlative
freely	most freely
intelligent	most intelligent
understanding	most understanding

CONNECT

Comparing two or more things is an important component of critical thinking and analysis. We compare cars before we buy them, we compare political candidates before we vote, and we compare poems in literature class. Comparative and superlative forms of modifiers are integral to the process. For example, we might say that the Chevy gets the *best* gas mileage, and the Ford is *cheaper* than the Toyota.

SPELLING ALERT

Remember this exception: If a two-syllable adjective ends in -*y*, change the *y* to *i*, and add -*est*.

Adjective	Superlative
friendly	friendliest
heavy	heaviest

GRAMMAR ALERT !

Never use the -*est* superlative form with *most*.

No: *Ian is the <u>most friendliest</u> person on campus.*

Yes: *Ian is the <u>friendliest</u> person on campus.*

No: *Biology is my <u>most importantest</u> class this term.*

Yes: *Biology is my <u>most important</u> class this term.*

17.14 ACTIVITY

Next to each adjective or adverb in the list below, write the correct superlative form.

EXAMPLES   easy _____*easiest*_____   desirable _____*most desirable*_____

1. angry   _angriest_   7. happy   _happiest_

2. loudly   _most loudly_   8. tired   _most tired_

3. short   _shortest_   9. smart   _smartest_

4. important   _most important_   10. completely   _most completely_

5. careful   _most careful_   11. cautiously   _most cautiously_

6. careless   _most careless_   12. fast   _fastest_

17.15 ACTIVITY

Fill in each blank in the following sentences with the correct superlative form of the adjective or adverb in parentheses.

EXAMPLE   (successful)   Lou is the ___*most successful*___ quarterback in the school's history.

1. (fair)   Dr. Petrakis has a reputation for being one of the _fairest_ professors on campus.

2. (deadly)   The venom of the brown recluse spider is one of the _deadliest_ poisons in nature.

3. (deep)   Fully clothed, the young child jumped into the _deepest_ section of the pool.

4. (annoyed)   This is the _most annoyed_ I have ever seen you.

5. (ambitious)   Jamal is the _most ambitious_ employee in the accounting department.

6. (fiercely)   Of everyone on the gymnastics squad, Gwen competes the

<u>most fiercely</u>   .

Write a sentence according to the directions given for each item below.

EXAMPLE   Use the comparative form of *moody:*

Helen has been moodier since Miguel left town.

1.   Use the comparative form of *quiet:*

quieter

2.   Use the comparative form of *wise:*

wiser

3.   Use the comparative form of *cheaply:*

more cheaply

4.   Use the comparative form of *important:*

morc important

5.   Use the superlative form of *seriously:*

most seriously

6.   Use the superlative form of *clear:*

clearest

7.   Use the superlative form of *old:*

oldest

8.   Use the superlative form of *difficult:*

most difficult

COMPARING TWO OR MORE THINGS USING GOOD, WELL, BAD, AND BADLY

The comparative and superlative forms of *good, well, bad,* and *badly* are irregular. If you are unsure about these forms, check the following list when you use them.

CONNECT

An excellent way to study is to write your reactions, insights, and questions in the margins of your books. When you do, note how critical the adjectives and adverbs are, as you write things like "*surprising* statistics," "*weak* example," and "*strongly* agree."

Adjective or Adverb	Comparative	Superlative
good	better	best
I had a good time.	*I had a better time last week.*	*I had the best time ever.*
well	better	best
He sings well.	*He sings better than I.*	*He is the best singer in the choir.*
bad	worse	worst
Karl had a bad idea.	*Karl's idea is worse than mine.*	*Karl's idea is the worst ever.*
badly	worse	worst
My back aches badly.	*My back aches worse than yours.*	*My back aches the worst of all.*

GRAMMAR ALERT !

Avoid *worser* in the speech and writing you use in college and on the job.

No: *I feel worser today than yesterday.*

Yes: *I feel worse today than yesterday.*

GRAMMAR ALERT !

Do not use *more* or *most* with the comparative and superlative forms.

No: *Jake's job is more better than yours.*

Yes: *Jake's job is better than yours.*

17.17 ACTIVITY

Fill in the blank in each of the following sentences with the correct comparative or superlative form of the adjective or adverb in parentheses.

EXAMPLE   (good)   Joanna likes rap music _____*better*_____ than alternative rock.

1. (good)   Professor Antonucci is the __*best*_____ teacher in the psychology department.

2. (well)   Mark pitches fast balls __*better*_____ than he pitches curve balls.

3. (bad)   I rewrote my introduction, but I think it is __*worse*_____ than the first version.

4. (badly)   Carol played the guitar __*worse*_____ after she sprained her wrist.

5. (good)   Business is __*better*_____ now that the store has lowered its prices.

6. (bad)   This production of *Hamlet* is the __*worst*_____ I have ever seen.

7. (well) Of all the people in the class, Kwame translates French

poetry <u>best.</u>

8. (good) You have always been the <u>best</u> bridge player in the
group because you never lose your concentration.

 IF ENGLISH IS YOUR SECOND LANGUAGE

In English, **count nouns** name persons, places, objects, emotions, or ideas that can be counted; that is, you can put a number in front of them. They include words such as these:

apple	car	girl	shoe
book	fear	hand	teacher
boy	friend	lake	tree

Yes: *one apple*

Yes: *three friends*

Noncount nouns name things that cannot be counted; that is, you cannot put a number in front of them. They include words such as these:

| air | furniture | honesty | pride |
| cereal | health | luggage | water |

1. Use *a* or *an* with a singular count noun whose specific identity is unknown to the reader, usually because it has not yet been mentioned.

   Jeff hired <u>a</u> tutor to help him with math. ["Tutor" is being mentioned for the first time; the specific identity is unknown.]

2. Use *the* before a singular count noun whose identity is known to the reader.

   Jeff hired Pilar to help him with math. <u>The</u> tutor charges ten dollars an hour. [The identity of the tutor is known to be "Pilar."]

3. Never use *a* or *an* with plural nouns.

   No: *I enjoy <u>an</u> eggs for breakfast.*
   Yes: *I enjoy eggs for breakfast.*

4. Never use *a* or *an* with noncount nouns.

   No: *I helped Henri move <u>a</u> furniture.*
   Yes: *I helped Henri move <u>the</u> furniture.*
   Yes: *I helped Henri move furniture.*

5. Use *the* with noncount nouns that name representatives of a larger group.

   No: *<u>A</u> coffee is very good at this restaurant.*
   Yes: *<u>The</u> coffee is very good at this restaurant.*

6. Use *the* to point out something specific.

   No: *<u>A</u> new major in hotel management is popular.*
   Yes: *<u>The</u> new major in hotel management is popular.*

Noncount nouns are also discussed on page 142.

RECHARGE

1. **Adjectives** describe nouns and pronouns, and **adverbs** describe, verbs, adjectives, and other adverbs.

   - The **demonstrative adjectives** are *this, that, these,* and *those.*
   - Adverbs often end in *-ly.*

2. *Good* is an adjective. It is often used after *taste, feel,* and *look. Well* is an adverb, unless it means "healthy"; then it is an adjective.

   You had a good idea.
   I always feel good after I exercise.
   Marta plays the piano well.
   I feel well, although I did not sleep last night.

3. *A* and *an* are **articles.** Use *an* before words that begin with a vowel sound, and use *a* with words that do not begin with a vowel sound.

4. Avoid **double negatives.**

5. Use the **comparative form** of adjectives and adverbs to compare two things; use the **superlative form** to compare more than two things.

17.18 CHAPTER REVIEW ACTIVITY

On a separate sheet, write sentences as directed.

1. Add adjectives and adverbs (whichever is appropriate) to describe the underlined words. Label each word you add as an adjective or adverb.

   EXAMPLE   The <u>child</u> <u>cried</u>.

             adj.   *adv.*
   The young child cried hysterically.

   A. A <u>storm</u> <u>is making</u> its way up the coast.
   B. The <u>business</u> needed a <u>loan</u> for <u>repairs</u> to its <u>plant.</u>
   C. The radio was playing <u>loudly</u> in the <u>room.</u>
   D. After the <u>concert,</u> the <u>performers</u> <u>waited</u> for their car to drive them to the <u>airport.</u>
   E. At noon, Professor Torres will give a(n) <u>lecture</u> on the results of his <u>research.</u>

2. Write sentences using the following words.
   A. *quiet*
   B. *quietly*
   C. *random*
   D. *randomly*
   E. *good*
   F. *well* (the adjective)
   G. *well* (the adverb)
   H. the comparative form of *graceful*
   I. the superlative form of *ugly*
   J. the comparative form of *good*

K. the comparative form of *well*
L. the superlative form of *bad*
M. the superlative form of *badly*

17.19 CHAPTER REVIEW ACTIVITY

Cross out the 12 incorrect forms in the following passage, and where necessary make corrections above the line.

The ~~more~~ healthier you are, the ~~more~~ better you can achieve all the objectives in your life. This is the reason that the fitness industry has become a multimillion-dollar business. Nonetheless, peak cardiovascular fitness may not be best for ~~no one~~ ^{someone} who wants to be ~~a~~ ^{an} astronaut, according to a study done at the University of Texas Southwestern Medical Center in Dallas.

Endurance athletes who are ~~high~~ ^{highly} trained develop hearts with different mechanical properties than those of less active people. As a result, their hearts fill with and pump out blood ~~different~~. ^{differently} It seems that ~~them~~ ^{these} endurance athletes respond ~~worser~~ ^{worse} to the reduced pressure conditions of no gravity than others do. In ~~a~~ ^{an} unusual experiment, athletes who ran 50 miles a week or cycled 250 miles a week were studied in a special tank which reduced the pressure on their lower bodies. When scientists studied the preliminary data, they were very surprised. The findings suggest that endurance athletes have a ~~more~~ larger decrease in the volume of blood pushed out with each heartbeat than less active people, which makes them unfit for space travel. Thus you won't ~~never~~ ^{ever} travel in space if you're ~~more~~ fitter than you need to be.

GETTING IN GEAR

thinking in writing: Think of a person who has played or currently plays an important role in your life. Write a list of words and phrases that describe that person.

writing from experience: Write a description of the person you selected for the previous activity.

writing in context: Assume the person who has played an important role in your life is being honored at an awards banquet and that you have been asked to deliver the testimonial speech. Write that speech.

CHAPTER 18

Using Participles and Infinitives to Describe

TIP

For a more detailed discussion of the present participle, see page 174.

TIP

For a more detailed discussion of the past participle, see page 159.

USING PARTICIPLES AND INFINITIVES TO DESCRIBE

The **present participle** is the *-ing* form of a verb. Thus, present participles are words such as these:

dancing	eating	loving	swimming	wanting
doing	going	seeing	walking	winning

Although the present participle is a verb form, it can function as an adjective by describing nouns and pronouns. Here are two examples.

Whistling, Joy walked past the cemetery. [*Whistling* describes *Joy.*]

Smiling, I told a joke I heard yesterday. [*Smiling* describes *I.*]

The present participle can be combined with other words to form a phrase that describes.

Whistling a familiar tune, Joy walked past the cemetery.

Smiling broadly, I told a joke I heard yesterday.

PUNCTUATION ALERT

As the previous examples show, you should place a comma after a participle or a participle phrase that comes at the beginning of a sentence.

The **past participle** is the *-ed* form of a regular verb. Thus, past participles are words such as these:

danced	helped	moved	started
feared	loved	solved	wanted

Some past participles are irregular. Instead of being formed with *-ed*, they are formed in a variety of ways. Here are some examples.

broken	found	seen	swollen
eaten	gone	spent	worn

Although the past participle is a verb form, it can function as an adjective when it describes nouns and pronouns. Here are some examples.

Helen put her tired feet on the sofa. [*Tired* describes *feet.*]

The child was exhausted. [*Exhausted* describes *child.*]

Annoyed, I refused to answer the question. [*Annoyed* describes *I.*]

The past participle can be combined with other words to form a phrase that describes.

Helen put her very tired feet on the sofa.

The child was exhausted from the picnic.

Instantly annoyed, I refused to answer the question.

PUNCTUATION ALERT ❗

Place a comma after a past participle or a past participle phrase that comes at the beginning of a sentence.

The **infinitive** is the *to* and the base form of the verb. Thus, infinitives are forms such as these:

to jump	to sing	to help	to run
to feel	to taste	to be	to realize

Although the infinitive is a verb form, it can function as an adjective by describing nouns and pronouns or as an adverb by describing verbs. Here are some examples.

The restaurant to try is The Lobster House. [*To try* describes *restaurant.*]

To illustrate, I will draw you a picture. [*To illustrate* describes *will draw.*]

The infinitive can be combined with other words to form a phrase that describes.

The restaurant to try as soon as possible is The Lobster House.

To illustrate my point, I will draw you a picture.

PUNCTUATION ALERT ❗

Place a comma after an infinitive or an infinitive phrase that comes at the beginning of a sentence *only* when it describes.

Infinitive describes: *To avoid a penalty, pay your bill now.*

Infinitive does not describe;
    it is the sentence subject: *To leave now is rude.*

POWER UP

Beginning sentences with present participles, past participles, and infinitives is a good way to vary sentence structure and create a fluid style. Find examples of sentences that begin with present participles, past participles, and infinitives in a magazine or newspaper. Do they make the passage more effective?

18.1 ACTIVITY

Combine the following sentence pairs into one sentence. First, change one sentence to a present participle or a present participle phrase. Then, join it to the beginning of the remaining sentence. Remember to use a comma after a participle or a participle phrase at the beginning of a sentence. (The sentences can be written more than one way.)

EXAMPLES   The bride and groom danced a waltz.
    They gazed into each other's eyes.

Gazing into each other's eyes, the bride and groom danced

a waltz.

or

Dancing a waltz, the bride and groom gazed into each other's eyes.

1. The wide receiver ran into the end zone.
   He was grinning.

   Grinning, the wide receiver ran into the end zone.

2. The child ran home immediately.
   He heard his mother call.

   Hearing his mother call, the child ran home immediately.

3. The storm was gathering force.
   It was approaching our town.

   Approaching our town, the storm was gathering force.

4. Carlos prepared to study.
   He sharpened his pencil and opened his book.

   Preparing to study, Carlos sharpened his pencil and opened his book.

5. The puppy ran in circles.
   He chased his tail.

   Chasing his tail, the puppy ran in circles.

6. Juliane told the waiter to take back her steak.
   She complained loudly.

   Complaining loudly, Juliane told the waiter to take back her steak.

7. Our car turned 360 degrees.
   It was sliding on the ice.

   Sliding on the ice, our car turned 360 degrees.

8. Stavros and Don stood on the street corner.
   They were waiting for a bus.

   Waiting for a bus, Stavros and Don stood on the street corner.

18.2 INDIVIDUAL OR GROUP ACTIVITY

Alone or with two classmates, add a present participle or a present participle phrase at the beginning of each sentence.

EXAMPLE   _Slurping loudly_ , Sue drank her coffee.

1.   Talking in the theater , Jonathan disturbed everyone nearby.

2.   Swerving wildly , the car narrowly missed striking a pedestrian.

3.   Whistling to myself , I strolled through the park.

4.   Shouting insults , Jan stormed out of the room.

5.   Gasping for breath , the marathon runner fell across the finish line.

6.   Offering encouragement , the instructor handed out the examination questions.

18.3 ACTIVITY

Combine each pair of sentences below by placing the underlined past participle or past participle phrase next to the word it describes. Remember to place a comma after a past participle or a past participle phrase at the beginning of a sentence.

CONNECT

Activity 18.3 asks you to combine two sentences into one for greater *economy* (brevity). In what writing contexts is economy an asset? Think about writing you do for different classes and writing you do (or will do) at work.

EXAMPLES   The children found all the Easter eggs.
The Easter eggs were <u>hidden in the grass.</u>

The children found all the Easter eggs hidden in the grass.

I didn't know what to do.
I was <u>torn in two directions.</u>

Torn in two directions, I didn't know what to do.

1. I decided to take a nap.
I was <u>tired after work.</u>

Tired after work, I decided to take a nap.

2. Frank threw the shirt away.
The shirt was <u>torn.</u>

Frank threw away the torn shirt.

3. Mrs. Chung gasped.
She was <u>surprised by what she saw.</u>

Surprised by what she saw, Mrs. Chung gasped.

4. Diane ran out of the room.
She was <u>embarrassed.</u>

<u>   Embarrassed, Diane ran out of the room.   </u>

5. We all admired the silver.
The silver was <u>brightly polished.</u>

<u>   We all admired the brightly polished silver.   </u>

6. The mother soothed the child.
The child was <u>distressed.</u>

<u>   The mother soothed the distressed child.   </u>

7. The cat arched its back and hissed.
The cat was <u>angered.</u>

<u>   The angered cat arched its back and hissed.   </u>

8. I could not sleep.
I was <u>worried about my job interview in the morning.</u>

<u>   Worried about my job interview in the morning, I could not sleep.   </u>

18.4 ACTIVITY

Select five of the following past participles or past participle phrases. On a separate sheet, write five sentences, each using one of your selections. In each sentence, draw an arrow to the noun or pronoun described by the past participle or the past participle phrase. Remember to place a comma after a past participle or a past participle phrase at the beginning of a sentence.

EXAMPLE   exhausted

<u>   *Exhausted, Lou fell asleep in the chair.*   </u>

determined to improve	hidden in the bushes
disgusted	neatly written
excited by the news	overheated
frozen solid	worried about the test

18.5 ACTIVITY

Combine each pair of sentences below by placing the infinitive or infinitive phrase in the second sentence at the beginning of the first sentence. Remember to use commas.

EXAMPLE   I set the alarm for six A.M.
I set the alarm to wake up early.

To wake up early, I set the alarm for six a.m.

1. Gloria hired a tutor.
   She hired a tutor to get better grades.

   To get better grades, Gloria hired a tutor.

2. You must score three more points.
   You must score the points to win.

   To win, you must score three more points.

3. Eduardo made an appointment with his adviser.
   He made the appointment to discuss changing his major.

   To discuss changing his major, Eduardo made an appointment with his adviser.

4. Mike and Catherine gave a big party.
   They gave the party to celebrate their engagement.

   To celebrate their engagement, Mike and Catherine gave a big party.

5. Fred questioned the student council candidates.
   He questioned them to learn their positions on the issues.

   To learn their positions on the issues, Fred questioned the student council candidates.

6. I painted the bedroom yellow.
   I painted it to make it more cheerful.

   To make it more cheerful, I painted the bedroom yellow.

18.6 ACTIVITY

Add an infinitive or an infinitive phrase to the beginning of each of the following sentences. Remember to use commas.

EXAMPLE   *To make the opening more interesting,* I revised the introduction of my essay.

1. To arrive on time, you will have to hurry.

2. To graduate in June, I must take another humanities course.

3. To improve her tennis game, _____ Cassie practiced three hours every day.

4. To prepare for company, _____ we cleaned the house thoroughly.

5. To gather evidence, _____ the police questioned all the suspects.

AVOID DANGLING MODIFIERS

If you fail to provide a logical word for a participle or infinitive to describe, you have a problem called a **dangling modifier.**

Knowing the answer, my hand was raised. [Did "my hand" know the answer?]

Depressed, Janine's tears flowed. [Were "Janine's tears" depressed?]

To eat less, fewer snacks were in the house. [Did "fewer snacks" want to eat less?]

To eliminate a dangling modifier, rewrite so the participle or infinitive has a nearby word to describe. You may need to rework some sentences extensively to accomplish this. Here are three examples:

Dangling modifier
(present participle):   *Knowing the answer, my hand was raised.*

Correction: *Knowing the answer, I raised my hand.* [Now the present participle can sensibly describe *I.*]

Dangling modifier
(past participle):   *Depressed, Janine's tears flowed.*

Correction: *Depressed, Janine cried hard.* [Now the past participle can sensibly describe *Janine.*]

Dangling modifier
(infinitive):   *To eat less, fewer snacks were in the house.*

Correction: *To eat less, Jack kept fewer snacks in the house.* [Now the infinitive can sensibly describe *Jack.*]

18.7 ACTIVITY

Rewrite the following sentences to eliminate dangling modifiers. Two sentences are correct as they are. For these, write "correct" in the blanks.

EXAMPLE   Riding my bike, the wheel fell off.

Riding my bike, I realized the wheel fell off.

1. Tired after work, a nap was what I wanted.

Tired after work, I wanted a nap.

2. Walking down the street, mud was splashed on me.

   Walking down the street, I was splashed with mud.

3. To quit smoking, a great deal of candy was in the house.

   To quit smoking, I kept a great deal of candy in the house.

4. Concerned about education reform, Martha decided to run for the school board.

   correct

5. Exploring the park with Carl, a lovely pond was discovered.

   Exploring the park with Carl, I discovered a lovely pond.

6. To do well in physics, a person needs good math skills.

   correct

7. Thrown into the deep underbrush, I lost the ball.

   Thrown into the deep underbrush, the ball was lost.

8. Chopping wood, splinters got in his eye.

   Chopping wood, he got splinters in his eye.

IF ENGLISH IS YOUR SECOND LANGUAGE

1. A participle or a participle phrase can appear before or after the word it describes.

   Pacing back and forth, Dr. Menendez delivered the lecture.
   Dr. Menendez, pacing back and forth, delivered the lecture.

2. Participles and participle phrases can come after linking verbs and can describe the subject.

   Cody was frightened by the loud noise.
   The eleven o'clock newscast was alarming.

RECHARGE

1. **Present participles** (*-ing* verb forms), **past participles** (*-ed* forms of regular verbs), and **infinitives** (*to* and the base form of verbs) can function as descriptive words.

   Present participle: *Singing,* I walked across campus.

   Past participle: *Fascinated,* Jan looked more closely at the painting.

   Infinitive: *To repeat,* I completely agree with you.

2. To avoid a **dangling modifier,** be sure the describing participle or infinitive has a stated word to describe.

   Dangling modifier: *Running quickly,* the bus passed me by.

   Correction: *Running quickly,* I missed the bus.

18.8 CHAPTER REVIEW ACTIVITY

Make corrections above the line to eliminate dangling modifiers.

To avoid oversleeping, ~~an alarm clock is used.~~ we use an alarm clock. Accustomed to this practice, ~~no thought is given to it by~~ give it no thought those of us who must wake up at a specific time. However, before 1787, alarm clocks were not available. It was in that year that Levi Hutchins hit upon the idea. Always oversleeping, ~~something to wake Levi up was what he needed.~~ Levi needed something to wake him up. In fact, he needed something to wake him up at the same time each day: four o'clock in the morning. Struck by a brainstorm, ~~a clever device was envisioned.~~ Levi envisioned a clever device Fixing a bell to the inside of one of his clocks, Levi rigged it so that when the hands pointed to 4:00, the bell would ring. The device worked, and as far as we know, Levi never overslept again.

As helpful as the alarm clock is, it did not solve one problem many of us have. Turning off the alarm and rolling over, ~~sleep overtakes us once more.~~ we are overtaken by sleep once more. To solve that problem, the snooze alarm was devised over a hundred years later. Plagued by an inability to get up easily in the morning, I for one am grateful for that improvement on Levi's invention.

18.9 CHAPTER REVIEW ACTIVITY

On a separate sheet, write three sentences using present participles or present participle phrases as modifiers, three sentences using past participles or past participle phrases as modifiers, and three sentences using infinitives or infinitive phrases as modifiers. Remember to use commas correctly, and remember to provide a nearby word for each participle or infinitive to describe.

GETTING IN GEAR

thinking in writing: Interview five students and record their responses to these questions: How has your life changed since you began college? Have the changes been positive or negative?

writing from experience: Write about how you or your life has changed since you began college, noting whether those changes have been positive or negative and why.

writing in context: Assume the role of student services director and write a piece for new college students that tells them about some of the more important changes they can expect in their first year of college. Your goal is to help new students prepare for the changes.

CHAPTER 19

Prepositions

Copyright © 2002, The McGraw-Hill Companies, Inc.

CHAPTER GOALS

By the end of this chapter, you will:

Recognize prepositions and prepositional phrases.

Know how to use prepositions correctly.

PREPOSITIONS AND PREPOSITIONAL PHRASES

Prepositions show how things are positioned in time or space. Here are two examples.

> *The wallet fell under the chair.* [*Under* is a preposition that shows how the wallet was positioned in space: it was *under* the chair.]
>
> *Laurie graduated in December.* [*In* is a preposition that shows how Laurie's graduation was positioned in time: it occurred *in* December.]

A good way to remember prepositions is to think of how a dog can be positioned in relation to a doghouse. The dog can be *in* the doghouse, *beside* the doghouse, *near* the doghouse, *by* the doghouse, or *on* the doghouse. Thus, *in, beside, near, by,* and *on* are prepositions. Although this test will not identify all prepositions, it will help you identify many of them.

Here is a partial list of prepositions. Studying it will help you recognize prepositions in writing.

about	before	from	through
above	behind	in	to
across	beside	into	toward
after	between	like	under
against	by	of	until
along	during	off	up
among	except	on	with
at	for	over	without

GRAMMAR ALERT !

A preposition can be more than one word. Here are some examples.

along with	in addition to
as well as	next to

The garage is next to the house.

A **prepositional phrase** is a preposition and the word or words that go with it. Here are some examples.

at first	*between* the red chairs	*in* the new car
at school	*by* now	*on* the roof
before this	*during* the night	*with* you

TIP

Some common prepositions also moonlight as other parts of speech. For example, *for* is sometimes a preposition and sometimes a coordinating conjunction. *Up* is sometimes a preposition and sometimes an adverb.

Prepositional phrases help a writer describe something, as the following examples show.

> *I left the keys in the new car.* [The prepositional phrase describes *left*.]
>
> *The meeting at school is running late.* [The prepositional phrase describes *meeting*.]
>
> *By now the game should be over.* [The prepositional phrase describes *should be*.]

19.1 ACTIVITY

Place brackets around each prepositional phrase and circle the preposition. A sentence can have more than one prepositional phrase.

EXAMPLE   We left [(in) the middle] [(of) the night.]

1. A compact disc looks [(like) a phonograph record,] but it does not work [(like) one.]
2. [(On) a record,] there are tiny grooves, and different sounds are recorded [(in) the grooves.]
3. The sounds are picked up [(with) a needle.]
4. A compact disc is covered [(with) microscopic pits] that form a digital code.
5. When you play a CD, a laser bounces [(off) it] and reads the little pits.
6. The laser translates the code [(into) electronic signals] and turns it [(into) sound.]
7. CDs are covered [(with) a thin layer] [(of) plastic,] to prevent scratching.
8. A needle never comes [(in) contact [(with) the CD,] so it never wears out.
9. People thought the high cost [(of) CDs] would bother consumers, but [(by) all accounts,] CDs are a huge success.
10. [(Without) a doubt,] CDs outsell all other forms [(of) recorded music.]

19.2 INDIVIDUAL OR GROUP ACTIVITY

Alone or with two classmates, add one or more prepositional phrases to each of the following sentences.

EXAMPLE   I went to a Dixie Chicks concert.

> *During spring break, I went to a Dixie Chicks concert with Liz.*

1. The traffic is terrible.

   During midafternoon, the traffic is terrible on this highway.

   _____

2. Dr. Phillips explained the research assignment.

   After class, Dr. Phillips explained the research assignment.

   _____

3. The police officer signaled me to pull over.

   At the intersection of Oak and Main, the police officer signaled me to pull over.

   _____

4. The fall trees are the most colorful.

   In October, the fall trees in this area are the most colorful.

   _____

5. The fans cheered.

   At the end of the first quarter, the fans cheered.

   _____

6. I dropped my keys.

   I dropped my keys between the seats of the car.

   _____

7. Bill told a story.

   During dinner, Bill told a story about Boris.

   _____

8. The City Council trimmed the budget.

   At its February meeting, the City Council trimmed the budget.

   _____

19.3 ACTIVITY

Combine each group of three sentences into one sentence. To do so, add the prepositional phrases in the second and third sentences to the first sentence.

EXAMPLE   I put my sweater on.
I put it on without looking.
I put it on inside out.

   Without looking, I put my sweater on inside out.

1. The instructor was pleased.
   She was pleased by the test scores.
   The test scores were those of her students.

   The instructor was pleased by the test scores of her students.

   _____

2. As a child, I fished every day.
   I fished in the lake.
   The lake was near my house.

   As a child, I fished every day in the lake near my house.

   _____

3. My car stalled.
    It stalled on the freeway.
    It stalled during rush hour.

    My car stalled on the freeway during rush hour.

4. Carmen gave a fascinating speech.
    His speech was about his summer trip.
    His trip was to Italy.

    Carmen gave a fascinating speech about his summer trip to Italy.

5. Half the audience left.
    They left during intermission.
    They left in disgust.

    Half the audience left in disgust during intermission.

6. The dog jumped.
    He jumped in the air.
    He jumped for the Frisbee.

    The dog jumped in the air for the Frisbee.

COMMON EXPRESSIONS WITH PREPOSITIONS

A number of expressions customarily use certain prepositions. Some of these expressions are listed below, with examples.

1. Use *accompanied by* with a person; use *accompanied with* with a thing or an object.

    The actor was <u>accompanied by</u> his agent.
    The fever was <u>accompanied with</u> a sore throat.

2. Use *angry with* and *upset with* with a person; use *angry at* and *upset at* with a thing or a situation.

    Peter is still <u>angry with</u> Troy.
    I am <u>upset at</u> your stubbornness.

3. Use *between* for two things; use *among* for more than two things.

    I cannot decide <u>between</u> the black suit and the brown one.
    I cannot decide <u>among</u> the black suit, the brown one, and the navy one

4. Use *correspond to* in a comparison; use *correspond with* to mean letter writing.

    Your facts <u>correspond to</u> mine.
    I have <u>corresponded with</u> Isaac for years.

5. Use *differ with* to mean "disagree with"; use *differ from* to mean "is unlike."

    I <u>differ with</u> you about who the best candidate is.
    This product <u>differs from</u> its picture in the magazine.

6. Use *different from*, not *different than*.

   No: *Your beliefs are <u>different than</u> mine.*
   Yes: *Your beliefs are <u>different from</u> mine.*

7. Use *disagree with* with a person; use *disagree on* with a topic or a thing.

   Julie <u>disagrees with</u> everyone.
   We <u>disagree on</u> the meaning of the novel.

8. Use *identical with*, not *identical to*.

   No: *Your shoes are <u>identical to</u> mine.*
   Yes: *Your shoes are <u>identical with</u> mine.*

9. Use *independent of*, not *independent from*.

   No: *This university is <u>independent from</u> the state.*
   Yes: *This university is <u>independent of</u> the state.*

10. Do not use *like* to mean "for example" or "such as."

    No: *Stephen King has written many books, <u>like Christine</u>, <u>Misery</u>, and <u>Needful Things</u>.*
    Yes: *Stephen King has written many books, <u>such as Christine</u>, <u>Misery</u>, and <u>Needful Things</u>.*
    Yes: *Stephen King has written many books. <u>For example</u>, he is the author of <u>Christine</u>, <u>Misery</u>, and <u>Needful Things</u>.*

PUNCTUATION ALERT !
Do not use a comma after "such as."

CONNECT

Different disciplines have common expressions using prepositions. For example, in literary studies, the expression "symbolism *of*" is frequently used, and in advertising, the expression "demographics *for*" is often used. What expressions with prepositions are heard in your major course of study?

11. Do not use *over to* or *over at* for *to* or *at*.

    No: *We went <u>over to</u> Janine's to eat.*
    Yes: *We went <u>to</u> Janine's to eat.*
    No: *We met <u>over at</u> Sue's.*
    Yes: *We met <u>at</u> Sue's.*

12. Use *respond with* with a reaction; use *respond to* with a procedure or an action.

    Responding with anger will not solve the problem.
    The upset child <u>responded to</u> my kindness.

13. Use *responsible for* with an action; use *responsible to* with a person.

    I am <u>responsible for</u> my own behavior.
    Senators must be <u>responsible to</u> the people who elected them.

14. Use *similar to*, not *similar with*.

    No: *Your schedule is <u>similar with</u> mine.*
    Yes: *Your schedule is <u>similar to</u> mine.*

15. Use *toward*, not *towards*.

    No: *We steered the boat <u>towards</u> the shore.*
    Yes: *We steered the boat <u>toward</u> the shore.*

19.4 ACTIVITY

Place a checkmark next to the sentence in each pair that uses prepositions correctly.

EXAMPLE ___✔___ Your schedule is different from mine.
                 _____ Your schedule is different than mine.

1. __√__ Lorenzo is working toward a degree in English.
   _____ Lorenzo is working towards a degree in English.

2. _____ The students were accompanied with a chaperon on their class trip to Disneyworld.
   __√__ The students were accompanied by a chaperon on their class trip to Disneyworld.

3. __√__ I divided the cake among the three of us.
   _____ I divided the cake between the three of us.

4. __√__ Rita Moreno has won many awards, such as the Tony, the Emmy, the Oscar, and the Grammy.
   _____ Rita Moreno has won many awards, like the Tony, the Emmy, the Oscar, and the Grammy.

5. __√__ The two candidates differ with each other about how to reduce the deficit.
   _____ The two candidates differ from each other about how to reduce the deficit.

6. _____ Let's go over to the student union and see a movie.
   __√__ Let's go to the student union and see a movie.

7. __√__ Karen is upset with herself for making a silly mistake.
   _____ Karen is upset at herself for making a silly mistake.

8. __√__ Authorities disagree on the significance of the research.
   _____ Authorities disagree with the significance of the research.

9. _____ This apartment is similar with the one I used to rent.
   __√__ This apartment is similar to the one I used to rent.

10. _____ Now that I have a job, I am independent from my family.
    __√__ Now that I have a job, I am independent of my family.

POWER UP

Review the list of common expressions with prepositions beginning on page 252, and pick five that you are unfamiliar with or have misused in the past. Then write each of these in a sentence.

IF ENGLISH IS YOUR SECOND LANGUAGE

1. See number 6 on page 64 for information on English verbs that are combined with prepositions and for information on when the prepositions can be separated from the verbs and when they cannot be separated.

2. Be aware of the uses of *in*, *on*, and *at* to show time and place.

   A. Use *in* for seasons, months, and years that do not include specific dates. Use *on* if a specific date appears.

   I was born in 1949.
   I was born on May 4, 1949.

B. Use *in* for a period of the day. Use *on* for a specific day. Use *at* for a specific time or period of the day.

> *I like to run two miles in the morning.*
> *I will run two miles on Wednesday.*
> *I like to run two miles at dawn.*

C. Use *in* for a location that is surrounded by something else. Use *at* for a specific location.

> *I lived in London for a year.*
> *Join me in the living room.*
> *I lived at 518 Tod Lane.*
> *Meet me at the crossroads.*

3. In English, the subject of a sentence cannot appear in a prepositional phrase, so cross out prepositional phrases before trying to identify the subject of a sentence.

> subject
> ~~In the morning,~~ [the sun] *rises over the ocean.*

4. Prepositional phrases that show place come before those that show time.

> No: *Edmund worked in 1992 in Mexico.*
> Yes: *Edmund worked in Mexico in 1992.*

RECHARGE

1. **Prepositions** show how things are positioned in time or space. They are words such as *at, by, near, through,* and *under.*
2. A **prepositional phrase** includes a preposition and the word or words that function with it. They are phrases such as *at noon, by now, through the tunnel,* and *under the water.*

19.5 CHAPTER REVIEW ACTIVITY

Cross out any incorrect prepositions in the following passage, and write the correct ones above the line.

The Monroe Doctrine is a statement of foreign policy issued by President James
Monroe. ~~On~~ [In] November 1823, he delivered a message ~~at~~ [to] Congress that included
many points that became known as the Monroe Doctrine—points ~~like~~ [such as] the following:

1. The American continents can no longer be colonized by Europe.
2. The European political system is different ~~than~~ [from] that of the United States.

   Therefore, efforts to extend the European system to the Western Hemisphere

   will be considered dangerous to the United States.
3. The United States will not interfere ~~of~~ [with] any existing European colonies.
4. The United States will not be responsible ~~to~~ [for] interfering in the internal affairs of

   European nations.

Sometimes the United States does not act in a way that is identical ~~to~~ ^{with} the principles of the Monroe Doctrine. For example, Theodore Roosevelt, in 1904, said the United States could interfere in the affairs of Latin America to keep Europe out. Still, as much as possible, the United States does try to respond to situations in a way that is compatible with the Monroe Doctrine.

Of course, many people maintain that the United States should extend the principles of the Monroe Doctrine to its behavior with non-European nations. These people say that this country interferes too much ~~on~~ ⁱⁿ the affairs of Asian, African, and Middle Eastern nations. They believe that countries are independent ~~from~~ ^{of} each other, so we should leave countries alone to work out their own problems.

GETTING IN GEAR

thinking in writing: Think about the benefits of being very good looking. In a column, list those benefits. Now think about the benefits of being very intelligent. List those benefits in a column.

writing from experience: Based on your own experience and observation, which would you rather have: great physical attractiveness or superior intelligence? Be sure to give reasons to support your view.

writing in context: Which do you think people value more: physical beauty or intelligence? Give examples to support your view, and explain why you think people value one more than the other.

PART FIVE REVIEW

Activity: Modifiers and Prepositions

Cross out and write corrections above the line to eliminate five errors with adjectives and adverbs, one incorrect article, two dangling modifiers, one double negative, and four errors with prepositions.

Almost all parts of the world celebrate something ~~similarly~~ [similar] to April Fools' Day. This almost-universal celebration is ~~an~~ [a] day when practical jokes are played ~~to~~ [on] friends and neighbors. Although ~~explained several ways,~~ [it has been explained several ways,] we are not sure how April Fools' Day began. One theory of origin, however, seems more ~~likelier~~ [likely] than others.

This theory states that April Fools' Day started with the French. When the calendar was reformed, the first nation to adopt it was France. Charles IX ordered, ~~on~~ [in] 1564, that the year should ~~definite~~ [definitely] begin January 1. Until then, New Year's visits and the exchange ~~with~~ [of] New Year's gifts had been associated with a different date, April 1.

After Charles issued his decree, visits and gifts became associated with the first of January. However, many people were unhappy ~~by~~ [with] the change. Refusing to go along with it, ~~jokes were played on these people.~~ [these people had jokes played on them.] The jokesters made fun of them by giving them mock gifts; they pretended to visit them, and they invited them to mock New Year's celebrations—all on the first of April. In other words, the jokesters made these people April Fools—people who still felt April was the ~~more better~~ [better] beginning of the new year. Thus, the custom of fooling people on April 1 started with the mock gifts and celebrations directed at those who would not ~~never~~ give in to Charles's decree.

Although this explanation is only one of many, it functions to explain the origin of April Fools' Day as ~~good~~ [well] as any other one. So the next time you play an April Fools' Day prank on someone, you might as well remember the thanks you owe to France's King Charles.

Activity: Modifiers and Prepositions

Cross out and write corrections above the line to eliminate four errors with adjectives and adverbs, three incorrect articles, two dangling modifiers, one double negative, and two errors with prepositions.

Marian Anderson was the first African American to sing at the Metropolitan Opera. She was known ~~primary~~ [primarily] for her rich voice and wide range. Named to the National Arts Hall of Fame, ~~her contribution to the American performing arts~~ [she made contributions to the American performing arts that] cannot ~~never~~ be overestimated. She was also cited at the first annual Kennedy Center

Honors in 1978. In addition to her noteworthy opera career, Anderson was ac-

claimed even more ~~wide~~ widely for her singing of spirituals.

Anderson first sang ~~at~~ in church choirs. To obtain the training necessary for her

career, ~~her race made it necessary for her to overcome great difficulties.~~ Anderson had to overcome great difficulties because of her race. In 1935,

she sang for Arturo Toscanini, who said that she had a voice that comes once in ~~an~~ a

hundred years. However, four years later, the Daughters of the American

Revolution denied her access to Washington's Constitution Hall for a concert.

Eleanor Roosevelt then arranged her concert on the steps of the Lincoln Memorial

before ~~a~~ an audience of 75,000.

After that, Anderson was named by the government as ~~a~~ an alternate United

Nations delegate. She sang ~~in~~ at the inaugural balls of Presidents Eisenhower and

Kennedy. She made many recordings and was noted ~~wide~~ widely for the deep timbre and

style of her singing.

Anderson retired after one of her most ~~successfulest~~ successful concert tours in 1965.

Improving Sentences

CHAPTER GOALS

By the end of this chapter, you will:

Know what parallelism is.

Know how to achieve parallelism with series and pairs.

Know how to achieve parallelism with pairs of conjunctions.

CHAPTER 20

Achieving Parallelism

Which of the following sentences is more pleasing to your ear?

> *Juan is known as an excellent swimmer, a strong runner, and he does the high jump well.*
>
> *Juan is known as an excellent swimmer, a strong runner, and a good high jumper.*

If you picked the second sentence, then you already recognize that a sentence with parallelism reads better than a sentence without parallelism.

PARALLELISM WITH WORDS IN SERIES AND PAIRS

Parallelism means that items that form a pair (two things) or items that form a series (more than two things) have the same grammatical form. In the following examples, the parallel items are underlined.

> Parallel pair: *Before bed, I like <u>watching</u> the 11 o'clock news and <u>drinking</u> milk.*
>
> Parallel series: *This coffee is <u>cold</u>, <u>weak</u>, and <u>bitter</u>.*

Notice how much less appeal the sentences have without parallelism.

> *Before bed, I like watching the 11 o'clock news and to drink milk.*
> *This coffee is cold, weak, and it is bitter.*

To eliminate problems with parallelism, place all the items in a series or pair in the same form. Here are two examples.

> Lacks parallelism: *The instructor told me <u>to study more</u> and <u>that I should get a tutor</u>.*
>
> Correction 1:   *The instructor told me <u>to study more</u> and <u>to get a tutor</u>.*
>
> Correction 2:   *The instructor told me <u>that I should study more</u> and <u>that I should get a tutor</u>.*
>
> Lacks parallelism: *The movie is <u>dull</u>, <u>pretentious</u>, and <u>it is too long</u>.*
>
> Correction 1:   *The movie is <u>dull</u>, <u>pretentious</u>, and <u>too long</u>.*
>
> Correction 2:   *The movie is <u>dull</u>, <u>it is pretentious</u>, and <u>it is too long</u>.*

20.1 ACTIVITY

POWER UP

One of the most familiar phrases in American history and politics is this example of parallelism: "government of the people, by the people, and for the people." Would anything be lost if the phrase had been worded like this: "government of the people, by the people, and government that is intended to be for the people as well"? Explain.

Circle the element in each item below that is not parallel. Write the parallel form in the blank.

EXAMPLE
young
innocent
full of ambition
clever
ambitious

1. tall
   athletic
   feeling cheerful
   intelligent
   cheerful

2. to sail
   swimming
   to ski
   to fish
   to swim

3. in the woods
   by the stream
   behind the house
   lakeside
   beside the lake

4. eating in good restaurants
   small parties
   political lectures
   modern art museums
   good restaurants

5. charity for the homeless
   being kind to strangers
   help for the ill
   friendship for the lonely
   kindness to strangers

6. Study daily.
   Ask questions.
   Take notes.
   Be sure to read assignments.
   Read assignments.

7. hair that shines
   radiant skin
   twinkling eyes
   lovely smile
   shining hair

8. She explains points well.
   She answers questions thoroughly.
   Her sense of humor is appealing.
   She enjoys students.
   She has an appealing sense of humor.

9. feeling alarmed by the thunder
   blown by the wind
   drenched by the rain
   pelted by the hail
   alarmed by the thunder

10. Stop smoking.
    Reduce my salt intake.
    Limit sugar.
    That I should exercise daily.
    Exercise daily.

20.2 ACTIVITY

In each pair of sentences below, place a checkmark next to the sentence that achieves parallelism.

EXAMPLE ✔ Our new apartment needs a coat of paint, a new dishwasher, and new carpeting.

_____ Our new apartment needs a coat of paint, a new dishwasher, and the carpeting is worn.

1. _____ Before school, I might study or taking a walk sounds pleasant.

   √ Before school, I might study or take a walk.

2. _____ With the fish you can have salad, soup, or coleslaw is available.

   __✓___ With the fish you can have salad, soup, or coleslaw.

3. _____ The police officers told the spectators to stand back, to let the firefighters through, and that they should then leave the scene.

   __✓___ The police officers told the spectators to stand back, let the firefighters through, and then leave the scene.

4. __✓___ On vacation, I enjoy sleeping late, reading, and eating in restaurants.

   _____ On vacation, I enjoy sleeping late, reading, and I like to eat in restaurants.

5. __✓___ We can buy it now for full price, or we can buy it on sale at the end of the month.

   _____ We can buy it now for full price, or at the end of the month it will be on sale.

6. _____ After being in this country six months, Rico had made many friends, had learned to like rap music, and he had acquired a taste for pizza.

   __✓___ After being in this country six months, Rico had made many friends, had learned to like rap music, and had acquired a taste for pizza.

7. __✓___ I looked for the missing book under my bed, behind the sofa, and in the back seat of my car.

   _____ I looked for the missing book under my bed, behind the sofa, and I looked in the back seat of my car.

8. _____ I like small, intimate restaurants, and large, noisy truck stops are nice.

   __✓___ I like small, intimate restaurants and large, noisy truck stops.

20.3 INDIVIDUAL OR GROUP ACTIVITY

Alone or with two classmates, fill in the blanks with a parallel word or words.

EXAMPLE Most people like Edward because he is friendly, honest, and _____ *funny.* _____

1. Lesley no longer eats chocolate because it gives her a headache and _acne._____

2. If you study every day, you will keep up with your assignments, reduce stress, and _feel confident._____

3. Although she is 80 years old, Aunt Hattie is in good shape because she exercises regularly, stays active, and _eats properly._____

4. In my freshman orientation class, I learned how to add and drop classes, where to find a tutor, and _how to use the library._____

5. When traveling at night, be sure to have a full tank of gas, directions to your destination, and _a flashlight._____

6. After I ran five miles, my ankles hurt and my back ached.

7. Dr. Goldberg's lectures are always inspiring, informative, and humorous.

8. You will find him in his room or in the library.

20.4 ACTIVITY

The underlined element in each of the following sentences is not parallel. Rewrite the sentences to achieve parallelism.

EXAMPLE   I was hoping to leave by noon and <u>that we would arrive by supper</u>.
I was hoping to leave by noon and to arrive by supper.

1. The beef is tough, stringy, and <u>it is overcooked</u>.
   The beef is tough, stringy, and overcooked.

2. The six-inch snowfall closed schools, stalled traffic, and <u>it disrupted business</u>.
   The six-inch snowfall closed schools, stalled traffic, and disrupted business.

3. Nigel's favorite activities are watching MTV, and <u>he likes to play billiards in the student union</u>.
   Nigel's favorite activities are watching MTV and playing billiards in the student union.

4. After a day at the beach, I was sunburned, chafed by the salt air, and <u>feeling tired</u>.
   After a day at the beach, I was sunburned, chafed by the salt air, and tired.

5. Dale decided to go to graduate school because he wanted a better job, he wanted to advance his education , and <u>to have an opportunity to teach</u>.
   Dale decided to go to graduate school because he wanted a better job, he wanted to advance his education, and he wanted an opportunity to teach.

6. Senator Jorgenson opposes free trade agreements, higher taxes, and <u>he is against federally funded daycare</u>.
   Senator Jorgenson opposes free trade agreements, higher taxes, and federally funded daycare.

7. We drove over the embankment, across the median, and <u>traveled into oncoming traffic</u>.
   We drove over the embankment, across the median, and into oncoming traffic.

8. With some paint, wallpaper, and <u>if we hang new drapes</u>, this apartment will look better.

   With some paint, wallpaper, and new drapes, this apartment will look better.

PARALLELISM WITH PAIRED CONJUNCTIONS

Conjunctions are joining words. A number of conjunctions work in pairs. Four of these paired conjunctions are:

both . . . and   neither . . . nor
either . . . or   not only . . . but also

To achieve parallelism when you use paired conjunctions, follow each conjunction with the same grammatical form.

Lacks parallelism: *You must not only <u>pass</u> the test, but also <u>you must</u> earn a high B.* ["Not only" is followed by a verb, and "but also" is followed by a subject and a verb.]

Achieves parallelism: *Not only <u>must you</u> pass the test, but also <u>you must</u> earn a high B.* ["Not only" and "but also" are both followed by subjects and verbs.]

Lacks parallelism: *I either <u>get</u> a job or <u>I drop</u> out of school.* ["Either" is followed by a verb, and "or" is followed by a subject and a verb.]

Achieves parallelism: *Either <u>I get</u> a job or <u>I drop</u> out of school.* ["Either" and "or" are both followed by subjects and verbs.]

Lacks parallelism: *This waffle both <u>is</u> cold and <u>soggy</u>.* ["Both" is followed by a verb and a descriptive word, and "and" is followed by just a descriptive word.]

Achieves parallelism: *This waffle is both <u>cold</u> and <u>soggy</u>.* ["Both" and "and" are followed by descriptive words.]

20.5 ACTIVITY

Place a checkmark next to the sentence in each pair below that achieves parallelism.

EXAMPLE ___✓___ Either we leave now, or we will be late.

_____ We either leave now, or we will be late.

1. __✓___ The children neither watched the television nor turned it off.

_____ The children watched neither the television nor turned it off.

2. _____ Carla not only bought the hat but also the scarf to go with it.

__✓___ Carla bought not only the hat but also the scarf to go with it.

3. __✓___ Majoring in special education is both challenging and rewarding.

_____ Majoring in special education both is challenging and rewarding.

4. __✓___ Ruth volunteers not only at nursing homes but also at the senior citizens' center.

_____ Ruth not only volunteers at nursing homes but also at the senior citizens' center.

5. _____ Either the exam will be postponed until Tuesday or Thursday.

    __✓___ The exam will be postponed until either Tuesday or Thursday.

6. __✓___ Clarice is amazing because she is both a talented painter and an accomplished musician.

    _____ Clarice is amazing because she both is a talented painter and an accomplished musician.

7. __✓___ Recycling not only helps the environment but also saves money.

    _____ Recycling helps not only the environment but also saves money.

8. __✓___ The candidate's speeches are either too long or too technical.

    _____ The candidate's speeches either are too long or too technical.

POWER UP

Alone or with a classmate, compose three sentences with parallel structure and three that lack parallelism. Give them as a quiz to other classmates.

20.6 ACTIVITY

Circle the paired conjunctions in each of the following sentences, determine what grammatical forms appear after them, and then decide whether parallelism has been achieved. If it has, write "correct" in the blank. If not, rewrite the sentence to achieve parallelism.

EXAMPLE   I [neither] enjoy handball [nor] racquetball.

I enjoy neither handball nor racquetball.

1. Candace can [either] play the female lead in the production, [or] he can be the understudy.

    Either Candace can play the female lead in the production, or she can be the understudy.

2. The new restaurant on the corner of Broad Street and Fifth Avenue is [both] reasonably priced [and] attractively decorated.

    correct

3. Igor was [not only] Dave's roommate, [but also] he was his best friend.

    Igor was not only Dave's roommate but also his best friend.

4. I can [neither] reach Joy at her home [nor] at her office.

    I can reach Joy neither at her home nor at her office.

5. Mohammed wants to live [either] in Los Angeles [or] in Houston after graduation.

    correct

6. The door is [either] bolted from the inside, [or] the lock is broken.

    Either the door is bolted from the inside, or the lock is broken.

7. This pudding is [not only] delicious [but also] fat-free.

   correct _____

   _____

8. Shopping at this store is [both] convenient [and] economical.

   correct _____

   _____

IF ENGLISH IS YOUR SECOND LANGUAGE

Consult the following list if you need help with the meanings and uses of the paired conjunctions.

1. *Either . . . or* indicates choice.

2. *Not only . . . but also* indicates addition.

3. *Neither . . . nor* indicates negative choice.
   (*Neither . . . nor* does not usually join clauses.)

4. *Both . . . and* indicates addition.
   (*Both . . . and* does not usually join clauses.)

RECHARGE

To achieve **parallelism**, be sure that elements in a series, in a pair, or after paired conjunctions have the same grammatical form.

Parallel pair: I like running on a treadmill or running on a beach.

Parallel series: The mayoral candidate promised a pay hike for police officers, tax incentives for new businesses, and road repairs.

Paired conjunctions: Either fix the car or buy a new one.

20.7 CHAPTER REVIEW ACTIVITY

Some of the sentences in the following passage lack parallelism. Cross out the problems and write any needed corrections above the lines.

No one knows who invented the ball, but we do know that people have played with balls from the earliest times. In fact, all civilizations—both early ones and ~~ones that are existing today~~ *existing ones*—have played games using some kind of ball. Some early people wove reeds into rounded shapes, ~~and leather was stuffed with feathers by others~~ *others stuffed leather with feathers.* The Greeks and Romans added a new idea—they used a blown-up leather ball to play catch.

Balls have been made from many materials, depending on what was available in the region. Deer hide, wrapped tissue, and ~~balls made with~~ vegetable gum have been used. It was the vegetable gum ball, used by Central American Indians, that led to the present-day use of a bouncy rubber ball.

Many modern ball games ~~either began as~~ began as either religious or magical ceremonies. Often the games told of old beliefs about war, gods, devils, life, and ~~about~~ death. Ancient Egyptians, for example, used a wooden ball and sticks for a ceremonial contest between two gods. Whoever knocked the ball through the opposing goal won a victory for that team's god. The Egyptians were among the first to have ceremonial ball games.

GETTING IN GEAR

thinking in writing: Think about things that appeal to teenagers and why those things are important by mapping the subject. (If you need to learn more about mapping, see page 8.) Begin by writing and circling this subject in the middle of a page: "things that appeal to teenagers."

writing from experience: Write about something that appealed to you as a teenager (and your peers) but not to the rest of the population—a particular form of dress, a certain kind of music, a special television program, or a way of talking, for instance. Explain why this element appealed to you and your peers.

writing in context: Many adults find it difficult to understand why teenagers like the things they do. For those people, select something that today's teenagers like and explain why it appeals to teens. Your goal is to increase understanding.

CHAPTER 21

Special Sentence Structure Challenges

SIMPLE SUBJECTS AND VERBS THAT DO NOT MAKE SENSE TOGETHER

The **simple subject** is the most important word in the complete subject. Simple subjects never appear in prepositional phrases (see page 51).

Sentence:	*The end of the movie was disappointing.*
Complete subject:	*the end of the movie*
Prepositional phrase:	*of the movie*
Simple subject:	*end (The <u>end</u> ~~of the movie~~ <u><u>was</u></u> disappointing.)*

A sentence structure problem can result when a verb works with a word in a prepositional phrase, rather than with the simple subject.

No:	*The purpose of the shot prevents the flu.* [The simple subject is *purpose. Purpose* does not prevent the flu; *shot* does. However, *shot* is part of the prepositional phrase *of the shot.*]
Correction 1:	*The <u>shot</u> <u><u>prevents</u></u> the flu.*
Correction 2:	*The <u>purpose</u> of the shot <u><u>is</u></u> to prevent the flu.*

21.1 ACTIVITY

Underline the simple subject once and the verb twice in each of the following sentences, and then check to see if they work logically together. If they do, write "correct" in the blank. If they do not, rewrite the sentence to eliminate the problem. Two sentences are correct.

EXAMPLE   The <u>role</u> of corresponding secretary <u><u>answers</u></u> all mail and writes all letters.

The corresponding secretary answers all mail and writes

all letters.

1.   The <u>increase</u> in the number of education majors <u><u>is growing</u></u> each semester.

The number of education majors is growing each semester.

2. The <u>amount</u> of vinegar in this salad dressing <u>tastes</u> very strong.

    The vinegar in this salad dressing tastes very strong.

3. The <u>excuse</u> for your absence <u>is</u> understandable.

    correct

TIP

After drafting, try reading your writing out loud. If you hear something that sounds off, check to see whether you have a subject and verb that do not work together.

4. The <u>difficulty</u> of the third question on the exam <u>was</u> hard to answer.

    The third question on the exam was hard to answer.

5. The <u>reason</u> for the popularity of this movie <u>is</u> hard to explain.

    correct

6. The <u>purpose</u> of vinyl <u>was meant</u> to be as durable as leather but less expensive.

    Vinyl was meant to be as durable as leather but less expensive.

7. The <u>position</u> of a secretary no longer <u>runs</u> the boss's errands.

    A secretary no longer runs the boss's errands.

8. The <u>desire</u> of a new employee <u>hopes</u> to make a good impression as quickly as possible.

    A new employee hopes to make a good impression as quickly as possible.

ILLOGICAL EQUATIONS WITH FORMS OF *BE*

Forms of the verb *be* (*am, is, are, was, were, been,* and *being*) can act like an equal sign (=). When this is the case, the form of *be* equates the subject with a word or words after the verb.

> *Jane* [*is*] *an excellent violinist.*
> *Jane = violinist*

> *My dentist* [*was*] *my uncle.*
> *dentist = uncle*

A sentence structure problem occurs when a form of *be* sets up an illogical equation.

Illogical equation:	*At one time, a teacher was a career for women only.* [Teacher = career?]
Explanation:	*A "teacher" is a person, not a "career."*
Correction:	*At one time, teaching was a career for women only.*

Illogical equation:	*A popular major at this school is hospitality manager.* [Major = manager?]
Explanation:	*A "major" is a thing, not a "manager."*
Correction:	*A popular major at this school is hospitality management.*

To correct sentences with illogical equations, you may have to rewrite by adding words.

Illogical equation:	*My instructor's reaction to my essay was too short and choppy.*
Correction:	*My instructor's reaction to my essay was that it was too short and choppy.*

21.2 ACTIVITY

Fill in the blanks to show the equation set up with the form of *be*. Then decide whether the equation is logical. If it is not, rewrite to correct the problem. For the two sentences that are correct, write "correct" in the blank.

EXAMPLE Real charity is a person who gives anonymously.

charity = *person*

Real charity is giving anonymously.

1. The study of the lake's pollution is too high for swimming.

   study = too high

   The lake's pollution is too high for swimming.

2. The columnist's criticism of the television show is too violent.

   criticism = too violent

   The columnist's criticism of the television show is that it is too violent.

3. Our view of his artwork is shoddy and overpriced.

   view = shoddy and overpriced

   Our view of his artwork is that it is shoddy and overpriced.

4. College instructors are a good place to ask about job opportunities in your major.

   instructors = place

   College instructors are good people to ask about job opportunities in your major.

5. The most important traits of my high school guidance counselor were gentle and intelligent.

traits _____ = _gentle and intelligent_____

The most important traits of my high school guidance counselor were gentleness and

intelligence.

6. The most frightening part of the movie was the conclusion.

part _____ = _conclusion_____

correct

7. A necessary asset of a distance runner is enduring.

asset _____ = _enduring_____

A necessary asset of a distance runner is endurance.

8. The most entertaining section of your essay is the beginning.

section _____ = _the beginning_____

correct

IS . . . WHEN, IS . . . WHERE, THE REASON . . . IS BECAUSE

Problems with sentence structure result when writers use *is . . . when, is . . . where,* or *the reason . . . is because.*

To avoid sentence structure problems, do not use *is . . . when* or *is . . . where* in definitions. Here are two examples.

No: *Exam anxiety is when students get so nervous about tests that they freeze up and cannot perform.* ["Exam anxiety" is a problem, not a time, so *when* is inaccurate. To correct the sentence, rewrite it.]

Correction: *Exam anxiety causes students to get so nervous about tests that they freeze up and cannot perform.*

No: *Unrestrained jealousy is where you can never be happy with what you have.* ["Unrestrained jealousy" is a condition, not a place, so *where* is inaccurate. To correct the problem, rewrite the sentence.]

Correction: *Unrestrained jealousy means you can never be happy with what you have.*

Because means "the reason is that." If you use "the reason is because," you will be saying, "the reason is the reason is that."

No: *The reason I got the job is because I have good communication skills.*

Yes: *The reason I got the job is that I have good communication skills.*

Yes: *I got the job because I have good communication skills.*

CONNECT

When writing about causes and effects, proofread carefully for *is . . . because* and *the reason . . . is because.* For example, in a history class, you may explain the causes of the Teapot Dome scandal, or in a physical therapy class, you may explain the effects of tendonitis. Don't weaken your writing with sentence structure problems you can find and fix.

21.3 INDIVIDUAL OR GROUP ACTIVITY

A. Alone or with two classmates, complete each of the following sentences by adding an explanation.

EXAMPLE   The reason you lost your job is *that you were always late.*

1. The reason I got lost was *that I had to take a detour.*

2. One reason Harry got an A on his essay is *that he supported his points well.*

3. The reasons everyone likes you are *that you are kind, helpful, and patient.*

B. Alone or with two classmates, complete each of the following sentences by adding a definition.

EXAMPLE   True maturity is *accepting people for what they are.*

4. Math anxiety is *the fear of all math classes and math tests.*

5. A blind date is *usually an experiment in hope.*

6. Freedom of speech is *the lifeblood of the democratic process.*

MIXED SENTENCE STRUCTURES

Here are two sentences that use different structures to convey the same idea.

Structure 1:   *By switching to a better grade of gasoline, I reduced the engine noise.*

Structure 2:   *Switching to a better grade of gasoline reduced the engine noise.*

If a writer begins a sentence with one sentence structure and switches to another sentence structure, a problem with **mixed sentence structures** results. Here is an example of mixed sentence structures resulting from mixing structure 1 and structure 2.

Mixed sentence structures: *By switching to a better grade of gasoline reduced the engine noise.*

To correct the problem, use one sentence structure or the other.

Mixed sentence structures: *Because the superintendent closed the school means the test is postponed.*

POWER UP

Pair up with a classmate and take turns reading your drafts out loud to listen for mixed sentence structures.

Correction (structure 1):	*Because the superintendent closed the school, the test is postponed.*
Correction (structure 2):	*The superintendent's closing of the school means the test is postponed.*

Mixed sentence structures often result when a writer begins by making a statement but switches to asking a question.

A statement:	*The band director asked whether everyone remembered the music.*
A question:	*The band director asked, "Does everyone remember the music?"*
Mixed sentence structures:	*The band director asked does everyone remember the music.*

To correct the problem, either make a statement or ask a question.

Mixed sentence structures:	*The instructor wanted to know did anyone have a question.*
Correction 1 (a statement):	*The instructor wanted to know whether anyone had a question.*
Correction 2 (a question):	*The instructor asked, "Does anyone have a question?"*

21.4 ACTIVITY

Cross out and rewrite above the lines to correct the sentences with mixed structures. (It is possible to rewrite more than one way.) Two sentences are correct.

By falling down on a patch of ice ~~hurt my knee~~ _{I hurt my knee}. Because of the swelling and pain, ~~caused~~ Leo ~~to take~~ _{took} me to the emergency room. After three hours, I still had not seen a doctor. Leo finally asked the receptionist how long ~~did we have~~ _{we had} to wait. When I finally saw the doctor _{, it was} ~~was~~ two hours after that. The doctor asked ~~do I have~~ _{whether I had} any allergies. I replied that I was allergic to long waits. While laughing ~~told~~ _{, the doctor told} me I would need surgery. ~~By having~~ _{Having} knee surgery allowed me to resume my basketball career.

IF ENGLISH IS YOUR SECOND LANGUAGE

1. In some languages, the subject is repeated, but in English, it is not repeated.

   No: *Your new haircut, it is very attractive.*

   Yes: *Your new haircut is very attractive.*

   No: *Caffeine and nicotine, they can cause headaches.*

   Yes: *Caffeine and nicotine can cause headaches.*

2. Do not use a pronoun to refer to a word already referred to by *who, which,* or *that.*

   No: *Someone stole my wallet, which I left it on the desk.*

   Yes: *Someone stole my wallet, which I left on the desk.* [*Which* already refers to *wallet,* so *it* is unnecessary.]

   No: *The pill that Raymond took was difficult to swallow it.*

   Yes: *The pill that Raymond took was difficult to swallow.* [*That* already refers to *pill,* so *it* is unnecessary.]

3. In English, subjects are not omitted, except in some commands and requests.

   No: *Studying takes up a great deal of time. Is what I do six hours a day.*

   Yes: *Studying takes up a great deal of time. It is what I do six hours a day.*

   No: *In the United States watch television too much.*

   Yes: *In the United States people watch television too much.*

4. Try to think in English when you speak and write. If you think in your native language and then attempt to translate into English, you are more likely to have problems with your English sentence structure.

RECHARGE

Sentence structure problems occur when

- A verb functions with a word in a prepositional phrase.
- A form of *be* sets up an illogical equation.
- *Is . . . when, is . . . where, the reason . . . is because* are used.
- Different sentence structures are mixed in the same sentence.

21.5 CHAPTER REVIEW ACTIVITY

In the following passage, seven sentences have sentence structure problems. Revise to eliminate the problems.

The best exercise program ~~is where you~~ begin with a 3- to 5-minute warm-up to increase respiration, circulation, and body temperature. ~~The purpose of a~~ warm-up also stretches muscles, tendons, and connective tissue to reduce the risk of injury. After the warm-up comes the conditioning period. ~~By conditioning~~ Conditioning increases cardiovascular fitness. You should exercise at a moderate rate—not at an exhaustive level. ~~If you exercise~~ Exercising regularly and gradually ~~increase~~ increasing the intensity level improves fitness. Your goal should be 30 to 60 minutes of conditioning at least three times a week. The reason the range is 30 to 60 minutes is ~~because~~ that the amount of time depends on how strenuous the activity is and your general health. After

exercising, cool down for a few minutes. Don't stand still or lie down after

exercising. ~~If you walk~~ ^{Walking} around for a few minutes lets your body adjust to the

decreased physical demands.

Don't let exercise be a fad. Regular workouts mean cardiovascular fitness

that can improve the quality of life. For healthy people, regular exercise is a

lifetime commitment. If, however, you have any doubts about your ability to

exercise, be sure to consult your doctor. Remember, the goal of any exercise

program is ~~healthy and strong~~ ^{health and strength}.

GETTING IN GEAR

thinking in writing: Each of us plays a number of roles during any given period of life. We can be student, spouse, parent, child, Little League coach, Girl Scout leader, salesclerk, soccer player, clarinet player, cheerleader, Sunday school teacher, and so forth. Make a list of all the roles you are currently playing.

writing from experience: Write about one of your roles. Describe and illustrate one of its chief features, using your own experience for details. For example, if you write about your role as mother, you might say that part of being a mother is being a diplomat. To illustrate that feature, you might describe your attempts to tell your son that his favorite shirt does not look good on him.

writing in context: Sometimes roles come into conflict. For example, a student-athlete who must travel to a game and miss a test in class finds the roles of student and athlete in conflict. Role conflict can be a significant source of stress. Discuss a common role conflict and consider ways society can make that conflict less stressful. For example, to make the conflict between being a parent and employee less stressful, you might recommend day care centers at the workplace.

CHAPTER 22

Varying Sentence Openers

Read the following passage out loud:

> *I saw the car cross the center line and come toward me. I slammed on my brakes. I quickly went into a skid. The car weaved back and forth all over the road. It finally came to a stop. It was resting in a drainage ditch.*

While nothing is grammatically wrong with this passage, you probably noticed how choppy it sounds because every sentence begins the same way—with the subject. To avoid such unpleasant choppiness in your own writing, follow the suggestions in this chapter for varying sentence openers. They will help you write more like this:

> *When I saw the car cross the center line and come toward me, I slammed on my brakes. Weaving back and forth all over the road, I quickly went into a skid. Finally, the car came to a stop. It was resting in a drainage ditch.*

OPEN WITH ONE OR TWO ADVERBS

Adverbs are descriptive words that often end in *-ly*. They are words such as these:

cautiously	loudly	slowly
fearfully	quickly	tenderly

Try opening some of your sentences with an adverb.

> *Thoughtfully, Delores read her assignment.*
> *Earnestly, Kevin explained the reason for his view.*

To open with an adverb, you may only need to rearrange words.

> *Dominic slowly pushed his shopping cart down the aisle.*
> *Slowly, Dominic pushed his shopping cart down the aisle.*

PUNCTUATION ALERT !

As the above examples show, an opening adverb is followed by a comma.

Try opening some sentences with a pair of adverbs.

> *Slowly and carefully, I ironed the expensive shirt.*
> *Quickly but skillfully, Helene painted my portrait.*
> *Gently, lovingly, Harry covered the sleeping infant.*

PUNCTUATION ALERT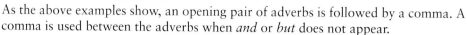

As the above examples show, an opening pair of adverbs is followed by a comma. A comma is used between the adverbs when *and* or *but* does not appear.

22.1 ACTIVITY

Combine each pair of sentences below into one sentence. To do so, open with the adverb or pair of adverbs given in the second sentence. Remember to use commas correctly.

EXAMPLE   The children argued over whose turn it was.
They argued noisily.

Noisily, the children argued over whose turn it was.

CONNECT

Varying your sentence openers is important for creating interest in your writing. Variety is also important in other areas. For example, to maintain their interest in exercise, people often vary their workout routines. Where else is variety important for maintaining interest?

1. I ran up and down the street looking for my puppy.
I ran frantically.

Frantically, I ran up and down the street looking for my puppy.

2. The speaker demanded an end to wasteful government policies.
The speaker demanded forcefully.

Forcefully, the speaker demanded an end to wasteful government policies.

3. Carmen disinfected Scott's wound and then drove him to the hospital.
Carmen disinfected the wound efficiently.

Efficiently, Carmen disinfected Scott's wound and then drove him to the hospital.

4. The German shepherd looked me in the eye and growled.
He did so menacingly.

Menacingly, the German shepherd looked me in the eye and growled.

5. I double-checked my answers before handing in the test.
I double-checked quickly but carefully.

Quickly but carefully, I double-checked my answers before handing in the test.

6. The dancer leaped into the air.
She leaped powerfully but gracefully.

Powerfully but gracefully, the dancer leaped into the air.

7. I asked the personnel director whether I got the job.
I asked anxiously.

Anxiously, I asked the personnel director whether I got the job.

8. Donald volunteered to help with the city cleanup campaign.
   He volunteered eagerly and happily.

   Eagerly and happily, Donald volunteered to help with the city cleanup campaign.

22.2 ACTIVITY

Pick five of the adverbs and adverb pairs below, and use them to open sentences. Write the sentences on a separate sheet, and remember to use commas correctly.

cautiously	loudly and angrily
fearlessly	quickly but carefully
gently	slowly, patiently

OPEN WITH A PRESENT PARTICIPLE OR A PRESENT PARTICIPLE PHRASE

The **present participle** is the *-ing* form of a verb. Here are some examples of present participles.

believing	eating	running
dancing	moving	seeing

The present participle can be combined with one or more words to form a **present participle phrase.** Here are some present participle phrases.

believing in you	eating lunch	running across campus
dancing slowly	moving quickly	seeing the sunset

Try opening some of your sentences with present participles and present participle phrases.

TIP

For additional discussions of present participles and present participle phrases, see pages 174 and 239. Dangling modifiers are discussed on page 245.

Singing. Henry walked through the park.
Singing show tunes. Henry walked through the park.
Laughing. I left the room.
Laughing loudly. I left the room.

PUNCTUATION ALERT
As the previous examples illustrate, an opening present participle or participle phrase is followed by a comma.

GRAMMAR ALERT
Be sure your present participle or present participle phrase is followed by a word the participle can sensibly describe, or you will have a **dangling modifier.**

Dangling modifier:	*Sleeping peacefully, the alarm woke me up.* [Was the alarm sleeping peacefully?]
Correct:	*Sleeping peacefully, I woke up to the alarm.*

22.3 ACTIVITY

Change one sentence in each pair below to a present participle or a present participle phrase, and open the remaining sentence with it. Remember to use a comma after the opening participle or phrase. (The sentences can be written more than one way.)

EXAMPLES   Dad was asleep on the couch.
He snored loudly.

Snoring loudly, Dad was asleep on the couch.

or

Sleeping on the couch, Dad snored loudly.

1. Stavros walked past the cemetery at midnight.
He whistled.

Whistling, Stavros walked past the cemetery at midnight.

2. Jan tried to sleep.
She was coughing.

Coughing, Jan tried to sleep.

3. Lillian played the car radio loudly.
She drove down the highway.

Playing the car radio loudly, Lillian drove down the highway.

4. I stirred the sauce on the stove.
I talked on the phone.

Talking on the phone, I stirred the sauce on the stove.

5. Chuck dribbled the ball down the basketball court.
He smiled at the crowd.

Dribbling the ball down the basketball court, Chuck smiled at the crowd.

6. The audience jumped to its feet.
The audience was applauding enthusiastically.

Applauding enthusiastically, the audience jumped to its feet.

POWER UP

To determine whether your writing would benefit from varying sentence openers, read it aloud. If it sounds singsongy or choppy, you probably have too many sentence openings alike.

7. The Girl Scouts were ringing doorbells in the neighborhood.
They were trying to sell cookies.

Trying to sell cookies, the Girl Scouts were ringing doorbells in the neighborhood.

8. Sylvia and Juan sat on a park bench at noon.
They were eating their lunches.

Eating their lunches, Sylvia and Juan sat on a park bench at noon.

22.4 INDIVIDUAL OR GROUP ACTIVITY

Working alone or with two classmates, add an opening present participle or an opening present participle phrase to each of the following sentences. Follow the opening participle or phrase with a comma.

EXAMPLE   _Watching television,_   I fell asleep on the couch.

1. Scratching their heads,   the students walked out of the classroom.

2. Kicking the surf,   Enrico jogged along the beach.

3. Seeing a squirrel,   the cat jumped from the window ledge.

4. Standing by the car,   the police officer wrote Randy a ticket for speeding.

5. Muttering under her breath, Chu Yen stormed angrily out of the room.

6. Rocking in her chair,   Grandma told the story of how she met Grandpa.

7. Holding hands,   we ran three blocks to get to the theater on time.

8. Smiling,   the 10-year-old raced down the street on her new red bicycle.

22.5 ACTIVITY

Pick five of the present participles and present participle phrases listed below, and use them to open sentences. Write the sentences on a separate sheet, and remember to use a comma after an opening participle or participle phrase.

chuckling	smiling broadly
humming	trying to understand the assignment
screaming	whistling a familiar tune

OPEN WITH A PAST PARTICIPLE OR A PAST PARTICIPLE PHRASE

The **past participle** is the *-ed* form of a regular verb. Past participles are words such as these:

believed	loved	started
flirted	moved	walked

Some past participles are irregular. Instead of being formed with *-ed*, they are formed in a variety of ways. Here are some examples.

driven	given	seen
eaten	gone	written

The past participle can be combined with one or more words to form a **past participle phrase,** such as one of these:

driven home	given half a chance	seen at night
eaten quickly	gone for good	written on a postcard

TIP

For additional discussions of past participles, see pages 159 and 239.

Try opening some of your sentences with past participles and past participle phrases.

Exhausted, Roy took a nap.

Exhausted after work, Roy took a nap.

Confused, Delia asked a question.

Confused about the assignment, Delia asked a question.

PUNCTUATION ALERT !

As the above examples illustrate, an opening past participle or participle phrase is followed by a comma.

GRAMMAR ALERT !

Be sure your past participle or past participle phrase is followed by a word the participle can sensibly describe, or you will have a **dangling modifier.**

Dangling modifier: *Worn out, a vacation was needed.* [Was the vacation worn out?]

Correction: *Worn out, I needed a vacation.*

TIP

Dangling modifiers are discussed on page 245.

22.6 ACTIVITY

Combine each pair of sentences below into one sentence. To do so, open the first sentence with the past participle or past participle phrase from the second sentence. Write your sentences in the following blanks, and remember to use commas after opening participles and participle phrases.

EXAMPLE   I complained to the landlord.
I was irritated by the dripping faucet.

   Irritated by the dripping faucet, I complained to the landlord.

1. Zahava laughed loudly at the joke.
She was amused.

   Amused, Zahava laughed loudly at the joke.

2. Ross changed his major to anthropology.
He was fascinated by other cultures.

   Fascinated by other cultures, Ross changed his major to anthropology.

3. Ivan organized a food drive on campus.
He was concerned about the plight of the poor.

   Concerned about the plight of the poor, Ivan organized a food drive on campus.

4. Blake quit the football team before the first game.
   He was tired of the long practices.

   Tired of the long practices, Blake quit the football team before the first game.

5. Marion and Lucy moved to New York to audition for parts in the theater.
   They had been bitten by the acting bug.

   Bitten by the acting bug, Marion and Lucy moved to New York to audition for parts in

   the theater.

6. The tractor trailer rig was blocking traffic.
   It was stalled in the middle of the highway.

   Stalled in the middle of the highway, the tractor trailer rig was blocking traffic.

7. The Jerrolds were given the city's humanitarian award.
   The Jerrolds are known for their charity work.

   Known for their charity work, the Jerrolds were given the city's humanitarian award.

8. We could not tell Lee about the surprise party.
   We were sworn to secrecy.

   Sworn to secrecy, we could not tell Lee about the surprise party.

22.7 ACTIVITY

Add an opening past participle or participle phrase to each of the following sentences. Be sure to use commas correctly.

EXAMPLE   *Annoyed by the loud band,* we left the party early.

1. Worried about her average,   Conchetta thought about how to improve her grades.

2. Concerned about my health,   the doctor told me to get more rest.

3. Angered by the outburst,   the umpire warned the first baseman to watch his temper.

4. Frightened by the noise,   the dog began howling.

5. Distracted,   the table server spilled the hot coffee all over the floor.

6. Amused,   I laughed to myself as I crossed campus.

7. Frustrated,   Dale threw the vase across the room.

8. Tired from working two jobs,   Daniel decided to take a much needed vacation.

22.8 ACTIVITY

Pick five of the past participles and past participle phrases listed below, and use them to open sentences. Write your sentences on a separate sheet, and remember to use a comma after an opening past participle or past participle phrase.

amused	disgusted
angered	frightened by the movie
cooked too long	worn out from the race

OPEN WITH A PREPOSITIONAL PHRASE

A **preposition** shows how things are positioned in time or space. Prepositions are words such as these:

around	behind	during	near	to
at	by	in	of	under

*I live **near** you.* [*Near* shows position in space.]
*I will leave **before** you.* [*Before* shows point in time.]

A **prepositional phrase** is a preposition and the word or words that go with it. Here are some examples.

at noon	by the garage	in the summer
behind the couch	during May	under the table

Try opening some of your sentences with prepositional phrases.

Before now, I never understood you.
During my lunch hour, I walk a mile.
In his pocket, Lou found a $5 bill.

To open with a prepositional phrase, you may only need to rearrange words.

Sentence: *Carlos found an abandoned kitten by the road*
Rearranged: *By the road, Carlos found an abandoned kitten.*

TIP

For a more complete discussion of prepositions and prepositional phrases, see Chapter 19.

PUNCTUATION ALERT

As the above sentences illustrate, an opening prepositional phrase is usually followed by a comma.

You can, however, omit the comma after a two-word phrase.

With a comma: *By noon, the meeting was over.*
Without a comma: *By noon the meeting was over.*

22.9 ACTIVITY

Rewrite the following sentences by adding opening prepositional phrases. Remember to use commas correctly.

EXAMPLE   Many audience members left.

     During the first act, many audience members left.

1. Jack lost his wallet yesterday.

     At the mall, Jack lost his wallet yesterday.

2. City council considered whether it should rewrite the city charter.

   All week, city council considered whether it should rewrite the city charter.

   _____

3. The new play opened to rave reviews.

   Over the weekend, the new play opened to rave reviews.

   _____

4. The couple began arguing very loudly.

   After dessert, the couple began arguing very loudly.

   _____

5. Voter turnout was surprisingly small.

   On election day, voter turnout was surprisingly small.

   _____

6. The coach decided that the team needed additional practice.

   During spring training, the coach decided that the team needed additional practice.

   _____

22.10 ACTIVITY

On a separate sheet, write five sentences that begin with prepositional phrases. Remember to use commas correctly.

OPEN WITH A DEPENDENT CLAUSE

> **TIP**
>
> For a more complete discussion of dependent clauses, see page 84.

A **dependent clause** has a subject and a verb, but it cannot stand alone as a sentence. Here are some examples of dependent clauses.

when the discussions were over
before you leave
although I disagree with you

Try opening some of your sentences with dependent clauses.

If I were you, I would find another job.
Because the lead singer is ill, the concert has been canceled.
Although I respect his view, I disagree with it.

To open with a dependent clause, you may only need to rearrange words.

The athletic program may be eliminated since the school levy failed.
Since the school levy failed, the athletic program may be eliminated.

PUNCTUATION ALERT
As the previous sentences illustrate, an opening dependent clause is followed by a comma.

22.11 ACTIVITY

Join each pair of sentences below into one sentence. First, change the second sentence into a dependent clause beginning with one of the following words.

after	because	if	when
although	before	since	while

Then use the dependent clause you created to open the first sentence. Be sure to use a comma after an opening dependent clause.

EXAMPLE   Jeffrey sneezes violently around cats and dogs.
He is allergic to animal dander.

Because he is allergic to animal dander, Jeffrey sneezes

violently around cats and dogs.

1. I curse my luck.
    A teacher calls on me for the only question I can't answer.

    When a teacher calls on me for the only question I can't answer, I curse my luck.

2. He tries to find books in the online catalog.
    Ben checks for magazines in *The Reader's Guide.*

    Before Ben checks for magazines in *The Reader's Guide,* he tries to find books in the online

    catalog.

3. The Writing Center tutors are very helpful.
    You want a sensitive, thoughtful reading of your draft.

    If you want a sensitive, thoughtful reading of your draft, the Writing Center tutors are

    very helpful.

4. *Phantom of the Opera* is my favorite play.
    I do not usually enjoy musicals.

    Although I do not usually enjoy musicals, *Phantom of the Opera* is my favorite play.

5. Crystal will attend summer school.
    She wants to graduate a semester early.

    Because she wants to graduate a semester early, Crystal will attend summer school.

6. The race for township trustee is a close one.
    Both candidates have long, distinguished political careers.

    Since both candidates have long, distinguished political careers, the race for township

    trustee is a close one.

7. I will be happy to drive you to work.
    Your car is in the shop for repairs.

    While your car is in the shop for repairs, I will be happy to drive you to work.

POWER UP

Select a piece of writing that you produced earlier this term. What sentence openers did you use? Do you need to increase the variety of sentence openers? If so, rewrite to do so. Test out the two versions on a classmate. Which did he or she prefer? Why?

8. I gained weight, but I felt better.
   I quit smoking.

   After I quit smoking, I gained weight, but I felt better.
   _____

22.12 ACTIVITY

Use five of the dependent clauses below to open sentences. Write your sentences on a separate sheet, and remember to use a comma after each opening dependent clause.

Because students experience stress   Since registration begins soon

Before Helen begins a race   Until the votes are counted

If I were you   When I was young

IF ENGLISH IS YOUR SECOND LANGUAGE

1. Varying your sentence openers is less important than grammatical correctness. Thus, do not consider whether or not you need to work on sentence openers until after you are sure you have made all the necessary changes in grammar.

2. If you are not sure whether or not your sentence openings need to be varied, ask a reliable reader (perhaps a Writing Center tutor) to read your work out loud and help you decide.

3. If you open some of your sentences with dependent clauses, be sure you understand the meanings of any subordinating conjunctions that open the clauses. You can check these meanings by looking back to page 94.

POWER UP

Punch up a professional's writing! Take a paragraph from a magazine or newspaper and rewrite a few sentences drawing on what you have learned about adding adverbs, participles, dependent clauses, and prepositional phrases. Compare the two versions. Do you like yours better? Why or why not?

RECHARGE

To avoid choppiness, vary your sentences in the following ways:

• Open with one or two adverbs.

  Anxiously, I awaited the doctor's report.

• Open with a present participle or present participle phrase.

  Seeing my opportunity, I slipped out the door.

• Open with a past participle or past participle phrase.

  Disturbed by the violence, we left the movie.

• Open with a prepositional phrase.

  Beside the pond, two ducks sunned themselves.

• Open with a dependent clause.

  Because I need more money, I will ask for a raise.

22.13 CHAPTER REVIEW ACTIVITY

On a separate sheet, write sentences according to the directions given.

1. Open with a prepositional phrase.
2. Open with a present participle.
3. Open with a past participle phrase.
4. Open with a dependent clause.
5. Open with two adverbs.

6. Open with a present participle phrase.
7. Open with a past participle.
8. Open with one adverb.

22.14 CHAPTER REVIEW ACTIVITY

The following passage would read better with a variety of sentence openers. Rewrite the passage, rearranging word order in some sentences to vary sentence openers with adverbs, present and past participles, participle phrases, prepositional phrases, and dependent clauses. More than one satisfactory rewrite is possible, so your work will differ from your classmates' work.

George Washington Carver was one of the world's greatest agricultural scientists. His parents were the black slaves of Moses Carver. George's father died soon after *[Soon after George was born, George's father died.]* George was born. The baby and his mother were kidnapped by bandits a few *[A few months later, the baby and his mother were kidnapped by bandits.]* months later. Moses Carver was able to buy George back, although the mother was *[Although the mother was never found, Moses Carver was able to buy George back.]* never found. The Carvers raised George themselves.

George showed a love for growing things at an early age. The neighbors called *[Because he used to care for and cure sick plants, the neighbors called him the plant doctor.]* him the plant doctor because he used to care for and cure sick plants. He later *[Seeking an education and performing jobs to pay for it, he later wandered about the United States. Finally, he entered Iowa State College.]* wandered about the United States seeking an education and performing jobs to pay for it. He finally entered Iowa State College. He was the first black person to graduate from the college, and he became its first black teacher.

Carver, appointed head of the agriculture department, joined the staff of *[Appointed head of the agriculture department, Carver joined the staff of Tuskegee Institute in 1896.]* Tuskegee Institute in 1896. He taught at Tuskegee for nearly 50 years. He worked *[Seeking ways to help the poor southern farmers, he worked long hours.]* long hours seeking ways to help the poor southern farmers. He introduced the peanut, pecan, and sweet potato to enrich soil worn out by cotton farming. He discovered new uses for these crops in his laboratory, including making butter, *[Asking no profit for himself, Carver gave his discoveries to the world.]* rubber, flour, coffee, and ink. Carver gave his discoveries to the world, asking no *[Freely, he advised anyone who consulted him.]* *[Although he received many high-paying job offers, he preferred to remain at Tuskegee and teach.]* profit for himself. He freely advised anyone who consulted him. He received many high-paying job offers. He preferred to remain at Tuskegee and teach. His work is carried on today through the George Washington Carver Foundation, which provides scholarships in agricultural research to black youth.

thinking in writing: Make a list of memorable moments you have spent with one or more members of your family. You can focus both on the distant and on the recent past.

writing from experience: Tell about a memorable moment you have spent with one or more members of your family. Be sure to make clear why the moment is so memorable.

writing in context: What do you consider to be the biggest problem facing the American family? Write an article suitable for *Parents Magazine* that notes what the problem is and that suggests a possible solution.

PART SIX REVIEW

Activity: Parallelism and Special Sentence Structure Challenges

Cross out and write above the line to correct two problems with parallelism and five problems with sentence structure.

Have you every wondered how ~~did~~ some things ^got^ ~~get~~ their names? ^Learning^ ~~By learning~~ about word histories is a good way to enrich our knowledge of language. Consider "cops," which has come to mean "police officers." One theory says ~~the reason is~~ ^that^ ~~because~~ in the nineteenth century many policemen wore big copper badges. People began referring to the police as "coppers" because of these badges. "Cops" ^occurred^ ~~was~~ when people shortened "coppers."

"Motel" is another interesting coinage. The combination of "motor" and "hotel" ~~come together to form~~ ^forms^ the word "motel." This word was coined by Arthur Heinman, who opened the first motel in California in 1925.

"Denim," "trivia," and ~~the word~~ "Gypsy" also have interesting origins. Both "denim" and "trivia" come from foreign languages. "Denim" got its name from the French town of DeNimes, where it was first made. "Trivia" comes from the Latin *trivium*, which means either "public square" or ~~it can mean~~ "where three roads meet." The plural Latin form is *trivia*, which means "street talk." "Gypsy" comes from the middle letters of *Egypt*, since Gypsies were originally believed to be from Egypt.

Activity: Parallelism, Special Sentence Structure Problems, and Sentence Openings

Cross out and write above the line to correct two problems with parallelism and two problems with sentence structure. Also, eliminate choppiness by increasing the variety of sentence openings.

Valentine's Day is an important holiday for many people. The reason is ^that^ ~~because~~ they can express their affection for those they care the most about. ~~Most~~ ^Although most people do not know the origin of the holiday,^ ~~people do not know the origin of the holiday, although~~ they celebrate it with enthusiasm. It actually began in ancient Rome, where February 14 was the day to honor Juno. Juno was the queen of Roman gods and goddesses, the goddess of women, and ~~she was~~ the goddess of marriage.

The lives of young boys and girls were strictly separate in ancient Rome. ^During the Lupercalia Festival, however, boys^ ~~Boys, however,~~ would get to pick the names of young girls from a ~~vase during the~~ ^vase.^ ~~Lupercalia Festival.~~ The boys became partners with the girls they chose. ^Then the^ ~~The~~ pairs of children ~~then~~ danced with each other for the duration of the festival. The pairing of children sometimes lasted an entire year. ~~By pairing~~ ^{Pairing} off for so long caused many to fall in love and later marry.

The first valentine was created many years later. It was a poem sent in 1415 by Charles, Duke of Orleans, to his wife. In the United States, Esther Howland receives credit for sending the first valentine's cards. Commercial valentines were introduced in the 1800s. Now the holiday has become tremendously commercialized. Friends and lovers feel obliged either to send flowers or ^{to} ~~they feel they must~~ send other gifts.

Spelling Correctly

CHAPTER **23**

Spelling

TEN WAYS TO BECOME A BETTER SPELLER

If you do not currently spell well, the following suggestions can help.

1. WAIT UNTIL YOU EDIT TO CHECK SPELLINGS. If you check during drafting and revising, you may check a word that you take out later. Furthermore, if you check spellings too soon, your attention will be diverted from the drafting and revising concerns. However, always be careful with spelling throughout.

2. USE A DICTIONARY WHEN YOU EDIT. Check *every* word you are unsure of. If you have even the slightest doubt, look up the word. To make checking more convenient, buy two dictionaries—one to keep where you usually write and another for your book bag to have at school.

3. USE AN ELECTRONIC SPELL CHECKER. Use either a handheld model or one that is part of your word processing program. However, be sure you understand the limits of these tools. They will not flag incorrect words that are correctly spelled, so if you write *hear* instead of *ear,* the spell checker will not notice.

4. KEEP A PERSONAL SPELLING LIST. Write the correct spelling of any word you misspell in any of your classes. Study the list every day, and have your classmates quiz you weekly. Then return the favor for them. Try underlining the troublesome parts of words, like this:

*defin**i**tely*

5. SPELL BY SYLLABLES. Long words, in particular, may be easier to spell if you sound them out syllable by syllable.

cit•i•zen•ship

6. SPELL PART BY PART.

hand•book   ground•work;   un•break•able

7. PRONOUNCE WORDS CORRECTLY. If you do so, you are more likely to spell them correctly. For example, you may misspell "athlete" if you pronounce it incorrectly as "ath**e**lete," with an extra syllable.

8. USE MEMORY TRICKS. For example, you may spell "tragedy" correctly if you remember that it contains the word "rage" and that characters in a tragedy are often filled with rage.

9. EDIT VERY SLOWLY. Pause for a few seconds over every word to think about the spelling.

10. LEARN THE RULES EXPLAINED IN THIS CHAPTER.

IDENTIFYING VOWELS AND CONSONANTS

To apply many of the spelling rules in this chapter, you must know the difference between vowels and consonants.

These letters are vowels:

a, e, i, o, u

All other letters, except *y*, are always consonants.

b, c, d, f, g, h, j, k, l, m, n, p, q, r, s, t, v, w, x, z

Y can be a consonant or a vowel, depending on the way it sounds.

y as a vowel sound:	*silly why company*
y as a consonant sound:	*yellow young yodel*

23.1 ACTIVITY

If the first underlined letter is a vowel, write "V" in the blank; if it is a consonant, write "C." Then write "V" or "C" in the second blank, to indicate whether the second underlined letter is a vowel or a consonant. Remember, *y* is sometimes a vowel and sometimes a consonant.

EXAMPLE   fri<u>e</u>ndl<u>y</u>   _____C_____   _____V_____

1. <u>ye</u>l<u>p</u>   _____C_____   _____C_____

2. r<u>ui</u>n   _____V_____   _____C_____

3. prom<u>is</u>e   _____V_____   _____C_____

4. l<u>u</u>ck<u>y</u>   _____V_____   _____V_____

5. <u>ti</u>red   _____C_____   _____V_____

6. ap<u>pl</u>e   _____C_____   _____C_____

7. <u>ye</u>sterday   _____C_____   _____V_____

8. <u>ha</u>ndle   _____C_____   _____V_____

9. <u>or</u>ange   _____V_____   _____V_____

10. tur<u>ke</u>y   _____C_____   _____V_____

CONNECT

Ask three instructors how they feel about spelling errors in student work.

RULE 1. ADDING A PREFIX

A **prefix** is one or more letters added to the *beginning* of a word to create a new word with a new meaning.

Prefix	+	Word	=	New Word with New Meaning
il	+	legal	=	illegal
im	+	mature	=	immature
un	+	eaten	=	uneaten

When a prefix is added, the spelling of the base word does not change.

im + mobile = immobile   over + run = overrun

in + audible = inaudible   un + nerved = unnerved

SPELLING ALERT !

The prefix rule often results in double letters, as the following examples show.

immobile   overrun   unnerved

23.2 ACTIVITY

Fill in each blank with the correct spelling of the word given.

EXAMPLE un + certain = _____uncertain_____

1. im + passable = impassable
2. il + legible = illegible
3. un + noticed = unnoticed
4. dis + appear = disappear
5. mis + spent = misspent
6. over + come = overcome
7. in + appropriate = inappropriate
8. un + necessary = unnecessary
9. in + audible = inaudible
10. un + discovered = undiscovered
11. im + mortal = immortal
12. un + knowing = unknowing
13. over + rule = overrule
14. un + nerved = unnerved
15. dis + service = disservice
16. im + partial = impartial
17. mis + judge = misjudge
18. il + legitimate = illegitimate
19. un + natural = unnatural
20. mis + spell = misspell

RULE 2. ADDING ENDINGS TO WORDS WITH A FINAL -Y

When you add an ending to a word with a final -*y*, change the -*y* to an *i* if there is a consonant before the -*y*. Keep the -*y* if a vowel appears before it.

Consonant before the final -*y*: Change the -*y* to *i*

cry + ed = cried   kindly + ness = kindliness

happy + est = happiest   study + ed = studied

Vowel before the final -*y*: Keep the -*y*

boy + s = boys   play + er = player

enjoy + ment = enjoyment   relay + ed = relayed

SPELLING ALERT !

Here are some exceptions to the rule, for you to memorize.

day + ly = daily   pay + ed = paid
dry + ly = dryly   say + ed = said
gay + ly = gaily   shy + ly = shyly
lay + ed = laid

When you add the ending *-ing*, keep the *-y*.

employ + ing = employing   say + ing = saying
enjoy + ing = enjoying   try + ing = trying

23.3 ACTIVITY

Fill in each blank below with the correct spelling of the word given.

EXAMPLES   ugly + er = *uglier*   joy + s = *joys*

1. study + ed = studied
2. tempt + ing = tempting
3. cry + ed = cried
4. happy + ness = happiness
5. marry + ed = married
6. stay + ed = stayed
7. deny + al = denial
8. hurry + ing = hurrying
9. clumsy + ness = clumsiness
10. fly + er = flier

11. destroy + er = destroyer
12. delay + ed = delayed
13. play + er = player
14. eat + ing = eating
15. likely + hood = likelihood
16. fly + ing = flying
17. crazy + est = craziest
18. pretty + est = prettiest
19. occupy + ed = occupied
20. lonely + ness = loneliness

RULE 3. ADDING ENDINGS TO WORDS WITH A FINAL *-E*

When you add an ending to a word with a final *-e*, drop the *-e* if the ending begins with a vowel. Keep the *-e* if the ending begins with a consonant.

Endings beginning with a vowel: Drop the -e

dine + <u>e</u>r = diner [One -e is dropped.]
drive + <u>ing</u> = driving
love + able = lovable
move + <u>e</u>d = moved [One -e is dropped.]

Endings beginning with a consonant: Keep the '-e

care + less = careless   place + ment = placement
false + <u>h</u>ood = falsehood   plate + <u>ful</u> = plateful

SPELLING ALERT !

Here are some exceptions for you to memorize.

acknowledge + ment = acknowledgment

argue + ment = argument

awe + ful = awful

courage + ous = courageous

judge + ment = judgment

mile + age = mileage

nine + th = ninth

notice + able = noticeable

true + ly = truly

23.4 ACTIVITY

Fill in each blank below with the correct spelling of the word given.

EXAMPLES wake + ing = _____waking_____

wake + ful = _____wakeful_____

1. hope + ing = _____hoping_____
2. create + ion = _____creation_____
3. spite + ful = _____spiteful_____
4. wide + ly = _____widely_____
5. advise + ing = _____advising_____
6. judge + ed = _____judged_____
7. take + s = _____takes_____
8. settle + ment = _____settlement_____
9. use + less = _____useless_____
10. continue + ing = _____continuing_____
11. sense + ible = _____sensible_____
12. life + like = _____lifelike_____
13. graze + ing = _____grazing_____
14. retire + ment = _____retirement_____
15. relate + ion = _____relation_____
16. love + ly = _____lovely_____
17. taste + ful = _____tasteful_____
18. fine + est = _____finest_____
19. bake + ed = _____baked_____
20. move + ment = _____movement_____

RULE 4. DOUBLING THE FINAL CONSONANT IN ONE-SYLLABLE WORDS

When you add an ending to a one-syllable word, double the final consonant if:

1. The ending begins with a vowel (-*ing*, -*ed*, -*er*, -*est*, and so forth).

and

2. The last three letters of the word are consonant-vowel-consonant (C-V-C).

One-Syllable Word Ending in C-V-C	+	Ending Beginning with a Vowel	=	Final Consonant Doubled
CVC run	+	er	=	runner
CVC g rab	+	ing	=	grabbing
CVC s lim	+	est	=	slimmest

POWER UP

Are you one of those people who cannot look up a word in a dictionary because you do not know how to spell it? If so, buy a pronunciation dictionary that lets you find words according to the way they sound rather than the way they are spelled.

Do not double the final consonant when the word does not end in C-V-C.

One-Syllable Word Not Ending in C-V-C	+	Ending Beginning with a Vowel	=	Final Consonant Not Doubled
VVC cl⌐ear⌐	+	est	=	clearest
VVC p⌐eel⌐	+	ing	=	peeling
VVC f⌐ear⌐	+	ed	=	feared

SPELLING ALERT ⚡

Here are some exceptions to memorize.

box + ing = boxing
bus + ing = busing [Bussing means "kissing"!]
saw + ed = sawed

23.5 ACTIVITY

Circle the last three letters of each of the following words, and label each letter "C" (consonant) or "V" (vowel). Then write in the blank the word formed with the ending given, being careful to apply the rule for doubling consonants.

EXAMPLES
CVC
⌐hop⌐ + ed = *hopped*

VVC
ch⌐eap⌐ + er = *cheaper*

CVC
1. ⌐sit⌐ + ing = ___sitting___

CVC
11. ⌐dip⌐ + er = ___dipper___

VVC
2. cl⌐ear⌐ + er = ___clearer___

VCC
12. s⌐end⌐ + ing = ___sending___

CVC
3. ⌐sad⌐ + en = ___sadden___

VCC
13. c⌐ool⌐ + er = ___cooler___

CVC
4. ⌐fat⌐ + en = ___fatten___

CVC
14. ⌐tap⌐ + ed = ___tapped___

VVC
5. c⌐oil⌐ + ed = ___coiled___

VVC
15. l⌐oot⌐ + ing = ___looting___

VCC
6. ⌐ask⌐ + ing = ___asking___

CVC
16. ⌐tan⌐ + ed = ___tanned___

CVC
7. t⌐hin⌐ + est = ___thinnest___

VCC
17. t⌐all⌐ + est = ___tallest___

CVC
8. ⌐wet⌐ + er = ___wetter___

CVC
18. ⌐red⌐ + er = ___redder___

CVC
9. w⌐rap⌐ + ed = ___wrapped___

CVC
19. d⌐rug⌐ + ist = ___druggist___

CVC
10. s⌐kip⌐ + ing = ___skipping___

VVC
20. b⌐oil⌐ + ed = ___boiled___

RULE 5. DOUBLING THE FINAL CONSONANT IN WORDS WITH MORE THAN ONE SYLLABLE

When a word has more than one syllable, double the final consonant if *all three* of the following conditions are met.

1. The ending begins with a vowel (*-ed*, *-ing*, *-er*, *-est*, and so forth).
2. The last three letters of the word are consonant-vowel-consonant (C-V-C).
3. The accent (stress or emphasis) is on the last syllable (begín).

Two or More Syllable Word Ending in C-V-C with Accent on Last Syllable	+	Ending Beginning with a Vowel	=	Final Consonant Doubled
CVC begin	+	er	=	beginner
CVC regret	+	ed	=	regretted
CVC permit	+	ing	=	permitting

If one or more of the three conditions is not met, do not double the final consonant.

1. If the ending does not begin with a vowel, do not double the consonant.

    commit + ment = commitment

2. If the last three letters are not C-V-C, do not double the consonant.

    befriend + ed = befriended

3. If the accent is not on the last syllable, do not double the consonant.

    visit + or = visitor

Do not double the final consonant if the accent moves from the last syllable when the ending is added.

Accent on last syllable: *prefer*
Accent moves to first syllable: *preference* [Do not double the consonant.]

SPELLING ALERT

Here are some exceptions to memorize.

cancel + ation = cancellation
equip + ed = equipped
excel + ence = excellence
excel + ent = excellent

23.6 ACTIVITY

Circle the last three letters of each of the following words, and mark each letter "C" for consonant or "V" for vowel. Next, determine which syllable is accented. Then spell the word with the given ending, being careful to double consonants according to the rule.

EXAMPLES ad⟨mit⟩ + ed = _admitted_   la⟨bor⟩ + er = _laborer_
CVC   *CVC*

VCC
1. rep⟨ent⟩ + ing =   repenting   11. la⟨bor⟩ + ed =   labored   CVC
CVC
2. ex⟨pel⟩ + ed =   expelled   12. per⟨mit⟩ + ed =   permitted   CVC
CVC
3. an⟨swer⟩ + ing =   answering   13. ord⟨ain⟩ + ed =   ordained   VVC
CVC
4. be⟨gin⟩ + ing =   beginning   14. re⟨fer⟩ + ence =   reference   CVC
VCC
5. pret⟨end⟩ + ed =   pretended   15. en⟨ter⟩ + ed =   entered   CVC
CVC
6. sub⟨mit⟩ + ed =   submitted   16. oc⟨cur⟩ + ed =   occurred   CVC
CVC
7. tra⟨vel⟩ + ing =   traveling   17. mo⟨tor⟩ + ist =   motorist   CVC
CVC
8. pa⟨trol⟩ + ed =   patrolled   18. ev⟨ict⟩ + ing =   evicting   VCC
VCC
9. ac⟨cept⟩ + ance =   acceptance   19. con⟨fer⟩ + ed =   conferred   CVC
CVC
10. go⟨ssip⟩ + ing =   gossiping   20. o⟨mit⟩ + ed =   omitted   CVC

RULE 6. ADDING -S OR -ES

Most nouns add -s to form the plural.

Singular Noun	Plural Noun
girl	girls
hat	hats
shoe	shoes
umbrella	umbrellas

Most verbs add -s in the present tense when their subject is *he, she, it,* or a singular noun.

It
The chef
He   } makes, stirs, cooks, eats, sleeps, feels
She

If a word ends in -s, -x, -z, -ch, or -sh, add -es.

address + es = addresses   mix + es = mixes
birch + es = birches   waltz + es = waltzes
dish + es = dishes

If a word ends in a consonant and -y, change the -y to -i and add -es. If the word ends in a vowel and -y, just add -s.

Consonant and -y   **Vowel and -y**
C   *V*
f⟨ly⟩   flies   t⟨oy⟩   toys
C   *V*
gup⟨py⟩   guppies   b⟨oy⟩   boys
C   *V*
la⟨dy⟩   ladies   k⟨ey⟩   keys

If a word ends in a consonant and -*o*, add -*es*. If the word ends in a vowel and -*o*, just add -*s*.

Consonant and -*o*

$\overset{C}{he\boxed{ro}}$ heroes

$\overset{C}{torna\boxed{do}}$ tornadoes

Vowel and -*o*

$\overset{V}{pat\boxed{io}}$ patios

$\overset{V}{rat\boxed{io}}$ ratios

SPELLING ALERT !

Many words related to music add -*s*. Some of these are exceptions to the rule above, and some are not.

altos	radios	sopranos
pianos	solos	trios

23.7 ACTIVITY

Add -*s* or -*es*, whichever is correct.

EXAMPLES   church _____churches_____   television _____televisions_____

1. puppy	puppies	11. do	does
2. chair	chairs	12. fox	foxes
3. wax	waxes	13. enjoy	enjoys
4. potato	potatoes	14. brush	brushes
5. stitch	stitches	15. genius	geniuses
6. tomato	tomatoes	16. dictionary	dictionaries
7. candy	candies	17. marry	marries
8. crash	crashes	18. joy	joys
9. monkey	monkeys	19. echo	echoes
10. boy	boys	20. miss	misses

RULE 7. CHOOSING BETWEEN *IE* AND *EI*

Here is an old rhyme that can help you decide whether *ie* or *ei* is correct.

> Use *i* before *e*
> Except after *c*
> Or when sounded like *a*,
> As in "neighbor" and "weigh."

1. Use *i* before *e*:

achieve	chief	priest
believe	grief	yield

2.   Except after *c* (that is, use *ei* after *c*):

ceiling   deceive   receipt

conceive   perceive   receive

3.   Or when sounded like *a,* as in "neighbor" and "weigh" (that is, use *ei* when the sound is a long *a*):

freight   sleigh   veil

neighbor   their   weigh

4.   The previous three rules apply when *ie* and *ei* are pronounced as one syllable. They do not apply when the letters are divided between two syllables. Usually when the letters are divided between two syllables, you can tell the spelling by the sound, as the following examples show.

deity   diet   science

SPELLING ALERT:
Here are some exceptions to memorize.

ancient   height   protein

caffeine   leisure   seize

either   neither   weird

23.8 ACTIVITY

Fill in the blanks in the following words with *ie* or *ei.*

EXAMPLES   r __ei__ gn

br __ie__ f

1. p __ie__ ce

2. w __ei__ ght

3. ach __ie__ ve

4. fr __ie__ nd

5. f __ie__ ld

6. sl __ei__ gh

7. soc __ie__ ty

8. conc __ei__ ve

9. f __ie__ rce

10. v __ei__ n

11. rec __ei__ ve

12. sh __ie__ ld

13. __ei__ ght

14. misch __ie__ f

15. rel __ie__ f

16. bel __ie__ f

17. b __ei__ ge

18. fr __ei__ ght

19. exper __ie__ nce

20. aud __ie__ nce

POWER UP

Tape a list of words you frequently misspell to your computer monitor so you can easily check these words as you write.

SPELLING LIST

Below is a list of 50 words people often misspell. Study a few of the words every day, review often, and you will be on your way to becoming a better speller.

Frequently Misspelled Words

absence	disappear	immediately	parallel
accommodate	embarrass	important	personnel
across	environment	integration	possess
answer	exaggerate	jewelry	recipe
athlete	familiar	judgment	reference
beginning	February	knowledge	rhythm
calendar	forty	license	separate
career	fourth	mathematics	strength
cemetery	government	miscellaneous	temperature
colonel	grammar	necessary	thorough
conscience	harass	occasion	until
desperate	height	occurred	Wednesday
different	illegal		

23.9 ACTIVITY

Form a group with two classmates. Each group member should select five different words from the list of frequently misspelled words to quiz the other group members on. Any time a word is missed, it should be written down and studied until everyone in the group can spell all 15 words.

IF ENGLISH IS YOUR SECOND LANGUAGE

The characteristics of your native language can make mastering English spelling difficult. For example, since Spanish has no *wh* sound, speakers of Spanish may spell *which* as *wich*. Similarly, speakers of Japanese may reverse *l* and *r*. For this reason, keeping a personal spelling list is very important. As you discover words you cannot spell, add them to your list and study them daily.

RECHARGE

To become a better speller,

- Use a dictionary or spell checker.
- Learn the rules for
  - Adding a prefix.
  - Adding endings to words with a final -*y*.
  - Adding endings to words with a final -*e*.
  - Doubling the final consonant in one-syllable words.
  - Doubling the final consonant in words with more than one syllable.
  - Forming noun plurals.
  - Using *ie* and *ei*.

23.10 CHAPTER REVIEW ACTIVITY

A. Write the correct spellings of the following words in the blanks. If you are unsure, consult the rules in parentheses or check your dictionary.

1. un + natural = _unnatural_ (rule 1)
2. shove + ed = _shoved_ (rule 3)
3. bat + er = _batter_ (rule 4)
4. carry + ed = _carried_ (rule 2)
5. dip + ed = _dipped_ (rule 4)
6. care + ful = _careful_ (rule 3)
7. walk + ing = _walking_ (rule 4)
8. feel + ing = _feeling_ (rule 4)
9. prefer + ence = _preference_ (rule 5)
10. flat + en = _flatten_ (rule 4)
11. run + ing = _running_ (rule 4)
12. friendly + er = _friendlier_ (rule 2)
13. regret + ed = _regretted_ (rule 5)
14. enchant + ment = _enchantment_ (rule 2)
15. re + evaluate = _reevaluate_ (rule 1)
16. admit + ed = _admitted_ (rule 5)
17. enjoy + able = _enjoyable_ (rule 2)
18. visit + ed = _visited_ (rule 5)
19. mis + spoke = _misspoke_ (rule 1)
20. love + able = _lovable_ (rule 3)

B. Write the correct spellings of the following words in the blanks. If you are unsure, check your dictionary or consult rules 6 and 7.

EXAMPLES   memo + (s or es) = _memos_

for _ei_ gn (ie or ei)

1. match + (s or es) = _matches_
2. mosquito + (s or es) = _mosquitoes_
3. th _ei_ r (ie or ei)
4. fix + (s or es) = _fixes_
5. w _ei_ ght (ie or ei)
6. reach + (s or es) = _reaches_
7. h _ei_ r (ie or ei)
8. moss + (s or es) = _mosses_
9. Cheerio + (s or es) = _Cheerios_

10. perc ___ei___ ve (ie or ei)

11. veto + (s or es) = ___vetoes___

12. grow + (s or es) = ___grows___

23.11 CHAPTER REVIEW ACTIVITY

The following paragraph has eight spelling errors. Find the errors by studying each word, syllable by syllable. Cross out each misspelled word and write the correct spelling above it. If necessary, consult your dictionary for the correct spelling.

If you want to buy an American-made car, you may have to do some detective work. Determining the origin of a vehicle can be tricky. With ~~internattional~~ *international* wheeling and ~~dealling~~ *dealing*, a car or truck ~~manufacturred~~ *manufactured* by a company in one country may ~~actualy~~ *actually* be sold by a company in another country. For example, many so-called domestic ~~autoes~~ *autos* now come from ~~foriegn~~ *foreign* factories ~~lisenced~~ *licensed* to overseas ~~companys~~ *companies*. Similarly, many midsize cars that carry Japanese labels roll off the assembly lines in Michigan and Indiana. What is a person to do? The answer may come in the form of legislation requiring car manufacturers to note clearly where their vehicles are made.

GETTING IN GEAR

thinking in writing: Make a list of things that you do well, such as making the perfect omelette, entertaining young children, throwing a fast ball, or choosing the right birthday presents. Then make a second list of things you wish you could do better.

writing from experience: Select a procedure you do well and explain how you have benefited from knowing how to do that thing well. As an alternative, pick a procedure you wish you could do better, and explain the problems that have resulted from not being able to perform the procedure as well as you wish.

writing in context: Select a magazine and write an article for its readership that explains how to do something that you do well. For example, if you are good at arranging flowers, explain how to do that for the readers of *Home and Garden*.

CHAPTER 24

Frequently Confused Words

A/AN

For an explanation of how to use these frequently confused words, see page 228.

A LOT/ALOT

The correct form is **a lot**.

ACCEPT/EXCEPT

1. **Accept** means "receive" or "get." It is a verb.

    Jonathan does not <u>accept</u> help easily.

2. **Except** means "excluded" or "other than." It is a preposition.

    All of the senators <u>except</u> Senator Howard answered the roll call vote.

Memory Tip: To remember that *except* means "excluded," remember that both begin with *ex-*.

24.1 ACTIVITY

A. Fill in the blanks in the following sentences with *accept* or *except*.

1. I hope you can find it in your heart to <u>accept</u> my apology.

2. People are happiest when they <u>accept</u> their limitations.

3. I finished all the problems <u>except</u> the last one.

4. <u>Except</u> for Carlos, everyone decided to attend the economics lecture in the auditorium.

5. Jane and Larry broke up because they could not <u>accept</u> each other's faults.

6. Every weather forecaster <u>except</u> the one on Channel 9 is predicting snow for Christmas.

B. On a separate sheet, write two sentences using *accept* and two using *except*.

ADVICE/ADVISE

1. **Advice** is a suggestion or an opinion. It is a noun.

    If you have a problem, ask Lee for <u>advice</u>.

2. **Advise** means "offer a suggestion." It is a verb.

    I <u>advise</u> you to get your tickets early.

Memory Tip: Remember that *advice* contains the word *vice*, and a person with a "vice" needs "advice."

24.2 ACTIVITY

A. Fill in the blanks in the following sentences with *advice* or *advise*.

1. My <u>advice</u> to you is to study harder.

2. I <u>advise</u> you to study harder.

3. If <u>advice</u> is what you want, you have come to the wrong person.

4. Imran wants Dr. Barolsky to <u>advise</u> him about how to apply to a good journalism school.

5. Most people listen to David's <u>advice</u> and then do the opposite of what he recommends.

6. No one can <u>advise</u> you better than your own conscience.

B. On a separate sheet, write two sentences using *advice* and two using *advise*.

AFFECT/EFFECT

1. **Affect** means "influence." It is a verb.

    High humidity <u>affects</u> my sinuses.

2. **Effect** means "result." It is a noun.

    The <u>effect</u> of the tax hike is not yet clear.

3. **Effect** can also be a verb meaning "bring about."

    Congress will try <u>to effect</u> a change in our trade agreement with Japan.

Memory Tip: Remember that *effect* means "result" by remembering that the first syllable of *effect* rhymes with the first syllable of *result*.

24.3 ACTIVITY

A. Fill in the blanks in the following sentences with *affect* or *effect*.

1. The most serious <u>effect</u> of the hurricane is the loss of life.

2. A person's genetic makeup will __affect__ his or her life expectancy.

3. Nothing can __affect__ my mood as much as music.

4. The tuition increase will __affect__ enrollment.

5. The __effect__ of the tuition increase will be dramatic.

6. As student government president, Jan hopes to __effect__ a change in the university's honor code.

B. On a separate sheet, write two sentences using *affect* and two using *effect*.

ALL READY/ALREADY

1. **All ready** means "all set" or "prepared."

   I am all ready to go with you.

2. **Already** means "previously," "by a specific time," or "by this time." It is an adverb.

   We are already an hour late for dinner.

Memory Tip: To remember that *all ready* means "all set," remember that they are both two words.

24.4 ACTIVITY

A. Fill in the blanks in the following sentences with *all ready* or *already*.

1. The reporters were __already__ at the scene when the police arrived.

2. I am __already__ a week ahead on my reading assignments, but I want to work a little longer.

3. The plane was __all ready__ for departure, but some of the passengers had not arrived yet.

4. Once the sound crew completes its work, we will be __all ready__ for the light crew to begin.

5. Once Martha gets a transcript of her grades, her scholarship application will be __all ready__ to mail.

6. Ivan __already__ told you not to wait for him.

B. On a separate sheet, write two sentences using *all ready* and two using *already*.

ALL RIGHT/ALRIGHT

In formal situations, do not use **alright. All right** is the acceptable form in college and on the job.

BEEN/BEING

1. **Been** is the past participle of *to be*. To form a complete verb, *been* is used with *have*, *has*, or *had*.

   You *have been* my best friend since seventh grade.
   Charlie *has been* here before.
   I *had been* angry until you apologized.

For a complete discussion of the past participle and its uses, see Chapter 11.

GRAMMAR ALERT
Be sure to use *have*, *has*, or *had* with *been*.

   No: The car *been* parked in a tow-away zone.
   Yes: The car *had been* parked in a tow-away zone.

2. **Being** is the present participle (the *-ing* form) of *to be*. To form the complete verb, it is used with *am*, *is*, *are*, *was*, or *were*.

   I *am being* stubborn about this.
   The car *is being* delivered this afternoon.
   We *are being* fair to you.
   He *was being* rude last night.
   The letters *were being* mailed to you.

For a complete discussion of the present participle and its uses, see Chapter 12.

GRAMMAR ALERT
Be sure to use *am*, *is*, *are*, *was*, or *were* with *being*.

   No: You *being* very understanding.
   Yes: You *are being* very understanding.

24.5 ACTIVITY

A. Fill in the blanks in the following sentences with the correct form: *been* or *being*. Also, circle the helping verb (*have*, *has*, *had*, *am*, *is*, *are*, *was*, or *were*).

1. The rowdy fans (were) being _____ asked to leave.

2. You (are) being _____ a very good friend to Jerry.

3. Before you arrived, I (had) been _____ cleaning the basement.

4. The children (have) been _____ very patient.

5. If I (am) being _____ unfair, I apologize.

6. Royce DePizzo (has) been _____ a baseball coach for 25 years.

B. On a separate sheet, write two sentences using *been* and two using *being*.

BESIDE/BESIDES

1. **Beside** means "alongside."

   Put the table *beside* the chair.

2. **Besides** means "in addition to."

Besides a fever, I have a sore throat.

Memory Tip: To remember that *besides* means "in addition to," think of the second *s* in *besides* as functioning in addition to the first *s*.

A. Fill in the blanks in the following sentences with *beside* or *besides*.

1. _Besides_____ going to the mall, we can shop downtown.

2. Do you mind if I sit _beside_____ you?

3. _Beside_____ the student center, the university planted a beautiful flower garden.

4. No one, _besides_____ you, believes that the final exam will be difficult.

5. _Besides_____ studying, I have to practice my clarinet tonight.

6. The child placed her favorite doll _beside_____ her on the couch.

B. On a separate sheet, write two sentences using *beside* and two using *besides*.

> **POWER UP**
>
> Explain the different meanings of these two sentences: "I have a desk in my room beside the bed" and "I have a desk in my room besides the bed."

BUY/BY

1. **Buy** means "purchase." It is a verb.

I cannot afford to buy those shoes.

2. **By** means "near" or "a means of." It is a preposition.

We can travel to Toronto by train.

Memory Tip: Remember that *buy* means "purchase" by thinking of the *u* in both words.

A. Fill in the blanks in the following sentences with *buy* or *by*.

1. When I get my paycheck, I can _buy_____ tickets to the concert.

2. For your birthday, Josie will _buy_____ you dinner at your favorite restaurant.

3. _By_____ my calculations, we will be out of money before the end of the week.

4. Wanda asked José to meet her _by_____ the clock tower at noon.

5. This article was written _by_____ a noted sociologist.

6. This month, every time you _buy_____ a hamburger at Carl's, two cents will be donated to the hospital's children's ward.

B. On a separate sheet, write two sentences using *buy* and two using *by*.

CAN/COULD

Can is a present tense form used for writing about something that is happening *now*. **Could** is a past tense form used for writing about something that happened *before now*.

Present: *When I am bored, I <u>can</u> sleep all day.*
Past: *When I was bored, I <u>could</u> sleep all day.*

24.8 ACTIVITY

A. Fill in the blanks in the following sentences with the correct form: *can* or *could*.

1. You _could_____ tell that Bebe was crying because her eyes were red.

2. If you are willing to take her advice, Inez _can_____ help you.

3. This morning, Professor Hyatt said that we _could_____ leave class early.

4. When spring arrives, I _can_____ notice everybody's mood improving.

5. Last semester, you _could_____ decide between an American and a British history class, and this semester you _can_____ decide between a French and a German class.

6. Now when I see chocolate, I _can_____ no longer resist it.

B. On a separate sheet, write two sentences using *can* and two using *could*.

> **TIP**
>
> If you often make mistakes with some of the frequently confused words, tape them—along with their definitions—to your computer screen as a reminder.

GOOD/WELL

For an explanation of how to use these frequently confused words, see page 227.

HAVE/OF

Some writers mistakenly use **of** instead of the helping verb **have**. This error most frequently occurs after one of these verbs: *could, would, should, may, must, might,* and *will,* probably because *of* sounds like *have* in phrases such as *could have. Of* is never correct in these constructions.

No: *I <u>could of</u> won the race.*
Yes: *I <u>could have</u> won the race.*

No: *She <u>must of</u> lost her way.*
Yes: *She <u>must have</u> lost her way.*

No: *Jan <u>should of</u> tried harder.*
Yes: *Jan <u>should have</u> tried harder.*

On a separate sheet, write sentences using any four of the following: *could have, would have, should have, may have, might have, must have,* and *will have.*

HEAR/HERE

1. **Hear** means "listen." It is a verb.

   We cannot hear you over the radio.

2. **Here** means "a nearby place." It is an adverb.

   Joseph will pick you up here at three o'clock.

Memory Tip: Hear, which means "listen," has the word *ear* in it: h⟨ear⟩.

A. Fill in the blanks in the following sentences with *hear* or *here.*

1. Let's move up front so we can __hear__ better.

2. __Here__ are the reports you are looking for.

3. To __hear__ Lionel tell it, he saved the day single-handedly.

4. Donna has lived __here__ for 30 years.

5. Dane refuses to admit that he cannot __hear__ very well.

6. An important Civil War battle was fought __here__ .

B. On a separate sheet, write two sentences using *hear* and two using *here.*

ITS/IT'S

1. **Its** shows ownership. It is a pronoun.

   This coat has a hole in its pocket.

2. **It's** means "it is" or "it has."

   It's raining again.
   It's been raining all day.

Memory Tip: Do not use *it's* unless you can substitute "it is" or "it has."

A. Fill in the blanks in the following sentences with *its* or *it's.*

1. __It's__ been three years since I met you.

2. During the tornado, the house was lifted off __its__ foundation.

3. I wonder if __it's__ too late to call Lucinda.

4. _It's_ been a pleasure working with Henry.

5. The company reduced _its_ workforce by 15 percent to save money.

6. Our dog buries _its_ bones under the porch.

B. In the blanks below, write two sentences using *its* and two using *it's*.

KNOW/NO AND KNEW/NEW

1. **Know** means "understand" or "have knowledge of." It is a verb.

   Juan knows CPR and first aid.

2. **No** expresses a negative idea.

   No, you may not come with me.

3. **Knew** is the past tense of *know*.

   Larry knew the answer, but he forgot it.

4. **New** means "not old."

   Sylvia's new car is sporty.

24.12 ACTIVITY

A. Fill in the blanks in the following sentences with *know, no, knew,* or *new.*

1. The _new_ philosophy professor is a fascinating lecturer.

2. Eleni _no_ longer works in the library.

3. If I _knew_ you were coming, I would have made more for supper.

4. We all _know_ Lucy to be honest and sincere.

5. Most Americans believe that anything _new_ is better.

6. Mike _knew_ he would have to lose 10 pounds to wrestle in the lighter weight classification.

7. I _know_ what I want to say, but I can't think of the right word.

8. There is _no_ reason to be angry.

B. On a separate sheet, write one sentence using each of these words: *know, no, knew,* and *new.*

LIE/LAY

1. **Lie** is an irregular verb meaning "rest on a surface." It has the following forms: *lie, lying, lay, lain.*

Present:	*lie(s)*	*I lie down every day at three o'clock.*
Present participle:	*lying*	*Raul is lying down for an hour.*

	Past:	*lay* *She lay down for a nap an hour ago.*
	Past participle:	*lain* *Margo has lain down for awhile.*

2. **Lie** is also a regular verb meaning "to not tell the truth." It has these forms: *lie, lying, lied, lied*.

	Present:	*lie(s)* *If you lie, I will know it.*
	Present participle:	*lying* *Dorrie can tell if I am lying.*
	Past:	*lied* *He was sorry he lied to you.*
	Past participle:	*lied* *The child has lied about his grade.*

3. **Lay** is an irregular verb meaning "put down" or "place." It has these forms: *lay, laying, laid, laid*.

	Present:	*lay(s)* *Sheila lays her keys on the table.*
	Present participle:	*laying* *You are laying that in the wrong place.*
	Past:	*laid* *I thought I laid my book on the bed.*
	Past participle:	*laid* *Mario has laid the tools on the bench.*

24.13 ACTIVITY

A. Fill in the blanks in the following sentences with the correct form of *lie* or *lay*.

1. Mahammed _lay_ down under a tree to read a book.

2. Whenever I _lie_ about something important, I become angry with myself.

3. Andy _laid_ his lunch by his schoolbooks and then left without it.

4. I fell asleep _lying_ on the couch.

5. When you set the table, you should _lay_ the forks to the left of the plates.

6. Doris has _lied_ about her accomplishments too often, and now nobody believes her.

7. We can't remember where we _laid_ our sunglasses.

8. I _lay_ down in the hammock and fell asleep instantly.

9. They have _lain_ on the grass so long that their clothes are grass-stained.

10. Mother is gently _laying_ the teddy bear next to the sleeping baby.

B. On a separate sheet, write two sentences using some form of the *irregular* verb *lie*, two using some form of the *regular* verb *lie*, and two using some form of the irregular verb *lay*.

LOOSE/LOSE

1. **Loose** means "not tight." It is an adjective.

   Since I have been exercising, my pants are <u>loose</u>.

2. **Lose** means "misplace" or "not win." It is a verb.

   I <u>lose</u> my keys once a week.
   You will <u>lose</u> the match if you do not concentrate more.

Memory Tip: Loose has two o's and lose has only one. You can remember that *lose* means "to misplace" if you think, One o has been misplaced.

24.14 ACTIVITY

A. Fill in the blanks in the following sentences with *loose* or *lose*.

1. Put your registration materials in a safe place so you will not
   <u>lose</u> them.

2. If we <u>lose</u> this game, we will not make it to the district championship.

3. <u>Loose</u> clothing is more comfortable than tight clothing.

4. My credit card numbers are recorded in my drawer, in case I
   <u>lose</u> my wallet.

5. The door is squeaking because a hinge is <u>loose</u> .

6. Have you heard the expression "<u>Loose</u> lips sink ships"?

B. On a separate sheet, write two sentences using *loose* and two using *lose*.

PASSED/PAST

1. **Passed** is the past tense of the verb *pass*. It means "went by" or "handed."

   The police car <u>passed</u> us at 80 miles an hour.
   When Rajá <u>passed</u> the milk, she knocked over the vase of flowers.

2. **Past** means "previous time." It also means "by."

   I am not proud of my <u>past</u>.
   Drive <u>past</u> Maurice's house to see if he is home.

Memory Tip: To remember that *past* means "previous time," remind yourself of the *p* and the *t* in both *past* and *previous time*.

24.15 ACTIVITY

A. Fill in the blanks in the following sentences with *passed* or *past*.

1. Our <u>past</u> experiences influence what we become in the future.

2. The speeding car __passed__ us in the inside lane.

3. In the __past__ , Carlotta considered dropping out of school.

4. It's time to let go of the __past__ .

5. As the parade __passed__ the reviewing stand, the band members tipped their hats.

6. The relay runner __passed__ the baton to the fastest runner on the team.

B. On a separate sheet, write two sentences using *passed* and two using *past*.

PRINCIPAL/PRINCIPLE

1. **Principal** means "main" or "most important." It is an adjective. It can also be a noun meaning "the head of a school" (the main or most important person in the school).

   The principal problem here is that you will not compromise.
   The principal closed the school because the water pipes froze.

2. **Principle** is a truth or a standard. It is a noun.

   You cannot play on our team because you do not understand the principles of fair play.

Memory Tip: Principal includes the word *pal,* and a principal should be a student's pal.

24.16 ACTIVITY

A. Fill in the blanks in the following sentences with *principal* or *principle.*

1. Now that Leah Stanich is the __principal__ of Woodside Elementary School, she misses teaching.

2. I agree with the __principle__ of freedom of the press but not when people's privacy is invaded.

3. The __principal__ matter before the school board is whether to change the high school curriculum.

4. I understand the __principle__ behind this algebra problem, but I do not know the procedure for solving it.

5. Right now, my __principal__ concern is for the well-being of my children.

6. Lucinda will not back down because she believes in the __principle__ she is fighting for.

B. On a separate sheet, write two sentences using *principal* and two using *principle.*

POWER UP

To appreciate how important it is to use the correct word, consider these sentences: "The principal is correct" and "The principle is correct." How do the meanings differ?

QUIET/QUIT/QUITE

1. **Quiet** means "without noise" or "calm."

    Joyce cannot sleep unless the house is completely quiet.

2. **Quit** means "stop" or "give up." It is a verb.

    Peter finally quit smoking.

3. **Quite** means "exactly" or "very."

    This is not quite the birthday Eleni hoped for.
    I am quite surprised by your actions.

24.17 ACTIVITY

A. Fill in the blanks in the following sentences with *quiet, quit,* or *quite.*

1. Mario studies in the library because it is _quiet_ .

2. I am not _quite_ sure how to help you.

3. Thomas _quit_ the basketball team because he tore a ligament in his knee.

4. Grandmother is _quite_ capable of taking care of herself.

5. The _quiet_ in the country helps me relax.

6. Marla's New Year's resolution is to _quit_ biting her nails.

B. On a separate sheet, write two sentences using *quiet,* two using *quit,* and two using *quite.*

RISE/RAISE

1. **Rise** is an irregular verb meaning "get up" or "go up." It has these forms: *rise, rising, rose, risen.*

Present:	rise(s)	*Terry rises every day at dawn.*
Present participle:	rising	*The sun is rising in the east.*
Past:	rose	*I rose to greet Father Clooney.*
Past participle:	risen	*The choir has risen from its seats.*

2. **Raise** is a regular verb meaning "lift up" or "force up." It has these forms: *raise, raising, raised, raised.*

Present:	raise(s)	*She raises her hand and waves.*
Present participle:	raising	*Kyle is raising his feet so I can sweep under them.*
Past:	raised	*I raised the curtain to start the play.*
Past participle:	raised	*Dominic has raised the shelf an inch.*

A. Fill in the blanks in the following sentences with the correct forms of *rise* or *raise*.

1. He _raised [raises]_ the curtain to reveal the grand prize.

2. The sun _rises [rose]_ over the Atlantic Ocean.

3. The mayor had _risen_ to speak when the lights went out.

4. Every morning, Jeremy _raised [raises]_ the flag.

5. She has _raised_ the blinds to let the sun in.

6. Lee and Chris are _raising_ the heavy trunk onto the table.

7. Each day, he _rose [rises]_ at three o'clock to feed the baby.

8. When Helena entered the room, the guests _rose_ to greet her.

9. I always _raise_ my arm to hail a taxi.

10. Sam is _rising_ early to go fishing.

B. On a separate sheet, write two sentences using some form of *rise* and two using some form of *raise*.

SIT/SET

1. **Sit** is an irregular verb meaning "sit down" or "rest." It has these forms: *sit, sitting, sat, sat.*

Present:	sit(s)	The cat <u>sits</u> by the fire.
Present participle:	sitting	I am <u>sitting</u> next to Brad.
Past:	sat	We <u>sat</u> in the back of the church.
Past participle:	sat	I have <u>sat</u> in one spot all day.

2. **Set** is an irregular verb meaning "place" or "arrange." It has these forms: *set, setting, set, set.*

Present:	set(s)	The caterer <u>sets</u> a lovely table.
Present participle:	setting	We were <u>setting</u> the chairs in a row.
Past:	set	Margery <u>set</u> her books on the desk.
Past participle:	set	I had <u>set</u> my briefcase on the roof of the car before driving off.

A. Fill in the blanks in the following sentences with the correct forms of *sit* or *set*.

1. Joyce _set_ the controls on the VCR to record her favorite program, and then she left the house.

2. Every day at five o'clock, Kwame _sets [set]_ the table for dinner.

3. We have <u>sat</u> here long enough.

4. The students <u>set</u> their first drafts on the instructor's desk before leaving class.

5. The passengers are <u>sitting</u> on the plane, patiently listening to the preflight instructions.

6. I <u>sat</u> in the library for an hour waiting for you.

7. Because Hank and I are nearsighted, we usually <u>sit</u> up front in theaters.

8. The mourners were filing by the coffin and <u>setting</u> flowers on it.

9. We have <u>sat</u> in these bleachers so long that our backs hurt.

10. Yesterday, Ira and Marco <u>set</u> up the tables for the garage sale.

B. On a separate sheet, write two sentences using some form of *sit* and two using some form of *set*.

SUPPOSE/SUPPOSED

1. **Suppose** means "assume." Its past tense form is *supposed*.

   I <u>suppose</u> Lesley will be joining us for dinner.
   Everyone <u>supposed</u> the snow storm would ruin the weekend.

2. When **supposed** comes between a helping verb (*am, is, are, was, were*) and *to*, it means "should."

   My sister <u>is supposed to</u> pick us up here.
   I <u>was supposed to</u> help Jan with the decorations.
   We <u>are supposed to</u> study together at noon.

GRAMMAR ALERT !

Because the *d* at the end of *supposed* and the *t* at the beginning of *to* are pronounced as one sound, writers may mistakenly omit the *d* in *supposed*.

No: *You were <u>suppose</u> to go with me.*
Yes: *You were <u>supposed</u> to go with me.*

No: *A student is <u>suppose</u> to study.*
Yes: *A student is <u>supposed</u> to study.*

24.20 ACTIVITY

A. Fill in the blanks in the following sentences with *suppose* or *supposed*.

1. If I finish my work in time, I <u>suppose</u> I will go to a movie.

2. Who do you <u>suppose</u> will win the Academy Award for best actor?

3. The test is <u>supposed</u> to cover the first four chapters of the textbook and our class notes.

4. I <u>suppose</u> I can go with you if you leave early enough.

5. The children were <u>supposed</u> to clean their rooms before playing outside.

6. Someone was <u>supposed</u> to tell you where to meet us.

B. On a separate sheet, write two sentences using *suppose* and two using *supposed*.

THAN/THEN

1. **Than** is used to compare.

   Diana is taller <u>than</u> Sue.

2. **Then** refers to time.

   I should be ready by <u>then</u>.

Memory Tip: Think of the *a* in *than* and *compare*; think of the *e* in *then* and *time*.

24.21 ACTIVITY

A. Fill in the blanks in the following sentences with *than* or *then*.

1. Dr. Dodge explained the assignment and <u>then</u> dismissed the class.

2. Skinless chicken is healthier <u>than</u> beef.

3. First preheat the oven and <u>then</u> assemble the ingredients.

4. It is more difficult to be a teenager <u>than</u> many adults realize.

5. If you leave <u>then,</u> you will miss dessert.

6. I would rather be intelligent <u>than</u> good-looking.

B. On a separate sheet, write two sentences using *than* and two using *then*.

THERE/THEIR/THEY'RE

1. **There** refers to direction or place. It can also be used as a sentence opener.

   Put your packages down <u>there</u>.
   <u>There</u> are no seats left.

2. **Their** shows ownership.

   The children played with <u>their</u> toys.

3. **They're** means "they are."

   If Phil and Janet come, <u>they're</u> sure to complain all evening.

Memory Tip: Use *they're* only when you can substitute "they are."

24.22 ACTIVITY

A. Fill in the blanks in the following sentences with *there*, *their*, or *they're*.

1. Many people lost __their__ homes when the Mississippi River flooded.

2. I thought I put my books over __there__ .

3. __There__ are no acceptable excuses for such behavior.

4. If __they're__ late, we will have to leave without them.

5. All the trees in the courtyard have lost __their__ leaves.

6. I enjoy visiting Ruth and Enrico because __they're__ always so entertaining.

B. On a separate sheet, write two sentences using *there*, two using *their*, and two using *they're*.

THREW/THROUGH

1. **Threw** is the past tense of *throw*. It is a verb.

   Hank <u>threw</u> the ball to second base.

2. **Through** means "in one side and out the other." It is a preposition. It can also be an adjective meaning "finished."

   The train passed <u>through</u> the tunnel.
   The play will be <u>through</u> at ten o'clock.

24.23 ACTIVITY

A. Fill in the blanks in the following sentences with *threw* or *through*.

1. I was the first one __through__ with the history test.

2. Lanie was so angry she __threw__ her keys across the room.

3. Nigel wadded up the paper and __threw__ it into the wastebasket.

4. The chef put the beef __through__ the meat grinder.

5. Dale __threw__ the ball up in a desperation shot.

6. We drove __through__ Pennsylvania on our way to New York.

B. On a separate sheet, write two sentences using *threw* and two using *through*.

TO/TOO/TWO

1. **To** means "toward." It is a preposition. It is also used with a verb to form the infinitive, as in "to eat."

   Let's go <u>to</u> class now.   I hate <u>to</u> take pills.

2. **Too** means "also" or "excessively." It is an adverb.

   Christina needs a menu <u>too</u>.   *It is <u>too</u> cold in here.*

3. **Two** is a number.

   Scott has <u>two</u> brothers.

24.24 ACTIVITY

A. Fill in the blanks in the following sentences with *to, too,* or *two.*

1. My roommate and I are going <u>to</u>   the dining hall.

2. <u>To</u>   get there on time, we must leave now.

3. <u>Two</u>   movies are playing in the student union tonight.

4. You <u>too</u>   can learn karate.

5. Stephen King books are <u>too</u>   scary for Kim.

6. We will leave at <u>two</u>   o'clock.

B. On a separate sheet, write two sentences for each of these words: *to, too,* and *two.*

USE/USED

1. **Use** is a verb meaning "make use of." Its past tense form is *used.*

   I hope you can <u>use</u> this sweater I bought you.
   Henri <u>used</u> the last towel and did not replace it.

2. When followed by **to, used** means "in the habit of."

   When I was younger, I <u>used to</u> sleep late on Saturday.
   I <u>used to</u> like spicy food, but now I do not.

GRAMMAR ALERT

Because the *d* at the end of *used* and the *t* at the beginning of *to* are pronounced as one sound, writers may mistakenly omit the *d* from *used.*

No: *Harriet <u>use</u> to live here.*
Yes: *Harriet <u>used</u> to live here.*
No: *I am <u>use</u> to a harder mattress.*
Yes: *I am <u>used</u> to a harder mattress.*

24.25 ACTIVITY

A. Fill in the blanks in the following sentences with *use* or *used.*

1. Carlotta is not <u>used</u>   to so much free time, so she does not know what to do with herself.

2. If you <u>use</u>   a plate, please wash it and put it away.

3. I gave Michael the book because he can <u>use</u> it more than you can.

4. Eventually, my brother became <u>used</u> to the extreme heat of the tropics.

5. I would like to leave for the gym and <u>use</u> the weights for an hour.

6. It often takes a full year for people to get <u>used</u> to college life.

B. On a separate sheet, write two sentences using *use* and two using *used*.

WERE/WE'RE/WHERE

1. **Were** is the past tense of *are*.

   They <u>were</u> late because of heavy traffic.

2. **We're** means "we are."

   <u>We're</u> happy to help you.

3. **Where** refers to location.

   <u>Where</u> are you going?

Memory Tip: Like *here*, *where* refers to location, and *where* contains the word *here*:

   w[here]

Memory Tip: Do not use *we're* unless you could substitute "we are."

24.26 ACTIVITY

A. Fill in the blanks in the following sentences with *were*, *we're*, or *where*.

1. <u>We're</u> not sure which road to take, so we should check the map.

2. <u>Where</u> do you think I should go for vacation?

3. I don't know about you, but <u>we're</u> happy to be here.

4. Joan and I thought the waiters in that restaurant <u>were</u> very rude.

5. This is the town <u>where</u> my father was raised.

6. The critics <u>were</u> charmed by the lead actor's performance.

B. On a separate sheet, write two sentences using *were*, two using *we're*, and two using *where*.

WHO'S/WHOSE

1. **Who's** means "who is" or "who has."

   <u>Who's</u> going with you?   *<u>Who's</u> been sitting here?*

24.30 CHAPTER REVIEW ACTIVITY

Fill in each of the following blanks with a frequently confused word that fits the definition given. Choose words from the list below.

accept	here	principal	they're
except	its	principle	threw
advice	it's	quiet	through
advise	know	quit	to
affect	no	quite	too
effect	knew	raise	two
all ready	new	rise	we're
already	lay	set	were
beside	lie	sit	your
besides	lose	than	you're
buy	loose	then	
by	passed	there	
hear	past	their	

1. Past tense of *throw:* _threw_

2. Understand: _know_

3. Shows exclusion: _except_

4. Influence: _affect_

5. Purchase: _buy_

6. It is: _it's_

7. Not old: _new_

8. A truth or standard: _principle_

9. Offer a suggestion: _advise_

10. Used to compare: _than_

11. Also: _too_

12. Stop: _quit_

13. In one side and out the other: _through_

14. Previously: _already_

15. Most important: _principal_

16. Receive: _accept_

17. Near: _by_

18. Very: _quite_

19. Previous time: _past_

20. In addition to: _besides (too)_

21. Not tight: _loose_

22. They are: _they're_

23. A sentence opener: <u>there</u>

24. Negative: <u>no</u>

25. Listen: <u>hear</u>

26. Alongside of: <u>beside</u>

27. Misplace: <u>lose</u>

28. Shows ownership by more than one person: <u>their</u>

29. You are: <u>you're</u>

30. A nearby place: <u>here</u>

31. Went by: <u>passed</u>

32. Result: <u>effect</u>

33. Past tense of *are:* <u>were</u>

34. Shows ownership by something not human: <u>its</u>

35. Without noise: <u>quiet</u>

36. Toward: <u>to</u>

37. All set: <u>all ready</u>

38. Past tense of *know:* <u>knew</u>

39. Suggestion or opinion: <u>advice</u>

40. We are: <u>we're</u>

41. 2: <u>two</u>

42. Get up: <u>rise</u>

43. Place: <u>set</u>

44. Lift up: <u>raise</u>

45. Rest on a surface: <u>lie</u>

24.31 CHAPTER REVIEW ACTIVITY

The following passage contains 12 errors with frequently confused words. Cross out the incorrect words and write the correct ones above them.

Everyone ~~heres~~ (hears) about the child ~~whose~~ (who's) more interested in playing with the wrapping paper, bows, and boxes than with his or her birthday presents. Parents, you should learn a lesson and heed this ~~advise~~ (advice): stop spending huge sums of money on preschoolers; ~~your~~ (you're) not ~~suppose~~ (supposed) to. Instead, use your imagination to entertain youngsters.

~~Accept~~ (Except) for sharp or very small objects, old items that are ~~all ready setting~~ (already sitting) around make excellent toys. For example, pots and pans, measuring cups, and ordinary kitchen utensils amuse curious toddlers, although they won't keep your house very quiet. Empty shoe boxes and cartons can make suitable toys, ~~to~~ (too). Just tie them together to form trains and dollhouses. Outdoor play can include fingerpainting with pudding and dabbling with tubs of cornmeal, water, and plastic cups.

    Remember, children do not require expensive, sophisticated toys. ~~There~~ *They're* capable of amusing themselves ~~quit~~ *quite* well with ordinary household objects. Such play is just as instructive as play with the newest "hot" toy, especially when that toy gets pushed aside in favor of the box it came in. Remember the last time you spent $50 on a toy? You probably could ~~of~~ *have* spent much less—or maybe nothing at all.

GETTING IN GEAR

thinking in writing: Write a mapping with this phrase at the center: the role of athletes in society. If you need to review mapping, see page 8.

writing from experience: Do you enjoy sports? In a page or so, explain why or why not. Be sure to give specific examples to explain why you feel as you do.

writing in context: Many professional athletes have multimillion dollar contracts. Explain whether or not you think we should reward athletes that generously and why you believe as you do.

PART SEVEN REVIEW

Activity: Spelling and Frequently Confused Words

The following passage has 10 errors with frequently confused words and 9 misspellings. Cross out and write above the line to correct the mistakes.

      People ~~generaly~~ *generally* love a good magic show. These days, magicians perform spectacular tricks, ~~makeing~~ *making* things like the Empire State Building and tigers ~~dissappear~~ *disappear*. Even so, people still love the old standards. For example, we ~~no its~~ *know it's* not really happening, but ~~its~~ *it's* hard not to gasp when the ~~magicain~~ *magician* begins to saw through the box toward the trapped woman's abdomen. This popular ~~ilusion~~ *illusion* is designed so that a woman appears to be ~~laying~~ *lying* full length in a box that rests on a table. Her hands and head protrude through holes in the ends of the box. In some versions of the trick, her hands and ~~ankels~~ *ankles* are tied with ropes, which come ~~threw~~ *through* the sides. The magician ~~procedes~~ *proceeds* to saw the box in half. The two halves are ~~than~~ *then* ~~seperated~~ *separated*, but you can't see inside because metal sheets have slid down over the cut ends of the box. Finally, the two halves are pushed together again, the sheets of metal are removed, and miraculously the woman is whole and very much alive.

      How is this done? The fact is, the ~~ilusion~~ *illusion* involves ~~to~~ *two* women. When the props are brought onto the stage, one woman is ~~all ready~~ *already* hidden in the table. As the woman on stage climbs into the box, the one ~~whose~~ *who's* hidden climbs up into the box through a trap in the table and pokes her feet out the end. She ~~sets~~ *sits* up, with her head bent forward between her knees. The other woman draws her knees up to her chin. Only an empty space lies in the path of the descending saw.

Capitalizing and Punctuating

PART EIGHT

CHAPTER **25**

Capitalization and End Marks

USING CAPITAL LETTERS

A number of rules govern when writers should use capital letters.

RULE 1. CAPITALIZE NAMES OF PEOPLE AND ANIMALS

Capitalize:

Bill Clinton	Lucinda	Puffy
Hank	Malcolm X	Rover

Do not capitalize:

man	girl	cat
boy	leader	dog

I asked Gloria if I should name my dog Rags.

Capital letters appear in *German shepherd* and *French poodle* because nationalities are capitalized.

RULE 2. CAPITALIZE TITLES BEFORE PEOPLE'S NAMES

Capitalize:

Aunt Helen	President Bush	Rabbi Schwartz
Judge Tipton	Private Williams	Reverend Jones
Mayor Browning	Professor Smith	Senator Hernandez

Do not capitalize:

my aunt	a president	a rabbi
a judge	a private	the reverend
the mayor	a professor	our senator

The guest of honor, Governor Ruiz, who used to be the mayor of our city, shook hands with my Uncle Roy and your aunt.

The word *President* is commonly capitalized when it refers to the President of the United States.

RULE 3. ALWAYS CAPITALIZE THE PERSONAL PRONOUN *I*

Lesley and I are leaving for a weekend vacation.

RULE 4. CAPITALIZE NAMES OF NATIONALITIES, LANGUAGES, AND RELIGIONS

In both noun and adjective form, the names of nationalities, languages, and religions should be capitalized.

Capitalize:

African art	Canadian border	Chinese food	Irish
American	Catholic	German	Judaism

We went to the museum to see the exhibit of Indian jewelry and then went out for Thai food.

25.1 ACTIVITY

Fill in the blanks according to the directions given.

EXAMPLE   Use a nationality:
I have never been fond of ___Mexican___ cooking.

1. Use a language:
   Mario regrets that he never studied ___Italian___.

2. Use the name and title of a senator:
   Several politicians attended the fund-raiser, including ___Senator Glenn___.

3. Use the name of an animal:
   As a child, I had a parakeet named ___Max___.

4. Use the name and title of a religious leader:
   The sermon was delivered by ___Father Esposito___.

5. Use a nationality:
   Circle Cinema is showing a series of ___French___ films this weekend.

6. Refer to yourself with a pronoun:
   Marcus hopes that ___I___ will help him.

RULE 5. CAPITALIZE NAMES OF SPECIFIC GEOGRAPHIC LOCATIONS

Capitalize:

Blue Ridge Mountains	Nashville, Tennessee	Route 66
Grand Canyon	Oregon	the South
Lake Michigan	Pacific Ocean	South America

Do not capitalize:

the mountains	a city	the highway
canyon	state	south
a lake	the ocean	continent

We drove on Route 80 and then on a two-lane highway until we got to the foothills of the Allegheny Mountains.

RULE 6. CAPITALIZE NAMES OF SPECIFIC ORGANIZATIONS, COMPANIES, INSTITUTIONS, COLLEGES, AND BUILDINGS

CONNECT

List 10 words or phrases requiring capital letters that are used in your major. For example, if you are an English major, you can note specific book or poem titles; if you are a business major, you can note the names of specific corporations; if you are a music major, you can note the names of specific music compositions.

Capitalize:

American Red Cross	Friars Club	Republican Party
Chrysler Corporation	General Foods	St. Elizabeth Hospital
Disneyland	Ohio University	Sears Tower

Do not capitalize:

organization	club	political party
car manufacturer	company	hospital
amusement park	university	building

Jerry applied for a job with General Foods, but he really wanted to work for an insurance company.

RULE 7. CAPITALIZE NAMES OF HISTORIC EVENTS, DOCUMENTS, AND PERIODS

Capitalize:

Battle of Gettysburg	Magna Carta	Roaring Twenties
Declaration of Independence	Renaissance	Vietnam War

Do not capitalize:

important battle	charter	wild era
document	historical period	war

The peace treaty following World War I did not end all wars.

RULE 8. CAPITALIZE REFERENCES TO GOD AND SACRED BOOKS AND DOCUMENTS

Capitalize words that refer to God or a supreme being of any religion, as well as the pronouns that refer to these words. Also capitalize the names of sacred books and documents.

Capitalize:

Allah	God	the Lord	the Torah
the Bible	the Koran	the Old Testament	the Trinity

Do not capitalize:

a deity	the gods	a sacred scroll

Many people who do not believe in any religion still pray to the Almighty and ask Him for help.

25.2 ACTIVITY

Fill in the blanks in the following sentences according to the directions given.

EXAMPLE   Use a specific geographic location:

I wish I could travel to *Houston, Texas* .

1. Use the name of a specific company or business:

After graduation, I would like to work for General Motors .

2. Use a specific historic event, period, or document:

    I have always wanted to learn more about the Civil War   .

3. Use the name of a sacred book or document:

    In religion class, the children are studying Genesis   .

4. Use the name of a specific organization:

    This year I will make a charitable donation to the Salvation Army   .

5. Use the names of specific geographic locations:

    When I lived in Pittsburgh   , I enjoyed visiting Falling Water   .

6. Use specific historic events, periods, or documents:

    I did well on the part of the test covering World War I   , but I had

    trouble with the part on the League of Nations   .

RULE 9. CAPITALIZE NAMES OF MONTHS, DAYS, AND HOLIDAYS

Capitalize:

    Independence Day   January   Tuesday

Do not capitalize:

    holiday   month   day   spring

My favorite holiday is Thanksgiving, which is always on the same day: Thursday.

RULE 10. CAPITALIZE SPECIFIC BRAND NAMES

Capitalize:

Buick	Jello	Pepsi
Cheerios	Nike tennis shoes	Pillsbury brownie mix

Do not capitalize:

car	gelatin	cola
cereal	tennis shoes	brownie mix

With my birthday money, I bought a London Fog raincoat, Reeboks, and a wool sweater.

RULE 11. CAPITALIZE THE FIRST AND LAST WORDS OF A TITLE AND EVERYTHING IN BETWEEN EXCEPT ARTICLES, CONJUNCTIONS, AND PREPOSITIONS

In titles, always capitalize the first and last words. In between, capitalize everything except articles (*a*, *an*, and *the*), conjunctions (joining words such as *and*, *but*, *or*, and *since*), and prepositions (words such as *of*, *at*, *to*, *from*, *by*, and *in*).

In the Heat of the Night   *The Sound of Music*
Sleepless in Seattle   *The Once and Future King*

I hate it when schools ban books, particularly when they are as good as The Catcher in the Rye.

POWER UP

Circle the first 10 capital letters in a newspaper or magazine article. (Do not circle the capital letters that begin sentences.) Explain the reason for each capital.

POWER UP

Write a sentence that illustrates each of the capitalization rules given in this chapter.

RULE 12. CAPITALIZE NAMES OF SPECIFIC COURSES

Capitalize:

Algebra 112	Introduction to Psychology	Principles of Accounting
History 101	Physics Fundamentals	Spanish III

Do not capitalize:

math	psychology	accounting
history	physics	language course

This semester I am enjoying Survey of Modern Drama, but I am struggling with Economics 101. I find economics boring.

25.3 ACTIVITY

Fill in the blanks in the following sentences according to the directions given.

EXAMPLE   Use a brand name:

This week _Oreos_ are on sale at the market.

1. Use the name of a movie with at least three words in the title:

    One of my favorite movies is _Gone with the Wind_ .

2. Use a month:

    My birthday is in _May_ .

3. Use products with brand names (e.g., Wilson tennis racquet):

    I only want a(n) _Sony disc player_ and a(n) _Timex watch_ for my birthday.

4. Use specific course titles:

    The professor teaching _Physics I_ is new this year, but the one

    teaching _Introduction to Psychology_ is ready to retire.

5. Use the name of a specific holiday and a month:

    My favorite holiday is _Halloween_ , partly because it is celebrated in

    October .

6. Use the title of a book with at least three words:

    I already own a copy of _The Diary of Anne Frank_ .

ENDING SENTENCES

The period (.), the question mark (?), and the exclamation point (!) make the reader's job easier because they show where sentences end. They also convey meaning. To appreciate this fact, notice the different messages expressed in the following sentences, each with the same words.

The test is today. [A statement of fact.]

The test is today! [Shows strong emotion, perhaps surprise or fear.]

The test is today? [Asks a question: Is the test today?]

THE PERIOD

Use a **period** (.) to end a sentence that makes a statement, makes a request, or gives an order.

Makes a statement:	*Today is Harry's birthday.*
Makes a request:	*Please open the window.*
Gives an order:	*Leave me alone.*

25.4 ACTIVITY

In the blanks below, write sentences according to the directions given. Use a period at the end.

EXAMPLE   Make a statement:

Joyce has moved here from Santa Fe.

1. Make a statement:

Tomorrow is my birthday.

2. Make a request:

Help me lift this box.

3. Give an order:

Stop that racket now.

THE QUESTION MARK

Use the **question mark** (?) to end a sentence that asks a direct question. Here are some examples.

May I join you?
Where is the nearest gas station?
How is that possible?

Some sentences pose a question, but that question is not in the speaker's or writer's exact words. These sentences are **indirect questions,** and they end with periods, not question marks.

Direct question:	*When does the play begin?*
Indirect question:	*I wonder when the play begins.*
Direct question:	*Joel asked, "Will you help me?"*
Indirect question:	*Joel asked whether I would help him.*

25.5 ACTIVITY

On a separate sheet, write three sentences that ask direct questions. Be sure to use question marks.

THE EXCLAMATION POINT

Use an **exclamation point** (!) to express strong feeling. Here are three examples.

> *The house is on fire!*
> *I can't believe you said that!*
> *Get out of here before it's too late!*

Do not overuse the exclamation point. You should rely on your words to carry most of your strong feelings.

PUNCTUATION ALERT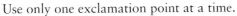

Do not use the exclamation point with a period or a question mark.

No: *Why are you doing that!?*
Yes: *Why are you doing that?*

PUNCTUATION ALERT

Use only one exclamation point at a time.

No: *Leave me alone!!*
Yes: *Leave me alone!*

25.6 ACTIVITY

On a separate sheet, write three sentences that show strong feeling. End each one with an exclamation point.

 IF ENGLISH IS YOUR SECOND LANGUAGE

1. If your native language is not based on the English alphabet (that is, if your language is Arabic, Chinese, Japanese, or another language that uses a different alphabet or hieroglyphics), you may have some trouble seeing the importance of the difference in size between capital and lowercase letters. Try to pay particular attention to this feature of English when you read.

2. If your native language is a Romance language, you may not be accustomed to capitalizing the names of languages, religions, nationalities, and days of the week, so pay particular attention to the need to capitalize these words in English.

3. Remember that word order is different for direct and indirect questions.

   A. In a direct question, the helping verb *comes before* the subject.

   > *Is Alice going with us?*

   Helping verb: *is*
   Subject: *Alice*
   Main verb: *going*

B. In an indirect question, the helping verb *comes after* the subject in the part of the sentence that suggests the question.

I asked whether Alice is going with us.

Helping verb: *is*

Subject: *Alice*

Main verb: *going*

C. In an indirect question, do not place all or part of the verb before the subject.

No: *The student asked why is the answer wrong.*
                                                  V   S

Yes: *The student asked why the answer is wrong.*
                                                  S   V

RECHARGE

1. Capitalize

    *   Names of people and animals (*Lorenzo, Spot*).
    *   Titles before people's names (*Professor Lorca, Uncle Henry*).
    *   The personal pronoun *I*.
    *   Nationalities, languages, and religions (*Spanish art, English*).
    *   Specific geographic locations (*Lake Michigan, Idaho*).
    *   Specific organizations, companies, institutions, colleges, and buildings (*American Legion, United Nations, Ford Motor Company*).
    *   Historic events, documents, and periods (*the Constitution, the Civil War*).
    *   References to God and sacred books and documents (*the Bible, Jehovah*).
    *   Months, days, and holidays (*March, Monday, Christmas*).
    *   Specific brand names and specific courses (*Coca Cola, Reynolds Wrap, Introduction to Organic Chemistry*).
    *   First and last words in a title and everything in between except articles, conjunctions, and prepositions (*From Here to Eternity*).

2. End sentences with a period for a statement of fact, a question mark for a question, or an exclamation point for strong emotion.

    *   *I can come.*
    *   *Can I come?*
    *   *I can come!*

25.7 CHAPTER REVIEW ACTIVITY

Circle the letters in the following sentences that should be capitalized.

EXAMPLE   After my breakfast of Ⓦheaties, I took a walk down Ⓕireside Ⓛane.

1. We were surprised to learn that Ⓒouncilwoman Hernandez did not support Ⓜayor Jefferson's campaign to be governor.

2. In recent years, the pollution in lake erie has been cleaned up, so people can once again use the lake for recreation.

3. On our trip west, i bought several pieces of indian pottery and acquired a taste for mexican food, especially burritos.

4. Kyle applied for a job at burger king and two other fast-food restaurants to earn money for summer school.

5. When we moved to south carolina, I fell in love with the atlantic ocean.

6. Some people say that the boy scouts of america should admit girls.

7. When we visited new york city, we saw *much ado about nothing* at radio city music hall.

8. An important civil war battle was fought in murfreesboro, tennessee, the town where I lived when I attended middle tennessee state university.

9. Sue bought her first car, a used chevrolet, for a very good price.

10. In september, aunt ama and uncle morty moved to state street.

25.8 CHAPTER REVIEW ACTIVITY

In the following passage, circle the letters that should be capitalized.

Elections were first held thousands of years ago by the ancient hebrews and greeks. The early kings of israel were elected, as were the generals in ancient greek armies. The idea of elections eventually came to britain with the anglo-saxon conquerors about 1,500 years ago. From england, the idea of electing public officials traveled with the colonists to america. Thus, even before the american revolution, elections occurred in local assemblies and town meetings.

Unfortunately, in the united states, voting was usually limited to free white males who met certain property and religious requirements. For example, in 1860, blacks and women could not vote. Voting privileges were gained by these groups— privileges they should have had in the first place—only after hard-fought battles.

After the civil war, the constitution was amended to give the vote to black men. In 1920, the nineteenth amendment allowed women to vote. Thus, while elections have been around for thousands of years, the right to vote has only recently been extended to many.

25.9 CHAPTER REVIEW ACTIVITY

Write sentences according to the directions given. Be prepared to explain your choice of end punctuation.

1. Write a sentence that might be spoken in a restaurant. The sentence should make a statement.

   The vegetables are cold.

   _____

2. Write a sentence that might be spoken in the classroom. The sentence should ask a direct question.

   May I borrow your notes?

   _____

3. Write another sentence that might be spoken in the classroom. This sentence should ask an indirect question.

   Professor Williams asked whether anyone needed extra help.

   _____

4. Write a sentence that expresses strong feeling.

   Call an ambulance right now!

   _____

5. Write a sentence that a parent might speak to a child. This sentence should make a request.

   Please clean up your room today.

   _____

6. Write a sentence that a police officer might speak to a suspect. This sentence should give a command.

   Show me your identification.

   _____

25.10 CHAPTER REVIEW ACTIVITY

Place appropriate end punctuation in the blanks below. Be prepared to explain your choices.

My 17-year-old son came home two weeks ago very upset because he got a speeding ticket _._ He felt the police officer should have just given him a warning because it was his first offense _._ I asked Marcus how fast he was going _._ He said he was going 48 mph in a school zone. I screamed, "You have got to be out of your mind _!_ " I then explained the dangers of speeding, but he still felt the ticket was unfair _._ Why do teenagers fail to realize that they can get hurt or hurt others _?_ In traffic court, the judge suspended my son's license for a month and fined him $63 _._ I asked

Marcus if he learned his lesson __.__ He responded, "What do you

think __?__ " I could tell from his dejected look that he would not speed

again __.__ Frankly, I am glad he got the ticket. It is teaching him a valuable

lesson __.__ Now I wonder what the next crisis will be __.__

GETTING IN GEAR

thinking in writing: Make a list of your favorites in five of the following categories: books, magazines, movies, vacation spots, cars, politicians, movie and television stars, television programs, holidays, websites, and CDs.

writing from experience: Select one of the favorites you listed and write about why it is one of your favorites.

writing in context: Assume you are a popular culture critic for the Sunday magazine supplement of your local newspaper, and write a review of a television program, CD, website, movie, or book that you have strong feelings about.

CHAPTER 26

Commas

CHAPTER GOALS

By the end of this chapter, you will:

Know how to apply the most common comma rules to your own writing.

COMMAS TO SEPARATE ITEMS IN A SERIES

A **series** is made up of three or more items. Use commas to separate the items in a series.

> *I bought <u>milk, bread, and cheese</u> at the store.*
> *The audience <u>clapped loudly, stood up, and cheered</u> on opening night.*
> *We searched for the kitten <u>under the porch, in the garage, behind the house, and in the basement.</u>*

As the above examples show, no comma appears after the last item in a series.

PUNCTUATION ALERT !

Do not use a comma with a pair.

> *We ate <u>a sandwich and soup.</u>*

Do not use a comma if the items in a series are separated by *and* or *or*.

> *Peg enjoys <u>skiing and surfing and swimming.</u>*
> *We can <u>visit Grandma or go to a movie or stay at home.</u>*

26.1 ACTIVITY

Write a sentence using each of the following series or pairs. Be careful to use commas when they are needed.

EXAMPLE   calculus   trigonometry   or advanced geometry

> *I will take calculus, trigonometry, or advanced geometry in summer school.*

1. Kenny   Miguel   or Phil

   Kenny, Miguel, or Phil will be the starting quarterback for Saturday's game.

2. the sweater   or the jacket

   Wear the sweater or the jacket because it is chilly.

3. swims daily   lifts weights   and eats a low-fat diet

Hildegard swims daily, lifts weights, and eats a low-fat diet to stay in shape.

4. Memphis   and Nashville   and Knoxville

On our trip to Tennessee, we visited Memphis and Nashville and Knoxville.

5. paint the living room   and repair the roof

For 500 dollars, Lee will paint the living room and repair the roof.

6. roast beef   mashed potatoes   and gravy

Roast beef, mashed potatoes, and gravy are forbidden on this diet.

7. ate supper   studied   watched television   and went to bed

After class, Gwen ate supper, studied, watched television, and went to bed.

8. listen carefully   take notes   and ask questions

Listen carefully, take notes, and ask questions to do well in the class.

9. hard work   and ambition

Hard work and ambition lead to success.

10. at home   at work   or at the gym

This evening I will be at home, at work, or at the gym.

COMMAS AFTER INTRODUCTORY ELEMENTS

An **introductory element** is a word, phrase, or clause that comes before the subject of a sentence. Here are some examples.

Introductory word: *Surprisingly,* [*John*] *agreed with us.* (subject)

Introductory phrase: *Without a doubt,* [*this snowfall*] *will close the schools.* (subject)

Introductory clause: *If you are not busy,* [*I*] *would like you to come with me.* (subject)

Place a comma after an introductory word, phrase, or clause.

Introductory word:	*Smiling, I walked away.*
Introductory phrase:	*In the cellar, we have a Ping-Pong table.*
Introductory clause:	*Since you enjoy live theater, Joe bought you season tickets to the Community Playhouse.*

26.2 ACTIVITY

Place a comma after each introductory word, phrase, or clause in the following sentences.

1. Interestingly, many people are allergic to dairy products.
2. At the end of the month, Lorenzo and Tillie will celebrate their anniversary.
3. Since the election is next week, my mail includes many campaign brochures.
4. Traveling at a high rate of speed, the truck almost caused an accident.
5. Tired, Betty was unable to join us.
6. After I got my contact lenses, I could see much better.
7. Annoyed by the sexist humor, many people left the theater.
8. Unable to sleep, Nicole read three magazines.
9. Because the band raised several thousand dollars, they could purchase new uniforms.
10. In our age of information, knowledge is power.

CONNECT

Opening sentences with introductory elements is a good way to achieve a pleasing style. For more on this, see Chapter 22 on varying sentence openers.

26.3 INDIVIDUAL OR GROUP ACTIVITY

Alone or with two classmates, choose six of the words, phrases, and clauses given below, and use them to begin sentences that you compose. Be sure to follow each word, phrase, or clause with the subject of the sentence. Also, be sure to use commas after the introductory elements. Use a separate sheet.

EXAMPLE   at noon

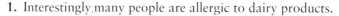

At noon, I always break for lunch.

at midnight	laughing
before you leave	under the bed
concerned	when the game ended
confused	while you were gone
in the middle of the night	whistling softly

COMMAS WITH COORDINATION

In Chapter 5, you learned that an **independent clause** has a subject and a verb and can stand as a sentence. Now is a good time to review that material.

Independent clause:	*the dog barked all night*
Sentence:	*The dog barked all night.*
Independent clause:	*we could not sleep*
Sentence:	*We could not sleep.*

TIP

For more on coordinating conjunctions, see page 70.

Coordination is the joining of two independent clauses in one sentence, using one of the following **coordinating conjunctions.**

and   for   or   yet

but   nor   so

The dog barked all night, so we could not sleep.

In Chapter 5, you learned that when you join independent clauses with a coordinating conjunction, you should place a comma before the conjunction. Here are some examples.

The doctor stitched the wound ⌐ *, and* ⌐ *she wrote a prescription for pain.*

I asked you a question ⌐ *, but* ⌐ *you did not answer.*

You can leave with Lauren now ⌐ *, or* ⌐ *you can leave with Alonzo later.*

The street department closed the road ⌐ *, so* ⌐ *workers could repair the water pipe.*

PUNCTUATION ALERT !

Do not use a comma unless an independent clause appears on *both* sides of the coordinating conjunction.

No comma: *I parked the car and went into the house.* [There is no independent clause after *and*.]

26.4 ACTIVITY

Use a coordinating conjunction to combine each pair of independent clauses into one sentence. Remember to use commas correctly.

EXAMPLE   the telephone was ringing
we were too tired to answer it

The telephone was ringing, but we were too tired to

answer it.

1. Katrina sprained her ankle
    she bruised her knee

    Katrina sprained her ankle, and she bruised her knee.

2. traffic was backed up for miles
    we still managed to arrive on time

    Traffic was backed up for miles, but we still managed to arrive on time.

3. Clarice hoped to get into medical school
    she was studying constantly

    Clarice hoped to get into medical school, so she was studying constantly.

4. the teenagers were planning a party
    their parents were out for the evening

    The teenagers were planning a party, for their parents were out for the evening.

    _____

5. you can meet me at the library
    you can meet me at the student center

    You can meet me at the library, or you can meet me at the student center.

    _____

6. I planted the seeds and watered them daily
    none of them sprouted

    I planted the seeds and watered them daily, but none of them sprouted.

    _____

26.5 ACTIVITY

Place commas where they are needed in the following sentences. Two sentences are correct.

1. Our electricity was not restored for two days, so all the food in the refrigerator spoiled.
2. The lecture series was well publicized, but very few people attended.
3. We asked you to chair the committee, for you are the most organized member.
4. I woke up to a heavy snowfall and went out to shovel the driveway.
5. Kevin jumped over the fence, and then he ran across the backyard.
6. I will not vote for Pelligrini, and I will not campaign for him.
7. The tutors in the Writing Center can react to your draft, or they can answer specific questions about writing.
8. Gretchen arrived early enough to eat with us but too late to see Harold.
9. Luigi has been in this country for only a year, yet he speaks our language well.
10. Frank is the best ball handler on the team, so he usually sets up all the plays.
11. National Public Radio is interesting to listen to, and it is entertaining as well.
12. I will tell you what happened, but I am not sure you will believe me.

COMMAS WITH NONESSENTIAL ELEMENTS

A **nonessential element** is a word, phrase, or clause that is not necessary (it is "nonessential") for identifying a person, place, object, emotion, or idea referred to. In the following examples, the underlined elements are nonessential.

> *The governor, <u>who is running for reelection,</u> will visit our town.*
> ["Who is running for reelection" is nonessential because it is not necessary for identifying who will visit.]
>
> *Carl, <u>anxious to make the team,</u> is lifting weights daily.* ["Anxious to make the team" is nonessential because it is not necessary for identifying who is lifting weights.]
>
> *Hilton Head, <u>a beautiful coastal town,</u> is our destination.* ["A beautiful coastal town" is nonessential because it is not necessary for identifying the destination.]

POWER UP

To appreciate the difference commas can make, consider the different meanings of these two sentences: (1) The child, who fell off his bike, is crying. (2) The child who fell off his bike is crying.

Nonessential elements are set off with commas. Use two commas if the nonessential element is in the middle of the sentence and one comma if it is at the end of the sentence.

Nonessential element
in the middle: *My guitar teacher, Al Smith, plays in a rock band.*

Nonessential element
at the end: *I had an interview with the personnel director, an interesting person.*

Words, phrases, and clauses necessary for identifying a person, place, object, emotion, or idea are **essential elements.** They are *not* set off with commas. Here is an example.

No commas: *The hotel that I visited had clean rooms.* ["That I visited" is necessary to identify which hotel is referred to.]

26.6 ACTIVITY

Underline the nonessential elements in the following sentences, and then set them off with commas. One sentence is correct.

EXAMPLE   The truckers' strike, now in its second week, shows no sign of ending.

1. Kevin Costner, the star and director of *Dances with Wolves*, will visit our city.
2. Hans and Carrie bought a house, a two-bedroom cottage.
3. Nashville, known as "Music City, USA," is an exciting place to live.
4. I have always admired my grandmother, who raised four children by herself during the Great Depression.
5. Rita Rudner, who is a gifted comedian, is currently appearing at Carnegie Hall.
6. You should take your broken watch to Claude Kingsley, who is a reputable jeweler and watch repairperson.
7. The woman who works here is also a township trustee.
8. I just finished reading *Killer Angels*, a Pulitzer prize-wining book about the Battle of Gettysburg.
9. Monopoly, which has been a popular game for many years, is still a best-seller.
10. Carly had to say good-bye to Mandy, her best friend for 10 years.

COMMAS WITH PARENTHETICAL ELEMENTS

A **parenthetical element** interrupts the flow of a sentence. It can be omitted without significant loss of meaning. Parenthetical elements are expressions like these:

as a matter of fact	however	of course
believe it or not	in fact	on the other hand
by the way	in my opinion	therefore
for example	it seems to me	without a doubt

Notice in the following examples that the underlined parenthetical expressions can be removed with no significant loss of meaning:

With parenthetical
    expression: *This restaurant, <u>it seems to me</u>, has excellent service.*

Without parenthetical
    expression: *This restaurant has excellent service.*

Parenthetical elements are set off with commas. Use one comma for a parenthetical element that comes first or last. Use two commas for a parenthetical element in the middle.

<u>Therefore</u>, that answer is wrong.
More people, <u>if you ask me</u>, oppose violent programming.
Phillips is the best choice for mayor, <u>in my opinion</u>.

POWER UP

If commas were never used, how do you think readers would be affected? Consider the following sentence: Without asking the boy the woman took his shovel pail and goggles and as far as I could tell she left.

26.7 ACTIVITY

Write sentences in the following blanks according to the directions given. Be sure to use commas correctly.

EXAMPLE   Use "of course" in the middle:

    You can, of course, make up your own mind.

1. Use "as a matter of fact" at the beginning:

    As a matter of fact, everyone disagrees with you.

2. Use "in fact" at the beginning:

    In fact, our team won the relay by two seconds.

3. Use "in my opinion" in the middle:

    The best candidate, in my opinion, won the election.

4. Use "without a doubt" in the middle:

    The army will, without a doubt, help John mature.

5. Use "however" at the end:

    Carlos cannot go; Phyllis can go, however.

6. Use "it seems to me" at the end:

    Voters are becoming increasingly apathetic, it seems to me.

Copyright © 2002, The McGraw-Hill Companies, Inc.

POWER UP

Pair up with a classmate and together write a sentence to illustrate each comma rule in this chapter.

COMMAS WITH DATES AND ADDRESSES

Two rules govern the use of commas with dates and addresses.

1. Use commas to separate items in dates.

    The baby was born on Tuesday, November 2, 1993, in Northside Hospital.
    Saturday, October 30, is my wedding day.

If no day is given, then a comma is not used between the month and the year.

    The new manager begins work in June 1995.

2. Use commas to separate items in addresses.

    Orlando, Florida, is the home of Disney World.
    My address is 5171 Sampson Drive, Youngstown, Ohio 44505.

As the above example shows, no comma is used before the zip code.

26.8 ACTIVITY

Complete the following sentences according to the directions given, being sure to use commas correctly.

1. Complete the sentence with the date of your birth:

    I was born May 4, 1967.

2. Complete the sentence with your address:

    Currently, I live at 501 Tod Lane, San Diego, California.

3. Complete the sentence with the month and year you entered college:

    I began college in August 2000.

4. Complete the sentence with a city and state you would like to visit:

    I wish I could go to Charleston, South Carolina.

MISUSED COMMAS

If you keep the following in mind, you will not use commas incorrectly.

1. Do not use a comma with a pair.

    No: *We ate a sandwich, and soup.*
    Yes: *We ate a sandwich and soup.*

2. Do not use a comma if the items in a series are separated by *and* or *or*.

    No: *Peg enjoys skiing, and surfing, and swimming.*
    No: *We can visit Grandma, or go to a movie, or stay at home.*
    Yes: *Peg enjoys skiing and surfing and swimming.*
    Yes: *We can visit Grandma or go to a movie or stay at home.*

3. Do not use a comma after *and* in a series.

    No: *My birthday presents included a sweater, a CD, and, a bracelet.*
    Yes: *My birthday presents included a sweater, a CD, and a bracelet.*

4. Do not use a comma between a subject and verb.

No: *The children on the playground, ran in circles.*

Yes: *The children on the playground ran in circles.*

IF ENGLISH IS YOUR SECOND LANGUAGE

1. If your native language does not use English script, punctuation may be new to you. Ask a Writing Center tutor or someone else you trust to help you edit for punctuation.

2. Do not use a comma whenever you would pause in speaking. This method, used in some languages, is unreliable in English.

RECHARGE

1. Use commas to separate items in a series.

   In Spain, we saw beautiful churches, historic mosques, and breathtaking mountains.

2. Use a comma after an introductory word, phrase, or clause.

   Because of the fog, our flight was canceled.

3. Use a comma before a coordinating conjunction joining independent clauses.

   Ricky Martin is a teen sensation, but adults like him too.

4. Use commas to set off nonessential words, phrases, and clauses.

   The child, barely four years old, already knew how to read.

5. Use commas to set off parenthetical elements.

   The stock market, in my opinion, is too volatile right now.

6. Use commas to set off items in dates and addresses.

   The wedding has been rescheduled for Saturday, May 29, 2004, at 5:00.
   The Metropolitan Museum in New York City, New York, is a national treasure.

26.9 CHAPTER REVIEW ACTIVITY

Add commas where they are needed in the following passages. Be prepared to explain the reason for every comma you use.

A. The gazelle, a kind of antelope, is a member of the cattle family. Usually found in Africa or Asia, the gazelle is a graceful animal with horns that sweep upward. Depending on the animal's species, the horns may be heavy, streamlined, or bent into a V or U shape. These horns can be 14 inches long. All the males have horns, and in some species the females also have horns. About 26 inches high at the shoulder, the gazelle is very fast. It can,in fact,outrun a greyhound. The gazelle is one of the swiftest land animals,and it is one of the most graceful as well.

B. Kareem Abdul-Jabbar,with his extraordinary height of 7 feet, 2 inches,is the top record-holder in basketball. When he retired in 1989,he became the first player to score more than 38,000 points. Among his other records were seasons played,games played,field goals,and shots blocked.

Abdul-Jabbar,the man who invented the skyhook,was born Ferdinand Lewis Alcindor Jr. on April 16,1947,in New York City,New York. He adopted his Arabic name in 1971,six years after he joined the Black Muslim movement. As a high school basketball player,Lew Alcindor led his team to a 95–6 record and scored 2,067 points. He received more than 100 offers of college scholarships and chose the University of California at Los Angeles. He enrolled there,and he led UCLA to three consecutive National Collegiate Athletic Association championships. He was the only player chosen three times as the collegiate All-American.

Upon graduation from UCLA,Abdul-Jabbar was the leading draft choice for the professional teams and was soon claimed by the Milwaukee Bucks. At center position,he continued to play spectacularly. In 1970,he was rookie of the year. The next year,he was awarded the Maurice Podoloff Trophy,which is presented annually to the most valuable player in the National Basketball Association. This award,incidently,is one Abdul-Jabbar went on to win six times. In 1980,he was traded to the Los Angeles Lakers. He helped the Lakers win the championship in 1980,1982,1985,1987,and 1988. He became the second NBA player to score more than 30,000 career points,and he became the NBA's all-time field-goal scoring leader. When he finished his twentieth season in the NBA in 1989,this great athlete retired.

GETTING IN GEAR

j   s   g: Write two lists, one that notes the advantages of being your gen-der (male or female) and one that notes the disadvantages.

writing from experience: Explain one of the advantages or disadvantages of being your gender, using your own experience and observation to illustrate your point.

writing in context: If you are male, assume you are writing for a magazine with a pre-dominantly female readership (*Glamour,* for example). If you are female, assume you are writing for a magazine with a predominantly male readership (*GQ,* for example). Keeping your audience in mind, write about the chief disadvantage(s) of being your gender. Your goal is to help members of the opposite sex understand one or more of the problems people of your gender face.

CHAPTER **27**

Apostrophes

CHAPTER GOALS

By the end of this chapter, you will:

Know how to use the apostrophe (') to spell contractions.

Know how to use the apostrophe (') to form possessives.

APOSTROPHES WITH CONTRACTIONS

A **contraction** is formed when two words are combined and one or more letters are omitted. An apostrophe (') stands for what is omitted. Some common contractions are shown in the list below.

Two Words	One-Word Contraction with Apostrophe for Omitted Letter(s)	Omitted Letter(s)
are not	aren't	o
cannot (exception)	can't	n o
could not	couldn't	o
did not	didn't	o
do not	don't	o
does not	doesn't	o
he is	he's	i
he will	he'll	w i
I am	I'm	a
I had	I'd	h a
I have	I've	h a
I will	I'll	w i
is not	isn't	o
it is/it has	it's	i/h a
let us	let's	u
she did	she'd	d i
she will	she'll	w i
should not	shouldn't	o
there is	there's	i
they are	they're	a
they would	they'd	w o u l
we are	we're	a
were not	weren't	o
where is	where's	i
who has	who's	h a
who is	who's	i
you are	you're	a
you have	you've	h a

Note: The contraction form of *will not* is the unusual form *won't*.

TIP

To be sure you understand the difference between the contraction *it's* and the possessive *its*, see page 314.

SPELLING ALERT

Be sure to place the apostrophe at the site of the omitted letter or letters.

No: *did'nt*

Yes: *didn't*

27.1 ACTIVITY

CONNECT

Contractions are not appropriate in the most formal writing, and some instructors may prefer that you avoid them. Ask three instructors how they feel about contractions in student writing. Report your findings to the class.

Fill in the following blanks with the correct contraction forms. Remember to use apostrophes for omitted letters.

EXAMPLE   he will = _____ *he'll* _____

1. I am = _____ I'm _____   6. he is = _____ he's _____

2. we are = _____ we're _____   7. she did = _____ she'd _____

3. cannot = _____ can't _____   8. it is = _____ it's _____

4. I will = _____ I'll _____   9. will not = _____ won't _____

5. they would = _____ they'd _____ 10. should not = _____ shouldn't _____

27.2 ACTIVITY

Underline each contraction in the following sentences. Then write what the contraction stands for in the blank.

EXAMPLE   _____ *Here is* _____ Here's the book I've wanted.

   _____ *I have* _____

1. ___They will___   They'll be here in an hour.

2. ___cannot___   I can't go because it's late.

   ___it is___

3. ___she would___   The receptionist said she'd be with me in a minute.

4. ___It has___   It's been years since I've seen you.

   ___I have___

5. ___I will___   I'll help you if you're sure your instructor won't mind.

   ___you are___

   ___will not___

6. ___would not___   I wouldn't worry just yet because you've still got time to

   ___you have___   solve your problem.

7. ___Let us___   Let's try to figure out who can't come to the party.

   ___cannot___

8. <u> Where is </u> Where's the picture frame you said you <u>didn't</u> want

    <u> did not </u> anymore?

27.3 ACTIVITY

Write the contraction forms above the underlined words in the following sentences. Remember to use apostrophes for omitted letters.

EXAMPLE   *It's*
<u>It is</u> hard to understand what *you're* <u>you are</u> doing.

POWER UP

Look through a recent newspaper or magazine and find six different pairs of words that could be written as contractions (*did not, have not, I will,* and so forth). Write out the word pairs and then note the contraction forms. Why were contractions not used in the originals? Would you have used them?

1. You <u>should not</u> *(shouldn't)* wait any longer to begin the paper because <u>it is</u> *(it's)* due in a week.
2. *(That's)* <u>That is</u> a beautiful sweater <u>you are</u> *(you're)* wearing.
3. Many writers <u>do not</u> *(don't)* receive the attention they deserve until after <u>they are</u> *(they're)* dead.
4. *(We're)* <u>We are</u> responsible for what <u>we have</u> *(we've)* done.
5. If <u>they will</u> *(they'll)* help us, <u>we will</u> *(we'll)* help them.
6. *(There's)* <u>There is</u> little medical science can do for people who smoke and drink too much.

27.4 ACTIVITY

From the list on page 356, pick six contractions, including any that are new to you or that you have not used correctly in the past. On a separate sheet, write sentences using the contractions you have chosen.

SHOWING OWNERSHIP

Possessive forms show ownership. In other words, possessive forms show that one person or thing belongs to another person or thing. Here are some examples.

> *Jake's flute* [The flute belongs to Jake.]
> *Maria's idea* [The idea belongs to Maria.]
> *the hotel's towels* [The towels belong to the hotel.]

27.5 ACTIVITY

In each of the following items, write the word that shows what is owned in the first column below. Write the word that identifies the owner in the second column.

		What Is Owned	**The Owner**
EXAMPLE	the cat's toy	*toy*	*cat*

		What Is Owned	**The Owner**
1.	the employee's schedule	schedule	employee
2.	the moon's glow	glow	moon

3. the student's grade   grade _____   student _____

4. my mother's ring   ring _____   mother _____

5. a child's smile   smile _____   child _____

6. one person's problem   problem _____   person _____

USING APOSTROPHES TO SHOW POSSESSION

The following rules will help you use apostrophes to show possession.

1. If a *noun* does not end in -s, form the possessive by adding an apostrophe and an s. Use this rule for both singular and plural nouns.

    Noun Not Ending in -s + 's = Possessive

    dog + 's = dog's   The dog's collar is too tight.
    car + 's = car's   The car's transmission must be replaced.
    children + 's = children's   The children's toys are lost.

2. If a *singular noun* ends in -s, form the possessive by adding an apostrophe and an s.

    Singular Noun Ending in -s + 's = Possessive

    Doris + 's = Doris's   Doris's ankle is sprained.
    Mr. Stills + 's = Mr. Stills's   Mr. Stills's garden is beautiful.
    dress + 's = dress's   The dress's hem is torn.

3. If a *plural noun* ends in -s, form the possessive by adding just an apostrophe.

    Plural Noun Ending in -s + ' = Possessive

    neighbors + ' = neighbors'   My neighbors' houses were robbed.
    boys + ' = boys'   The boys' basketballs need air.
    parents + ' = parents'   Some parents' discipline techniques are questionable.

GRAMMAR ALERT !

Possessive pronouns do not take an apostrophe.

Yes	No
mine	mine's
yours	your's
his	his's
hers	her's
its	it's [*it's* means "it is" or "it has"]
ours	our's
their	their's

GRAMMAR ALERT !

Do not use an apostrophe with plurals that do not show possession.

No: *The students' asked several questions.*
Yes: *The students asked several questions.*

CONNECT

Name three important people, living or dead, in your major area of study. Then show how to form the possessive forms of the names.

27.6 ACTIVITY

Rewrite the following phrases so that ownership is shown with possessive forms. Remember to use apostrophes.

EXAMPLES   the coat belongs to Mohammed _Mohammed's coat_

the books belong to the boys _the boys' books_

1. the hat belongs to the girl _the girl's hat_

2. the hats belong to the girls _the girls' hats_

3. the house belongs to Boris _Boris's house_

4. the equipment belongs to the worker _the worker's equipment_

5. the equipment belongs to the workers _the workers' equipment_

6. the question belongs to James _James's question_

7. the boots belong to the soldier _the soldier's boots_

8. the boots belong to the soldiers _the soldiers' boots_

9. the papers belong to the men _the men's papers_

10. the poem belongs to John Keats _John Keats's poem_

11. the vote belongs to the senator _the senator's vote_

12. the votes belong to the senators _the senators' votes_

13. the responsibility belongs to the boss _the boss's responsibility_

14. the stories belong to O'Henry _O'Henry's stories_

15. the victory belongs to the players _the players' victory_

27.7 ACTIVITY

Combine each pair of sentences below into one sentence by using a possessive form.

EXAMPLE   The return policy is liberal.
The return policy belongs to the store.

The store's return policy is liberal.

1. Dr. Carlito has new office hours.
The office hours are posted on his door.

Dr. Carlito's new office hours are posted on his door.

2. Although I was careful, I tore the blouse.
   The blouse belonged to Cassandra.

   Although I was careful, I tore Cassandra's blouse.

3. The carpenters were pounding.
   The pounding gave me a headache.

   The carpenters' pounding gave me a headache.

4. Rosa has a new car.
   The new car already has a scratch on it.

   Rosa's new car already has a scratch on it.

5. The meetings are held in the library.
   The meetings are for hospital volunteers.

   The hospital volunteers' meetings are held in the library.

6. The techniques are controversial.
   The techniques belong to the filmmaker.

   The filmmaker's techniques are controversial.

7. The conclusion was weak.
   The conclusion belonged to the essay.

   The essay's conclusion was weak.

8. The sale attracted many new customers.
   The sale belonged to the business. [*Hint:* "Business" is singular.]

   The business's sale attracted many new customers.

9. The profits were the highest in recent history.
   The profits belonged to the businesses. [*Hint:* "Businesses" is plural.]

   The businesses' profits were the highest in recent history.

10. The car is double-parked.
    The car belongs to Luis.

    Luis's car is double-parked.

27.8 ACTIVITY

Write sentences on a separate sheet using the possessive forms of the terms below.

1. friend   **3.** teacher   **5.** Ms. Sykes

2. friends   **4.** teachers   **6.** children

IF ENGLISH IS YOUR SECOND LANGUAGE

You may find the forms *its* and *it's* confusing. Remember the following:

1. **Its** is a pronoun that shows ownership; it does not have an apostrophe, just as other pronouns that show ownership do not have apostrophes (*his, hers, theirs*).

The toy train came off its tracks.

2. Use **it's** (with an apostrophe) only to mean *it is* or *it has*.

It's not easy to work and attend school. [It is not easy.]
It's been years since you began studying yoga. [It has been years.]

RECHARGE

1. Use an apostrophe to form contractions.

- A contraction is formed when two words are combined and one or more letters are left out. The apostrophe takes the place of the missing letter or letters.
- Contractions include words such as *didn't (did not)*, *you're (you are)*, and *there's (there is)*.

2. Use an apostrophe to show ownership.

- Add an *'s* to form the possessive of nouns that do not end in -s *(car + 's = car's engine; men + 's = men's room)*.
- Add an *'s* to form the possessive of singular nouns ending in -s *(boss + 's = boss's report)*.
- Add an *'* to plural nouns ending in -s *(trees + ' = trees' leaves)*.

27.9 CHAPTER REVIEW ACTIVITY

Fill in the blanks in the following sentences according to the directions given.

1. Use the contraction form of *it is*:

I explained that _it's_____ too late to add a class.

2. Use the possessive form of *tree*:

The _tree's_____ branches should be pruned.

3. Use the contraction form of *does not:*

   If _doesn't_ rain soon, the crops will die.

4. Use the possessive form of *animals:*

   This zoo tries to reproduce the _animals'_ natural habitats.

5. Use the contraction form of *who is:*

   Who's responsible for this mix-up?

6. Use the possessive form of *Chris:*

   Chris's plan has several advantages.

7. Use the contraction form of *they are:*

   If _they're_ right, we must congratulate them.

8. Use the possessive form of *salespeople:*

   I like to shop here because I trust the _salespeople's_ advice.

9. Use the contraction form of *are not:*

   Students who _aren't_ computer literate should take a computer science course.

10. Use the possessive form of *crowd:*

    The _crowd's_ cheering distracted the quarterback.

27.10 CHAPTER REVIEW ACTIVITY

Write in the correct possessive and contraction forms where they are needed in the following paragraph.

Wal-Mart shoppers are accustomed to finding a range of products in the store, but it came as a surprise when Cleveland County Civil and Criminal Superior Court used the store to fill its need for jurors. However, thats exactly what happened in Shelby, North Carolina, when Judge Don Bridges asked the sheriffs office to solve the courts problem. Apparently, the court ran out of prospective jurors. The court needed last-minute jurors because some people didnt show up for jury duty, and others were disqualified. Judge Bridges's order gave the sheriffs deputies three hours to round up 55 people, so deputies went to Wal-Mart and started handing out the judges subpoenas. Some shoppers timelines were very tight; they had only 30 minutes to report to court. Some shoppers complained, but deputies said they had no choice. They admitted that it wasnt the best solution to the problem, but they werent aware of anything else they could do. Fortunately, the jurors sense of civic duty—to say nothing of their sense of humor—kept them good-natured about the proceedings.

thinking in writing: Skim all the articles on the front page of your local newspaper. Then freewrite for about 15 minutes on one of the subjects you read about.

writing from experience: Drawing on your own experience, observation, and reading of the newspaper, tell what you think the most serious problem is facing the United States today. Be sure to note why you think that problem is the most serious.

writing in context: Select a problem that has been written about in your local newspaper, and write a letter to the editor suggesting a possible solution to the problem. Be sure to explain why your solution will work.

CHAPTER 28

Punctuating Direct Quotations

CHAPTER GOALS

By the end of this chapter, you will:

Know what a direct quotation is.

Know the difference between a direct and an indirect quotation.

Be able to punctuate direct quotations.

DIRECT QUOTATIONS

A **direct quotation** is the reproduction of someone's exact spoken or written words. The exact words quoted are enclosed in quotation marks (" "). Here are some examples:

> *Marla said, "The soup is cold."* [The exact words Marla spoke are between the quotation marks.]
>
> *"Call me Ishmael," wrote Herman Melville.* [The exact words Melville wrote are between the quotation marks.]
>
> *"If I were you," Rami remarked, "I would take the job."* [The exact words Rami spoke are between two sets of quotation marks.]

A direct quotation has two parts:

- The exact words quoted
- A statement that notes who spoke or wrote the words

Here is an example:

> *Leo said, "I did well on the English test."*

Exact words quoted:	*I did well on the English test.*
Statement that notes who spoke:	*Leo said.*

Three arrangements are possible when you write direct quotations.

1. The exact words quoted can come at the beginning of the sentence.

   "Interest rates will rise if the trade agreement is signed," the economist predicted.

2. The exact words quoted can come at the end of the sentence.

   The economist predicted, "Interest rates will rise if the trade agreement is signed."

3. The exact words quoted can be divided between the beginning and the end of the sentence.

   "Interest rates will rise," the economist predicted, "if the trade agreement is signed."

CONNECT

Research papers generally include direct quotations from source material. Are research papers a part of your curriculum? In what subjects are you likely to write them?

28.1 ACTIVITY

Place quotation marks around the exact words quoted in the following sentences. Remember, exact words can come at the beginning, at the end, or both at the beginning and the end. Periods and commas go *inside* quotation marks.

EXAMPLES "You may not enter here," the security guard said.
"This model," the clerk explained, "is the best buy for the money."

1. Rhonda took a sip from the glass and gasped, "This milk is sour."
2. "I'll be with you shortly," the barber said.
3. "A computer," he remarked, "is a wise investment for a college student."
4. The cheerleaders shouted, "Get that ball and score!"
5. "We need to simplify our lives," I announced.
6. "Tell me what is wrong," the teacher said, "and I will try to help."

POWER UP

Write a direct quotation of two sentences containing important information from one of your textbooks.

PUNCTUATING DIRECT QUOTATIONS

To write direct quotations correctly, pay attention to these factors.

- Quotation marks
- Commas
- End punctuation
- Capitalization

How these four factors are handled will depend on the nature of the quotation and where the quotation is placed in the sentence. Each time you write a direct quotation, check the box that follows to be sure you are handling the four factors correctly.

HOW TO HANDLE DIRECT QUOTATIONS

1. *Placing the Quotation at the Beginning of the Sentence*

"We can leave now," she said.
"Can we leave now?" she asked.

Quotation marks:	Enclose the exact words quoted.
Comma:	Place a comma before the second quotation mark if the quotation makes a statement.
End punctuation:	Place a question mark before the last quotation mark if the quotation asks a question. Use a period at the end of the sentence.
Capitalization:	Capitalize the first word of the quotation. Do not capitalize the first word indicating who spoke unless it is a name, such as "Jeff" or "Ms. Akers."

2. *Placing the Quotation at the End of the Sentence*

The child whined, "I want a drink."
The child asked, "Can I have a drink?"

Quotation marks:	Enclose the exact words quoted.
Comma:	Place the comma after the statement of who spoke or wrote the words.

End punctuation:	Place the end punctuation inside the last quotation mark.
Capitalization:	Capitalize the first word of the quotation.

3. *Dividing the Quotation between the Beginning and the End of the Sentence*

"Before class is over," said Professor Samuels, "let me know if you have any questions."
"We should leave now," said Dan. "The concert is over."
"Is it true," Katrina asked, "that you resigned?"

Quotation marks:	Enclose the exact words quoted.
Comma:	Place a comma before the second quotation mark. Place another comma after the statement of who spoke or wrote the words when the first part of the quotation does not form a sentence.
End punctuation:	Place a period or a question mark before the last quotation mark. Place a period after the statement of who spoke or wrote the words when the first part of the quotation forms a sentence.
Capitalization:	Capitalize the first word of the quotation. Capitalize the first word of the second part of the quotation only when the first part of the quotation is a sentence.

Note: Thoughts may be handled either as direct quotations or as indirect quotations. (See page 369 on indirect quotations.)

Direct quotation:	*I said to myself, "I can do this."*
Indirect quotation:	*I told myself that I can do this.*

POWER UP

Write out a sentence you recently heard spoken at home. Be sure to indicate who spoke and to punctuate correctly. Place the quotation after the indication of who spoke. Then rewrite the sentence with the spoken words before the indication of who spoke.

28.2 ACTIVITY

The following sentences have a direct quotation at the beginning. Rewrite the sentences in the blanks below, using the correct punctuation and capitalization. If you are unsure, check the "How to Handle Direct Quotations" box.

EXAMPLE   This smoke detector needs batteries the fire inspector told me

"This smoke detector needs batteries," the fire inspector told me.

1. I need help in the garage Dad yelled

"I need help in the garage," Dad yelled.

2. There is no reason to be upset Mother explained

"There is no reason to be upset," Mother explained.

3. Is the clock fast I asked

"Is the clock fast?" I asked.

4. How can this be happening she wondered

    "How can this be happening?" she wondered.

    _____

5. I'm sorry to have bothered you the elderly man whispered

    "I'm sorry to have bothered you," the elderly man whispered.

    _____

6. This is ridiculous Sheila muttered to herself

    "This is ridiculous," Sheila muttered to herself.

    _____

28.3 ACTIVITY

The following sentences have direct quotations at the end. Rewrite the sentences in the blanks below, using the correct punctuation and capitalization. If you are unsure, check the "How to Handle Direct Quotations" box.

EXAMPLE   The teenager behind the counter asked do you want fries with your burger

The teenager behind the counter asked, "Do you want fries with your burger?"

1. The coach yelled watch out for the fast break

    The coach yelled, "Watch out for the fast break!"

    _____

2. The librarian said if you cannot be quieter, you will have to leave

    The librarian said, "If you cannot be quieter, you will have to leave."

    _____

3. I asked myself where did I go wrong

    I asked myself, "Where did I go wrong?"

    _____

4. Lydia announced I'm joining the army to see the world

    Lydia announced, "I'm joining the army to see the world."

    _____

5. The bus driver explained I can only accept exact change

    The bus driver explained, "I can only accept exact change."

    _____

6. Wanda replied if I were you, I would apply to graduate school

    Wanda replied, "If I were you, I would apply to graduate school."

    _____

28.4 ACTIVITY

The following sentences have direct quotations divided between the beginning and the end. Rewrite the sentences with the correct punctuation and capitalization. If you are unsure, check the "How to Handle Direct Quotations" box.

EXAMPLE   Before you leave said Donna I need to speak to you

"Before you leave," said Donna, "I need to speak to you."

1. When I was your age my grandfather said we knew the value of a dollar

   "When I was your age," my grandfather said, "we knew the value of a dollar."

2. You can do it I told myself all you have to do is concentrate [*Hint:* The thought forms two sentences.]

   "You can do it," I told myself. "All you have to do is concentrate."

3. The first thing to do explained my teacher is read through the test questions

   "The first thing to do," explained my teacher, "is read through the test questions."

4. Why is it Laura asked that everything goes wrong at once

   "Why is it," Laura asked, "that everything goes wrong at once?"

5. If you believe in yourself I always say you can accomplish anything

   "If you believe in yourself," I always say, "you can accomplish anything."

6. Dinner is at six o'clock said Mimi please don't be late [*Hint:* The spoken words form two sentences.]

   "Dinner is at six o'clock," said Mimi. "Please don't be late."

28.5 ACTIVITY

On a separate sheet, write two sentences with direct quotations at the beginning. Then write two sentences with direct quotations at the end. Finally, write two sentences with direct quotations divided between the beginning and the end. If you need help, consult the "How to Handle Direct Quotations" box.

INDIRECT QUOTATIONS

An **indirect quotation** refers to someone's words or thoughts but does not reproduce those words or thoughts exactly. Instead, it reports *about* what the person said or thought. Indirect quotations do not appear in quotation marks.

Direct Quotation— Exact Words or Thoughts Are Reproduced	Indirect Quotation— Exact Words or Thoughts Are Not Reproduced
The clerk said, "I'll be back."	*The clerk said he would be back.*
Lee advised, "Count to ten before speaking in anger."	*Lee advised me to count to ten before speaking in anger.*
The waiter asked, "Do you want separate checks?"	*The waiter asked whether we wanted separate checks.*
I wondered, "Where are we going?"	*I wondered where we were going.*

28.6 ACTIVITY

Rewrite the indirect quotations in the following sentences to make them direct quotations. Consult the "How to Handle Direct Quotations" box if you need help with punctuation and capitalization.

EXAMPLE   I wondered whether I would get the job.

I wondered, "Will I get the job?"

POWER UP

When is a direct quotation more effective than an indirect quotation? When is an indirect quotation more appropriate?

1. Carlos said that he prefers morning classes.

    Carlos said, "I prefer morning classes."

2. The police officer explained that the crime may never be solved.

    The police officer explained, "The crime may never be solved."

3. Joseph replied that he was certain a compromise could be reached.

    Joseph replied, "I am certain a compromise can be reached."

4. The electrician said that rewiring the lamp costs $50.

    The electrician said, "Rewiring the lamp costs $50."

5. The usher asked where we were sitting.

    The usher asked, "Where are you sitting?"

6. Helga thought to herself that she would win the race.

    Helga thought to herself, "I will win the race."

28.7 ACTIVITY

Rewrite the direct quotations in the following sentences to make them indirect quotations.

EXAMPLE   Roberto said, "We can have the meeting at my apartment."

Roberto said that we could have the meeting at his apartment.

1. The hairdresser said, "Long hair is often considered unprofessional in the workplace."

    The hairdresser said that long hair is often considered unprofessional in the workplace.

2. The flight attendant said, "Fasten your seatbelts."

    The flight attendant said to fasten our seatbelts.

3. The teacher asked, "Does anyone need help with the assignment?"

    The teacher asked whether anyone needed help with the assignment.

4. The doctor told me, "You should have your tonsils taken out."

    The doctor told me that I should have my tonsils taken out.

5. Louisa muttered, "I never want to see Frankie again."

    Louisa muttered that she never wanted to see Frankie again.

6. Juan thought, "I need a tutor to help me."

    Juan thought that he needed a tutor to help him.

IF ENGLISH IS YOUR SECOND LANGUAGE

When you change from a direct to an indirect quotation, the following changes are often made:

1. Changes in the verb tense:

    Direct quotation: *Max said, "Helga <u>is</u> at the store."*
    Indirect quotation: *Max said that Helga <u>was</u> at the store.*

2. Changes in the pronoun:

    Direct quotation: *Phillipe mentioned, "<u>I</u> need a haircut."*
    Indirect quotation: *Phillipe mentioned that <u>he</u> needed a haircut.*

3. Changes in the adverb:

    Direct quotation: *Dr. Juarez said, "I want your papers <u>now</u>."*
    Indirect quotation: *Dr. Juarez said he wanted our papers <u>then</u>.*

4. Changes in the demonstrative adjective:

Direct quotation: *Chris asked, "May I have <u>this</u> candy?"*

Indirect quotation: *Chris asked if he could have <u>that</u> candy.*

RECHARGE

1. Direct quotations are punctuated according to where in the sentence the exact words appear.

Exact words at beginning:	"Your table is ready," the waiter said.
	"Is our table ready?" we asked.
Exact words at end:	The waiter said, "Your table is ready."
	The waiter asked, "Do you want the nonsmoking section?"
Exact words divided:	"Your table is ready," the waiter said. "Do you want the nonsmoking section?"
	"Your table is ready," the waiter said, "but it is in the smoking section."
	"Are you sure," the waiter asked, "that you want the chicken?"

2. Be sure to distinguish between direct and indirect quotations.

Direct quotation:	I said, "I will not pay $50 for that ticket."
Indirect quotation:	I said that I would not pay $50 for that ticket.

3. Thoughts are punctuated like direct quotations.

"I hope I can do this," I thought.

28.8 CHAPTER REVIEW ACTIVITY

Write sentences according to the directions given below.

EXAMPLE   Write a sentence you might hear spoken at a movie theater. Put the direct quotation at the beginning of the sentence and the statement of who spoke at the end.

    "I want to sit close to the screen," Marco said.

1. Write a sentence you might hear spoken in a shopping mall or grocery store. Place the direct quotation at the beginning of the sentence and the statement of who spoke at the end.

    _____

    _____

2. Write a sentence you recently heard in a classroom. Place the direct quotation at the end of the sentence and the statement of who spoke at the beginning.

    _____

    _____

3. Write two sentences a dentist might speak to a patient. Place the first sentence at the beginning and the second sentence at the end. In between, indicate who spoke the words.

   _____

   _____

4. Write an indirect quotation to complete the following sentence:

   The children asked whether _____

   _____

5. Write something you might say to yourself before an examination. Place the direct quotation at the end of the sentence and the statement of who thought the words at the beginning.

   _____

   _____

28.9 CHAPTER REVIEW ACTIVITY

The following passage has direct quotations that lack correct punctuation and capitalization. Correct the passage by adding the missing punctuation and capitalization.

A year after I married in 1970, we moved to Tennessee so my husband could attend graduate school. We arrived to discover that tuition had gone up, and we did not have enough money. To solve the problem, I applied for a job in the university's admissions office. "Can you type?" the director of admissions asked. Thinking of all the papers I had typed in college, I replied, "As a matter of fact, I can."

The director of admissions seemed interested. Apparently, someone had just quit abruptly, and he needed a replacement immediately. "How fast," he asked me, "can you type?" I really had no idea. I wondered what the average speed was, thinking I was probably average. For some reason, the number 80 popped into my brain. "I can type 80 words per minute," I said. The man seemed very pleased; in fact, he was grinning broadly. I thought, "I've got this job for sure."

Unfortunately, no one could be hired for the job without a typing test. The director asked if I minded taking one. The next thing I knew, I was sitting at an imposing machine, and a stop clock was ticking in the background. "I'm doomed," I said to myself.

And doomed I was. The test showed I didn't type anything like 80 words a minute. "I'm sorry, but you don't type very well at all," the director said. "However, if a nontyping position opens up, I will call you."

Fortunately, something did open up, and I helped pay my husband's tuition bill working as a records clerk—no typing required.

GETTING IN GEAR

thinking in writing: List the most important things you have learned—in or out of the classroom—about your ethnic or cultural heritage.

writing from experience: Consider something important you have learned about your heritage. Write about what you learned, how you learned it, and why it is so important.

writing in context: Write an editorial for a newspaper. Explain the chief value of making sure that ethnic and cultural heritage remains a significant emphasis of public school curricula.

PART EIGHT REVIEW

Activity: Capitalization and Punctuation

Edit each passage for capital letters, end punctuation, commas, apostrophes, and quotation marks.

1.   Sometimes truth is stranger than fiction—even in sports. Consider the story of a baseball player named Bert Haas who once used his breath to stop a run from scoring.

  Haas was playing third base for the montreal royals of the international league during a 1940 game. The jersey city giants had a runner at third base, when batter Woody Jensen tried to start a squeeze play. After Jensen dropped a bunt toward third base the ball rolled slowly along just inside the foul line.

  The runner at third ran for home and Jensen sprinted for first base. Bert Haas realized that he wouldnt be able to throw out the runner at either base so he got down on his knees and began to blow the ball toward the foul line. It kept rolling fair so he blew again and again. Keep blowing, screamed the montreal infielders. Just before the ball reached third base it rolled foul. The runner had to return to third base and the batter had to return to the plate.

  Strangely jersey city did not protest. However Frank Shaughnessy who was president of the international league thought he should say something. With a twinkle in his eye Shaughnessy proclaimed after this, no player is permitted to blow a ball foul.

2.   At the first stroke of midnight, the happy crowd on times square shouts, happy new year! You, too, are probably accustomed to celebrating each new year on january 1. However, no festival has been observed on so many different dates as the welcoming of another year. The ancient greeks for example started the new year with the new moon after june 21. Before the time of julius caesar the roman new year started on March 1.

  What about today? In most predominantly christian countries the year begins on January 1 but other countries and religions observe New Years Day on different dates. The chinese celebrate twice—once on january 1 and once on the New Years Day reckoned according to the chinese lunar calendar. This second date can occur any time between January 21 and February 19. People in Indonesia also celebrate twice—once on january 1 and once on the islamic new year. the russian orthodox church celebrates on a date determined by the julian calendar which places the day on January 14. The jewish New Year, rosh hashanah, is usually celebrated at the end of September or the beginning of October. In vietnam each new year usually

begins in February; Iran celebrates on March 21. Each religious group in India has
its own date for the beginning of the year. One H̲indu celebration comes in April or
May. The people of Morocco observe the beginning of the year on the tenth day of
M̲uharram, which is the first month of the I̲slamic year.

By the way, the custom of sending New Year's cards is a very old one. The
Chinese have been doing it for more than a thousand years. Their cards were used
when people visited. They carried the visitors' name but no greeting or message.

Reading and Writing Responses to Reading

CHAPTER 29

CHAPTER GOALS

Reading and Writing Responses to Reading

College work often requires you to read material thoughtfully and then respond to that material in writing. This is what is known as reading and writing *critically*. In this sense, *critically* does not mean "negatively," as is sometimes mistakenly thought. It is reading and writing energetically, responsively, and thoughtfully. To read and write critically, you must

- Understand what you read.
- Form opinions about the reading.
- Relate the reading to other facts and ideas.
- Express your reactions and conclusions in careful, considered writing.

STRATEGIES FOR THOUGHTFUL READING

   1. PREVIEW THE READING.   Get an idea of what is in store by doing the following:

- *Read the title*. Does it give you any clues to the selection? Sometimes it will and sometimes it won't. For example, "The Truth about Our Little White Lies" (page 411) gives you a pretty good indication of the theme of the essay, but "Big White" (page 382) suggests nothing.
- *Check the author's name*. If you have read anything else by this person or heard of him or her, you know something that you can bring to the selection.
- *Read introductory notes, headings, bold face type, charts, and captions* for another indication of what is coming up.

   2. MARK THE TEXT.   Read with a pencil in your hand and react to the material in the following ways:

- *Underline the main idea and important points*. Doing so will help you remember the significant ideas and will provide a study aid. Be careful not to underline too much—just get the main points. If you prefer not to write in the book, use post-it notes.
- *Circle words you do not know*. Check the meanings in your dictionary and write them in the margin.
- *Write your reactions in the margins*. If you like something, write a star or

exclamation point. If you agree with something, write "yes!" or "I agree." If you disagree, write "no." If you don't understand something, place a question mark. If a passage makes you think of something or causes you to wonder about something, say so: "Makes me think of Dr. Small's lecture on socialism" or "How can this be true?" Whatever your reactions, write them in the margins with comments such as "clever," "needs more proof," "good example," "seems harsh," "not fair," and so forth. Don't worry about being right or wrong—there is no right or wrong here. Just react. (An example of a marked text follows.)

3. REREAD AS NECESSARY. Sometimes one reading will be enough. More often, college reading demands more. To identify all the important ideas, understand everything, and respond thoughtfully, you will have to read the material two or more times. Each time you read, mark the text.

4. WRITE IN YOUR JOURNAL. Writing about what you read is an excellent way to help you remember ideas, and it is an excellent way to consider points, evaluate issues, and form responses. Journal entries can be anything you want. You might want to try the following:

- *Freewrite.* For 10 or 15 minutes write anything and everything that occurs to you about the reading. See page 4 for more on freewriting.
- *List the main points of the reading and your reactions to those points.* This is a particularly effective study tool.
- *Map the main points.* Mapping, discussed on page 8, is another effective study aid.
- *Write a set of test questions on the material.* Try swapping them with a classmate. Answer each other's questions. This technique also helps you remember what you have read.
- *Write a paragraph that relates the material to something you have experienced, to something you know, or to something you are studying in another class.*

A SAMPLE MARKED ESSAY

The essay here shows what a piece can look like when a critical reader marks it. Because marking a text is as individual as the reader, your marked texts will look different.

ON HOLIDAYS AND HOW TO MAKE THEM WORK
Nikki Giovanni

1   A proper holiday, coming from the medieval "holy day," is supposed to be a time of reflection on great men, great deeds, great people. Things like that. Somehow in America this didn't quite catch on. Take Labor Day. On Labor Day you take the day off, then go to the Labor Day sales and spend your devalued money with a clerk who is working. And organized labor doesn't understand why it suffers declining membership? Pshaw. Who wants to join an organization that makes you work on the day it designates as a day off? Plus, no matter how hidden the agenda, who wants a day off if they make you march in a parade and listen to some politicians talk on and on about nothing.

[margin note: What does she mean by this?]

[margin note: Not women?]

[margin note: Labor Day is depressing— means end of summer.]

[margin note: Shouldn't this be a question mark?]

why quotes?

2   Hey. I'm a laborer. I used to work in Walgreen's on Linn Street. We were open every holiday and I, being among the junior people, always "got" to work the time-and-a-half holidays. I hated those people who came in. Every fool in the Western world, and probably in this universe, knows that Christmas is December 25. Has been that way for over a thousand years, yet there they'd be, standing outside the door, cold, bleary-eyed, waiting for us to open so they could purchase a present. Memorial Day, which used to be Armistice Day until we got into this situation of continuous war, was the official start of summer. We would want to be out with our boyfriends barbecuing . . . or something, but there we were behind the counter waiting to see who forgot that in order to barbecue you need: (1) a grill, (2) charcoal, (3) charcoal starter. My heart goes out to the twenty-four-hour grocery people, who are probably selling meat!

Does she think people are stupid? Why is she so angry?

Missing subject

3   But hey. It's the American way. The big Fourth of July sales probably reduced the number of fatal injuries as people spent the entire day sober in malls, fighting over markdowns. Minor cuts and bruises were way up, though, I'll bet. And forget the great nonholiday, Presidents' Day. The damned thing could at least have a real name. What does that mean—President's Day? Mostly that we don't care enough to take the time to say to Washington and Lincoln: Well done. But for sure, as a Black American I've got to go for it. Martin Luther King, Jr.'s birthday has come up for the first time as a national holiday. If we are serious about celebrating it, Steinberg's will be our first indication: GHETTO BLASTERS 30% OFF! FREE TAPE OF "I HAVE A DREAM" WITH EVERY VCR PURCHASED AT THE ALL-NEW GIGANTIC MARTY'S BIRTHDAY SALE. Then Wendy's will, just maybe, for Black patrons (and their liberal sympathizers) Burn-A-Burger to celebrate the special day. Procter & Gamble will withhold Clorox for the day, respectfully requesting that those Black spots be examined for their liberating influence. But what we really want, where we can know we have succeeded, is that every Federated department store offers 50 percent off to every colored patron who can prove he or she is Black in recognition of the days when colored citizens who were Black were not accorded all the privileges of other shoppers. That will be a big help because everybody will want to be Black for a Day. Sun tanneries will make fortunes during the week preceding MLK Day. Wig salons will reap great benefits. Dentists will have to hire extra help to put that distinctive gap between the middle front teeth. MLK Day will be accepted. And isn't that the heart of the American dream?

It's the Amer. way—but not a good one?

First time? When was this written?

Very sarcastic! Very clever!

Why "colored" here?

given

4   I really love a good holiday—it takes the people off the streets and puts them safely in the shopping malls. Now think about it. Aren't you proud to be with Uncle Sam?

She means opposite. I disagree. Relaxing in malls is good and people like earning the xtra $

BIG WHITE
Skip Rozin

Skip Rozin, who often writes about sports, turns his attention to a common source of frustration in this 1975 essay first printed in Harper's. *In "Big White," it's human against machine—and the human is at a serious disadvantage.*

1   A strange calm settled over me as I stood before the large white vending machine and dropped a quarter into the appropriate slot. I listened as the coin clunked into register. Then I pressed the button marked "Hot Chocolate." From deep inside, a paper cup slid down a chute, crackling into place on a small metal rack. Through an unseen tube poured coffee, black as night and smoking hot.

2   I even smiled as I moved to my customary place at the last table, sat down, and gazed across to the white machine, large and clean and defiant. Not since it has been moved in between the candy machine and the sandwich machine had I known peace. Every morning for two weeks I had selected a beverage, and each time the machine dispensed something different. When I pushed the button for hot chocolate, black coffee came out. When I pushed the button for tea with sugar, coffee with half and half came out. So the cup of coffee before me was no surprise. It was but one final test; my plan had already been laid.

defiant (2) resisting authority

dispensed (2) gave out

3   Later in the day, after everyone else had left the building, I returned to the snack bar, a yellow legal pad in my hand and a fistful of change in my pocket. I approached the machine and, taking each button in order, began feeding in quarters. After the first quarter I pressed the button labeled "Black Coffee." Tea with sugar came out, and I recorded that on the first line of my pad. I dropped in a second quarter and pressed the button for coffee with sugar. Plain tea came out, and I wrote that down.

4   I pressed all nine of the buttons, noting what came out. Then I placed each cup on the table behind me. When I had gone through them all, I repeated the process, and was delighted to find the machine dispensing the same drinks as before.

5   None was what I had ordered, but each error was consistent with my list.

6   I was thrilled. To celebrate, I decided to purchase a fresh cup of chocolate.

7   Dropping in two dimes and a nickel and consulting my pad, I pressed the "Coffee with Sugar and Half and Half" button. The machine clicked in response, and a little cup slid down the chute, bouncing as it hit bottom. But that was all. Nothing else happened. No hot chocolate poured into my cup. No black coffee came down. Nothing.

livid (8) enraged

8   I was livid. I forced five nickels into the slot and punched the button for black coffee. A cup dropped into place, but nothing more. I put five more nickels in and pushed another button, and another cup dropped down—empty. I dug into my

pocket for more change, but found only three dimes. I forced them in, and got back a stream of hot water and a nickel change. I went berserk.

9   "White devil!" I screamed as I slammed my fists against the machine's clean enamel finish. "You white devil!"

10   I beat on the buttons and rammed the coin-return rod down. I wanted the machine to know what pain was. I slapped at its metal sides and kicked its base with such force that I could almost hear the bone in my foot crack, then wheeled in agony on my good foot, and with one frantic swing, sent the entire table of coffee-, tea-, and chocolate-filled cups sailing.

wheeled (10) turned

11   That was last night. They have cleaned up the snack bar since then, and I have had my foot X-rayed and wrapped in that brown elastic they use for sprains. I am now sitting with my back to the row of vending machines. I know by the steadiness of my hand as I pour homemade hot chocolate from my thermos that no one can sense what I have been through—except, of course, the great white machine over against the wall.

12   Even now, behind me, in the space just below the coin slot, a tiny sign blinks off and on:

13   "Make Another Selection," it taunts. "Make Another Selection."

ON WRITING

Rozin uses very specific words—words such as *clunked* and *crackling* in paragraph 1. Cite four other specific words in the piece. What does the specific word choice add?

READING CLOSELY

1. Paragraph 2 notes that the plan had been laid. What was the plan?
    The plan was to identify a pattern by which the vending machine dispensed its drinks so the narrator could use that pattern to get the desired drink.

2. Paragraph 8 says that the narrator was "livid" and "went berserk." Explain what caused the intensity of the reaction.
    The frustration was enormous because the narrator thought he had devised the perfect plan to best the machine and get what he wanted, but the machine found a new way of thwarting him.

3. *Personification* is giving living qualities to something that is not alive. Rozin uses personification in "Big White." For example, in paragraph 2, he says that the vending machine was "defiant." Since only people can be defiant, granting this quality to a machine is an example of personification. What other examples of personification are there in the piece?
    Paragraph 10 says that the machine can feel pain; paragraph 11 says that it can sense what the narrator has been through; paragraph 13 says that the machine is taunting.

4. Which of the following describes the theme of the story? Explain your choice(s). (You may have more than one answer.)
    A. Good versus evil.
    B. Human versus machine.
    C. Control versus helplessness.
    All responses are possible. The good versus evil theme becomes apparent when the machine is referred to as "white devil." The control versus helplessness theme is seen because the narrator loses control, but the machine does not. The human versus machine theme is the primary thrust of the narrative.

5. *vocabulary in context:* Using the clues in paragraphs 12 and 13, decide which word best defines *taunts* as it is used in paragraph 13: "says," "flashes," "shouts," or "teases"?

Taunts means "teases."

REFLECTING ON IDEAS

1. One possible lesson or moral to be taken from "Big White" is that in the battle between human and machine, the machine is likely to win. How seriously do you think Rozin wants the reader to take this lesson? Explain.

Rozin is probably serious about the fact that machines frustrate us, but his tongue is firmly in his cheek for any statement stronger than that.

2. Explain the meaning of the conclusion (paragraphs 12 and 13).

The machine has won; the narration ends with personification because like a human, the machine is capable of taunting.

3. Why does Rozin make the narrator's response so extreme?

The response is exaggerated to help Rozin achieve comic effect.

4. People say that the best humor has an element of truth in it. Is there an element of truth in "Big White"? Explain.

The humor points to the truth that machines can function in unpredictable ways and thereby create frustration.

GETTING IN GEAR

thinking in writing: How much frustration is added to our lives by malfunctioning machines? Are we enduring too much at the hands of modern devices? Are we slaves to the machines we have created? Respond to these questions in a page or two of freewriting. (Freewriting is explained on page 4.)

writing from experience: Develop a writing topic by filling in the blank in this sentence: "_____ is more trouble than it is worth." Fill in the blank with any device you wish (an alarm clock, a VCR, a car, a telephone, an answering machine, and so forth). If you like, you can make this piece humorous.

writing in context: Write a story for a science fiction magazine about an evil machine that takes over or an op-ed piece arguing for less reliance on a machine (for example, the computer).

connecting the readings: Like "Big White," the essay, "For One Teacher, a Lesson about E-Mail and Privacy" (page 400), treats a problem associated with a modern convenience. What other problems can you think of that are associated with modern conveniences? Do the benefits of the conveniences outweigh the problems?

THEY SHUT MY GRANDMOTHER'S ROOM DOOR
Andrew Lam

Award-winning writer Andrew Lam is an associate editor with the Pacific News Service. Born in Saigon, Vietnam, he came to the United States when he was 11-years-old. Drawing on his experiences in both Vietnam and the United States, Lam contrasts the two cultures' views of death and offers an explanation for those differences. You will probably have no trouble determining which view the author finds superior.

convalescent home (1) nursing home

Tet (1) New Year celebration

1   When someone dies in the convalescent home where my grandmother lives, the nurses rush to close all the patients' doors. Though as a policy death is not to be seen at the home, she can always tell when it visits. The series of doors being slammed shut remind her of the firecrackers during Tet.

2   The nurses' efforts to shield death are more comical to my grandmother than reassuring. "Those old ladies die so often," she quips in Vietnamese, "every day's like new year."

3   Still, it is lonely to die in such a place. I imagine some wasted old body under a white sheet being carted silently through the empty corridor on its way to the morgue. While in America a person may be born surrounded by loved ones, in old age one is often left to take the last leg of life's journey alone.

4   Perhaps that is why my grandmother talks now mainly of her hometown, Bac-Lieu; its river and green rich rice fields. Having lost everything during the war, she can now offer me only her distant memories: Life was not disjointed back home; one lived in a gentle rhythm with the land; people died in their homes surrounded by neighbors and relatives. And no one shut your door.

5   So it goes. The once gentle, connected world of the past is but the language of dreams. In this fast-paced society of disjointed lives, we are swept along and have little time left for spiritual comfort. Instead of relying on neighbors and relatives, on the river and land, we deal with the language of materialism: overtime, escrow, stress, down payment, credit cards, tax shelter. Instead of going to the temple to pray for good health we pay life and health insurance religiously.

escrow (5) money held as part of a contract

6   My grandmother's children and grandchildren share a certain pang of guilt. After a stroke which paralyzed her, we could no longer keep her at home. And although we visit her regularly, we are not living up to the filial piety standard expected of us in the old country. My father silently grieves and my mother suffers from headaches. (Does she see herself in such a home in a decade or two?)

filial (6) pertaining to a son or daughter

7   Once, a long time ago, living in Vietnam we used to stare death in the face. The war in many ways had heightened our sensibilities toward living and dying. I can still hear the wails of widows and grieving mothers. Though the fear of death and dying is a universal one, the Vietnamese did not hide from it. Instead we dwelt in its tragedy. Death pervaded our poems, novels, fairy tales and songs.

ON WRITING

Explain the use of the apostrophe in *patients'* (paragraph 1), *grandmother's* (paragraph 6), *America's* (paragraph 8), and *don't* (paragraph 14). Why do the apostrophes appear where they do?

8   But if agony and pain are part of Vietnamese culture, pleasure is at the center of America's culture. While Vietnamese holidays are based on death anniversaries, birthdays are celebrated here. American popular culture translates death with something like nauseating humor. People laugh and scream at blood and guts movies. The wealthy freeze their dead relatives in liquid nitrogen. Cemeteries are places of big

business, complete with colorful brochures. I hear there are even drive-by funerals where you don't have to get out of your own car to pay your respects to the deceased.

9   That America relies upon the pleasure principle and happy endings in its entertainments does not, however, assist us in evading suffering. The reality of the suffering of old age is apparent in the convalescent home. There is an old man, once an accomplished concert pianist, now rendered helpless by arthritis. Every morning he sits staring at the piano. One feeble woman who outlived her children keeps repeating, "My son will take me home." Then there are those mindless, bedridden bodies kept alive through a series of tubes and pulsating machines.

10   But despair is not newsworthy. Death itself must be embellished or satirized or deep-frozen in order to catch the public's attention.

11   Last week on her 82nd birthday I went to see my grandmother. She smiled her sweet sad smile.

12   "Where will you end up in your old age?" she asked me, her mind as sharp as ever.

wafting (13) floating through air

13   The memories of monsoon rain and tropical sun and relatives and friends came to mind. Not here, not here, I wanted to tell her. But the soft moaning of a patient next door and the smell of alcohol wafting from the sterile corridor brought me back to reality.

14   "Anywhere is fine," I told her instead, trying to keep up with her courageous spirit. "All I am asking for is that they don't shut my door."

READING CLOSELY

1.   What is the main difference between the way Americans and Vietnamese view death?
      The Vietnamese accept death as a natural part of life, whereas Americans hide from it.

2.   How is the attitude of Americans toward death reflected in American culture?
      Americans' attitude toward death is reflected in the fact that we celebrate birthdays, laugh at gory movies, freeze dead relatives, and have commercialized, dehumanized funeral services.

3.   How does Lam explain the Vietnamese attitude toward death?
      Lam points to the war in Vietnam and the ability of the Vietnamese to live "in a gentle rhythm with the land" as causes of their attitude toward death.

4.   In addition to their different attitudes toward death, what other contrasts between Vietnamese and Americans does Lam point out?
      Lam sees people in Vietnam as being one with nature; he considers life in the United States to be "disjointed," materialistic, and fast-paced.

5.   *vocabulary in context:* Using the clues in paragraph 4, decide which word best defines *disjointed* as it is used in the paragraph: "confusing," "disconnected," "unhappy," or "stressful?"
      Disjointed means "disconnected."

REFLECTING ON IDEAS

1. Which attitude toward death does Lam prefer? How can you tell?

   Lam prefers the Vietnamese attitude. In paragraphs 13 and 14, he states that he hopes to die among relatives and friends rather than isolated in a convalescent home.

2. What is the significance of the closed door?

   The door is a symbol of isolation. It is meant as a form of protection, shielding patients from death. But in reality it isolates them from life.

3. In paragraph 4, Lam says that for his grandmother, "Life was not disjointed back home." In paragraph 5, he says, "The once gentle, connected world of the past is but the language of dreams." What point do you think Lam is making when he contrasts the disjointed life and the connected world?

   Responses will vary, but some may note that the contrast emphasizes Lam's view by providing an alternative to the American way. The contrast also helps establish the error of the American way.

4. If you were a nursing home administrator, what procedure would you implement for dealing with the death of a resident?

   Responses will vary.

GETTING IN GEAR

thinking in writing: Freewrite for about 15 minutes to explore your feelings about aging, death, or funerals.

writing from experience: If you have ever visited a nursing home, write about the experience. Was it pleasant or unpleasant? Why? As an alternative, write about a time you witnessed or participated in the rituals of a particular culture or religion, including your own, for dealing with death. What purpose did the rituals serve? Did you find them comforting? Why or why not?

writing in context: The elderly are the fastest-growing age group in the United States. Without a doubt, a number of changes will occur as American society adapts to the large aging population. Assume the role of an advertising executive, and make recommendations for a campaign advertising a particular kind of car. Your recommendations should take into consideration the large segment of the population that is aging.

connecting the readings: "They Shut My Grandmother's Room Door" and the next selection, "Baby Names, Big Battles" below deal with customs surrounding birth and death. Tell about one or more of the customs in your family that surround birth or death.

BABY NAMES, BIG BATTLES
Tunku Varadarajan

Former bureau chief for the London Times *in New York and Madrid, Tunku Varadarajan is currently a freelance writer in New York. In the following op-ed piece that originally appeared in the* New York Times *in 1999, he notes that choosing a baby's name is an important process with lifelong impact. It is also a process that can be difficult for parents in the United States who are from a different culture.*

1   My wife has just given birth to a son. Tomorrow, the twelfth day after he was born, our family will perform an ancient but simple Hindu ritual. We will sing a

intoning (1) speaking in a particular tone of voice

Sanskrit (2) the traditional language of the Hindu religion

protracted (2) long

arduous (3) difficult

prayer and make a small offering to the gods, after which I will put my lips to his little ear and say to him three times: "Your name is 'Satya.' " Thirty-seven years ago, in Delhi, my father observed the same rite, intoning my name thrice into my right ear.

2   Satya [SUT-ya] is the Sanskrit word for "truth." For me, and for my wife, it has two clear virtues as a name: its meaning is a handsome one, and its brevity sits snugly with my protracted surname.

3   We arrived at Satya after a process that was as arduous, and almost as lengthy, as the boy's gestation. Parents will always quarrel over their child's name—with each other, with friends, with relatives. There is no privacy in the process, and a number of names, which I cherished fleetingly, fell by the wayside as soon as someone said, "You can't call him *that!*" These battles over a baby's name are magnified when a parent is, like I am, not from a Judeo-Christian background.

4   Although my American wife has her roots in North Carolina, she was rather keen that her son should have an Indian name. My initial protestations that he should, perhaps, be called "something American" were given the shortest shrift. Walter was simply out of the question, as was Lancelot.

5   My wife was right, of course. Saying, "Your name is Walter" would have sounded absurd at the end of a Hindu naamakaran, or naming ceremony.

6   Naming a child is not easy for parents in America who come from non-European backgrounds, from cultures where Ashutosh, Chae-Hyun, and Naeem are common names. We have to ask ourselves a number of important questions. How will the child's foreign name sound to American ears? (That test ruled out Shiva, my family deity; a Jewish friend put her foot down.)

7   Will it provoke bullies to beat him up on the school playground? (That was the end of Karan, the name of a warrior from the Mahabharata, the Hindu epic. A boy called "Karen" wouldn't stand a chance.)

8   Will it be as euphonic in New York as it is in New Delhi? (That was how Sameer failed to get off the ground. "Like a bagel with a schmear!" said one ruthless well-wisher.)

9   There were other questions: Does it make a jarring sound, especially when mispronounced—as it surely will be—by other people? Does it mean something rude in English? Will he have to spend the rest of his life spelling it out over the telephone, letter by wretched letter?

10   My wife and I could have resorted to an option that many Indian parents in the United States employ: going for a perfectly orthodox Indian name that "sounds American." Over the last few months, as our ear for names grew more acute, we've encountered children called Neel (Neil), Dev (Dave), Jai (Jay) and even Dilin (Dylan).

11   We've also noted names that sound American when shortened to nicknames, like Samar (Sam), Ishaan (Sean) and Sidhartha (Sid). Our problem with these Indian names—I call them "Ameronyms"—is that they limited us to a meager short list. Besides, they are growing to be rather common among Indians in this country.

12   But one evening, about a month ago, my wife called excitedly from the next room. She'd found a name for our son at last. Leafing through a book of Indian baby names—published in Bombay and purchased by us in Jackson Heights, Queens—she had come across Satya. Here was an Indian name that didn't sound American. It couldn't even be snipped or tweaked to sound American. But we loved it so much that we forgot America. We were naming him for ourselves, after all, and not for America. We can hardly wait, now, to whisper the words: "Your name is Satya."

ON WRITING

Cite two examples of parenthetical words or phrases set off with commas or dashes. (See page 351 for a discussion of commas and parenthetical words and phrases.) What effect do these constructions have on Varadarajan's prose?

READING CLOSELY

1. Why does the author think that Satya is a good name for his son?
   The name has a positive meaning (truth), and it is short so it goes well with the author's long last name.

2. What made choosing a name so difficult for the author and his wife?
   Choosing a name was difficult because the author is not from the United States, nor is he of a Judeo-Christian background.

3. A Jewish friend objected to the name Shiva. Why? If you do not know, ask someone who is Jewish or check a dictionary.
   For Jews, shivah is a seven-day mourning period that follows the funeral of a loved one.

4. What requirements did the author have for a suitable name for his son?
   The name had to be Indian, not jarring, not rude in English, and not too common.

5. *vocabulary in context:* Using the clues in paragraph 4, decide which phrase best defines *shortest shrift* as it is used in the paragraph: "briefest consideration," "immediate brush off," "immediate disbelief," or "briefest chuckle"?
   Shortest shrift means "briefest consideration."

REFLECTING ON IDEAS

1. Did the author put undue emphasis on the choice of a name for his son? Explain.
   Responses will vary.

2. Should the author and his wife have chosen an American name, such as John or Bill, for their son? Why or why not?
   Responses will vary.

3. Why do you think that many Indians are choosing Indian names that sound American for their children?
   Indian names that sound American allow Indians to maintain their cultural traditions at the same time their children can feel assimilated. Also, such names are not difficult for Americans to pronounce.

4. How does the author feel about his Indian heritage?
   The author is proud of his Indian heritage and wants to maintain his Indian identity and instill it in his son.

thinking in writing: How important is a person's first name? Freewrite on the answer to this question for about 15 minutes. (Freewriting is discussed on page 4.)

writing from experience: Do you like your first name? Explain why or why not and explain how your first name has affected you.

writing in context: Assume you are writing the introduction to a book of names for babies. For that introduction, explain the importance of choosing a baby's name.

connecting the readings: In "Back, but Not Home" (page 417), the author discusses her need to preserve her cultural heritage. Is naming a baby, the issue discussed in "Baby Names, Big Battles," an important way to preserve one's cultural heritage? Explain.

HAVE A NICE DAY
Thomas H. Middleton

"Have a nice day!" we are regularly told. But is the speaker sincere? Maybe not, says Thomas Middleton, but the sentence is harmless enough—and sometimes it even does some good. Interestingly, this essay originally appeared in 1979 in the Saturday Review, *yet it remains relevant today, as "Have a nice day" continues to be used routinely.*

quasi (1) seeming

1   Shortly after the quasi-annual Los Angeles fire disaster last year, we met Gordon Jenkins, the composer-conductor, and his wife, Beverly. The Jenkinses had lived in one of the oldest and most charming houses on Broad Beach Road in Malibu. Broad Beach was one of the areas most severely affected by the fire.

2   Mr. Jenkins told me that when the fire leaped down the hills and started blazing across the street from their home, and the smoke billowed in, they were forced to leave. They drove to a motel and checked in for the night. Early the next morning, they went back home. As you drive along Broad Beach, what you see from your car is a row of garages. As a rule, the garages hide the houses, which are built along the beach. The Jenkinses' garage, being made of cement, was intact. When they went around the garage to where their house had stood the day before, they found only ashes. They had lived in the house for over 31 years.

3   They went back to the motel for what I suspect was a crushingly dismal breakfast.

4   On their return to Broad Beach, they found that the police were blocking off the street. The policeman who stopped them told them no one but residents could enter the area. Mr. Jenkins told him that he was a resident, or that at any rate he had been a resident, his house having burned to the ground the day be-

fore. The cop checked his driver's license and waved them through, calling, "Have a nice day!"

5   The Jenkinses got about 200 feet down the road before the "Have a nice day" sank all the way in and their gales of laughter burst out. Surely, no other phrase could have made Gordon and Beverly Jenkins laugh all the way to the ashes of their home. That mindless pleasantry brightened a dark day.

ubiquitous (6) seeming to be everywhere

6   "Have a nice day" is ubiquitous these days, at least in this part of the country. It is said constantly by supermarket checkers, filling-station attendants, receptionists, and just about everyone else who deals regularly with the public.

curmudgeonly (7) easily angered

7   I have friends and relations, not necessarily curmudgeonly, who loathe the expression on the grounds that it is almost always said automatically and that, like most automatic utterances, it is almost always insincere.

admonition (8) warning

8   My own feeling is that it is a pleasant enough pleasantry. I grant that "Have a nice day" probably helps no more than my wife's admonition, "Don't fall down." That's what Jeannie says whenever I'm standing on a narrow ledge or a stepladder. I'd do my best not to fall down even if she didn't tell me not to. Still, it's good to know that she cares.

9   There is a difference between "Have a nice day" and "Don't fall down" in that the person who tells me to have a nice day may not be sincerely concerned over what kind of day I'll have, whereas if I should fall off the ladder, Jeannie's day could be seriously flawed.

peevishly (10) irritably

10   Years before I heard "Have a nice day," I was in the habit of telling people to have a good time, and I always meant it sincerely, for whatever good it might do. I remember long ago when I used to drive young Tom to school on those infrequent days when he'd miss the bus or the weather would be particularly foul. As I dropped him off, I always said, "Have a good time," and he always said, "Thanks," until one day, after my customary "Have a good time," he turned rather peevishly and said "*Geez*, I'm going to *school!*"

11   I said, "I know. Have a good time while you're learning something, or learn something while you're having a good time. They're not mutually exclusive." He brightened and said, "Hey, ri-i-ght! Thanks!"

12   I think "Have a nice day" provides one of those little indications that we do care, even if only slightly, about one another's welfare. It has taken its place for a time in the storehouse of phrases we use for civility's sake, and on at least one occasion it brought unexpected laughter in a time of heavy tragedy.

13   Have a nice day.

ON WRITING

Anecdotes are brief stories that can illustrate a point. For example, paragraphs 1 through 5 form an anecdote to illustrate that "Have a nice day," even when used mindlessly, can brighten a day. In addition to illustrating, anecdotes often add interest and liveliness to writing. What would this piece have been like without the anecdote?

1. In your own words, explain the main idea of the essay.

   One possibility: "Have a nice day" is a harmless expression that shows we care about people.

2. Do you find the essay humorous? If so, what parts are amusing to you? If not, why not?

   Responses will vary, but students may find paragraphs 8, 9, and 10 amusing.

3. According to the essay, why do some people think that those who say "Have a nice day" are almost always "insincere"?

   Paragraph 7 explains that the expression may be insincere because it is uttered automatically and unthinkingly.

4. The couple in the essay laughed when the police officer told them to have a nice day. Why?

   Perhaps the couple laughed as a release of tension following an emotional, traumatic event. The absurdity triggered the release.

5. *vocabulary in context:* Using the clues in paragraph 12, decide which word best defines *civility* as it is used in the paragraph: "humor," "sincerity," "conversation," or "politeness"?

   Civility means "politeness."

1. Why does Middleton use humor rather than treat his topic in a serious way?

   Middleton uses humor to entertain the reader. Because his subject is not that serious, a serious treatment is not necessary.

2. Do you routinely say, "Have a nice day"? Why or why not?

   Responses will vary.

3. Why do you think the policeman told the couple to "have a nice day"? Was his remark appropriate?

   The policeman's remark was not appropriate. Despite the tragedy, the policeman was probably numbed by the routine of his job and not thinking clearly.

thinking in writing: Paragraph 12 refers to the "storehouse of phrases we use for civility's sake." List some of the other things people say for the sake of civility. Think about what we say at events such as weddings, funerals, and graduations.

writing from experience: Pick a slang expression, ethnic term, or term of endearment used in your family, and explain what the term means and how it is used, relying on one or more anecdotes to illustrate.

writing in context: Select a sentence or expression commonly used in a particular situation. For example, people at funerals often say to mourners, "Call me if there is anything I can do." Imagine you are writing a book of etiquette. Explain whether the words are harmful or helpful.

connecting the readings: The expression "Have a nice day" is a pleasantry that may be insincere, but it is one "we use for civility's sake" (paragraph 12). Read "They Shut My Grandmother's Room Door" (page 384), and discuss the things we do and say at times of death for "civility's sake."

THANK YOU, M'AM
Langston Hughes

Best known as a poet, Langston Hughes is also respected as a playwright, critic, and fiction writer. He was an important figure in the 1920s' blossoming of literature and music known as the Harlem Renaissance. "Thank You, M'am" is his short story about a confrontation between a young boy and a savvy woman, an encounter that did not go at all as the boy expected. As you read, consider what you would have done in the woman's place.

1   She was a large woman with a large purse that had everything in it but hammer and nails. It had a long strap and she carried it slung across her shoulder. It was about eleven o'clock at night, and she was walking alone, when a boy ran up behind her and tried to snatch her purse. The strap broke with the single tug the boy gave it from behind. But the boy's weight, and the weight of the purse combined caused him to lose his balance so, instead of taking off full blast as he had hoped, the boy fell on his back on the sidewalk, and his legs flew up. The large woman simply turned around and kicked him right square in his blue jeaned sitter. Then she reached down, picked the boy up by his shirt front, and shook him until his teeth rattled.

2   After that the woman said, "Pick up my pocketbook, boy, and give it here."

3   She still held him. But she bent down enough to permit him to stoop and pick up her purse. Then she said, "Now ain't you ashamed of yourself?"

4   Firmly gripped by his shirt front, the boy said, "Yes'm."

5   The woman said, "What did you want to do it for?"

6   The boy said, "I didn't aim to."

7   She said, "You a lie!"

8   By that time two or three people passed, stopped, turned to look, and some stood watching.

9   "If I turn you loose, will you run?" asked the woman.

10   "Yes'm," said the boy.

11   "Then I won't turn you loose," said the woman. She did not release him.

12   "I'm very sorry, lady, I'm sorry," whispered the boy.

13   "Um-hum! And your face is dirty. I got a great mind to wash your face for you. Ain't you got nobody home to tell you to wash your face?"

14   "No'm," said the boy.

15   "Then it will get washed this evening," said the large woman starting up the street, dragging the frightened boy behind her.

16   He looked as if he were fourteen or fifteen, frail and willow-wild, in tennis shoes and blue jeans.

17   The woman said, "You ought to be my son. I would teach you right from wrong. Least I can do right now is to wash your face. Are you hungry?"

18   "No'm," said the being-dragged boy. "I just want you to turn me loose."

19   "Was I bothering *you* when I turned that corner?" asked the woman.

20   "No'm."

21   "But you put yourself in contact with *me*," said the woman. "If you think that that contact is not going to last awhile, you got another thought coming. When I get through with you, sir, you are going to remember Mrs. Luella Bates Washington Jones."

22   Sweat popped out on the boy's face and he began to struggle. Mrs. Jones stopped, jerked him around in front of her, put a half-nelson about his neck, and continued to drag him up the street. When she got to her door, she dragged the boy inside, down a hall, and into a large kitchenette-furnished room at the rear of the house. She switched on the light and left the door open. The boy could hear other roomers laughing and talking in the large house. Some of their doors were open, too, so he knew he and the woman were not alone. The woman still had him by the neck in the middle of her room.

half-nelson (22) a wrestling hold

23   She said, "What is your name?"

24   "Roger," answered the boy.

25   "Then, Roger, you go to that sink and wash your face," said the woman, whereupon she turned him loose—at last. Roger looked at the door—looked at the woman—looked at the door—*and went to the sink.*

26   "Let the water run until it gets warm," she said. "Here's a clean towel."

27   "You gonna take me to jail?" asked the boy, bending over the sink.

28   "Not with that face, I would not take you nowhere," said the woman. "Here I am trying to get home to cook me a bite to eat and you snatch my pocketbook! Maybe you ain't been to your supper either, late as it be. Have you?"

29   "There's nobody home at my house," said the boy.

30   "Then we'll eat," said the woman. "I believe you're hungry—or been hungry—to try to snatch my pocketbook."

31   "I wanted a pair of blue suede shoes," said the boy.

32   "Well, you didn't have to snatch *my* pocketbook to get some suede shoes," said Mrs. Luella Bates Washington Jones. "You could of asked me."

33   "M'am?"

34   The water dripping from his face, the boy looked at her. There was a long pause. A very long pause. After he had dried his face and not knowing what else to do dried it again, the boy turned around, wondering what next. The door was open. He could make a dash for it down the hall. He could run, run, run, run, *run!*

day-bed (35) an armless couch that serves as a bed by night and a sofa by day

35   The woman was sitting on the day-bed. After awhile she said, "I were young once and I wanted things I could not get."

36   There was another long pause. The boy's mouth opened. Then he frowned, but not knowing he frowned.

37   The woman said, "Um-hum! You thought I was going to say *but,* didn't you? You thought I was going to say, *but I didn't snatch people's pocketbooks.* Well, I wasn't going to say that." Pause. Silence. "I have done things, too, which I would not tell you, son—neither tell God, if he didn't already know. So you set down while I fix us something to eat. You might run that comb through your hair so you will look presentable."

38   In another corner of the room behind a screen was a gas plate and an icebox. Mrs. Jones got up and went behind the screen. The woman did not watch the boy to see if he was going to run now, nor did she watch her purse which she left behind her on the day-bed. But the boy took care to sit on the far side of the room where he thought she could easily see him out of the corner of her eye, if she wanted to. He did not trust the woman *not* to trust him. And he did not want to be mistrusted now.

39   "Do you need somebody to go to the store," asked the boy, "maybe to get some milk or something?"

40   "Don't believe I do," said the woman, "unless you just want sweet milk yourself. I was going to make cocoa out of this canned milk I got here."

41   "That will be fine," said the boy.

42   She heated some lima beans and ham she had in the icebox, made the cocoa, and set the table. The woman did not ask the boy anything about where he lived, or his folks, or anything else that would embarrass him. Instead, as they ate, she told him about her job in a hotel beauty-shop that stayed open late, what the work was like, and how all kinds of women came in and out, blondes, red-heads, and Spanish. Then she cut him a half of her ten-cent cake.

43   "Eat some more, son," she said.

44   When they were finished eating she got up and said, "Now, here, take this ten dollars and buy yourself some blue suede shoes. And next time, do not make the mistake of latching onto *my* pocketbook *nor nobody else's*—because shoes come by devilish like that will burn your feet. I got to get my rest now. But I wish you would behave yourself, son, from here on in."

45   She led him down the hall to the front door and opened it. "Goodnight! Behave yourself, boy!" she said, looking out into the street.

46   The boy wanted to say something else other than, "Thank you, m'am," to Mrs. Luella Bates Washington Jones, but he couldn't do so as he turned at the barren

ON WRITING

In Chapter 28, you learned about punctuating direct quotations. When you use conversation to reproduce someone's exact words, you are using direct quotations. Hughes uses a great deal of conversation in his story. What does it contribute? How would the story be different without the conversation?

stoop and looked back at the large woman in the door. He barely managed to say, "Thank you," before she shut the door. And he never saw her again.

READING CLOSELY

1. For what reason does Roger say that he tried to steal the purse?
    Roger wanted to buy a pair of blue suede shoes.

2. Was snatching Mrs. Jones's purse something that Roger planned? How can you be sure Roger is telling the truth about whether he planned to steal the purse?
    In paragraph 6, Roger notes that the theft was not premeditated; the reader may or may not believe him, but in paragraph 10 he did not lie about his willingness to run away.

3. Do you think the title of the story is a good one? Explain.
    Responses will vary, but many students will like that the title reflects Roger's respect for Mrs. Jones and the irony that a would-be thief is so polite.

4. Why does Mrs. Jones bring Roger to her house, even though he tried to mug her?
    Mrs. Jones seems to feel sorry for Roger and probably thinks she can reach out to help him. It was an act of kindness.

5. *vocabulary in context:* Using the clues in paragraph 46, decide which word best defines *barren* as it is used in the paragraph: "crumbling," "needing paint," "infertile," or "without interesting features"?
    Barren means "without interesting features."

REFLECTING ON IDEAS

1. Using the evidence in the essay for clues, list words and phrases that describe Roger. Then list ones that describe Mrs. Jones.
    Responses will vary, but the following are possibilities for Roger: poor, unsupervised, in need of direction, probably wanting to live decently, wanting more than he has, appreciative of Mrs. Jones, basically decent, polite. The following can describe Mrs. Jones: compassionate, strong-willed, savvy, having a checkered past, hardworking, in-charge, independent, fearless, aggressive.

2. What do you think of the way Mrs. Jones handled the situation with Roger? Explain your view.
    Responses will vary, but many may be impressed by her compassion.

3. Why is it significant to Mrs. Jones that Roger's face is dirty, and why is it important that she takes him home to wash it?
    To Mrs. Jones, the dirty face is a symbol of what is wrong with Roger: He lacks personal pride or devotion to basic virtues, like cleanliness being next to Godliness. Also, Mrs. Jones wants his face washed so he can "clean up his act," so to speak, and get himself righted.

4. Why does Roger ask Mrs. Jones if she needs him to go to the store?
    Responses will vary, but possibly Roger wanted to make a helpful gesture to repay her—or possibly he wanted to escape.

GETTING IN GEAR

thinking in writing: Mrs. Jones was just one person who made a difference. List ways just one person can make a difference. That is, list things one person can do to make the world a better place.

writing from experience: Have you ever tried to help someone? Or did someone ever try to help you? Explain what happened and what you learned as a result.

writing in context: Assume you are a member of a campus group that wants to undertake a project meant to improve life on your campus. Also assume that you have been asked to decide what that project will be. Determine what the project should be and write a report explaining the activity, why it is important, and how it will benefit your campus community.

connecting the readings: If Luella Bates Washington Jones had been the teacher in "For One Teacher, a Lesson about E-Mail and Privacy" (page 400), how would she have dealt with Rachel, the student in that essay?

A LIFETIME OF PRODUCTION
Michelle M. Ducharme

For the "My Turn" section of Newsweek *magazine, readers can submit essays on any topic. In 1996, on the occasion of her father's retirement, Michelle Ducharme wrote the following essay for the section, in which she reflects on the value of a lifetime of labor and considers what work should mean.*

1   I know how to prepare a French fold. It's simply a matter of layering the box flaps clockwise then lifting up the bottom one. The result is an interlocked seal and a surprisingly strong-bottomed box. Doing French folds is one of my parlor tricks, an uncomplicated skill, like changing fuses or checking tire pressure, that, when performed effortlessly, brands the doer as versatile and experienced.

2   The boxes on which I perform my magic are not cardboard. I'm talking about corrugated board—single and double wall. To confuse board of that sturdiness with the stuff of pastry boxes is a horrid blunder. As with most things, there is a culture behind box making. It is the corrugated industry that I know, and in my memory it includes the deep scent of steamed paper, a vending machine stocked with orange Dreamsicles and my father's slide rule.

corrugated (2) having ridges

3   I am the daughter of a man who has scheduled the production of corrugated board and boxes for 35 years and seven months. When I contemplate my father's career, I focus inevitably on the issue of job security. First, I think how fortunate my father was to have known an era when jobs could be had—and came with dental benefits. Then I move to gratitude that my father never fell under the shadow of downsizing. Unlike so many of his peers, he wasn't cast off with decades of service but just not enough to collect a pension. My father is leaving this summer by choice, and I am thankful that his job lasted to his retirement.

hoopla (4) noisy disturbance

4   He is grateful, too, and when he receives only a handshake and no hoopla on his last day, he won't complain. My father had his cake—a steady job for more than three decades—so he really doesn't expect any icing. These days, economic blessings

aren't so much opportunities bestowed as bullets dodged. Still, I have to believe that a person's working life transcends the exchange of labor for money. It has to matter that for more years than I have been alive, my father walked into that steam-scented plant and transformed box orders into an efficient production run.

5   It never was a glamorous job. His shared office had no window and contained tired furniture. Each day's objective was the same, though order specifications and grades of board varied. The challenge was to determine the best method for the next day's production, the one that would result in the least waste and the fewest machine setups. In between, there was paper to be ordered, rail delivery to be negotiated and inventory to be maintained. As the decades passed, the tools of the scheduling trade changed: the quiet slide rule was replaced first by a calculator, then by a computer.

6   My dad changed, too. He had come to that job feeling—as I do now—that everything was still possible. He'd served his time in the air force during the Korean War. Then, while my mother worked as a secretary to support them, he earned a college degree courtesy of the GI Bill. After graduation my father painted houses for a season until he was offered a position scheduling the production of corrugated board. He took it, though he has told me that he never planned to stay. It was not something he envisioned as his life's work. I try to imagine what it is like suddenly to look up from a stack of orders and discover that the job you started one December day has watched you age.

7   For 35 years, my father did his job well. He crafted production runs that fit like a dovetail joint. Always there were last-minute cancellations and order changes that required him to tear apart the runs, then rebuild them so that the company could fulfill its promises to customers. His days frequently lasted far beyond nightfall because he worked not just until the job was completed but until it was done right. Though it is never officially acknowledged, in the days before computers my father's manual scheduling enabled his Eastern-division plant to repeatedly hold the national record for producing the greatest yield of board with the lowest percentage of waste. Through it all, he kept his health problems to himself, cared for his aging parents on the weekends and, in partnership with my mother, raised three daughters.

8   Still, no merit raises, no accolades, not even an office window. As a child, I was unaware of these indignities. Instead, I saw the shining ice-cream machine, the soft-lead colored pencils and my father's swivel chair. Then there were the boxes, enough of them to form a tunnel across my front yard. We crawled through them, my sisters, me and every kid on the block. They were our toys, our Halloween costumes, and later they moved us to college, graduate school and adult lives.

GI Bill (6) benefits given to former military personnel

accolades (8) awards; honors

9   I realize that on some fronts we are all replaceable. After my father's retirement, someone else will do his job, and, as scheduling software advances, the position will become less and less specialized. But if technology has taught us anything, it's that a machine is only as skilled as its operator. It is people, not products or profits, who create meaning. And that's what desperately needs to be said. All of us need to know that our lifework has mattered, but in the swirling quest for bigger, better and faster, there is no time or space for affirmation. Even when it has been 35 years of a job well done.

mantra (10) words repeated often like a chant

10   The mantra of the bottom line attempts to convince us that our lives are secondary to the market. Like so many workers, my dad's skill and dedication to task helped his company remain competitive in a fluctuating economy. Still, the vocabulary of disposability, full of double-talk and sidestepping, is spoken with no context other than the latest quarterly report. Yesterday we were laid off, today we're downsized and tomorrow we'll be rightsized. If we happen to make it through, like my father did, there is only silence.

11   I want my father to know that by crafting production runs day after day, he did more than fulfill a job description. He created boxes, and they were marvelous units. In them, my sisters and I found unconditional love and all the hopes of childhood. They carried us through, their French folds never buckling. And now we breathe our "thank yous," grateful for him, his work and language that distinguishes us from timecards and machines.

READING CLOSELY

1. The author is thankful for a number of things related to her father's job. What are they?
   The author is thankful that her father had a job, that the job came with insurance benefits, and that he was not laid off after years of service but was able to work until retirement.

2. Was the author's father important to the company? Cite examples to support your view.
   Paragraph 7 makes clear that the author's father was important to the company: he did his job well for 35 years; he handled last-minute problems; he did not punch the clock but worked until the job was done; he worked well so his plant won awards; he kept his health problems to himself.

3. How does the author think the company treated her father?
   The author believes that the company was not appreciative of her father's accomplishments. He received only a handshake upon his retirement, and he never received merit raises or awards.

4. How does the author think the father changed after he began his job with the company? Can you be sure that this change took place? Explain.
   At first, the author says, her father did not think the job would be permanent; he was sure that more was in store, "that everything was still possible" (paragraph 6). The implication is that eventually her father gave up hope for anything better. The reader has only the author's word for this; there is no quote from her father.

5. *vocabulary in context:* Using the information in paragraph 4, decide which word best defines *transcends* as it is used in the paragraph: "goes beyond," "transforms," "negates," or "equals"?
    Transcends means "goes beyond."

REFLECTING ON IDEAS

1. What is the author's view of work?
    The author thinks that work should have meaning beyond the paycheck it earns.

2. Make a list of words and phrases that describe the author's father.
    Responses will vary but may include terms such as these: hardworking, able, uncomplaining, family man, responsible, dedicated.

3. In paragraph 11, Ducharme says that in the boxes her father created, she and her sisters found "unconditional love" and that the boxes "carried [them] through." Explain what you think Ducharme means.
    The boxes are a symbol of the father's sturdiness and strength, a sturdiness and strength that gave his family stability.

4. In paragraph 10, Ducharme says, "The mantra of the bottom line attempts to convince us that our lives are secondary to the market." What do you think she means? Do you agree? Explain.
    The quotation indicates that corporate America places profit before the well-being of workers. The profit motive leads to downsizing, subordination of employees to mechanization, and devaluing of people.

GETTING IN GEAR

thinking in writing: Use mapping to explore the features of your ideal job. In the center of a sheet of paper write "my ideal job" and proceed from there. If you need to review mapping, see page 8.

writing from experience: Ducharme says, "All of us need to know that our lifework has mattered" (paragraph 9). What work have you done—or what work do you hope to do—that "matters"? Explain the nature of the work and how it matters.

writing in context: Visit your campus career services or job placement office, and learn how the people there can help seniors find satisfying work after graduation. Then write a piece that explains how the office can help seniors. Your piece should be suitable for a brochure about the career services or job placement office.

connecting the readings: Both "A Lifetime of Production" and "Thank You, M'am" (page 393) are about people who make a difference. What do these essays tell you about living a life that allows a person to make a difference?

FOR ONE TEACHER, A LESSON ABOUT E-MAIL AND PRIVACY
Elizabeth Stone

In this 1999 New York Times *piece, college professor Elizabeth Stone explains that she once imagined chatting with students in the cafeteria over coffee. Little did she know that she would be chatting with them online—whether she found it convenient or not.*

1   It's 3 in the morning, and not a creature is stirring, except for the mouse. My mouse. I can't sleep, which is why I'm in my nightie, online at the computer, my study dark except for the light cast by my monitor.

2   Suddenly, there is the telltale tinkle of Instant Message, America Online's system for real-time communication among its members, followed by a note from a student— let's call her Rachel, or Elmo1972—across my screen. "HI PROFESSOR!! IT'S ME, RACHEL!!!" That presumes that I don't already know who Elmo1972 is.

3   Which I do.

4   Here we are again, I think, just the two of us, alone in the dark in the middle of the night.

undaunted (5) not discouraged

5   Undaunted by my failure to respond as instantly as the Instant Message genre suggests I should, Rachel types me another message.

genre (5) kind or type

6   "What are u doing up so late???!"

7   When I became a college professor, I imagined having conversations after class with students over coffee in the cafeteria. I did not imagine that I would be a presence on their Buddy Lists, someone to be dragooned into insomniac pajama parties in cyberspace.

dragooned (7) forced

8   Nor did I imagine that they might learn more about me than I care to have them know—like my nocturnal online habits. And I didn't envision that, like Rachel, they would be able to leap out of the cyberbushes at me, any time day or night.

nocturnal (8) night

9   "I'm marking your paper," I finally type back "That's what I'm doing." I remind myself I have to block Rachel's screen name so she won't know when I'm online, a way of drawing a curtain between my personal life and hers. I've said this to myself before and didn't do it, but this time I will, less because I don't want to be on call 24 hours a day (though I don't) than because I don't like being imagined in my nightgown.

10   "Marking my paper? Oh phat!!" she types back.

11   "Well, see you in class," I reply, hoping she'll take the hint.

12   She doesn't.

13   "How do u like it so far?"

14   "Can't go into it now or I'll never get them all done."

15   Eventually, I manage to end the conversation.

16   "Sleep tight," she types by way of adieu.

17   The day I first gave students my e-mail address, I knew it would add a new dimension to our professional relationship. And in the beginning, I thought it would be a simple one.

18   They could send me papers via e-mail.

19   I could use e-mail to send them back.

20   They could send me questions via e-mail.

21   I could use e-mail to send back answers.

22   Since I teach journalism, I could send them to websites to read the *Denver Post* the day after the Littleton killings or tell them to check out the new study on coffee posted at the National Institutes of Health or give them an assignment to find out as much information as they could about a classmate, armed with only that person's phone number.

23   I tried to mold this new aspect of our relationship around the traditional pedagogical core. I changed my screen name from ElizaS to the more restrained ElizStone. I was their teacher, after all.

24   Some of the initial rough spots were familiar ones, only in a new key. I found, to my chagrin, that I could misplace just as many e-mail papers as I did the hard-copy kind. For their part, excuses for missing work remained essentially unchanged. "I know I left it in your mailbox" altered not at all, while "my dog ate it," merely changed to "my computer ate it."

25   What I didn't anticipate were the options available to those students of mine who, like Rachel, were AOL subscribers—and that was nearly half of them, as it turned out. For users like us, the first part of an e-mail address is the screen name. Once my students knew my screen name, they could slap it onto their Buddy Lists.

26   Then whenever I went on line, my name would appear in a small window on their monitors.

Rear Window (27) an Alfred Hitchcock movie

27   I began to think of the Buddy List window as a sort of online *Rear Window*, from which they could secretly watch my comings and goings.

28   I knew more about them, too, than I once had, often from their screen names alone.

29   Sports zealots—like a Mets fan, Piazza1979—were obvious. When Flipper70 hobbled in on crutches one day saying her tendon had snapped, I figured out, correctly, that she was a gymnast.

30   Sometimes, though, what was right before my eyes proved mysterious. Gigglez122 is one of the most somber students I've ever had. Does she have a merry side? Does she yearn to? Sabachik is Irish. I don't know what to make of BluLady, Punkissa and Snowinlove. Last year, there was EatsDirt. I didn't dare inquire.

31   Recently, a screen name I didn't recognize emblazoned itself across my screen in an Instant Message note. "WAIT!" BBoop181 said, "DON'T SHUT ME OUT! IT'S ME, RACHEL!"

32   "What happened to Elmo?" I typed back.

font (33) the style of type

ON WRITING

In casual e-mail correspondence, people often use shorthand spellings because they can be quick and easy. Note, for example, the use of *u* for *you* in paragraphs 33 and 36. However, in more formal usage, whether for e-mail or not, use conventional spelling

33   "u blocked Elmo," she said, her font dripping with accusation. "I know because Ken and I were both online one day while we were talking on the phone. Ken could see u come online from his Buddy List, but I couldn't see u on mine. That's when I knew."

34   I had been caught. After years of teaching, I knew how to handle lots of ticklish problems—kids who were unhappy with their grades or depressed or falling asleep in class or on the verge of dropping out—but this ticklish Elmo issue was a new one.

35   But Rachel seemed oddly unfazed.

36   "So anyway, now that I reached u, could u do me a favor? That paper I e-mailed u yesterday? My printer is broken. Do u think u could print me out a hard copy?"

READING CLOSELY

1. How did Professor Stone anticipate using e-mail and online resources when she first gave students her e-mail address?
   Stone expected to use the Internet and e-mail as efficient tools for conducting class business and creating worthwhile assignments.

2. Now that students have her e-mail address, Stone is uncomfortable with the results. Why?
   Stone feels her privacy is being invaded because almost half of her students can monitor when she is online and attempt to communicate with her at will.

3. Stone finds her students' screen names interesting. Why?
   Stone is fascinated by the fact that sometimes students' screen names reflect their interests or personalities, and other times they are a contradiction or a mystery.

4. Explain the reference contained in the first sentence: "not a creature is stirring, except for the mouse."
   The reference is to the opening line of the poem " 'Twas the Night before Christmas."

5. *vocabulary in context:* Using the information in paragraph 23, decide which word best defines *pedagogical* as it is used in the paragraph: "respectful," "instructional," "old-fashioned," or "nontechnical."
   Pedagogical means "instructional."

REFLECTING ON IDEAS

1. Using her e-mail communication with Professor Stone for clues, how would you describe Rachel's personality?
   Rachel is pushy and inclined to overstep the bounds of decorum, as evidenced by her tendency to continue e-mailing when Professor Stone does not answer immediately and by her request for a print copy of her paper. She is also unaware and unable to take a hint, which is why she is "oddly unfazed" by having her screen name blocked.

2. Using the clues in the essay to help you decide, how would you describe Professor Stone?
   Responses will vary, but many will note that she is patient and student-centered, as evidenced by the fact that she was very gentle with Rachel.

3. If you were Professor Stone, would you feel as she does about AOL's Buddy List? Why or why not?
   Responses will vary.

4. If you were Professor Stone, how would you have handled the correspondence with Rachel and the invasion of privacy?
   Responses will vary.

GETTING IN GEAR

thinking in writing: List the ways computers make your life easier. List the ways they create problems.

writing from experience: If you use e-mail, explain how it affects your relationships with people.

writing in context: An increasing number of colleges are offering courses online. What do you think of this trend? Why?

connecting the readings: Both "For One Teacher, a Lesson about E-Mail and Privacy" and "Have a Nice Day" (page 390) deal with ways people communicate with each other. What conclusions can you draw from those essays about how the people communicate?

ONE OF THE BAD GUYS
Ray Hanania

Ray Hanania, an Arab-American who lives in Chicago, wrote this essay in 1998 for the "My Turn" section of Newsweek. *In it, he laments the Hollywood portrayal of Arabs. All he's asking, he says, is for "Hollywood to be fair."*

1   As a child in the 1960s, I thought my relatives were famous. It seemed like they were in many Hollywood movies, often playing similar roles. OK. They weren't the headliners, but they did appear alongside stars like Paul Newman (*Exodus*), Sophia Loren (*Judith*) and Kirk Douglas (*Cast a Giant Shadow*). My "relatives" always played the "terrorists."

2   As I grew older, though, I realized that those actors were not my relatives, at all. They just looked like them. They have that "terrorist" look, and so do I. I can safely assure you, though, I don't have the mannerisms. I'm tired of seeing my likeness wielding an AK-47, murdering innocent women and children, getting stomped by Arnold Schwarzenegger (*True Lies*), or Harrison Ford (*Indiana Jones and the Temple of Doom*), or Kurt Russell (*Executive Decision*), and now Bruce Willis (*The Siege*).

wielding (2) using

AK-47 (2) an automatic gun

3   I'm Arab-American. And for some reason, Hollywood seems to think it's OK to portray all Arabs—and all Muslims, for that matter—as the bad guys. I don't mean just bad. I mean *really* bad. It makes me so angry I want to get in my half-track

with my 50-caliber howitzer that's parked in my two-Hummer garage, drive to the center of town and start shooting! I mean, isn't that what you've come to expect Arabs to do?

4   After I was honorably discharged from the U.S. Air Force in 1975, the FBI opened a file on me. It began with the ominous suggestion that I might be involved in "suspected" terrorist organizations, but the investigation concluded two years and 23 pages later that I was concerned only about improving the condition of my community. The investigation seemed based on the assumption that because I was an Arab, I must also be a potential terrorist. Most of the juicy text was blocked out with heavy, black Magic Markered lines, so it's hard to know for sure.

5   Hollywood movies are founded on the same assumption, that the Arab is the terrorist. I once thought movies were just entertainment, but they're much more. It's at the movies that the public learns about people like me. And it's also where I compare myself to the characters on the screen and wonder if there really is something wrong with me. How did my look suddenly become something so sinister? My eyes become even darker and more deep set? My accent heavier? I begin to question myself. Why is this person who looks like me so angry he wants to murder and harm innocent people? What is it that makes him wreak havoc and wanton suffering upon an innocent world?

6   Occasionally, there is an upside to being pegged as a terrorist. Once at Miami International Airport, a gaggle of people all wearing the same light gray jackets were following me around the terminal. Finally, introducing themselves as airport security, they directed me to a room where they rifled through my bags and grilled me about my travel history. They held up the embarrassing evidence of my terrorism. Wood carved heads. Goofy-looking hats. And dirty clothes.

7   When they finally realized I was just a tourist-trap junkie, they excused themselves. Usually, it takes about 15 minutes before I am released from airport detention and I'm on my way. Meanwhile, the nonterrorist-looking commuters are left waiting in the long immigration lines, impatiently nudging luggage across the tile floor, complaining about the heat and delays. But the security officers always have a reason to stop me. At Miami, they said I looked like the suspect they were pursuing. And, they just happened to have a Polaroid picture of the "suspect." He wore a double-breasted, polyester leisure suit, with a wide-brimmed Panama hat. And he had olive skin, dark eyes and those skinny little fingers that fit neatly around the trigger of a gun, like mine do. Naturally, I was very impressed. It must be difficult to get a terrorist to stop long enough to pose for a Polaroid picture.

8   Look, I'm realistic. I don't think we can erase all of Hollywood's stereotypes. But the movies seem fixated on the exaggerated bad side of Arabs. To Hollywood,

ominous (4) threatening

sinister (5) threatening

wreak havoc (5) cause destruction

wanton (5) reckless; deliberate

the Arab is the wife-abuser who wants to buy Steve Martin's home in *Father of the Bride II*. Or the guy hanging from the missile in *True Lies* when Schwarzenegger pushes the launch button and says in his Austrian accent, "Yaw're fi-yard!" We Arabs murder innocent airline passengers in *Executive Decision* simply because it makes us feel good.

9   Even a company like Disney takes a shot at us, with these lyrics from the movie *Aladdin:* "Oh I come from a land, from a faraway place, where the caravan camels roam; Where they cut off your ear if they don't like your face; It's barbaric, but hey, it's home." (Disney responded to Arab-Americans' complaints by changing the last line for the video release.)

10   Must every Arab portrayed in the movies be the villain? Why can't we be the hero just once? There are plenty of overlooked role models to choose from. The first heart-transplant surgeon is an Arab-American, Michael DeBakey. Candy Lightner, who founded Mothers Against Drunk Drivers, is Arab, too. There were at least 74 Arab passengers aboard the Titanic when it sank. Half of them drowned. Director James Cameron had a good opportunity to highlight the human side of the Arab community. Instead, he chose to highlight a make-believe Irish wedding aboard the ship, rather than include one of the three Arab weddings that actually took place.

11   Arabs are everyday people. Doctors. Teachers. Football stars and team owners. Grocery-store clerks. Engineers. Elected officials. We're the mail carriers who deliver your mail. The nurses and emergency medical technicians who hold your hand through tragedy. The clerks who help you at the bank.

12   I'm not asking Hollywood to hate someone else. That would be wrong. But, I'm asking Hollywood to be fair. Don't just show the bad. Show our good side, too. But, if that can't be done, I do have one last question: are you still mad about the Crusades?

ON WRITING

Chapter 25 explains the need to use a question mark at the end of a sentence that asks a question. Notice that questions appear in paragraphs 3, 5, 10, and 12. However, these are a particular kind of question, known as a *rhetorical question*. A rhetorical question does not require or expect an answer. What effect do they have on this piece?

Crusades (12): Wars undertaken by Christians in the 11th–13th centuries to recover the Holy Land from the Muslims

READING CLOSELY

1.   According to Hanania, how does Hollywood portray Arabs?
     Hollywood portrays Arabs as terrorists, wife-abusers, and "bad guys" who murder for pleasure.

2.   Hanania has more than one reaction to Hollywood's portrayal of Arabs. What are those reactions?
     Hanania reacts to the portrayal of Arabs with anger. He also compares himself to the portrayal and wonders whether he is like it in some way and whether anything is wrong with him.

3.   Hanania explains a problem and then suggests a solution. What is that solution?
     Hanania's solution is to let Arabs be the heroes once in a while.

4. Why do you think the author finds it necessary to give examples of Arab role models (paragraph 10)?

   Hanania probably suspects that we are so conditioned to the stereotype that we need proof that Arabs can be admirable people.

5. *vocabulary in context:* Using the clues in paragraph 3, decide what the following words have in common: *half-track, howitzer,* and *Hummer.*

   All these words have a military application.

REFLECTING ON IDEAS

1. Hanania often uses exaggeration and sarcasm (saying one thing but meaning another). For example in paragraph 3, he does not really mean that he wants to start shooting. What other paragraphs include exaggeration or sarcasm? What do the exaggeration and sarcasm contribute?

   Sarcasm appears in paragraph 6, when he suggests there is an upside to being mistaken for a terrorist; in paragraph 7, when he says it must be difficult to get a Polaroid picture of a terrorist; and in paragraph 12, when he asks whether people are still mad about the Crusades.

2. Why do you think Hollywood persists in portraying Arabs as terrorists and villains?

   Responses will vary, but some may note that relying on a stereotype is easier than developing realistic, representative characters.

3. Because of his looks, Hanania is often perceived in a particular way. How is he perceived, and what do you think life is like for a person perceived in that way?

   Responses will vary, but some may note that Hanania experiences discrimination and that he probably finds it difficult to know that he is always viewed with suspicion.

4. What is the significance of the fact that "even a company like Disney" (paragraph 9) is guilty of stereotyping Arabs?

   The fact that a company known for children's movies is guilty of stereotyping is indicative of how pervasive the practice is.

GETTING IN GEAR

thinking in writing: The portrayal of Arabs as terrorists and murderers is not the only stereotyping seen in Hollywood movies. List other stereotypes frequently seen on the big screen.

writing from experience: Write about how you are treated as a result of a group you belong to or some aspect of who you are. For example, you can write about how people treat you because of your religion, race, ethnicity, socioeconomic status, height, weight, or gender. You can also write about how you are treated as a result of being a student athlete, piercing your body, having very long hair, and so forth.

writing in context: Write a letter to the editor of your campus or community newspaper calling for a boycott of movies that include stereotypical portrayals of Arabs or another cultural or ethnic group.

connecting the readings: "One of the Bad Guys" deals with ethnic pride, as does "The Fight" on page 408. After reading these essays, think about what can be done in schools to teach the value and richness of ethnic diversity. Write up your ideas.

THE FIGHT

Maya Angelou

The fight referred to in this excerpt from Angelou's autobiographical I Know Why the Caged Bird Sings *(1969) occurred in the 1940s, when African-American heavyweight champion Joe Louis fought to keep his title. For the blacks who cheered Louis on, the fight was not just another sporting event.*

1   The last inch of space was filled, yet people continued to wedge themselves along the walls of the Store. Uncle Willie had turned the radio up to its last notch so that youngsters on the porch wouldn't miss a word. Women sat on kitchen chairs, dining-room chairs, stools and upturned wooden boxes. Small children and babies perched on every lap available and men leaned on the shelves or on each other.

2   The apprehensive mood was shot through with shafts of gaiety, as a black sky is streaked with lightning.

3   "I ain't worried 'bout this fight. Joe's gonna whip that cracker like it's open season."

4   "He gone whip him till that white boy call him Momma."

5   At last the talking was finished and the string-along songs about razor blades* were over and the fight began.

6   "A quick jab to the head." In the Store the crowd grunted. "A left to the head and a right and another left." One of the listeners cackled like a hen and was quieted.

7   "They're in a clench, Louis is trying to fight his way out."

8   Some bitter comedian on the porch said, "That white man don't mind hugging that niggah now, I betcha."

contender (9) person who fights the title holder

9   "The referee is moving in to break them up, but Louis finally pushed the contender away and it's an uppercut to the chin. The contender is hanging on, now he's backing away. Louis catches him with a short left to the jaw."

10   A tide of murmuring assent poured out the doors and into the yard.

11   "Another left and another left. Louis is saving that mighty right . . ." The mutter in the Store had grown into a baby roar and it was pierced by the clang of a bell and the announcer's "That's the bell for round three, ladies and gentlemen."

12   As I pushed my way into the Store I wondered if the announcer gave any thought to the fact that he was addressing as "ladies and gentlemen" all the Negroes around the world who sat sweating and praying, glued to their "master's voice."[†]

*Singing commercials for Gillette razor blades.
[†]A famous advertising slogan for RCA, "His master's voice" was accompanied by a picture of a dog listening to a phonograph.

13   There were only a few calls for R. C. Colas, Dr. Peppers, and Hire's root beer. The real festivities would begin after the fight. Then even the old Christian ladies who taught their children and tried themselves to practice turning the other cheek would buy soft drinks, and if the Brown Bomber's victory was a particularly bloody one they would order peanut patties and Baby Ruths also.

14   Bailey and I lay the coins on top of the cash register. Uncle Willie didn't allow us to ring up sales during a fight. It was too noisy and might shake up the atmosphere. When the gong rang for the next round we pushed through the near-sacred quiet to the herd of children outside.

15   "He's got Louis against the ropes and now it's a left to the body and a right to the ribs. Another right to the body, it looks like it was low . . . Yes, ladies and gentlemen, the referee is signaling but the contender keeps raining the blows on Louis. It's another to the body, and it looks like Louis is going down."

16   My race groaned. It was our people falling. It was another lynching, yet another Black man hanging on a tree. One more woman ambushed and raped. A Black boy whipped and maimed. It was hounds on the trail of a man running through slimy swamps. It was a white woman slapping her maid for being forgetful.

17   The men in the Store stood away from the walls and at attention. Women greedily clutched the babes on their laps while on the porch the shufflings and smiles, flirtings and pinching of a few minutes before were gone. This might be the end of the world. If Joe lost we were back in slavery and beyond help. It would all be true, the accusations that we were lower types of human beings. Only a little higher than the apes. True that we were stupid and ugly and lazy and dirty and, unlucky and worst of all, that God Himself hated us and ordained us to be hewers of wood and drawers of water, forever and ever, world without end.

ordained (17) ordered

hewers (17) people who cut down trees

18   We didn't breathe. We didn't hope. We waited.

19   "He's off the ropes, ladies and gentlemen. He's moving towards the center of the ring." There was no time to be relieved. The worst might still happen.

20   "And now it looks like Joe is mad. He's caught Carnera with a left hook to the head and a right to the head. It's a left jab to the body and another left to the head. There's a left cross and a right to the head. The contender's right eye is bleeding and he can't seem to keep his block up. Louis is penetrating every block. The referee is moving in, but Louis sends a left to the body and it's the uppercut to the chin and the contender is dropping. He's on the canvas, ladies and gentlemen."

21   Babies slid to the floor as women stood up and men leaned toward the radio.

22   "Here's the referee. He's counting. One, two, three, four, five, six, seven . . . Is the contender trying to get up again?"

23   All the men in the store shouted, "NO."

24   "—eight, nine, ten." There were a few sounds from the audience, but they seemed to be holding themselves in against tremendous pressure.

25   "The fight is all over, ladies and gentlemen. Let's get the microphone over to the referee . . . Here he is. He's got the Brown Bomber's hand, he's holding it up . . . Here he is . . ."

26   Then the voice, husky and familiar, came to wash over us—"The winnah, and still heavyweight champeen of the world . . . Joe Louis."

ambrosia (27) food of the gods

27   Champion of the world. A Black boy. Some Black mother's son. He was the strongest man in the world. People drank Coca-Colas like ambrosia and ate candy bars like Christmas. Some of the men went behind the Store and poured white lightning in their soft-drink bottles, and a few of the bigger boys followed them. Those who were not chased away came back blowing their breath in front of themselves like proud smokers.

28   It would take an hour or more before the people would leave the Store and head for home. Those who lived too far had made arrangements to stay in town. It wouldn't do for a Black man and his family to be caught on a lonely country road on a night when Joe Louis had proved that we were the strongest people in the world.

ON WRITING

Explain the reason for each of the following capital letters: *Momma* (paragraph 4), *Christian* (paragraph 13), *Baby Ruths* (paragraph 13), *Himself,* (paragraph 17), *Brown Bomber's* (paragraph 25) *Christmas,* (paragraph 27).

READING CLOSELY

1. Which paragraphs tell something of what life was like for African Americans during slavery? What do those paragraphs say life was like?
   Paragraphs 16 and 17 show that white people generally abused and sometimes murdered African Americans.

2. What image of white people is presented in the selection?
   White people are portrayed as cruel.

3. One of the elements of the story that helps set it in the 1940s is the description of the store. Cite two other references that help identify the time.
   The fact that they are listening to a fight on the radio and not watching it on television is a clue to the time, as is the overpowering awareness of racial tension.

4. What connection exists between the outcome of the fight and the pride of the African-American community?
   Paragraphs 16 and 17 reveal that African-American pride rests on the outcome of the fight.

5. *vocabulary in context:* In paragraph 15, the boxing announcer says that Louis was "against the ropes." This boxing term has worked its way into broad usage outside the boxing ring. When someone is "against the ropes" that person is which of the following: "near defeat," "in pain," "tied up," or "fighting hard"?
   Against the ropes means "near defeat."

REFLECTING ON IDEAS

1. Why do you think that "the old Christian ladies who taught their children and tried themselves to practice turning the other cheek" (paragraph 13) supported the fight?

   Even though supporting the fight contradicted the women's belief that fighting was wrong, the women seemed to support the fight because of what it represented.

2. Why do you think Angelou makes this statement: "It wouldn't do for a Black man and his family to be caught on a lonely country road on a night when Joe Louis had proved that we were the strongest people in the world" (paragraph 28)?

   Angelou suggests that white people would be angry because a white man lost to an African American. Thus, African Americans would not be safe on the streets.

3. For what purpose do you think Angelou tells the story of the fight?

   Angelou tells the story because it represents an important time for African Americans. It was a rare moment when an African American was in a position to best a white man.

4. What is the significance of the fight and the story?

   The fight is significant because it represents the African-American struggle for freedom, the possibility of winning instead of losing to white people.

GETTING IN GEAR

thinking in writing: In the 1930s, Joe Louis was a symbol of pride, hope, victory, and strength for African Americans. Think about what today's sports figures symbolize by doing a mapping. To begin, write "what sports figures symbolize" in the center of a page and draw a circle around it. If you do not know how to complete a mapping, see page 8.

writing from experience: Tell a story about a time you participated in an athletic event or were a spectator at an athletic event, a time that was significant for some reason. Be sure to make clear the significance of the event.

writing in context: As a sport, boxing is controversial. Critics say that the sport is violent and that those who enjoy it are guilty of encouraging brutality. Defenders cite the skill of the participants and the excitement of the sport. Argue for or against banning boxing.

connecting the readings: After reading "The Fight" and "America's Scapegoats" (page 414), write about how we react to people with visible ethnicity.

THE TRUTH ABOUT OUR LITTLE WHITE LIES
Karen S. Peterson

You probably know that lying is common, but did you know that, according to some researchers, it keeps things running smoothly? See if you agree that some forms of lying are not harmful—and even helpful. This essay first appeared in USA Today. *After reading it, ask yourself why that publication is a good one for this piece.*

1   Gail Safeer, a graduate student in suburban Washington, DC, doesn't let on to people that two of her three children were born during a previous marriage. "I don't

correct people when they assume all three are my husband's," she says. "It's nobody's business. It's a little white lie of omission, like not telling somebody her husband is running around. . . . White lies are not daily currency in my life," adds Safeer. "But we all do it."

omission (1) leaving out

2   Indeed we do. Each of us fibs at least 50 times a day, says psychologist Jerald Jellison of the University of Southern California in Los Angeles, who has spent a decade musing on the truth about our lies. He says we lie most often about the Big Three—age, income and sex—areas where our egos and self-images are most vulnerable. To protect them we even lie non-verbally with gestures, silences, inactions and body language. "You can even lie with your emotions," says Jellison. "The smile you don't mean, or the classic nervous laugh. A man asks a woman, 'Your place or mine?' and then chuckles. If she's offended, he can always elaborate on that laugh by saying, 'Can't you take a joke? I was only kidding.' "

musing (2) thinking about

3   These types of lies are what Jellison calls "little white lies," the kind we throw around as casually as old sneakers but which he claims are our "social justifications." "We lie because it pays," he says. "We use (lies) to escape punishment for our small errors. . . . Also, our social justifications help us avoid disapproval. 'I gave at the office,' or 'I'm sorry.' "

4   Our most common reason for lying is to spare someone else's feelings, says Jellison. "We often tell ourselves that, but usually we're trying to protect our own best interests. I'll feel that if I tell you the truth, you'll get mad." Adds B. L. Kintz, a psychology professor at Western Washington University in Bellingham: "We lie so often, with such regularity and fluency, so automatically and glibly that we're not even aware we're doing it. The little self-serving deceptions, the compliments we don't mean, stretching the point in a social situation—they are part of reality. Lying is simply something that is."

fluency (4) smoothness

glibly (4) spoken smoothly or too smoothly to be convincing

5   Jellison couldn't agree more. He believes that white lies are the oil for the machinery of daily life. "Society actually functions fairly well on many small deceptions. They contribute the little, civilized rituals that comfort us. . . . The idea that we must always tell the truth is too simplistic," he says. "Is lying 'right' or 'wrong'? is an impossible question to answer."

ON WRITING

A *metaphor* is a comparison formed without using the words *like* or *as*. What metaphor appears in paragraph 5?

6   Be it right or wrong, we have become so accustomed to lying and being lied to that we only see it as harmful in daily life when we don't realize that it's happening to us. "We take for granted some degree of lying from politicians, government, business, advertising," says psychiatrist Dr. Irving Baran of the USC San Diego Medical School. "We don't get excited about an ad that hypes some product in a way we know isn't true. But the rub comes when we go to someone we need and trust and

hypes (6) promotes with exaggeration

are deceived. A banker for a loan who says he's got the best interest rate going. A real estate agent who convinces us his is the best package available. An insurance agent pushing an unsound policy. An auto dealer who doesn't tell you the product's safety record. Then our backs go up, and what isn't true—hurts."

READING CLOSELY

1. According to the essay, when are people most likely to lie?
    We are most likely to lie when our self-image is most vulnerable, which means we are likely to lie about age, income, or sex. We are also likely to lie to spare someone's feelings.

2. How does the essay say that society at large is affected by white lies?
    White lies help society run smoothly on a day-to-day basis.

3. Are people likely to think lying is bad? Explain.
    No, we are upset about lying only when we do not realize we are being lied to by someone we need and trust.

4. In your own words, write a definition of the white lie.
    Responses will vary, but will be something like this: A white lie is an untruth told to protect the liar's self-image or to protect the feelings of another; it does not cause any serious harm.

5. *vocabulary in context:* Think of what it means when a cat arches its back, and then decide the meaning of this phrase in paragraph 6: "Then our backs go up."
    The phrase refers to being angry, since a cat raises its back when angry.

REFLECTING ON IDEAS

1. Paragraph 4 notes that we lie so often and so well that we are often not even aware that we are lying. How can this be so? Explain.
    One possibility is that because we all lie so frequently it becomes second nature, something not thought about on a conscious level.

2. Do you think that the lie of omission, referred to in paragraph 1, is as serious as telling a lie outright? Explain.
    Responses will vary.

3. Paragraph 5 says that determining whether lying is right or wrong is impossible. Do you agree? Explain.
    Responses will vary, but students are likely to hold their opinions strongly.

4. Are there any times when you would rather be lied to than told the truth? Explain.
    Responses will vary.

GETTING IN GEAR

thinking in writing: List the white lies that you tell in day-to-day life.

writing from experience: Tell about a time you lied or were lied to, being sure to explain the consequences of the lie.

writing in context: Assume you are fulfilling an assignment for an ethics class, and write an argument in favor of lying. Your strategy should be to explain what life would be like if everyone told the truth all of the time.

connecting the readings: "The Truth about Our Little White Lies" discusses the frequency with which we tell little white lies and the reasons we do so. What about the expression, "Have a nice day" (see "Have a Nice Day" on page 390)? Are we telling a little white lie when we use that expression? Explain.

scapegoats (title) people or groups made to bear the blame for others

AMERICA'S SCAPEGOATS
Chang-Lin Tien

Chang-Lin Tien is an accomplished professional who immigrated to the United States many years ago. In "America's Scapegoats," which first appeared in 1994 in Newsweek's "My Turn" column, he argues that we should take pride in our immigrant heritage.

1   My life has been far more satisfying than I dreamed possible when I arrived in the United States, 38 years ago. I am privileged to head a world-class institution, the University of California, Berkeley. My former Ph.D. students are professors at major universities. My engineering research has contributed to America's space technology, nuclear-reactor, safety and energy technology.

2   Yet no matter the scope of my accomplishments, when many Americans see my face and hear my Chinese accent, they think of me as an immigrant, first and foremost. In the eyes of many, that has come to mean a drain on public services, a competitor for jobs and a threat to a cohesive society.

3   I have watched the campaign to discourage immigration with growing concern. Whether we preside over universities or work the fields, immigrants are becoming the scapegoats for America's ills. I don't object to controlling the volume of immigration. Today, with unprecedented shifts in the global population, no nation can afford to throw its borders wide open. But we are in danger of forgetting that America was built by immigrants, and that our immigrant heritage is the wellspring of our nation's strength and vitality.

4   Even as a university chancellor, I am no stranger to the sharp sting of anti-immigrant hostility. Perhaps the most dramatic incident took place when I represented Berkeley a few years ago at a football rally after the Citrus Bowl. As I walked to the stage, a few people in the audience chanted, "Buy American, Buy American." This was profoundly disturbing. I am American and proud of it.

5   Just looking like an immigrant can make you the target of heckling. Any of us of Asian, Latin American and Middle Eastern heritage knows this. Several friends and family members have been subjected to taunts of "Go back to your own country." It's difficult for them to respond; like Bruce Springsteen, they were born in the U.S.A. This anti-immigrant mood is not new. Throughout our history, whenever the

economy suffered, immigrants became easy targets. But today, it is not only the immigrants who suffer. Ultimately, all Americans stand to lose, native and foreign born alike.

formidable (6) powerful

constituencies (6) resident groups

6   Now our nation faces the formidable challenge of forging a unified society from highly diverse constituencies. The population is undergoing a rapid transformation, and by the middle of the 21st century, the majority of Americans will trace their roots to Latin America, Africa, Asia, the Middle East and the Pacific Islands.

7   Evolving into a cohesive society based on respect and understanding is far from automatic. Throughout human history, racial and ethnic tensions have divided and destroyed peoples and countries. The ethnic strife that ripped apart Brooklyn's Crown Heights and South-Central Los Angeles is a sobering reminder of the challenge posed by rapid diversification.

8   Yet if there is a nation that promises to be a model for how to make diversity work, it is the United States. This is the nation with the strongest and deepest democratic roots. This is a nation with a living Constitution that guarantees rights to all its citizens. This is a nation that has taken pride not in its homogeneity, but in its immigrant heritage.

9   It was America's promise that drew me here in 1956. Even as a penniless graduate student from China, I believed I could make a contribution in this land of opportunity. Indeed, I am deeply grateful to America for offering opportunities difficult to find anywhere else in the world.

rivet (10) hold

10   Today, however, in the headlong rush to restrict immigration, we are jeopardizing this promise. Hundreds of state and federal measures have been introduced to curb legal and illegal immigration. The backers of these proposals often rely on inflammatory anti-immigrant rhetoric to rivet the attention of Americans, ignite their rage and move them to action.

11   In the hoopla, the debate is now moving away from the legitimate question of how much immigration America can sustain. Instead, we're blaming immigrants for many of our most urgent problems and trying to convince ourselves that we'll solve them by simply restricting immigration.

12   Effective immigration policy must be grounded in reason, not emotion. Racial and cultural hostilities fanned by the present anti-immigration frenzy must cool down. Then I am confident, we can make immigration work for America, just as it has from the time of our nation's infancy.

Jim Crow segregation (13) policy of discrimination against African Americans

13   After all, in my 38 years here, I have seen this nation make amazing progress. When I came here to study in the South, I encountered Jim Crow segregation.

Whites rode in the front of buses and blacks in the back. This racial system did not apply to Asian-Americans and left us in an ugly limbo. It troubled me and left a life-long impression. The rest of the country was not free from racial discrimination. When I joined the Berkeley faculty, in 1959, my wife and I could not live in certain Bay Area neighborhoods.

14   In less than four decades I have seen the enactment of civil-rights legislation that has created opportunities for all Americans. I have seen universities open doors to students who reflect our diverse society. I have seen women and men of all backgrounds become leaders in government, business, science, arts and education. Now I look forward to seeing the promise of America fulfilled. We can turn our national motto of *e pluribus unum*, or "one out of many," into more than an expression in a dead language. What it will take is the same kind of unwavering commitment that forged one nation from highly diverse colonies more than two centuries ago.

15   Immigrants are not the cause of America's major problems. It's time America stopped putting all the blame on immigrants and started facing up to the difficult reality of a world in transition. Let's seize the opportunity to transform America into a model of diversity for the future.

ON WRITING

In sentence 2 of paragraph 5, notice that the singular verb *knows* is used with the indefinite pronoun *any*. As explained on page 207, *any* can be either singular or plural, depending on meaning. In this case, it has the singular sense of "any *one* of us."

READING CLOSELY

1. The author is a highly educated, unusually productive United States citizen. Yet often he is not perceived as such because he looks like an immigrant. How is he often perceived?

    The author is often perceived as someone responsible for the United States's most pressing problems and as a drain on the country's resources and as a "competitor for jobs and a threat to a cohesive society" (paragraph 2).

2. Explain the meaning of the United States motto *e pluribus unum*, which translates to "one out of many."

    The motto refers to the fact that the United States brought diverse colonies together into one unified country and to the fact that it brings diverse populations together.

3. When people try to pass laws to severely limit immigration, what important fact are they forgetting?

    People who try to restrict immigration forget that the United States was built by immigrants and that immigrants are a source of our vitality and strength.

4. Why does the author believe the United States is the country that stands the best chance of becoming a model for successful diversity?

    The author feels that the United States has the strongest democracy and a Constitution that ensures equal rights for all. It is also a country that is proud of its immigrant heritage.

5. *vocabulary in context:* Using the clues in the sentence in which it appears, decide which word best defines *homogeneity* as it is used in paragraph 8: "difference," "sameness," "purity," or "newness"?

    Homogeneity means "sameness."

REFLECTING ON IDEAS

1. In paragraph 12, the author says that "we can make immigration work for America, just as it has from the time of our nation's infancy." What do you think this statement means?

   Since the United States is, with the notable exception of Native Americans, a country settled and developed by immigrants, all that we are is a result of our immigrant population.

2. In your own words, explain Chang-Lin Tien's position on immigration and why he feels as he does. Do you agree with him? Why or why not?

   The author favors a rational discussion of how much immigration the United States can sustain and becoming, within that limit, a model for diversity.

3. Why do you think some people blame immigrants for America's problems?

   Responses will vary, but many will note that people find it easier to blame immigrants rather than identify the real problems and develop effective solutions.

4. The author closes by calling for us to "transform America into a model of diversity for the future" (paragraph 15). Suggest two or three ways we can heed his call.

   Responses will vary.

GETTING IN GEAR

thinking in writing: Freewrite for about 15 minutes on what you think life is like in this country for a recently arrived immigrant. If you are from another country, write about your own experience.

writing from experience: Interview several international students on your campus or immigrants in your neighborhood to learn what their experience has been like so far. Write up your findings in a paper that includes something about what you can learn from people from other countries or what you can do to help them have a more positive experience in the United States.

writing in context: Check with the appropriate campus office (perhaps the office for international students, the admissions office, or the student services office) to learn how much diversity exists on your campus. Then write a position paper for your campus newspaper arguing that your school should (or should not) increase its efforts to create a diverse student population.

connecting the readings: A **stereotype** is a fixed, overgeneralized, and oversimplified image applied to all members of a group. For example, it is a stereotype that used car dealers are dishonest. Both "America's Scapegoats" and "One of the Bad Guys" (page 404) deal with stereotypes. Describe these stereotypes and explain the danger of stereotypical thinking.

BACK, BUT NOT HOME
Maria L. Muñiz

When Maria Muñiz left Cuba, she was only five years old. She left behind many family members and a piece of herself. In 1979, when she was 20, she wrote "Back, but Not Home" for the New York Times. *In it, she reveals her sense of loss.*

1   With all the talk about resuming diplomatic relations with Cuba, and with the increasing number of Cuban exiles returning to visit friends and relatives, I am

exiles (1) outcasts

constantly being asked, "Would you ever go back?" In turn, I have asked myself, "Is there any reason for me to go?" I have had to think long and hard before finding my answer. Yes.

2   I came to the United States with my parents when I was almost five years old. We left behind grandparents, aunts, uncles and several cousins. I grew up in a very middle-class neighborhood in Brooklyn. With one exception, all my friends were Americans. Outside of my family, I do not know many Cubans. I often feel awkward visiting relatives in Miami because it is such a different world. The way of life in Cuban Miami seems very strange to me and I am accused of being too "Americanized." Yet, although I am now an American citizen, whenever anyone has asked me my nationality, I have always and unhesitatingly replied, "Cuban."

3   Outside American, inside Cuban.

4   I recently had a conversation with a man who generally sympathizes with the Castro regime. We talked of Cuban politics and although the discussion was very casual, I felt an old anger welling inside. After 16 years of living an "American" life, I am still unable to view the revolution with detachment or objectivity. I cannot interpret its results in social, political or economic terms. Too many memories stand in my way.

regime (4) government or military rule

5   And as I listened to this man talk of the Cuban situation, I began to remember how as a little girl I would wake up crying because I had dreamed of my aunts and grandmothers and I missed them. I remembered my mother's trembling voice and the sad look on her face whenever she spoke to her mother over the phone. I thought of the many letters and photographs that somehow were always lost in transit. And as the conversation continued, I began to remember how difficult it often was to grow up Latina in an American world.

6   It meant going to kindergarten knowing little English. I'd been in this country only a few months and although I understood a good deal of what was said to me, I could not express myself very well. On the first day of school I remember one little girl's saying to the teacher: "But how can we play with her? She's so stupid she can't even talk!" I felt so helpless because inside I was crying, "Don't you know I can understand everything you're saying?" But I did not have words for my thoughts and my inability to communicate terrified me.

relegated (7) assigned

7   As I grew a little older, Latina meant being automatically relegated to the slowest reading classes in school. By now my English was fluent, but the teachers would always assume I was somewhat illiterate or slow. I recall one teacher's amazement at discovering I could read and write just as well as her American pupils. Her incredulity astounded me. As a child, I began to realize that Latina would always mean

proving I was as good as the others. As I grew older, it became a matter of pride to prove I was better than the others.

8   As an adult I have come to terms with these memories and they don't hurt as much. I don't look or sound very Cuban. I don't speak with an accent and my English is far better than my Spanish. I am beginning my career and look forward to the many possibilities ahead of me.

9   But a persistent little voice is constantly saying, "There's something missing. It's not enough." And this is why when I am now asked, "Do you want to go back?" I say "yes" with conviction.

10   I do not say to Cubans, "It is time to lay aside the hurt and forgive and forget." It is impossible to forget an event that has altered and scarred all our lives so profoundly. But I find I am beginning to care less and less about politics. And I am beginning to remember and care more about the child (and how many others like her) who left her grandma behind. I have to return to Cuba one day because I want to know that little girl better.

11   When I try to review my life during the past 16 years, I almost feel as if I've walked into a theater right in the middle of a movie. And I'm afraid I won't fully understand or enjoy the rest of the movie unless I can see and understand the beginning. And for me, the beginning is Cuba. I don't want to go "home" again; the life and home we all left behind are long gone. My home is here and I am happy. But I need to talk to my family still in Cuba.

12   Like all immigrants, my family and I have had to build a new life from almost nothing. It was often difficult, but I believe the struggle made us strong. Most of my memories are good ones.

13   But I want to preserve and renew my cultural heritage. I want to keep "la Cubana" within me alive. I want to return because the journey back will also mean a journey within. Only then will I see the missing piece.

ON WRITING

In Chapter 2, you read that examples help a writer show and not just tell. Notice that the example in paragraph 6 helps Muñiz show how people reacted to her in school because she did not speak much English. What other paragraph has an example that helps the author show and not just tell?

READING CLOSELY

1.   Why does Muñiz want to return to Cuba?
      Muñiz feels that she needs to know her Cuban family, her Cuban heritage, in order to be complete or to move forward. Going back will allow her to examine herself and achieve self-awareness and understanding.

2.   What does Muñiz tell the reader about her experiences in school?
      School was painful for Muñiz. On her first day, she was labeled "stupid" by another child, a label that apparently stuck with her.

3.   How was Muñiz affected by her school experiences?
      Because she was Latina, she always had to prove she "was as good as the others" (paragraph 7) and was automatically placed in the lower groups.

4. What political issues does Muñiz raise in the essay? Why does she mention them?

   In paragraph 4, Muñiz mentions the Castro political regime, pointing out that she is unable to view the events of the revolution objectively because of her memories. In paragraph 10, she explains that while the revolution drastically changed many lives, she is now finding herself focusing on its personal effects on "the child . . . who left her grandma behind."

5. *vocabulary in context:* Using the clues in paragraph 7, decide which word best defines *incredulity* as it is used in the paragraph: "bigotry," "hatred," "stupidity," or "surprise."

   Incredulity means "surprise."

REFLECTING ON IDEAS

1. In paragraph 9, Muñiz says, "There's something missing." What do you think is missing?

   Responses will vary but should pertain to Muñiz's sense of cultural heritage and personal identity.

2. Do you think going back to Cuba will help Muñiz find what's missing? Explain.

   Responses will vary.

3. What does Muñiz mean when she says that "the journey back will also mean a journey within" (paragraph 13)?

   Going back to Cuba would force Muñiz to examine who she was before becoming "Americanized"—she would be examining her Cuban family and life as they related to her and influenced her identity.

4. Do you think Muñiz is bitter about her school experiences? Explain.

   Muñiz feels the pain of her childhood, but she believes her struggles strengthened her (paragraph 12).

GETTING IN GEAR

thinking in writing: Think about a family member you have not seen for a long time. Write a letter to this person that expresses what you want him or her to know about you. Also ask any questions that you have.

writing from experience: Tell about a time when you felt like an outsider, when you felt different from everyone else. For example, you can write about your first day in a new school, moving into a new neighborhood, or attending a party where you did not know very many people.

writing in context: Do you think immigrants should preserve their cultural heritage or become as Americanized as possible? Explain and defend your view in an opinion piece for a sociology class.

connecting the readings: "Back, but Not Home" deals with the desire to preserve and embrace one's cultural heritage. How is that desire revealed in the essay and in "One of the Bad Guys" (page 404)?

Photo Gallery with Writing Topics

WRITING TOPIC:

Write a story that tells what led up to the moment depicted in the photograph.

WRITING TOPIC:

If your home were destroyed by a natural disaster, which of your possessions would you miss the most? Why?

WRITING TOPIC:

Write about what you think it is like to be this woman. As an alternative, write about what you imagine she is thinking.

WRITING TOPIC:

Adults influence children in important ways, both obvious and subtle. Tell how an adult influenced you when you were a child, and consider to what extent that influence is still with you.

WRITING TOPIC:

Write about the role you think luck plays in people's lives. Support your view with one or more examples.

WRITING TOPIC:

Do you have a special friend? If so, explain what makes that friend so special.

WRITING TOPIC:

Is this photograph a good symbol of the American middle-class way of life? Explain why or why not.

WRITING TOPIC:

Write a letter to one of your Congressional Representatives or Senators urging that person to continue or discontinue funding for the space program. Be sure to provide reasons for your view.

Appendix

The Parts of Speech

The **parts of speech** are the words from which sentences are made. The eight parts of speech are:

nouns	adverbs
pronouns	prepositions
verbs	conjunctions
adjectives	interjections

A word can be one part of speech in one sentence and a different part of speech in another sentence. Here is an example, using the word *love*.

As a verb: *I <u>love</u> New York in June.*

As a noun: *His <u>love</u> of opera is passionate.*

The parts of speech are mentioned and explained throughout this text; they are discussed together here as a guide you can refer to as needed.

NOUNS

A **noun** names a person, a place, an object, an emotion, or an idea.

Persons:	*teacher, plumber, Joyce, Karl, Dr. Mann, sisters, doctors*
Places:	*yard, Chicago, Argentina, city, bedrooms, township*
Objects:	*boats, shoe, Kmart, stores, window, Buick, paint, house*
Emotions:	*jealousy, love, anxiety, hatred, happiness*
Ideas:	*thought, wisdom, cowardice, beliefs, democracy*

<u>Lonnie</u> brought his <u>notes</u> on <u>economics</u> to <u>class</u>

PRONOUNS

A **pronoun** substitutes for a noun or refers to a noun. Here are some of the most commonly used pronouns:

I, me, my, mine	it, its
you, your, yours	we, us, our, ours
he, him, his	they, them, their, theirs
she, her, hers	

Mario brought <u>his</u> daughter to work, but <u>his</u> boss said <u>she</u> could not stay.

The students told their teacher that the book was unclear, so they did not understand it.

For a more complete discussion of pronouns, see Chapters 14, 15, and 16.

VERBS

1. Some verbs are **action verbs** because they express action, a process, or thought. They are words such as these:

consider	eat	go	love	think
do	enjoy	hit	talk	try

    The artist sells his paintings cheaply.

2. Some verbs are **linking verbs** because they link the subject to a word or words that rename or describe that subject. These are the linking verbs:

am	was	appear	taste
be	were	feel	smell
is	been	seem	look
are	being	sound	become

    That salesperson is grouchy. [*Is* links the subject "salesperson" to "grouchy," which describes "salesperson."]

    My brother was class president. [*Was* links the subject "brother" to "class president," which renames "brother."]

3. A verb can be more than one word; it can be made up of an action verb or a linking verb and one or more of the following **helping verbs:**

am	were	must	do	had
be	been	might	did	shall
is	being	could	does	will
are	may	would	have	
was	can	should	has	

    The plane will be on time.
    We should have left an hour ago.

    For a more detailed explanation of verbs, see the discussion beginning on page 57.

ADJECTIVES

Adjectives describe nouns and pronouns.

This milk is sour.

The new red car is parked on a steep hill.

For a more detailed discussion of adjectives, see Chapter 17.

ADVERBS

Adverbs describe verbs, adjectives, or other adverbs.

The sun is shining brightly. [*Brightly* describes the verb "is shining."]
Helga's humor is very sarcastic. [*Very* describes the adjective "sarcastic."]
You are speaking too loudly. [*Too* describes the adverb "loudly."]

For a more detailed discussion of adverbs, see Chapter 17.

PREPOSITIONS

Prepositions show how things are positioned in time or space. They are words such as these:

at	by	of	to
before	in	on	under
between	near	through	with

The dog ran between the trees and into the doghouse.
I thought you would be gone by now.

For a more detailed discussion of prepositions, see Chapter 19.

CONJUNCTIONS

Conjunctions are joining words. There are three kinds of conjunctions: *coordinating conjunctions, subordinating conjunctions,* and *conjunctive adverbs.*

1. **Coordinating conjunctions** join words, phrases, and clauses of equal importance in a sentence. The coordinating conjunctions are

and	for	or	yet
but	nor	so	

    Bill and Theresa are brother and sister. [The coordinating conjunctions join words of equal importance.]
    You will find the keys on the table or in the car. [The coordinating conjunction joins phrases of equal importance.]
    I heard what you said, but I don't believe it. [The coordinating conjunction joins clauses of equal importance.]

2. **Subordinating conjunctions,** which begin dependent clauses, join the dependent clauses to independent clauses. Some common subordinating conjunctions are

after	because	unless
although	before	until
as	if	when
as if	since	while

    While you were out, your boss called.
    We bought the house cheaply because the owner was anxious to sell.

    For a detailed discussion of subordinating conjunctions, dependent clauses, and independent clauses, see Chapters 5 and 6.

3. **Conjunctive adverbs** are used with semicolons to join independent clauses. Some common conjunctive adverbs are

consequently	instead	therefore
furthermore	meanwhile	thus
however	nevertheless	

    The violent storm knocked out the town's electricity; furthermore, it left thousands of people injured.

    For more on using conjunctive adverbs to join independent clauses, see page 73.

INTERJECTIONS

Interjections express strong emotions. They are words such as these:

hooray   ouch   wow

oh   whew   yikes

Interjections can be punctuated with a comma or an exclamation point.

Oh, I remember you.

Wow! I got the highest grade on the test.

Acknowledgments

Angelou, Maya: "The Fight," from *I Know Why the Caged Bird Sings* by Maya Angelou. Copyright © 1969 & 1997 by Maya Angelou. Reprinted by permission of Random House, Inc.

Ducharme, Michelle M.: "A Lifetime of Production," from *Newsweek*, 1996. All rights reserved. Reprinted by permission.

Giovanni, Nikki: "On Holidays and How to Make Them Work," from *Sacred Cows and Other Edibles* by Nikki Giovanni. Copyright © 1988 by Nikki Giovanni. Reprinted by permission of HarperCollins Publishers, Inc.

Hanania, Ray: "One of the Bad Guys," from *Newsweek*, 1998. All rights reserved. Reprinted by permission.

Hughes, Langston: "Thank You, M'am," from *Short Stories* by Langston Hughes. Copyright © 1996 by Ramona Bass and Arnold Rampersad. Introduction copyright © 1996 by Arnold Rampersad. Compilation and editorial contribution copyright © 1996 by Akiba Sullivan Harper. Reprinted by permission of Hill and Wang, a division of Farrar, Straus and Giroux, LLC.

Lam, Andrew: "They Shut My Grandmother's Room Door." Andrew Lam is associate editor of Pacific News Service and a short story writer.

Middleton, Thomas H.: "Have a Nice Day." Reprinted by permission of *The Saturday Review*, © 1979, General Media International, Inc.

Muñiz, Maria L.: "Back, But Not Home." Copyright © 1979 by the New York Times Co. Reprinted by permission.

Peterson, Karen S.: "The Truth about Our Little White Lies." Copyright 1983, *USA TODAY*. Reprinted with permission.

Rozin, Skip: "Big White." Reprinted with permission of the author.

Stone, Elizabeth: "For One Teacher, a Lesson about E-Mail and Privacy." Copyright © 1999 by the New York Times Co. Reprinted by permission.

Index